Developing Reading Versatility

NINTH EDITION

W. ROYCE ADAMS
Emeritus, Santa Barbara City College

BECKY PATTERSON
Emerita, University of Alaska, Anchorage

Australia Canada Mexico Singapore Spain United Kingdom United States

Developing Reading Versatility, Ninth Edition
W. Royce Adams/Becky Patterson

Publisher: Michael Rosenberg
Acquisitions Editor: Stephen Dalphin
Development Editor: Cathlynn Richard Dodson
Production Project Manager: Lianne Ames
Marketing Manager: Carrie Brandon
Print Buyer: Mary Beth Hennebury
Compositor: WestWords, Inc.

Project Manager: Jami L. Darby
Photography Manager: Sheri Blaney
Permissions Manager: Sarah Harkrader
Photo Researcher: Deborah Nicholls
Cover Desiger: Ha Nguyen
Text Designer: WestWords, Inc.
Printer: Edwards Brothers

Cover Art: *The Bridge* by Wassily Kandinsky, © 2004 Artists Rights Society (ARS), New York/ADAGP, Paris. **Photo Credit:** © Erich Lessing/Art Resource, NY

Printed in the United States of America.
2 3 4 5 6 — 07 06 05

For more information contact Thomson Wadsworth, 25 Thomson Place, Boston, Massachusetts 02210 USA, or you can visit our Internet site at http://www.thomson.com

ISBN: 1-4130-0255-2

Library of Congress Control Number: 2004101787

Preface

This ninth edition of *Developing Reading Versatility,* as with the previous editions, can be used as the central component of a developmental reading course or as a supplemental textbook in reading labs or learning centers. The diverse readings and extensive practice exercises provide enough flexibility to adapt this text to the needs of their students and course requirements.

As before, the text is divided into three major sections: Literal, Critical, and Affective Comprehension. Literal comprehension, the most basic level of understanding, is developed through practices in vocabulary development and through numerous comprehension questions based on reading selections from newspapers, magazines, and textbooks. The varied literal practices help students learn, among other skills, to develop their vocabulary, recall main ideas, understand paragraph patterns and how they can aid comprehension, identify facts, identify the difference between an author's subject and thesis, and develop reading-rate flexibility. Reading selections range from short paragraphs to longer essays with some timed reading practices spaced throughout the text.

Skills practiced in the Critical Comprehension section help students learn to distinguish between fact and opinion; recognize an author's intent, attitude, and tone; detect bias and propaganda techniques; and recognize inferences and form conclusions using inductive and deductive reasoning. Some timed-reading selections are provided to help the student continue developing flexibility in their reading rates.

Affective comprehension practices, often ignored in many reading-skills textbooks, help students define and develop a personal aesthetic reaction to imaginative literature. Exercises in this section teach students strategic ways necessary to recognize and appreciate affective language. Approaches to reading short stories, poems, and imaginative essays are provided.

The ninth edition of *Developing Reading Versatility* maintains the fundamental skills of previous editions and improves upon them through the following additions and changes:

- Twenty new reading selections have replaced outdated or no-longer-relevant material.
- A new chapter on reading on the Internet has been added in the Literal Comprehension section.

- The study reading chapter in the last edition has been slimmed and moved to the Appendix. Many reviewers have told us that such skills are often taught in separate study-skills classes rather than in reading-development courses. However, the Appendix contains sufficient material for those instructors who like to present study skills in their classes.
- Many new and revised comprehension and vocabulary practices can be found.
- A section on reading rate and flexible rates now appears in the Literal Comprehension section rather than in the study-skills section.
- Many comprehension questions now require written responses rather than just multiple-choice selections.

An answer key is available on request, ISBN: 1-4130-0256-0.

Our intent in revising this edition, as before, is to help students understand that reading is complex; that background, purposes, and motivation determine the quality of comprehension; and that there are not always right or wrong answers to some questions.

It is only due to the helpful advice of students and instructors who use *Developing Reading Versatility* that this book has reached its ninth edition. For their help in bringing this edition to fruition, we want to thank our editors Cathlyn Richard Dodson, Stephen Dalphin, Lianne Ames, and other members of the editorial and production staff at Thomson Wadsworth, as well as project manager Jami Darby and copyeditor Cheryl Adam. The following reviewers supplied us with excellent advice and suggestions for which we thank them:

Belinda Adams, *Navarro College*
Delia DuRoss, *Long Beach Community College*
Caren Kessler, *Blue Ridge University*
Johnie Scott, *California State University, Northridge*
Barry Selinger, *Nevada Community College*

To the Student

Your "No-Money-Back Guarantee"

This book offers you no money-back guarantee if you fail to read any better after completing it than you do now. It is quite possible that you could do well on every exercise in this book and still continue to read the way you do now. Why? Because you might fail to *use* the information gained from this book when you read material outside the book. In other words, unless you practice in *all* your reading what you do and learn in this book, there will be no transfer of skills. You will just be kidding yourself that you are reading better. Thus, while we can guarantee that the book may be helpful, we can't be sure of *you.* So, no money-back guarantee.

However, to get the most for your money, here are some points and suggestions for you to consider.

1. *Turn to the Contents.* Notice that this book is divided into three units. Each unit provides you with a variety of exercises in one level of comprehension. Together, these three different levels of understanding will bring you closer to a total comprehension of what you read. Actually, no Great Reading God in the Sky said, "Let there be three levels of comprehension. Zap!" These divisions are made only to help you see the many facets of comprehension.
2. *Don't feel obligated to do every practice in each unit.* How much practice you need depends on how much more competent you want to be in each area.
3. *Become conscious of your reading rate.* Some of the explanations and practices throughout this book deal with reading rate. If you are a very slow reader—averaging, say, 150 words per minute—you will find these drills very beneficial. These practices will help you break your slow reading-rate habits.
4. *Increase your speed.* In each chapter, some of the practices in this book are timed for speed. The pressure of speed is used to prod you from your normal reading habits and get you used to faster rates. But don't make speed your entire goal. Your speed will automatically increase as a by-product of the good reading habits you will learn here. Reading speeds vary depending on purpose, material, and vocabulary levels.
5. *Don't expect overnight miracles.* Lifetime results can be obtained from the practices you do here if you learn from your mistakes as well as your successes. It takes time, effort, and patience to change reading habits you have developed over many years.

6. *Develop your discussion skills.* Some of the practice questions can't be answered in a key, and in these cases the class should discuss them. Discussion is necessary for developing comprehension skills. Engage in class discussion; don't just sit back and listen to others, especially when you are working in Unit Three.
7. *Keep records.* A Student Record Chart is provided so you can keep a record of your various practice work. Don't be worried about ups and downs in rate and comprehension scores. It's normal to fluctuate. Also, don't be fooled into thinking that because your scores go up on the chart, you are reading better in materials outside the text. Only you can actually determine how much success you are feeling.

With these things said, you are ready to get down to work. Just remember: The responsibility for learning and transfer of learning is yours. Are you willing to place a money-back guarantee on yourself?

Brief Contents

Contents

UNIT ONE

LITERAL COMPREHENSION

Comprehension is the act of understanding or the capacity to understand. But as you know, the act of understanding is not always simple. In order to help you develop your ability to comprehend better, this book is divided into three levels of comprehension: literal, critical, and affective. None of these levels is actually a separate entity. Each of the three depends on the others. Think of total comprehension as a diamond. If we want to look more closely at that diamond, we can look separately at each of its facets or polished sides. The more facets, the more glimmer to the diamond.

You are going to be working separately with three facets of comprehension. Each of the three facets will be further broken down so that you can "polish" the skills necessary to get maximum comprehension of what you read. If you *look at the diagram* that follows on page 2, you will notice that each leg of the triangle represents one level of comprehension. Literal comprehension is at the bottom of the triangle; it's the most basic, the foundation for understanding. Literal comprehension skills include such things as vocabulary knowledge, understanding main ideas and supporting details, scanning, and rate flexibility.

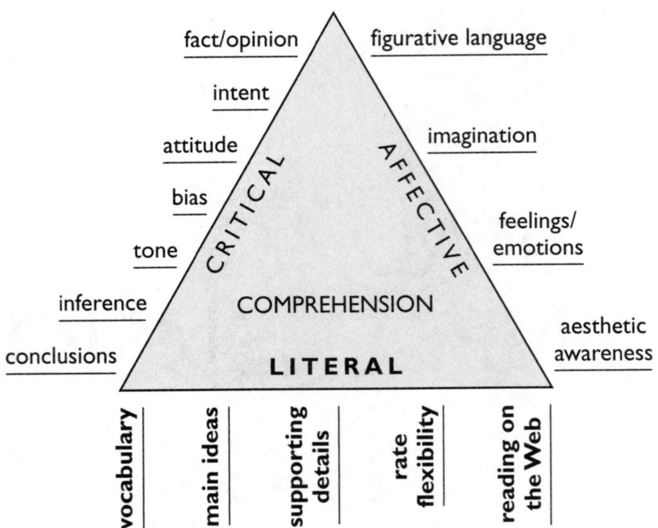

The second leg of the triangle is critical comprehension, which requires separating fact from opinion; recognizing an author's intent, attitude, tone, and bias; being able to draw inferences; and drawing conclusions. All of these skills are presented for your practice in Unit Two—along with continued practice of the skills from Unit One.

The third part of the triangle represents affective comprehension, which requires an understanding of figurative language, use of the imagination and feelings, and an awareness of the aesthetics of imaginative and expository writings. Unit Three deals with these skills. By the time you have finished with the last unit, you will have had continual practice using all three levels of comprehension. It is important as you work through this book to keep in mind that each skill eventually builds upon the others.

What Is Literal Comprehension?

This first unit deals with just one of three complex levels of total comprehension, the literal level. Literal comprehension is that basic level of understanding that entails the ability to recognize words accurately, to identify main ideas and supporting details, to understand a sequence of events, to recognize cause-and-effect relationships, to interpret directions, and to understand organizational patterns used in various types of reading matter. It is the level of comprehension you use when you follow a cooking recipe or the directions for putting a swing set together. It is also the level of comprehension necessary for understanding the main ideas in a news story, a magazine article, or a chapter from a textbook. More simply put, it is the most basic level of understanding, providing the foundation for the development of the two higher levels, namely, critical and affective comprehension.

Of the three levels of comprehension, literal comprehension is probably the most used. That is because everyday reading skills, such as skimming and scanning telephone directories, catalogs, and movie and television listings, and even reading the newspaper or a favorite magazine, seldom require anything but literal comprehension. In addition, most training in reading courses from the early grades through college classes places greater emphasis on literal recall than on critical or affective comprehension. This is not to say that there is no training in these areas, but an examination of materials and tests used in reading courses, as well as in other subjects, reveals a strong reliance on literal comprehension with more stress on recall than on forming judgments, evaluations, or personal reactions at the critical and affective levels. In spite of daily use, however, most people do not read as well as they could at the literal level.

Reading is much more than just recognizing words on a page. Knowing the meaning and function of words you are reading is naturally basic, but you must also understand those words in their context. Then it becomes important to understand the author's main points, the details and how they are being used, and the organization of the material. When these basics are mastered, speed of comprehension is increased and the basis is laid for developing your critical and affective levels of awareness.

What Does This Unit Cover?

In this unit, the practices deal with the development of all facets of *literal comprehension.* Practices are as basic as learning a new vocabulary word and as complex as separating main ideas from supporting details and recognizing writing patterns. A variety of reading experiences will help you feel comfortable with each skill.

There are three chapters in this unit. Chapter One offers methods for vocabulary development, an important area for the improvement of reading at any level. Chapter Two deals with the development of literal recall, stressing reading for main ideas and supporting details, understanding paragraph patterns, and recognizing an author's thesis. Chapter Three offers you practice in developing skills necessary for reading on the Internet. All chapters contain reading practices of various styles and subject matter with vocabulary, comprehension, and rate practice. "Putting It All Together" sections at the end of each chapter help you put together all the skills you have learned in that chapter.

There are two points about the reading practices that can't be overstated. One is that you should not worry about mistakes you make. Turn your mistakes into "learning experiences." When you miss a question, learn from it. Try to understand what caused you to make an error. If you can't figure it out on your own, get help from your instructor. The second point is to take what you learn here and apply it to your reading outside this text. Whether or not this text helps you to read any better is really up to you. While many students do well as they proceed through the work required of them in this book, they fail to apply the techniques to other required or pleasure readings. This book is designed to develop an awareness of what is required of an intelligent person when reading certain types of materials. Apply this awareness to all of your reading by completing the applications activities in each chapter.

What Should You Know after Completing This Unit?

Even though it may take quite a while to complete the practices that will be assigned to you, in this unit you should have some goals and objectives in mind that you want to achieve before going on to the next unit. Here are some objectives to consider. You may want to add some of your own. When you have finished this unit, you should be able to:

1. Write a thorough definition of literal comprehension.
2. Select a method that aids you in the continuing development of your vocabulary, and use it regularly.
3. Find main ideas and supporting details in a variety of materials.
4. Identify the following writing patterns as an aid in comprehension: definition, example, comparison/contrast, description, sequence of events, and narration.
5. Understand the differences in reading on the Internet and traditional printed material.
6. Know how to search for information on the Internet.
7. Apply flexible reading rates and read expository reading matter at least 100 words per minute faster with no loss in comprehension.

These are not unrealistic objectives to keep in mind as you work through this unit. With proper practice, you will achieve them all. If you have any objectives of your own, write them down in the space below and share with your instructor.

Personal reading objectives for Unit One: ______________________________

____

____

____

____

____

____

CHAPTER ONE

Developing Vocabulary Skills

Introduction to Vocabulary Development

One of the first places to begin developing reading versatility is with vocabulary. Without a good vocabulary, reading is slow and comprehension is poor. In order to understand what you read, you need to recognize not only the definitions of the words being read but also, more important, the way words are used in context.

Think of strategies for increasing vocabulary that you have tried in the past. What do you do when you run across unfamiliar words? In the selection that follows, "How I Discovered Words: A Homemade Education," one famous figure, Malcolm X, tells about his strategy for increasing his vocabulary and learning new words. Throughout this book, we have placed brief biographies and quotes from authors or public figures to inspire you by their examples as well as their words. Start by reading about Malcolm X.

Another way to find current information, quotations, or pictures of Malcolm X is to use the World Wide Web. Using a search engine such as Google, go2net.com, or AltaVista, type his name under "Search."

Introducing Malcolm X

Malcolm X was a controversial Black Muslim leader who became one of the most powerful and articulate blacks to focus on the plight of the urban black poor in the 1960s. Born Malcolm Little, he drifted into the world of drugs, prostitution, and crime as a very young man. While imprisoned for robbery, he converted to the Nation of Islam, or Black Muslims, a rigid sect that brought discipline into the lives of its members. During this period, Little took the name Malcolm X, the letter X standing for what he felt was his lost African name. Also while in prison, Malcolm X pursued his "homemade education."

After prison, he was assigned a Muslim temple in Harlem, where he preached black pride and the rejection of integration and called for a separate black nation. He soon became one of the most powerful and articulate blacks of the 1960s, caus-

ing jealousy among the members of the Nation of Islam and fear among many whites. Expelled from the Nation of Islam in 1963, Malcolm X formed his own group, the Organization of Afro-American Unity.

Eventually, he softened his stance, rejecting racism of all kinds and lecturing on the need for the common bond linking humanity. In 1965, he was shot to death by three Black Muslim loyalists while giving a speech in Harlem.

Malcolm X was a self-educated man who felt the need and desire for an academic education. In *The Autobiography of Malcolm X,* he states:

> My greatest lack has been, I believe, that I don't have the kind of academic education I wish I had been able to get. . . . I have always loved verbal battle, and challenge. You can believe me that if I had the time right now, I would not be one bit ashamed to go back into any New York City public school and start where I left off at the ninth grade, and go on through a degree. Because I don't begin to be academically equipped for so many of the interests that I have. For instance, I love languages. I wish I were an accomplished linguist. I don't know anything more frustrating than to be around people talking something you can't understand.
>
> I would just like to *study.* I mean ranging study, because I have a wide-open mind. I'm interested in almost any subject you can mention.

Now, read the following selection to learn how Malcolm X increased his vocabulary.

HOW I DISCOVERED WORDS: A HOMEMADE EDUCATION

Malcolm X

1 It was because of my letters that I happened to stumble upon starting to acquire some kind of a homemade education.

2 I became increasingly frustrated at not being able to express what I wanted to convey in letters that I wrote, especially those to Mr. Elijah Muhammad. In the street, I had been the most articulate hustler out there—I had commanded attention when I said something. But now, trying to write simple English, I not only wasn't articulate, I wasn't even functional. How would I sound writing in slang, the way I would say it, something such as, "Look, daddy, let me pull your coat about a cat. Elijah Muhammad—"

3 Many who today hear me somewhere in person, or on television, or those who read something I've said, will think I went to school far beyond the eighth grade. This impression is due entirely to my prison studies.

4 I had really begun in the Charleston Prison, when Bimbi first made me feel envy of his stock of knowledge. Bimbi had always taken charge of any conversation he was

in, and I had tried to emulate him. But every book I picked up had few sentences which didn't contain anywhere from one to nearly all of the words that might as well have been in Chinese. When I just skipped those words, of course, I really ended up with little idea of what the book said. So I had come to the Norfolk Prison Colony still going through only book-reading motions. Pretty soon, I would have quit even these motions, unless I had received the motivation that I did.

5 I saw that the best thing I could do was get hold of a dictionary—to study, to learn some words. I was lucky enough to reason also that I should try to improve my penmanship. I was sad. I couldn't even write in a straight line. It was both ideas together that moved me to request a dictionary along with some tablets and pencils from the Norfolk Prison Colony school.

6 I spent two days just riffling uncertainly through the dictionary's pages. I'd never realized so many words existed! I didn't know *which* words I needed to learn. Finally, just to start some kind of action, I began copying.

7 In my slow, painstaking, ragged handwriting, I copied into my tablet everything printed on that first page, down to the punctuation marks.

8 I believe it took me a day. Then, aloud, I read back, to myself, everything I'd written on that tablet. Over and over, aloud, to myself, I read my own handwriting.

9 I woke up the next morning, thinking about those words—immensely proud to realize that not only had I written so much at one time, but I'd written words that I never knew were in the world. Moreover, with a little effort, I also could remember what many of these words meant. I reviewed the words whose meaning I didn't remember. Funny thing, from the dictionary first page right now, that "aardvark" springs to my mind. The dictionary had a picture of it, a long-tailed, long-eared, burrowing African mammal, which lives off termites caught by sticking out its tongue as an anteater does for ants.

10 I was so fascinated that I went on—I copied the dictionary's next page. And the same experience came when I studied that. With every succeeding page, I also learned of people and places and events from history. Actually the dictionary is like a miniature encyclopedia. Finally the dictionary's A section had filled a whole tablet—and I went on into the B's. That was the way I started copying what eventually became the entire dictionary. I went a lot faster after so much practice helped me to pick up handwriting speed. Between what I wrote in my tablet, and writing letters, during the rest of my time in prison I would guess I wrote a million words.

11 I suppose it was inevitable that as my word-base broadened, I could for the first time pick up a book and read and now begin to understand what the book was saying. Anyone who has read a great deal can imagine the new world that opened. Let me tell you something: from then until I left that prison, in every free moment I had, if I was not reading in the library, I was reading on my bunk. You couldn't have gotten me out of books with a wedge. Between Mr. Muhammad's teachings, my correspondence, my visitors—usually Ella and Reginald—and my reading of books, months passed without my even thinking about being imprisoned. In fact, up to then, I never had been so truly free in my life.

Here is a man whose life was changed for the better by discovering the power of words. "I saw that the best thing I could do was get hold of a dictionary—to study, to learn some words," Malcolm X tells us. And because he took the time to do so, he "could for the first time pick up a book and read and now begin to understand what the book was saying."

How well you can read and understand begins at the same place it did for Malcolm X—with words. As a first step in developing reading versatility, this chapter will provide you with some methods and practice in vocabulary building, understanding words in context, and learning word parts and roots.

Vocabulary development means more than just adding new words to those you already know. It also means learning how to change words to different parts of speech, how to add or delete prefixes and suffixes, how to recognize the root elements of a word and its relationship to other words with that root, how synonyms and antonyms form families of words, as well as how to use words correctly in your own speech and writing.

While this book is not a vocabulary textbook, a strong emphasis is placed on vocabulary building because no real reading improvement can take place without it. Several approaches for building your vocabulary are presented in the following pages. Some may seem more helpful to you than others, but give them all a try. Many words will be presented not only in this chapter but also throughout the book as part of the reading comprehension and vocabulary practices. Be selective and learn words that you feel you need to learn. You might want to start with those words you "sort of" know but can't really use well. Devote some part of your day to working on your vocabulary. There is no getting around the work part. Building up your vocabulary is like staying in shape. It requires concentrated effort and regular workouts. No one can do it for you.

The first part of this chapter presents three methods for learning words you really want to make your own. Try all three methods before deciding which one you will use during this course.

The second part deals with words in context. For instance, the word *run* can have many different meanings, depending on how it is used in context. Notice these samples:

> There was a run on the bank.
> She had a run in her stocking.
> Run to the store for me.

In each case, and there are many others with the word *run,* the meaning is different, depending on the contextual use of the word. Learning to use contextual clues can also save you many trips to the dictionary.

The third section of this chapter deals with word structure, that is, prefixes, roots, and suffixes. Learning how words are structured and what certain commonly used prefixes, roots, and suffixes mean can help you unlock the meanings of many unfamiliar words. Useful Greek and Latin word roots are presented in practices to help you develop this aspect of vocabulary building.

Vocabulary development is a lifelong process. This chapter is meant only to get you started, not to be a complete course. It will be up to you to continue to use the information provided in this chapter. Select a method that aids you in the continuing development of your vocabulary, and use it regularly.

A. Learning New Words: Three Methods

Method 1: A Vocabulary Notebook or Computer Compilation

One way to develop your vocabulary is to keep a notebook of the words you want to learn. If you intend to write the words down on paper, an $8\frac{1}{2}'' \times 11''$ spiral notebook is best. Write the words you want to learn, their definitions, and sentence examples using the words. For instance, a typical entry might look like this:

> *perspicacious* = having keen insight, judgment, or understanding; shrewd
> If he had been more perspicacious, he might not have lost so much money on the stock market.

What type entries are made is up to you. Some students prefer to include the sentence where the word is first encountered and then write an example sentence of their own. In addition, some students also write in the phonetic spelling of the word, especially if it is one they have never heard before.

If you use a computer, find a program that allows you to manipulate your new vocabulary. You may want to alphabetize them, show only the words so you can supply the definition, or scramble the order. The advantages to the compilation method are that it is a convenient way to keep all new words together and a good source for constant review of older entries as new ones are made. The disadvantage is that the notebook or computer can, if you let them, become nothing more than lists of words unless you take the effort to review your entries constantly.

Method 2: The Column Folds

With this method, you take a regular piece of notebook paper and fold it into three or four columns, three if you do not need to learn the phonetic spelling of the word you want to learn. In the first column, you write the words you wish to learn. In the second column, you write the phonetic spelling. In the third column, you write the definition of the word, and in the fourth column, an example sentence using the word, but instead of writing in the word, you place a blank. You can usually get about ten or twelve words on one sheet of paper.

You can then practice learning the words in several ways. One way is to fold the paper so only the words show. You then see if you can remember the definitions; if not, you unfold the paper and check the answer; another way is to fold the paper so only the definitions show and see if you can identify the word that belongs to that definition. Still another way is to fold the paper so only the sentences show and try to remember the word that goes in the blank. And still another way is to fold the paper so that the phonetic spelling shows and try to pronounce the word and give its definition.

The advantage to this method is that it provides you with a means of studying with immediate feedback to the answers. The disadvantage is that the paper can become rather tattered after a while if you require much time to learn the words.

Method 3: Vocabulary Cards

You have probably seen boxed sets of vocabulary cards for foreign languages as well as for English. In such sets, each card has a word on one side and its definition on the other. These ready-made cards can be helpful, but chances are you will already know many of the words on the cards.

You can easily personalize the vocabulary card method by making up your own 3" × 5" index file cards. Here's all you need to do:

1. On the front of a card, print the word you want to learn. Use ink, so that after much use it will still be legible. Underneath the word print the phonetic spelling unless you already know how to pronounce the word.
2. On the back of the card, put as much information as needed to help you learn the word. It is recommended that besides the definition you include a synonym (a

word that has a similar meaning) and an antonym (a word that has the opposite meaning) if possible. A sentence using the word is also advised, either the sentence in which you found the word or an example of your own.

mnemonic

(nēmon′ik)

aiding or designed to aid the memory: a device to help remember

Vocabulary cards are mnemonic devices used to remember newly learned words.

3. Be selective and make vocabulary cards only for the words you want to overlearn. It is important to overlearn new words, not just memorize them, because you will gradually forget their meanings if you do not use them. All the words you presently know you have already overlearned and use without thinking. The only way to have a truly larger vocabulary is to overlearn new words the way you have the ones you now use regularly.
4. Try to learn at least five words a week, more if you can. Practice daily by quickly flashing only the front of the vocabulary card and pronouncing the word to yourself and providing the word's meaning. Try not to refer to the back of the card unless you can't recall the definition.
5. Carry a small stack of cards around in your purse or pocket so you can refer to them often. At odd times during the day—between classes, while waiting for a friend, on a bus—practice flashing your cards. If you have a friend who is also using this method, practice flashing each other's cards. The more you practice, the sooner you will begin to overlearn the words and recognize them by sight.
6. As the weeks go by and you accumulate fifty to a hundred or so cards, put aside the cards for words you feel you know very well and probably will never forget. At a later date, review the cards you put aside and see if you still remember them. If there are some you don't remember, put them back in your active stack of cards.

The advantage to this method is that it is a convenient way to learn words. If you have your cards with you, practice can take place anywhere, anytime. Rather than learning words from a list where association with other words on the list takes place, flash cards can be shuffled and mixed up. Once you have all the information you need on a card, you never have to look up the word again. The disadvantage is that making up cards does take time, but the advantages far outweigh this.

All this may seem like too much work. Perhaps it's not the method for you, but it has worked very well for many students. Of the three methods mentioned, the personalized vocabulary card method is the one most recommended.

Application I: Learning New Words

Select one of the three vocabulary development methods and use it on new vocabulary for another class. Have another student test you on your words. Turn in the results and a brief summary of how your vocabulary development method worked for you.

CHECK TEST

Directions: Answer the following questions in the blanks provided.

1. What is meant by vocabulary development? ______________________________
____
____

2. What are the three methods just discussed for developing vocabulary? __________
____
____

3. Explain Method 1. ____
____
____

4. Explain Method 2. ____
____
____

5. Explain Method 3. ____
____
____

6. Which method is most recommended? ______________________________
____
____

7. Why is this method recommended over the others? ____________________
____
____

8. What is meant by overlearning new words?__________________________
____
____

9. Why is developing your vocabulary vital to developing reading versatility? _______
____
____

10. Which method do you think you will use once you have tried all three?__________
____

Why?____
____
____

Name ______________________________ Section __________ Date __________

B. Learning Words in Context

This section provides practice in figuring out a word's meaning by its use in context. A close look at the context in which a word is used can often, though not always, eliminate the need to use a dictionary.

Contextual Hints

Several different types of context clues will be covered in this section. The first is **contextual hints.** For instance, in the following sentence notice how the meaning of the word *lucid* is hinted at:

> His lucid lectures, along with his clearly presented explanations, made it easy to take notes.

The phrases "clearly presented explanations" and "easy to take notes" give clues to the meaning of the word *lucid*—easy to understand, clear. Thus, it's generally a good idea not to stop on words you don't know but rather to read on a bit and see if hints or other clues to the word's meaning might be given.

Here's another sentence written with a contextual hint to a key word's meaning:

> It was imprudent for Lisa to skate on the ice without checking to see how thick it was.

Since we know that skating on ice without making sure it is thick enough is dangerous, we can guess that Lisa was not very wise, perhaps foolish for doing so. Therefore, *imprudent* must mean unwise, rash, or foolish.

PRACTICE B-1: Contextual Hints

Directions: Define the italicized words in the following sentences, and explain the contextual hints.

1. Their *vociferous* chatter made me wish I had earplugs.

a. *vociferous* means ______________________________

b. The clue is ______________________________

2. He was so *impudent* to his mother that I would have spanked him if he talked to me that way.

a. *impudent* means ______________________________

b. The clue is ______________________________

3. When asked if she liked her aunt's new hat, she *candidly* gave her frank view that it was ugly.

a. *candidly* means ______________________________

b. The clue is ______________________________

4. The toy is a *lethal* weapon; the kid almost killed me with it!

   a. *lethal* means ______________________________

   b. The clue is______________________________

5. My dad is so *punctilious* that he always corrects my sloppy speech or points out my incorrect use of certain words.

   a. *punctilious* means ______________________________

   b. The clue is______________________________

6. They think of themselves as the *elite* group on campus, looking down their noses at others.

   a. *elite* means ______________________________

   b. The clue is______________________________

   Make vocabulary cards for any words that gave you trouble, or use whatever method you have decided to use to develop your word power.

Signal Words

Sometimes there are contextual **signal words** in a sentence that indirectly help define an unknown word. Signal words are just that: words that signal that a change is about to occur. Just as stoplights and road signs signal that you should slow down, look for curves, and watch out for cross streets while you're driving, signal words are used by writers to help you follow their thoughts. For instance, consider the following sentence:

> While his subjects were grieving over their dead, the king was filled with exultation over his military victory.

Notice how the signal word *while* contrasts the way the subjects feel with the way the king feels. The subjects are grieving (sad) while the king is exulting (happy). So if we didn't know what *exultation* meant, the signal word *while* alerts us that it means the opposite of grieving.

Here's another example:

> Despite his fear of the snake, Paul managed to subdue his true feelings as it coiled around his arm.

The signal word here is *despite,* meaning in spite of, or even though. Here we have someone who has a fear of snakes, but despite that fear he subdues it; or, as we can guess from the context, Paul manages to control his true feelings.

Here are some signal words that you probably already know but may never have thought about using in this way. In the future, let them help you unlock the meanings to words you may not know.

Signal Words

but	while	in spite of	in contrast
however	despite	rather	although
nevertheless	even though	yet	instead

PRACTICE B-2: Signal Words

Directions: Using the signal words, figure out the meaning of the italicized words in the following sentences.

1. Although the patient is usually *morose,* she seems happy today.
   - **a.** *morose* means ____________________
   - **b.** signal word ____________________
2. He is usually *loquacious,* but tonight he's rather silent.
   - **a.** *loquacious* means ____________________
   - **b.** signal word ____________________
3. The boxer *feigned* a punch with his left rather than actually jabbing.
   - **a.** *feigned* means ____________________
   - **b.** signal word ____________________
4. Even though our camp spot was rather *remote,* I was afraid other people might discover it.
   - **a.** *remote* means ____________________
   - **b.** signal word ____________________
5. She usually is a *laggard;* however, today she was energetic and did her share.
   - **a.** *laggard* means ____________________
   - **b.** signal word ____________________
6. Although his parents were *indigent,* they somehow managed to provide Tommy with proper food and clothing.
   - **a.** *indigent* means ____________________
   - **b.** signal word ____________________

Make vocabulary cards or use some other method to learn any words that gave you trouble.

Contextual Examples

Another way you can frequently determine an unknown word's meaning is through **contextual examples.** Writers often provide examples of things or ideas that help define a word. For instance, look at these sentences:

> Luis must be very affluent. He wears expensive clothes and jewelry, drives a Rolls-Royce convertible, and owns a $1,750,000 house in Beverly Hills.

Notice all the examples that help define the word *affluent:* expensive clothes, jewelry, car, house in Beverly Hills. All of these are items that require money or wealth. So it doesn't take much work to figure out that *affluent* means wealthy or well-to-do.

Let's look at another instance of the use of contextual examples:

> The navy recruiting officer offered him several inducements to join up, such as the promise of a college education, the opportunity to fly jets, and the chance to be stationed in Hawaii.

If the word *inducements* is unclear to begin with, a look at the examples of what the recruitment officer promised gives us a hint that the word must mean reasons or motives for joining the navy.

Now try using this technique on the following sentences.

PRACTICE B-3: Contextual Examples

Directions: Define the italicized words in the following sentences and give the example clues.

1. In order to show *clemency,* the judge reduced the fine to one dollar and merely gave the man a warning.
   - **a.** *clemency* means ______________________________
   - **b.** example clues ______________________________
2. Burning the village to the ground, shooting all the villagers, and plundering the area for valuables, the rebels committed one of the most *heinous* acts of the war.
   - **a.** *heinous* means ______________________________
   - **b.** example clues ______________________________
3. Sara is very *astute;* she borrowed money at a very low interest rate and built it into a small fortune through wise investments.
   - **a.** *astute* means ______________________________
   - **b.** example clues ______________________________

4. Jerry is so *indolent!* He sleeps late, never does chores unless yelled at, and would rather lounge around the house than look for a job.

   a. *indolent* means ______________________________

   b. example clues ______________________________

5. Carnegie was very *frugal.* Even though he did not earn a lot, he saved most of his money and lived on very little until he saved $10,000 for the investment that was to make him rich.

   a. *frugal* means ______________________________

   b. example clues ______________________________

6. They *enhanced* the property by pulling weeds, mowing the lawn, and planting trees around the house.

   a. *enhanced* means ______________________________

   b. example clues ______________________________

Make vocabulary cards or use some other method to learn the words that gave you trouble.

Definition Clues

The easiest of context clues to recognize is the **definition clue.** Some sentences actually define the unknown word right in the sentence itself. Notice how that is done in the following example:

> Sue, serving as the chairperson, presided at the meeting.

The phrase "serving as the chairperson" actually defines the word *preside,* which means to hold the position of authority, to be in charge.

Here's another example of a definition clue in a sentence:

> Luke's pretentious manner, standing up and shouting at Sue that he should be running the meeting just to give her a bad time, didn't win him any friends.

Based on Luke's bad manners, we can guess that *pretentious* has something to do with claiming or demanding something when it's unjustified.

While context clues are not always there to help you with unfamiliar words, they do appear with frequency. Take the time in your future readings to look for the various types of clues covered in this section.

PRACTICE B-4: Definition Clues

Directions: Define the italicized words in the following sentences.

1. I *presumed* or guessed that something was wrong when I smelled the smoke.

   presumed means ______________________________

2. I always felt the *rapport* between us was good, based on a relationship of trust.

   rapport means ______________________________

3. The most *salient* feature on his face is his chin; it's quite prominent.

   salient means ______________________________

4. Sherry's ill will or, more accurately, *malevolence* toward her brother became obvious when she tried to push him down the stairs.

   malevolence means ______________________________

5. Bret's *jocose* manner soon had all of us laughing and joking.

   jocose means ______________________________

6. Hans Zinsser said, "The rat, like men, has become practically *omnivorous*—it eats anything that lets it."

   omnivorous means ______________________________

Make vocabulary cards or use some other method to learn the words that gave you trouble.

PRACTICE B-5: Contextual Clues in Paragraphs

Directions: Read the following paragraphs and define each of the bold print words as they are used in context. Read each paragraph in its entirety before attempting to define the bold words or phrases.

Paragraph 1

Who makes the better boss: men or women? The debate has been **simmering** for some time both in scientific journals as well as in employees' intraoffice e-mails. In order to come to a final **verdict,** researchers at Northwestern University examined 45 studies on the subject that were conducted between 1985 and 2002. Though the difference found in each study was small, the conclusion reported in the *Psychological Bulletin* is that women make better bosses. Females are more likely to serve as role models and **mentors** for employees and to encourage creativity than are males.

a. simmering ______________________________

b. verdict ______________________________

c. mentors ______________________________

Paragraph 2

The findings of the study **beg the question:** If women make better bosses than men, why aren't more women in the higher levels of **corporate America?** The evidence suggests that women should be rising the **corporate ladder** at least as fast as men, if not faster. But it's not happening. Of the *Fortune 500*'s top jobs—senior vice president and above—only 6 percent are held by women.

a. beg the question ______________________________

b. corporate America ______________________________

c. corporate ladder ______________________________

Paragraph 3

In our **media-intensive** culture, it is not difficult to find differing opinions. Thousands of newspapers and magazines and dozens of radio and television talk shows **resound** with differing points of view. The difficulty lies in deciding which opinion to agree with and which "experts" seem the most credible. The more inundated we become with differing opinions and claims, the more essential it is to **hone** critical reading and thinking skills to evaluate these ideas. (From David L. Bender and Bruno Leone, series editors, *Opposing Viewpoints* series, Greenhaven Press, 2000.)

a. media-intensive ________________________________

b. resound ________________________________

c. hone ________________________________

Paragraph 4

It matters, if individuals are to **retain** any capacity to form their own judgments and opinions, that they continue to read for themselves. How they read, well or badly, and what they read, cannot depend wholly upon themselves, but why they read must be for and in their own interest. You can read merely to pass the time, or you can read with an **overt urgency,** but eventually you will read against the clock. Bible readers, those who search the Bible for themselves, perhaps exemplify the **urgency** more plainly than readers of Shakespeare, yet the quest is the same. One of the uses of reading is to prepare ourselves for change, and the final change alas is universal. (From Harold Bloom, *How to Read and Why*, Scribner, 2000, p. 21.)

a. retain ________________________________

b. overt ________________________________

c. urgency ________________________________

Paragraph 5

I became increasingly frustrated at not being able to express what I wanted to **convey** in letters that I wrote . . . In the street, I had been the most **articulate** hustler out there—I had **commanded** attention when I said something. But now, trying to write simple English, I not only wasn't articulate, I wasn't even **functional.** How would I sound writing slang the way I would say it, something such as, "Look, daddy, let me pull your coat about a cat." (From Malcolm X with Alex Haley, *Autobiography of Malcolm X*, Ballantine, 1965.)

Circle the correct response.

1. convey
a. transport
b. communicate
c. believe

2. articulate
a. funny
b. mean, tough
c. clear

3. commanded
a. ordered
b. overlooked
c. exercised authority

4. functional
a. workable
b. not usable
c. worthy

Paragraph 6

An antiliterature attitude exists among some people who feel that reading literature is **impractical** and holds little value. It's frowned upon as being little more than a pleasure-centered, leisure-time activity. Such literary interests are looked upon as **pretentious,** something an "upper-class" or **elite** person does. That may be because some people have tried to use literary knowledge in a snobbish way as a status symbol, which is unfortunate.

Circle the correct response.

1. impractical
- **a.** unknown
- **b.** unrealistic
- **c.** important

2. pretentious
- **a.** false
- **b.** showy
- **c.** smart

3. elite
- **a.** intelligent
- **b.** superior status
- **c.** enlightened

PRACTICE B-6: Quick Quiz

Directions: The following words are from the practices you've been doing on context clues. Define each word, and then write a sentence using it correctly in context.

1. *vociferous* (B-1, #1)

a. definition ______________________________

b. sentence ______________________________

____

2. *laggard* (B-2, #5)

a. definition ______________________________

b. sentence ______________________________

____

3. *loquacious* (B-2, #2)

a. definition ______________________________

b. sentence ______________________________

____

4. *frugal* (B-3, #5)

a. definition ______________________________

b. sentence ______________________________

____

5. *astute* (B-3, #3)

a. definition ______________________________

b. sentence ______________________________

____

6. *indolent* (B-3, #4)

a. definition ______________________________

b. sentence ______________________________

____

7. *rapport* (B-4, #2)

a. definition ______________________________

b. sentence ______________________________

____

8. *jocose* (B-4, #5)

a. definition ______________________________

b. sentence ______________________________

____

9. *articulate* (B-5, paragraph 5, #2)

   a. definition ______________________________

   b. sentence ______________________________

   ____

10. *pretentious* (B-5, paragraph 6, #2)

   a. definition ______________________________

   b. sentence ______________________________

   ____

Turn the quiz in to your instructor.

Name ______________________ Section __________ Date __________

C. Learning Word Parts and Structure

Another good way to develop your vocabulary is to learn some of the basic word parts that make up the English language. Many of our words are derived from other languages, and many prefixes, suffixes, and root word parts come from Latin and Greek. You probably already know many of them but have never taken the time to see how frequently they appear in our language or why certain words mean what they do. In this section, you will review and learn some of the commonly used word parts in English.

No doubt you know the word *phonograph.* This common word in English is actually made up of two Greek word roots—*phon,* meaning sound, and *graph,* meaning write or record. Technically, the grooves in a recording are a record of sound, or, if you will, sound written on a record. The advantage of knowing the meaning to word parts is that you can often figure out what an unknown word means by looking at its parts. Look at some of the words that contain the word part *phon:*

phone = informal verb meaning to telephone someone, as well as the informal word for telephone
phonate = to utter speech sounds
phoneme = one of the set of the smallest units of speech that distinguishes one utterance or word from another; the *b* in *bat* and the *m* in *mat* are phonemes.
phonemics = the study of phonemes
phonetic = representing the sounds of speech with distinct symbols
phonetician = an expert in phonetics
phonic = having sound
phonics = the study or science of sound
phonogram = a character or symbol representing a word or phoneme
phonology = the science of speech sounds
phonotype = text printed in phonetic symbols
symphony = a long sonata for orchestra (*sym* means together or in harmony)
euphony = good, pleasant sounds (*eu* means good)
cacophony = harsh, unpleasant sound (*caco* means bad)

Even though some of these words are speciality words, you are one step ahead when you know that all the words have something to do with sound.

Many words in English are made up of *prefixes* (small but meaningful letter groups added before a base word or root that change the root's meaning) and *suffixes* (letter groups that are added to the end of a base word or root). Learning the meaning of these word parts, together with the meaning of common base words and Greek and Latin roots, will give you the key for unlocking the meanings of hundreds of words.

Following are several practices dealing with word parts and structure. Some you will know, and some will be new to you. Make vocabulary cards for those you want to overlearn, or use whatever method you have decided upon for enlarging your vocabulary.

PRACTICE C-1: Prefixes That Express Negativity and Reversal

Directions: There are several prefixes (letter groups added before a root word that change the root's meaning) that have to do with negation or reversal. For instance, placing the prefix *dis* in front of the root word *approve* creates the word *disapprove,* changing the word to a negative one. Placing the prefix *dis* on the root word *arm* creates the word *disarm,* reversing the root's meaning.

Below are three columns. Column 1 contains some prefixes that express negative or reverse meanings. Column 2 contains words you should know. In column 3, you should write in the words from column 2, adding to each what you think is the correct prefix from column 1 to the root word's meaning. The first one has been done for you. Here are clues for using *il, im,* and *ir:*

use *il* with words beginning with *l*
use *im* with words beginning with *b, m,* and *p*
use *ir* with words beginning with *r*

Column 1	Column 2	Column 3
a	active	1. inactive
counter	comfortable	2. ______
de	expensive	3. ______
dis	logical	4. ______
non	violent	5. ______
il	fair	6. ______
im	regulate	7. ______
in	typical	8. ______
ir	pleasant	9. ______
un	settle	10. ______
	proper	11. ______
	legal	12. ______
	regular	13. ______
	polite	14. ______
	decisive	15. ______
	easy	16. ______
	movable	17. ______
	possible	18. ______
	rational	19. ______
	legitimate	20. ______

PRACTICE C-2: Prefixes That Express Time and Place

Directions: Below are some commonly used prefixes that express time and place. Study them carefully. Then fill in the blanks in the numbered exercises. The first one has been done for you.

Prefix	Meaning	Prefix	Meaning
intro, intra	inside, within	re	back, again
inter	between, among	super	above
pre	before	trans	across
de	away, undo	sub	under
ex	out, not any longer	retro	back, backward
post	after	circum	around

1. What is the opposite of *inflate* (to fill)? ______deflate______
2. If a patriot is a loyal countryman, what is an *expatriate?* ______________
3. What is the opposite of *activate?* ______________
4. If import means to bring in, *export* means ______________
5. If urban refers to the city, what is an *intraurban* truck line? ______________

   ____
6. Is *postgraduate* work done before or after you graduate from college? ______
7. A *prefix* is called what it is because it is fixed ______________ the root word.
8. If the root word *vive* refers to life, what does *revive* mean? ______________
9. A *transatlantic* voyage would take you ______________
10. If you *intercede* during an argument, what are you doing? ______________
11. *Intercollegiate* sports are activities that take place ________ different colleges.
12. *Intracollegiate* sports are activities that take place ______________
13. Is the *pre*-Victorian period before or after the Victorian period? ______________
14. *Mortem* refers to death; what is a *postmortem?* ______________
15. Who is higher in rank, a *subprincipal* or a principal? ______________
16. What is meant by a *superhuman* effort? ______________
17. What would it mean if your boss said you had some *retroactive* pay coming to you? ______________
18. What's the difference between *circumference* and diagonal measurements? ______

    ____
19. Why are *subways* called what they are? ______________
20. What is the difference between *interisland* ships and those that *circumnavigate?*

    ____

PRACTICE C-3: Miscellaneous Prefixes

Directions: Study the following miscellaneous prefixes and their meanings, then answer the questions that follow. The first one has been done for you.

Prefix	Meaning	Prefix	Meaning
anti	against	hetero	different
auto	self	mis, miso	wrong; hatred
bene	good, well	mal	bad, wrong
bi	two	poly	many
eu	good, nice		

1. If a newspaper is printed *bimonthly,* it is printed twice a month
2. If *phon* means sound, what does *euphonious* mean? ____________
3. If *toxin* means poison, what does *antitoxin* mean? ____________
4. If *gen* refers to types or kinds, what does *heterogeneous* mean? ____________
5. If *homogeneous* is the opposite of *heterogeneous,* what does it mean? ____________
6. If *sect* means to cut or divide, what does *bisect* mean? ____________
7. If *caco* means bad, or unpleasant, how would you form a word that means the opposite of *euphony?* ____________
8. Since *gam* refers to marriage, *misogamy* means ____________
9. Since *gyn* refers to women, a *misogynist* is ____________
10. What is a *polygamist?* ____________
11. Why is an *automatic* transmission called what it is? ____________
12. Which is better: a tumor that is *malignant* or *benign?* ____________
13. What is *malpractice?* ____________
14. Why are fundraisers often called *benefits?* ____________
15. Why is someone who donates money called a *benefactor?* ____________

PRACTICE C-4: Quick Quiz

Directions: Define the following prefixes and write a word that contains each prefix.

Prefix	Definition	Word Using Prefix
1. auto	______________________	______________
2. il	______________________	______________
3. intra	______________________	______________
4. in	______________________	______________
5. un	______________________	______________
6. ir	______________________	______________
7. anti	______________________	______________
8. a/an	______________________	______________
9. bi	______________________	______________
10. de	______________________	______________
11. dis	______________________	______________
12. hetero	______________________	______________
13. bene	______________________	______________
14. eu	______________________	______________
15. sub	______________________	______________
16. im	______________________	______________
17. mis	______________________	______________
18. post	______________________	______________
19. trans	______________________	______________
20. re	______________________	______________

Turn in the quiz to your instructor.

Name ______________________ Section __________ Date __________

PRACTICE C-5: Noun Suffixes

Directions: A noun, as you may remember, is frequently defined as a person, place, or thing: woman, John, city, farm, hammer, car—all are nouns. There are some suffixes (letters at the end of a word) that change root words into nouns. For instance, *er* on the end of the word *teach* (a verb) forms the word *teacher,* a noun. The suffix *dom* on the end of *free* creates the noun *freedom.*

Study the following list of suffixes. They all mean "a person who is or does something." Then answer the questions that follow. The first one has been done for you.

ent	ant	ist
er	ar	ee
or	ess	ard

1. Someone who acts is an ______actor, actress______
2. A person who is paid to serve in a household is a ______________
3. Someone who gets drunk much of the time is a ______________
4. A person who practices science is______________
5. A woman who waits on tables in a restaurant is a ______________
6. One who begs is a______________
7. A person who resides in an apartment is called a ______________
8. One who is elected to preside over an organization is called the______________

   ____
9. A payer ______________ while a payee______________
10. Someone who commits anarchy is an ______________
11. A friend who keeps your confidence is called a ______________
12. One who sails is a______________
13. Someone who practices biology is a______________
14. A person who narrates is a ______________
15. One who studies is a______________

PRACTICE C-6: More Noun Suffixes

Directions: Column 1 contains a list of suffixes that mean "a state or quality of being." For instance, *violence* is the state of being *violent; loyalty* is the state of being *loyal.* Column 2 contains some words that can be changed to nouns by adding the suffixes from column 1. Using the suffixes in column 1, write in the correct noun form in column 3. The first one has been done for you.

Column 1	Column 2	Column 3
ance	fail	1. ______failure______
ation	hero	2. ______________

Column 1	Column 2	Column 3
dom	amuse	3. ______
hood	friend	4. ______
ion	free	5. ______
ism	tense	6. ______
ity	necessary	7. ______
ment	repent	8. ______
ness	starve	9. ______
ty	royal	10. ______
ship	happy	11. ______
ure	seize	12. ______
	lively	13. ______
	content	14. ______
	moderate	15. ______

PRACTICE C-7: Miscellaneous Suffixes

Directions: Study the following list of suffixes and their definitions. Then, using the list, add suffixes to the words that follow. Some words may take more than one suffix. The first one has been done for you.

Suffix	Definition	Suffix	Definition
able, ible	able to	less	without
cy	state or condition	ize	to make
full, ous	full of	ly	a characteristic or in a certain manner
ic, al	related to		
ish, ive	inclined to, similar		

1. care *careful, careless, carefully, carelessly*
2. depend ______
3. instruct ______
4. infant ______
5. vocal ______
6. expend ______
7. form ______
8. permanent ______
9. care ______
10. tropic ______
11. active ______
12. popular ______

13. combat ______________________________
14. compete ______________________________
15. caution ______________________________
16. word ______________________________
17. history ______________________________
18. wonder ______________________________
19. nature ______________________________
20. defense ______________________________

PRACTICE C-8: Roots

Directions: Using the list below of word roots and their definitions, answer the questions that follow.

Root	Definition	Root	Definition
aud	hear	graph	write, record
chron	time	man, manu	hand
cred	belief	mort	death
dent	tooth	phil	love
dict	tell, say	phon	sound

1. If *meter* means measure, a chronometer ______________________________
____
2. If something is audible, you can ______________________________ it.
3. *Incredulous* means ______________________________
____
4. The suffix *ist* refers to a person; that's why someone who works on your teeth is called a ______________________________
5. If *contra* means against or opposite, *contradict* means ______________________________
____
6. A chronograph is ______________________________
____
7. The opposite of *automatic* is ______________________________
____
8. Does a *postmortem* occur before or after death? ______________________________
9. If *anthrop* refers to man or mankind, what is a philanthropist? ______________________________
____
10. If you talk into a *dictaphone*, you are recording the ______________ of your voice.

PRACTICE C-9: More Roots

Directions: Define the following words. Don't look back at any previous exercises. You should be able to define all of these words if you learned from the previous drills.

Root	Definition	Root	Definition
biblio	book	phobia	fear
bio	life	poly	many
gam	marriage	port	carry
gen	kinds, types	tele	far, distance
log(y)	study of	theo	god
mono	one	vis	see

1. bibliography ______________________________

2. biology ______________________________

3. biography ______________________________

4. monogamy ______________________________

5. polyphonous ______________________________

6. heterogeneous ______________________________

7. bibliophobia ______________________________

8. portable ______________________________

9. televise ______________________________

10. theology ______________________________

Application 2: Finding Word Parts in Other Readings

In your textbooks or other reading material, find at least ten words that use the roots you have learned. Write out the words and their definitions so that you can give them to your instructor.

PRACTICE C-10: Quick Quiz

Directions: Define the following words. You should be able to define all of these words if you have learned from previous drills.

1. dictation (C-8) ____________
2. credible (C-8) ____________
3. bibliography (C-9) ____________
4. philanthropist (C-8) ____________
5. bibliophile (C-9) ____________
6. incredulous (C-1), (C-8) ____________
7. audiometer (C-8) ____________
8. submariner (C-2) ____________
9. monogamy (C-9) ____________
10. autograph (C-3) ____________
11. misanthropist (C-3) ____________
12. intraoffice (C-2) ____________
13. deflate (C-2) ____________
14. heterogeneous (C-3), (C-9) ____________
15. antitheological (C-3) ____________
16. euphonious (C-3) ____________
17. bimotored (C-3) ____________
18. atypical (C-1) ____________
19. irrational (C-1) ____________
20. illogical (C-1) ____________

Turn in the quiz to your instructor. Make vocabulary cards for any words you missed or need to learn better.

Name ____________ Section ____________ Date ____________

D. Learning Dictionary Skills

There comes a time when context clues and knowledge of word parts are not enough to help you understand an unknown word's meaning. That usually means a trip to the dictionary. The dictionary is more than a recorder of a word's meaning. It gives information on the word's origin; its various meanings, pronunciation, parts of speech, spellings, synonyms and antonyms; and its formal and informal usage. If you don't have a good, up-to-date dictionary, you should get one. (In a later practice, you will read an essay entitled "What You Should Look for in a Dictionary," by Robert M. Pierson, which will help you select one appropriate for you.)

Here is a typical dictionary word entry:

[1]**com•pound** \käm-ˈpau̇nd, ˈkäm-ˌ\ *vb* [ME *compounen*, fr. MF *compondre*, fr. L *componere*, fr. *com-* together + *ponere* to put] **1** : COMBINE **2** : to form by combining parts ⟨~ a medicine⟩ **3** : SETTLE ⟨~ a dispute⟩; *also* : to refrain from prosecuting (an offense) in return for a consideration **4** : to increase (as interest) by an amount that can itself vary; *also* : to add to
[2]**com•pound** \ˈkäm-ˌpau̇nd\ *adj* **1** : made up of individual parts **2** : composed of united similar parts esp. of a kind usu. independent ⟨a ~ plant ovary⟩ **3** : formed by the combination of two or more otherwise independent elements ⟨~ sentence⟩
[3]**com•pound** \ˈkäm-ˌpau̇nd\ *n* **1** : a word consisting of parts that are words **2** : something formed from a union of elements or parts; *esp* : a distinct substance formed by the union of two or more chemical elements **syn** mixture, composite, blend, admixture, alloy
[4]**com•pound** \ˈkäm-ˌpau̇nd\ *n* [by folk etymology fr. Malay *kampung* group of buildings, village] : an enclosure containing buildings

In almost all dictionaries, the main word appears in bold type and is divided into syllables by dots. In the *Merriam-Webster Dictionary* used in these exercises, different definitions of the same word are given separate entries and are distinguished by superscript numerals preceding each word. The word *compound* in this entry thus has four quite different meanings. The first *compound* has four meanings; the second has three meanings; the third has two meanings; the last entry has only one meaning.

Following in parentheses are the pronunciation symbols. If you are unfamiliar with the symbols, a pronunciation key usually appears on the inside front or rear cover of the dictionary. The first exercise in this section will help you learn how to use pronunciation keys. Notice that the first entry of *compound* has a different pronunciation than the other three entries.

Next, abbreviated, is the word's part of speech. The abbreviation *vb* means verb, *adj* means adjective, and *n* means noun. The word can thus be a verb, adjective, or noun. It's important to understand what part of speech a word is so that you can use it correctly.

The bracketed section that appears near the beginning of an entry provides the word's etymology or its historical origin. In this case, the first entry originally came from the Middle English and Middle French. The fourth entry shows it came from a Malay word, *kampung:* group of buildings, village.

Notice that there are four definitions given for *compound* as a verb, three definitions as an adjective, and three definitions as a noun. In this dictionary, the word meanings are arranged from the oldest to the most recent, so the most common present-day definition of *compound* as a verb is "to increase (as interest) by an amount that can itself vary; also: to add to."

Sometimes the definitions given for words in some dictionaries are not easy to understand. Frequently, a word that is being used in a definition must also be looked up in the dictionary! All dictionaries are not the same, so be selective in your choice.

The following practices should help you become more familiar with how to get the most from whatever dictionary you buy.

PRACTICE D-1: Pronunciation Keys

Directions: Using the pronunciation key on page 36, answer the following questions. Answers with explanations follow each question.

1. The first *o* in the word *loquacious* (lō-kwā´-shəs)—meaning talkative—is pronounced like the *o* in key words such as ____________ or ____________.
   The key words are *bone* or *hollow.* Since the first *o* in loquacious is marked ō, it is necessary to scan the dictionary symbol column and find an ō listed. Such a symbol appears in the first column, seven up from the bottom. This sound is called the "long o" sound. The symbols appearing over the vowel letters are called diacritical marks.

2. The *a* in the word *loquacious* (lō-kwā´-shəs) is pronounced like the *a* in key words such as ____________ or ____________.
   The keys words are *day* or *fate.* The answer is found in the first column, sixth listing. This sound is called the "long a" sound. ____________

3. The ə symbol used in the pronunciation clues (lō-kwā´-shəs) symbolizes the sound of the letter ____________ as in the word circus.
   The symbol ə represents several sounds depending on what letter of the alphabet it represents. In this case, it represents the *u* sound as in the word circus.
   The symbol ə is called a "schwa."

4. The *a* in the word *chartreuse* (shär-trüz´)—meaning yellowish green—is pronounced like the *a* in the word ____________.
   The two small dots give the *a* a completely different sound, which is sometimes called the "short vowel" sound. The words *bother, father,* or *cot* are possible answers listed in the first column.

5. The *u* sound in *chartreuse* (shär-trüz´) is pronounced like the *u* in the words ____________ or ____________.
   The words *boot* or *few* contain the *ü* sound. See the second column.

6. The first *e* in the word *egocentric* (ē-gō-sen´-trik)—meaning self-centered—is pronounced like the *e* in the word ____________.
   The *ē* is the "long e" sound, and the correct answer is *beat* or *easy.*

7. The *dg* in the word *edge* appears as the letter ____________ as a pronunciation clue. Unless you already knew the answer, you needed to scan the key words column and look for the word *edge.* It is in the first column, in the twenty-first listing. To the left is the letter *j,* meaning that *dg* is sounded as a *j* sound.

8. Sometimes the letter *s* may be pronounced like the letter *z.* What is one word that has an *s* that sounds like *z?* ____________
In the pronunciation key, go to the letter *z.* Notice that the last key word is *raise,* which is the answer you should have written.

9. What letters besides *sh* are sometimes prononounced as *sh?* ____________.
Your answer should be *ss,* as in mission. Look for the letter *sh* in the second column and find which key words have that sound.

10. The *s* in *pleasure* is pronounced like the letters ____________.
Find the key word *pleasure* in the second column. Your answer should be *zh.*

PRONUNCIATION SYMBOLS

ə . . . . **a**but, c**o**llect, s**u**ppose
ˈə, ˌə h**u**mdr**u**m
ᵊ . . . . (in ᵊl, ᵊn) batt**le**, cott**on**; (in lᵊ, mᵊ, rᵊ) French ta**ble**, pris**me**, ti**tre**
ər . . . op**er**ation, f**ur**th**er**
a . . . . m**a**p, p**a**tch
ā . . . . d**ay**, f**a**te
ä . . . . b**o**ther, c**o**t, f**a**ther
ȧ . . . . a sound between \a\ and \ä\, as in an Eastern New England pronunciation of **au**nt, **a**sk
au̇ . . . n**ow**, **ou**t
b . . . . **b**a**b**y, ri**b**
ch . . . **ch**in, ca**tch**
d . . . . **d**i**d**, a**dd**er
e . . . . s**e**t, r**e**d
ē . . . . b**ea**t, **ea**s**y**
f . . . . **f**i**f**ty, cu**ff**
g . . . . **g**o, bi**g**
h . . . . **h**at, a**h**ead
hw . . . **wh**ale
i . . . . t**i**p, ban**i**sh
ī . . . . s**i**te, b**uy**
j . . . . **j**ob, e**dg**e
k . . . . **k**in, **c**oo**k**
k̲ . . . . German Ba**ch**, Scots lo**ch**
l . . . . **l**i**l**y, coo**l**
m . . . **m**ur**m**ur, di**m**
n . . . . **n**i**n**e, ow**n**
ⁿ . . . . indicates that a preceding vowel is pronounced through both nose and mouth, as in French bon \bōⁿ\
ŋ . . . . si**ng**, si**ng**er, fi**n**ger, i**n**k
ō . . . . b**o**ne, holl**ow**
ȯ . . . . s**aw**
œ . . . French b**œu**f, German H**ö**lle
œ̄ . . . French f**eu**, German H**ö**hle
ȯi . . . t**oy**
p . . . . **p**e**pp**er, li**p**
r . . . . **r**a**r**ity
s . . . . **s**our**ce**, le**ss**
sh . . . **sh**y, mi**ss**ion
t . . . . **t**ie, a**tt**ack
th . . . **th**in, e**th**er
th̲ . . . **th**en, ei**th**er
ü . . . . b**oo**t, few \ˈfyü\
u̇ . . . . p**u**t, pure \ˈpyu̇r\
ue . . . German f**ü**llen
ue̅ . . . French r**ue**, German f**ü**hlen
v . . . . **v**i**v**id, gi**v**e
w . . . **w**e, a**w**ay
y . . . . **y**ard, cue \ˈkyü\
ʸ . . . . indicates that a preceding \l\, \n\, or \w\ is modified by having the tongue approximate the position for \y\, as in French di**gne** \dēnʸ\
z . . . . **z**one, rai**se**
zh . . . vi**s**ion, plea**s**ure
\ . . . . slant line used in pairs to mark the beginning and end of a transcription: \ˈpen\
ˈ . . . . mark at the beginning of a syllable that has primary (strongest) stress: \ˈshə-fəl-ˌbōrd\
ˌ . . . . mark at the beginning of a syllable that has secondary (next-strongest) stress: \ˈshə-fəl-ˌbōrd\
- . . . . mark of a syllable division in pronunciations (the mark of end-of-line division in boldface entries is a centered dot •)
( ) . . . indicate that what is symbolized between sometimes occurs and sometimes does not occur in the pronunciation of the word: **bakery** \ˈbā-k(ə-)rē\ = \ˈbā-kə-rē, ˈbā-krē\

PRACTICE D-2: Word Entry Knowledge

Directions: Using the following dictionary word entry, answer the questions that follow.

[1]**out·side** \au̇t-ˈsīd, ˈau̇t-ˌsīd\ *n* **1** : a place or region beyond an enclosure or boundary **2** : EXTERIOR **3** : the utmost limit or extent
[2]**outside** *adj* **1** : OUTER **2** : coming from without ⟨~ influences⟩ **3** : being apart from one's regular duties ⟨~ activities⟩ **4** : REMOTE ⟨an ~ chance⟩
[3]**outside** *adv* : on or to the outside
[4]**outside** *prep* **1** : on or to the outside of **2** : beyond the limits of **3** : EXCEPT

1. In total, how many definitions are given for the word *outside?* ________________

2. For how many parts of speech can *outside* be used? ________________

3. Two ways to pronounce *outside* are given. What is the difference between the two?

____

____

4. What does it mean to say there is an outside chance you might win?

____

____

5. A phrase using *outside* in context is provided after the second definition of the word as an adjective. Explain in your own words what the phrase means. ________

____

____

6. What is one meaning of saying you're working *at the outside* of your ability? Hint: *outside* is used as a noun in this phrase, so look under the noun definitions.

____

____

7. Use *outside* as a noun in a sentence. ________________

____

8. Use *outside* as an adjective in a sentence. ________________

____

9. Use *outside* as an adverb in a sentence. ________________

____

10. Use *outside* as a preposition in a sentence. ________________

____

babble • back out 68

1 : to talk enthusiastically or excessively 2 : to utter meaningless sounds — **babble** *n* — **bab·bler** \-b(ə-)lər\ *n*

babe \ˈbāb\ *n* 1 : BABY 2 *slang* : GIRL, WOMAN

ba·bel \ˈbā-bəl, ˈba-\ *n, often cap* [fr. the Tower of *Babel*, Gen 11:4–9] : a place or scene of noise and confusion; *also* : a confused sound **syn** hubbub, racket, din, uproar, clamor

ba·boon \ba-ˈbün\ *n* [ME *babewin*, fr. MF *babouin*, fr. *baboue* grimace] : any of several large apes of Asia and Africa with doglike muzzles

ba·bush·ka \bə-ˈbüsh-kə, -ˈbu̇sh-\ *n* [Russ, grandmother, dim. of *baba* old woman] : a kerchief for the head

[1]**ba·by** \ˈbā-bē\ *n, pl* **babies** 1 : a very young child : INFANT 2 : the youngest or smallest of a group 3 : a childish person — **baby** *adj* — **ba·by·hood** *n* — **ba·by·ish** *adj*

[2]**baby** *vb* **ba·bied; ba·by·ing** : to tend or treat often with excessive care

baby boom *n* : a marked rise in birthrate — **baby boom·er** \-ˈbü-mər\ *n*

baby's breath *n* : any of a genus of herbs that are related to the pinks and have small delicate flowers

ba·by–sit \ˈbā-bē-ˌsit\ *vb* **-sat** \-ˌsat\; **-sit·ting** : to care for children usu. during a short absence of the parents — **ba·by–sit·ter** *n*

bac·ca·lau·re·ate \ˌba-kə-ˈlȯr-ē-ət\ *n* 1 : the degree of bachelor conferred by colleges and universities 2 : a sermon delivered to a graduating class

bac·ca·rat \ˌbä-kə-ˈrä, ˌba-\ *n* : a card game played esp. in European casinos

bac·cha·nal \ˈba-kən-ᵊl, ˌba-kə-ˈnal, ˌbä-kə-ˈnäl\ *n* 1 : ORGY 2 : REVELER

bac·cha·na·lia \ˌba-kə-ˈnāl-yə\ *n, pl* **bacchanalia** : a drunken orgy — **bac·cha·na·lian** \-ˈnāl-yən\ *adj or n*

bach·e·lor \ˈba-chə-lər\ *n* 1 : a person who has received the usu. lowest degree conferred by a 4-year college 2 : an unmarried man — **bach·e·lor·hood** *n*

bach·e·lor·ette \ˌba-chə-lə-ˈret\ *n* : a young unmarried woman

bachelor's button *n* : a European plant related to the daisies and having blue, pink, or white flower heads

ba·cil·lus \bə-ˈsi-ləs\ *n, pl* **-li** \-ˌlī\ [NL, fr. ML, small staff, dim. of L *baculus* staff] : any of numerous rod-shaped bacteria; *also* : a disease-producing bacterium — **bac·il·lary** \ˈba-sə-ˌler-ē\ *adj*

[1]**back** \ˈbak\ *n* 1 : the rear or dorsal part of the human body; *also* : the corresponding part of a lower animal 2 : the part or surface opposite the front 3 : a player in the backfield in football — **back·less** \-ləs\ *adj*

[2]**back** *adv* 1 : to, toward, or at the rear 2 : AGO 3 : so as to be restrained or retarded 4 : to, toward, or in a former place or state 5 : in return or reply

[3]**back** *adj* 1 : located at or in the back; *also* : REMOTE 2 : OVERDUE 3 : moving or operating backward 4 : not current

[4]**back** *vb* 1 : SUPPORT, UPHOLD 2 : to go or cause to go backward or in reverse 3 : to furnish with a back : form the back of

back·ache \ˈba-ˌkāk\ *n* : a pain in the lower back

back–bench·er \-ˈben-chər\ *n* : a rank-and-file member of a British legislature

back·bite \-ˌbīt\ *vb* **-bit** \-ˌbit\; **-bit·ten** \-ˌbit-ᵊn\; **-bit·ing** \-ˌbī-tiŋ\ : to say mean or spiteful things about someone who is absent — **back·bit·er** *n*

back·board \-ˌbōrd\ *n* : a board placed at or serving as the back of something

back·bone \-ˌbōn\ *n* 1 : the bony column in the back of a vertebrate that is the chief support of the trunk and consists of a jointed series of vertebrae enclosing and protecting the spinal cord 2 : firm resolute character

back·drop \ˈbak-ˌdräp\ *n* : a painted cloth hung across the rear of a stage

back·er \ˈba-kər\ *n* : one that supports

back·field \-ˌfēld\ *n* : the football players whose positions are behind the line

[1]**back·fire** \-ˌfīr\ *n* : a loud noise caused by the improperly timed explosion of fuel in the cylinder of an internal combustion engine

[2]**backfire** *vb* 1 : to make or undergo a backfire 2 : to have a result opposite to what was intended

back·gam·mon \ˈbak-ˌga-mən\ *n* : a game played with pieces on a double board in which the moves are determined by throwing dice

back·ground \ˈbak-ˌgrau̇nd\ *n* 1 : the scenery behind something 2 : the setting within which something takes place; *also* : the sum of a person's experience, training, and understanding

back·hand \ˈbak-ˌhand\ *n* : a stroke (as in tennis) made with the back of the hand turned in the direction of movement; *also* : the side on which such a stroke is made — **back·hand** *vb*

back·hand·ed \ˈbak-ˈhan-dəd\ *adj* 1 : INDIRECT, DEVIOUS; *esp* : SARCASTIC 2 : using or made with a backhand

back·hoe \ˈbak-ˌhō\ *n* : an excavating machine having a bucket that is drawn toward the machine

back·ing \ˈba-kiŋ\ *n* 1 : something forming a back 2 : SUPPORT, AID; *also* : a body of supporters

back·lash \ˈbak-ˌlash\ *n* 1 : a sudden violent backward movement or reaction 2 : a strong adverse reaction

[1]**back·log** \-ˌlȯg, -ˌläg\ *n* 1 : a large log at the back of a hearth fire 2 : an accumulation of tasks unperformed or materials not processed

[2]**backlog** *vb* : to accumulate in reserve

back of *prep* : BEHIND

back out *vb* : to withdraw esp. from a commitment or contest

PRACTICE D-3: Finding Information

Directions: Using the dictionary excerpt of "b" entries on page 38, look for the answers to the following questions. Write your answers in the blanks.

1. What is one slang meaning of *babe?*______________________________

____

2. *Babel* is the name of a city, but it also refers to a place of what? ______________

____

3. Which definition of *baby* is used in this example: "A woman in my book club *babies* her husband."____

4. Where is *baccarat* usually played?_____________________________________

____

5. What is the definition of *bachelor* that has to do with college? ________________

6. What part of speech is *back* in the following sentence: "He wrote *back* to my e-mail within a day." ____

7. Explain in your own words what *backbiting* means. _______________________

____

8. Use *backfire* in a sentence, being clear about which definition you are using. _____

____

9. What are some synonyms for *backhanded?* _____________________________

____

10. If you have a *backlog* of class assignments to do, what is the likely outcome? _____

____

PRACTICE D-4: Quick Quiz

Directions: The dictionary excerpt of "s" entries reproduced on page 41 has some items marked for your identification. Look at the circled material and fill in the blanks with the letter from the following list of items that best describes it. One has been done for you. When finished, turn in the exercise to your instructor.

a. etymology or word history

b. parts of speech

c. contextual examples of word usage

d. word used as several different parts of speech (*n, vb, adj, adv,* or *prep*)

e. definition based on history of word

f. synonyms

g. the preferred pronunciation of the word

h. word meaning in its original language

i. most current definition of the word

j. guide words that show the first and last word on each page

1. ______________________________
2. ______________________________
3. h_____________________________
4. ______________________________
5. ______________________________
6. ______________________________
7. ______________________________
8. ______________________________
9. ______________________________
10. _____________________________

shame • shaving

[2]**shame** *vb* **shamed; sham·ing** **1** : DISGRACE **2** : to make ashamed
shame·faced \ˈshām-ˌfāst\ *adj* : ASHAMED, ABASHED — **shame·faced·ly** \-ˌfā-səd-lē, -ˌfāst-lē\ *adv*
[1]**sham·poo** \sham-ˈpü\ *vb* [Hindi *cāpo*, imper. of *cāpnā* to press, shampoo] : to wash (as the hair) with soap and water or with a special preparation; *also* : to clean (as a rug) similarly
[2]**shampoo** *n*, *pl* **shampoos** **1** : the act or an instance of shampooing **2** : a preparation for use in shampooing
sham·rock \ˈsham-ˌräk\ *n* [Ir *seamróg*, dim. of *seamar* clover] : a plant of folk legend with leaves composed of three leaflets that is associated with St. Patrick and Ireland
shang·hai \shaŋ-ˈhī\ *vb* **shang·haied; shang·hai·ing** [*Shanghai*, China] : to force aboard a ship for service as a sailor; *also* : to trick or force into an undesirable position
Shan·gri–la \ˌshaŋ-gri-ˈlä\ *n* [*Shangri-La*, imaginary land depicted in the novel *Lost Horizon* (1933) by James Hilton] : a remote idyllic hideaway
shank \ˈshaŋk\ *n* **1** : the part of the leg between the knee and the human ankle or a corresponding part of a quadruped **2** : a cut of meat from the leg **3** : the narrow part of the sole of a shoe beneath the instep **4** : the part of a tool or instrument (as a key or anchor) connecting the functioning part with a part by which it is held or moved
shan·tung \ˌshan-ˈtəŋ\ *n* : a fabric in plain weave having a slightly irregular surface
shan·ty \ˈshan-tē\ *n*, *pl* **shanties** [prob. fr. CanF *chantier* lumber camp, hut, fr. F, gantry, fr. L *cantherius* rafter, trellis] : a small roughly built shelter or dwelling
[1]**shape** \ˈshāp\ *vb* **shaped; shap·ing** **1** : to form esp. in a particular shape **2** : DESIGN **3** : ADAPT, ADJUST **4** : REGULATE **syn** make, fashion, fabricate, manufacture, frame, mold
[2]**shape** *n* **1** : APPEARANCE **2** : surface configuration : FORM **3** : bodily contour apart from the head and face : FIGURE **4** : PHANTOM **5** : CONDITION — **shaped** \ˈshāpt\ *adj*
shape·less \ˈshā-pləs\ *adj* **1** : having no definite shape **2** : not shapely — **shape·less·ly** *adv* — **shape·less·ness** *n*
shape·ly \ˈshā-plē\ *adj* **shape·li·er; -est** : having a pleasing shape — **shape·li·ness** *n*
shard \ˈshärd\ *also* **sherd** \ˈshərd\ *n* : a broken piece : FRAGMENT
[1]**share** \ˈshar\ *n* : PLOWSHARE
[2]**share** *n* **1** : a portion belonging to one person or group **2** : any of the equal interests into which the capital stock of a corporation is divided
[3]**share** *vb* **shared; shar·ing** **1** : APPORTION **2** : to use or enjoy with others **3** : PARTICIPATE — **shar·er** *n*
share·crop·per \-ˌkrä-pər\ *n* : a farmer who works another's land in return for a share of the crop — **share·crop** *vb*
share·hold·er \-ˌhōl-dər\ *n* : STOCKHOLDER
[1]**shark** \ˈshärk\ *n* : any of various active, usu. predaceous, and mostly large marine cartilaginous fishes
[2]**shark** *n* : a greedy crafty person
shark·skin \-ˌskin\ *n* **1** : the hide of a shark or leather made from it **2** : a fabric (as of cotton or rayon) woven from strands of many fine threads and having a sleek appearance and silky feel
[1]**sharp** \ˈshärp\ *adj* **1** : having a thin cutting edge or fine point : not dull or blunt **2** : COLD, NIPPING ⟨a ~ wind⟩ **3** : keen in intellect, perception, or attention **4** : BRISK, ENERGETIC **5** : IRRITABLE ⟨a ~ temper⟩ **6** : causing intense distress ⟨a ~ pain⟩ **7** : HARSH, CUTTING ⟨a ~ rebuke⟩ **8** : affecting the senses as if cutting or piercing ⟨a ~ sound⟩ ⟨a ~ smell⟩ **9** : not smooth or rounded ⟨~ features⟩ **10** : involving an abrupt or extreme change ⟨a ~ turn⟩ **11** : CLEAR, DISTINCT ⟨mountains in ~ relief⟩; *also* : easy to perceive ⟨a ~ contrast⟩ **12** : higher than the true pitch; *also* : raised by a half step **13** : STYLISH ⟨a ~ dresser⟩ **syn** keen, acute, quick-witted, penetrative — **sharp·ly** *adv* — **sharp·ness** *n*
[2]**sharp** *adv* **1** : in a sharp manner **2** : EXACTLY, PRECISELY ⟨left at 8 ~⟩
[3]**sharp** *n* **1** : a sharp edge or point **2** : a character ♯ which indicates that a specified note is to be raised by a half step; *also* : the resulting note **3** : SHARPER
[4]**sharp** *vb* : to raise in pitch by a half step
sharp·en \ˈshär-pən\ *vb* : to make or become sharp — **sharp·en·er** *n*
sharp·er \ˈshär-pər\ *n* : SWINDLER; *esp* : a cheating gambler
sharp·ie *or* **sharpy** \ˈshär-pē\ *n*, *pl* **sharp·ies** **1** : SHARPER **2** : a person who is exceptionally keen or alert
sharp·shoot·er \ˈshärp-ˌshü-tər\ *n* : a good marksman — **sharp·shoot·ing** *n*
shat·ter \ˈsha-tər\ *vb* : to dash or burst into fragments — **shat·ter·proof** \ˈsha-tər-ˌprüf\ *adj*
[1]**shave** \ˈshāv\ *vb* **shaved; shaved** *or* **shav·en** \ˈshā-vən\; **shav·ing** **1** : to slice in thin pieces **2** : to make bare or smooth by cutting the hair from **3** : to cut or pare off by the sliding movement of a razor **4** : to skim along or near the surface of
[2]**shave** *n* **1** : any of various tools for cutting thin slices **2** : an act or process of shaving
shav·er \ˈshā-vər\ *n* **1** : an electric razor **2** : BOY, YOUNGSTER
shaves *pl of* SHAFT
shav·ing *n* **1** : the act of one that shaves **2** : something shaved off

Name ______________________ Section __________ Date __________

PRACTICE D-5: How Words Get in the Dictionary

Directions: The English language is continually changing, especially American English. Some words become archaic, meaning seldom or no longer used. At some point they are dropped from the dictionary. Other words are added as new technology and other languages make their way into American usage. A dictionary tries to reflect the words as used by most. Because a word appears in the dictionary does not necessarily mean the word is correctly used, only that it is used that way by enough people that it gets reported in the dictionary. The following essay gives you an idea of how new words get placed in a dictionary.

GIVE US YOUR SCUZZBUCKETS: "MULTITASK" AND "DAY TRADER" (BUT NOT "STALKERAZZI") GET THE NOD IN A NEW AMERICAN HERITAGE DICTIONARY

Walter Kim and Andrea Sachs

1 If you're still hoarding typewriter ribbons for the day when this whole computer thing blows over and still insist on calling pasta "noodles," maybe this will convince you that times have changed. According to the *American Heritage Dictionary,* whose fourth edition appears this fall, complete with 10,000 entries not found in the third edition of eight years ago, the following sentence is now legitimate English: "The dot-com brainiac went postal, big-time, spewing baba gannouj all over the food court, when some butthead with no sense of netiquette stole his def domain name."

2 Lexicographers are to words what INS agents are to immigrants: providers of legal residency. The words may have been in the country already and may have even gained a social foothold ("day trader," "erectile dysfunction"), but they weren't here officially, so to speak. They had to watch over their shoulders for the authorities. Viewed with suspicion by traditionalists because of foreign sounding names ("keiretsu") or unconventional customs ("air kiss"), such words risked deportation at any moment.

3 They can breathe easier now. In contrast to the more conservative gatekeepers at Merriam-Webster and *The Oxford English Dictionary,* the editors at American Heritage practice a linguistic open-door policy. Give us your "shock jocks," your "scuzzbuckets," they say. Give us your "digerati" yearning to "multitask." "People look at the dictionary as a normalizing thing," says executive editor Joseph Pickett. "It helps to give the word codified status." Not all words, thankfully. Take "stalkerazzi," which gained currency after Princess Diana's death. The term was considered for the dictionary but couldn't produce convincing credentials. Maybe it lost its place to "drug holiday" ("n. A usually brief period during which a drug that is typically taken on a daily basis, such as an antidepressant, is not taken . . . "), or "seaborgium," a term from physics that I have yet to look up but that I'm almost sure means blue-green slime.

4 Many of the fresh entries in the dictionary, like many of the nation's recent immigrants, have been admitted because they play a role in the new, high-tech economy. It's clear what we've been talking about for the past eight years: machines and money. "Usenet." "Comp time." "Bit stream." "Index fund." This is your heritage, America: a language that's forever evolving new terms for small computers ("subnotebook") and exotic lending practices ("reverse mortgage") but still has only one word for snow ("snow").

5 Who decides which words get in the dictionary? I do, actually. "We have a systematic program for reading publications like *TIME,*" says Pickett, "looking for exam-

ples of new words and new uses of old words." This knowledge is unsettling. Take "pizza face," a hurtful name once hurled at me as an acne-afflicted teen. Never do I want to see this epithet enshrined in a major dictionary, and yet by using it, as I just did, I've probably guaranteed its inclusion in the next edition.

6 There's a lesson here. Next time you're "cybersurfing" the "Web" and spot a new word, don't say it out loud. They might hear you, brainiac.

Answer the following questions in the spaces provided.

1. What dictionary and what edition are discussed in the article? ________________

____

2. How many more words appear in the new edition of the dictionary than in the last edition? ____

____

3. The authors use the analogy that lexicographers are to words what INS agents are to immigrants. What do they mean? ________________________________

____

____

4. Do all words people use get in the dictionary? Explain your answer. ____________

____

5. From what source do many of the new words in the dictionary come? ___________

____

6. Translate the last sentence in the first paragraph. ______________________

____

____

7. What, if any, of the words in that sentence have you used? _________________

____

PRACTICE D-6 "What You Should Look for in a Dictionary" by Robert M. Pierson

Directions: Answer the following questions.

1. What is your method or criteria for selecting a new dictionary? ________________

____

2. What do you think is an important characteristic of a good dictionary? __________

____

3. For what purpose do you most often use a dictionary? ___________________

____

The following selection provides much about dictionaries that you should know. Dictionaries are an important tool for increasing your vocabulary and should be chosen carefully. In the following article, the author not only gives you interesting information about what dictionaries do and don't do, but he also helps you evaluate dictionaries by looking at twelve different parts a good dictionary should contain.

Before you begin to read, take a moment to survey or skim over the article. It may seem long, but notice the twelve parts of a good dictionary are numbered and in bold print as an aid in reading. The point of this practice is to read and understand how these twelve parts can help you select a good dictionary.

WHAT YOU SHOULD LOOK FOR IN A DICTIONARY

Robert M. Pierson

1 First, does it describe or prescribe? Does it tell you how words *are* used or does it tell you how its compiler thinks words *should* be used? Most modern dictionaries do the former—most of the time. They are—or strive to be—objective reports of the state of the language. (The big exceptions are usage manuals and stylebooks—on which more below.) Editors of today's dictionaries may privately shudder at *presently* for *now*, at *hose* for *stockings*, at *cremains* for *ashes of people who have been cremated*, at *home* for *house*. But if Americans choose to use words so, editors are honor-bound to record that fact. The day is therefore past when you can defend the artistic effect of your use of a word by saying, "But I found it in the dictionary."

2 It was not always so. In centuries past, dictionaries existed primarily to establish and maintain good French—or whatever. Sometimes the motive was to replace Latin (a nearly frozen language) with something just as stable and "classic"; sometimes, to make one dialect (that of the capital?) supreme; sometimes, to encourage the use of a national language (as opposed to that of a foreign oppressor). Times have indeed changed.

3 Not that today's dictionaries are completely value-free. They identify some uses as slang, some as obsolete, some as dialectal, some as illiterate—and some words as taboo, even offensive. But even here they strive to explain how society in general views words, not how *the dictionaries* view them. They are not saying that it is "bad" to use *smashed* for *drunk*—only that most people will regard *smashed* as an informal way of putting it. Only you and your editor can decide whether, in a particular situation, you should write *smashed* or *drunk*—or *blotto* or *feeling no pain* or *intoxicated* or *inebriated* or *under the influence* (without, perhaps, saying of what!).

4 Some other points to note in dictionaries:

1. **Their scope.** Are they *general* or are they in some way *specialized?* Do they cover the language as a whole or are they in some way limited? Do they, for example, cover new words only? or slang only? or only the special vocabulary of science—or of one particular science? As a writer, you will surely want a general dictionary—plus one or more specialized ones, depending on your interests.
2. **Their scale** (a result of their *degree of selectivity*). Are they more or less complete—*unabridged*—or are they selective—*abridged?* If the latter, is abridgement a matter of less information about the same number of words or a matter of the same amount of information about fewer words—or, as is usually the case, mostly the latter but with some of the former? As a writer you may, deep in your heart, want an unabridged dictionary, plus a revolving stand to mount it on. You will probably find that an abridged dictionary designated, in its title, as "college" or "colle-

Excerpted from "A Writer's Guide to Dictionaries" by Robert M. Pierson. Originally published in *Writer's Digest*, November 1983, pp. 34–38. Reprinted by Permission.

giate" will meet your needs well enough—and with less pain to your wallet and your arm muscles. If you can afford to do so, get two such dictionaries and, when a problem arises, compare what they have to say.

3. **Their intended readership.** Are they for children or for adults? If for adults, for adults of what level of sophistication? Again, the "collegiate" dictionaries will probably best suit you as a writer: they will give you not only *the* meaning of each word they list but also other meanings, with labels to alert you to how words are likely to be received. They will also tell you a little about the origins and histories of the words they list.
4. **Their overall arrangement.** Basically, are they in one alphabetical sequence or in several? Opinions differ as to which way is best. Should place-names be in a separate list? What about personal names? foreign words widely used in English? abbreviations? How about new words and new uses of old words? Some dictionaries merge all categories into (as information scientists say) one file. Others lift out one or more categories and file them separately. The best solution, so far as users of dictionaries are concerned, is to look, first of all, at each dictionary's table of contents. And once you are within an alphabetical sequence, remember what I said before about word-by-word, letter-by-letter, and keyword-by-keyword alphabetizing. Remember, too, that *Mc* and *Mac* names may be filed as spelled, filed separately, or all filed as if spelled *Mac* (which is how most library catalogs do it, by the way). Again, don't struggle to remember which system is used: just be ready to shift gears.
5. **The order in which they list multiple definitions.** Here are two main sequences: "historical" sequence, with oldest extant uses defined first, newest last; and "frequence" sequence, with most common first, least common last. Historical sequence tends to be featured in Merriam-Webster titles; frequency, in most others. As a writer, you must be aware of all the ways in which the words you use *may* be understood, so always read the whole entry. Just bear in mind that the first meaning listed may or may not be the only most likely to come to mind.
6. **The readability of their definitions.** One of the attractive features of the *American Heritage* titles is their sheer readability. Occasionally, if the editors of dictionaries are not watchful, circular definitions, which leave you where you were, creep in—e.g., called a *prothesis* a *prosthetic appliance.* Sometimes definitions will seem duskier than the words they are said to illumine. On the other hand, dictionaries tend to be brief—and who said brevity always leads to clarity? If dictionary editors spun out their definitions to make them more readable, their products would weigh and cost much more. Still and all, try looking up some words in fields you know a *little* about and see how they read: if you look up words you already know a lot about, you may "read in" meaning not provided by their definitions; and if you look up totally unfamiliar words, you will be in no position to judge. Either way, try not to mistake oversimplification for genuine clarity: sure, it's "readable" to call an apricot "a delicious fruit of a pale creamy pinky yellow," but would not that definition apply equally well to nectarines and some grapefruits?
7. **Their labeling of meanings and uses.** As suggested earlier, it is helpful to know that *braces* in the sense of *suspenders* is British, as is *suspender* in the sense of *garter*—that in botanical usage, the Irish potato is a *stem,* strawberry not essentially a *fruit,* and a tomato only a *berry!* The constant reminder as to what is *standard* (unlabeled) and what is not really keep us on our toes—as writers. Not that labeling is always perfect: one dictionary I reviewed several years ago carefully labeled racial and religious slurs as offensive, e.g., *nigger* and *kike,* but did not so label *broad* ("woman") and *queer* ("homosexual")—surely just as offensive to those to whom the words are applied—although just possibly, I grant, those particular words are

not always *intended* to be offensive. But surely that is just the point. As writers, we need to express ourselves, yes, choosing the words that most exactly say—to us—what we mean; but if we are to communicate successfully, we must also think of how our words are likely to be received, regardless of our intentions. Hence the usefulness of labels. By the way, the American Heritage titles are particularly strong in respect to usage, with more concerning the "social status" of words than you find in other general dictionaries.

8. **What they may tell words besides their meanings.** Pronunciation, syllabification, grammatical inflections (plurals, past tense forms, etc.), origins and histories—and, of course, spelling! All these are likely to be indicated in "collegiate" dictionaries. Often the presentation of this material is extremely condensed and literally hard to read: I know one dictionary whose print is so small and so dull that it is hard to tell whether the little marks between syllables are only raised periods (meaning, in that dictionary, syllabic division) or actual hyphens (meaning to spell with hyphens). In an age when we are encouraged to read faster and faster, you may need to slow down, as if reading the thorniest Rossetti or Hopkins sonnet! And to be sure to study the system of symbols used—e.g., > for "derived from" and the "schwa" (ə) for the "uh" sound—and abbreviations too, like O.F. for "Old French." There may well be a key at the bottom of the page. Just don't assume that every new dictionary—or dictionary new to you—is, in this respect, like one you are used to.
9. **Their references to related words.** Often defining a word precisely is very difficult. One solution to that problem is to refer to words of more or less similar meaning (from *awkward* to *clumsy,* from *rude* to *boorish,* from *immaculate* to *clean*) or to words of opposite meaning (from *calm* to *agitated,* from *mellifluous* to *harsh*). The more a dictionary does this—and the more it explains subtle differences—the better for you as a writer. Sensitivity to such matters will give your writing precision.
10. **Their use of examples—including quotations—to clarify meaning.** These may be "made-up" illustrations of their usage or they may be quotations from published material. If the latter, observe their age. As a reader of old and new material, you may be helped by a quotation from the Bible or from Shakespeare. As a writer, you may be more helped by a quotation from *TIME* or *Natural History* or *Organic Gardening.* In any case, quotations—giving words in context—may hint at shades of meaning exceedingly difficult to convey otherwise.
11. **Their use of graphics, especially line drawings.** Again, the more the better—to label the parts of a Greek column, for instance, or the components of a threshing machine. I do not share the view that a picture is always worth a thousand words, but sometimes a picture can do what dozens of words fail to do—at least as you and I use them.
12. **The presence of encyclopedic information.** In theory, a dictionary is a word book; an encyclopedia, a subject-matter book. When you define *grizzly bear* so as to make it clear how grizzlies differ, basically, from American black bears, you are doing only what dictionaries traditionally do; when you tell what they feed on (cow parsnips, I am told) and how many are left—and go on to mention a good book on the subject—you are doing, in addition, what encyclopedias do. Some dictionaries go very far along this line, even to the point of giving lists of chemical elements, evolutionary trees for animals and plants and languages, maps of continents, rules of grammar and punctuation, even the text of the Constitution—you name it; some dictionary—some "word book"—will provide it. And when you get into specialized subject dictionaries, the tendency is even more marked—with *dictionary* used to designate just about any book featuring alphabetical sequence.

When it comes to selecting a general English-language dictionary of "desk size," my advice is this: don't buy a book on the basis of bonus features unless you really need the bonus features. How much space do you have for other books? Do you already own an encyclopedia? How far do you live from the public library?

5 My advice, then, is this: Get to know your dictionaries. Look at *all* their parts—including those little appendices and supplements at the back. Imagine how you might use what you find. Keep your dictionaries at hand, and form the habit of consulting them often. And read them for pleasure. Though not set up for consecutive reading, as are novels and treatises, they can be read in much the same way. Read in them again and again—and note your findings, whether in your "writer's journal," on note cards for orderly filing, or in that secret file at the back of your mind. Save all these bits and pieces. You never know when they will rise to the surface for you to hook them. They will be there "for you," like old friends, to enrich your creative output; to help you say what you mean, not just something close; to help you convey a sense of truth-telling, not of weary echoing of the thoughts and feelings of others; to help give your writing the sheen, the glow, the magic that we, all of us, strive for but so seldom achieve, let alone sustain.

Comprehension Check

Directions: In the spaces provided, answer the following questions about the selection you just read.

1. Some of the examples Pierson uses are words that have changed common meanings since he wrote this article. He says *stockings* would be preferred over *hose*, yet *hose* sounds more current to us. What is one other current term for this piece of clothing? ______________________________

____

____

The following are some of the points the author says to note when looking for a good dictionary. Explain briefly what he means by each:

2. scope ______________________________

____

3. scale ______________________________

____

4. intended readership ______________________________

____

5. overall arrangement ______________________________

____

6. What is one of the two ways some dictionaries list multiple definitions? __________

____

7. Explain what the author means by circular definitions. ______________________________

____

8. According to Pierson, if a Merriam-Webster dictionary lists several definitions of a word, the first definition is the

a. oldest

b. most common

c. slang definition

9. T/F Good dictionaries have more graphics or pictures.

10. T/F The author believes all dictionaries are basically the same.

Vocabulary Check

Directions: Define the following underlined words from the article.

1. First, does it describe or prescribe? Does it tell you how words *are* used or does it tell you how its compiler thinks words *should* be used? (paragraph 1)

____

2. Not that today's dictionaries are completely value-free. They identify some uses as slang, some as obsolete . . . (paragraph 3)

____

3. Only you and your editor can decide whether, in a particular situation, you should write *smashed* for *drunk*—or *blotto* or *feeling no pain* or . . . inebriated (paragraph 3) ______________________________

____

4. Are they more or less complete—unabridged—or are they selective—*abridged?* (point #2) ______________________________

____

5. Try not to mistake oversimplification for genuine clarity. (point #6) ______________

____

6. One dictionary I reviewed several years ago carefully labeled racial and religious slurs as offensive . . . (point #7) ______________________________

____

7. Pronunciation, syllabication, grammatical inflections (plurals, past tense forms, etc.) are all likely to be indicated in collegiate dictionaries. (point #8) ______________

____

8. Often the presentation of this material is extremely condensed and literally hard to read. (point #8) ______________________________

____

9. One solution to that problem is to refer to words of more or less similar meaning (from *awkward* to *clumsy,* from *rude* to boorish). (point #9)______________________________

____

10. Look at *all* their parts—including those little appendices and supplements at the back. (final paragraph)______________________________

____

After the results of the comprehension check and vocabulary check have been scored, record them on the Student Record Chart in the Appendix. Each answer for both checks is worth 10 percent for a total of 100 percent possible for comprehension and 100 percent for vocabulary.

Remember to make vocabulary cards for any words that gave you trouble.

Application 3: Evaluating Your Own Dictionary

Evaluate the dictionary you currently use according to any six of the twelve criteria for evaluating dictionaries in Robert Pierson's article. Briefly explain what this shows you about your personal dictionary that you didn't know before. Turn in your evaluation and explanation.

E. Putting It All Together

Following are two reading selections. Both are followed by comprehension and vocabulary checks; the second one is a timed reading. Increasing your ability to read well involves these three components: vocabulary, comprehension, and rate. In this chapter, you have worked primarily on the first component—vocabulary. If you don't recognize the words when you are reading, you will have a hard time understanding what you read. You will now be asked to answer comprehension questions, too, showing that you understand the selections you are reading. Much of this book will be devoted to increasing your comprehension of what you read. The final reading is a timed reading because if you read too slowly (under 180 words per minute [wpm]), your mind may wander and comprehension may fall. The comprehension questions and timed reading in this section are primarily to help you see what your understanding and reading rate are at the beginning of the book. Your scores at this point are less important than understanding why you may have missed a question. Always make certain you understand why you may have missed any questions. Learn from your mistakes.

Another way of increasing vocabulary is to read widely and well. Sherman Alexie has a lot to say about books, reading, and writing. Read about him to see if his work or life inspires you to new ways of vocabulary development. Another way to find current information, quotations, or pictures of this author is to use the World Wide Web. Using a search engine such as Google, go2net.com or AltaVista, type Sherman Alexie's name under "Search."

Introducing Sherman Alexie

Sherman Alexie is a Spokane/Coeur d'Alene Native American from Wellpinit, Washington, on the Spokane Indian Reservation. Alexie has published over 200 poems, stories, and translations in many magazines and journals. He is the winner of numerous prizes and awards, including a poetry fellowship from the National Endowment of the Arts in 1992. His publications include a best-selling collection of interlinked stories, *The Lone Ranger and Tonto Fistfight in Heaven* (1993); and a novel, *Reservation Blues,* about a Native American rock band called Coyote Springs. He wrote the script for the movie "Smoke Signals."

Simon Ortiz, himself a Native American writer, says this of Alexie: "His vision is an amazing celebration of endurance, intimacy, love, and creative insight. Alexie speaks for the spirit of Native American resistance, determination, and sovereignty." Prominent among the issues Alexie raises in his writing is the reconciliation of modern life with existence under the reservation system. Much of Alexie's work reflects the need and power of the imagination just to survive Indian circumstances on the reservation.

In an "On Tour" interview for *Hungry Mind Review* in which he was asked to respond to a question on the theme "Heroes and Villains," Alexie wrote:

> I've always been picky about heroes. Like most American males, I've always admired athletes, particularly basketball players. . . . Unlike many American males, I always admired writers as much as I admired athletes. I loved books and the people who wrote books. John Steinbeck was one of my earliest heroes because he wrote about the poor. Stephen King became a hero because he wrote so well of misfit kids, the nerds and geeks. Growing up on my reservation, I was a poor geek, so I had obvious reasons to love Steinbeck and King. I still love their novels, but I have no idea if they were/are spiritual, compassionate, and gracious men. There is so much spirit, compassion, and grace in their work, I want to assume that Steinbeck and King were/are good people. I would be terribly disappointed to find out otherwise. . . .
>
> Most of my heroes are just decent people. Decency is rare and underrated. I think my writing is somehow just about decency. Still, if I was keeping score, and I like to keep score, I would say the villains in the world are way ahead of the heroes. I hope my writing can help even the score.

PRACTICE E-1

Directions: Read the following selection and answer the questions that follow.

SUPERMAN AND ME

Sherman Alexie

1 I learned to read with a *Superman* comic book. Simple enough, I suppose. I cannot recall which particular *Superman* comic book I read, nor can I remember which villain he fought in that issue. I cannot remember the plot, nor the means by which I obtained the comic book. What I can remember is this: I was three years old, a Spokane Indian boy living with his family on the Spokane Indian Reservation in eastern Washington state. We were poor by most standards, but one of my parents usually managed to find some minimum-wage job or another, which made us middle class by

reservation standards. I had a brother and three sisters. We lived on a combination of irregular pay-checks, hope, fear, and government-surplus food.

2 My father, who is one of the few Indians who went to Catholic school on purpose, was an avid reader of westerns, spy thrillers, murder mysteries, gangster epics, basketball-player biographies, and anything else he could find. He bought his books by the pound at Dutch's Pawn Shop, Goodwill, Salvation Army, and Value Village. When he had extra money, he bought new novels at supermarkets, convenience stores, and hospital gift shops. Our house was filled with books. They were stacked in crazy piles in the bathroom, bedrooms, and living room. In a fit of unemployment-inspired creative energy, my father built a set of bookshelves and soon filled them with a random assortment of books about the Kennedy assassination, Watergate, the Vietnam War, and the entire twenty-three-book series of the Apache westerns. My father loved books, and since I loved my father with an aching devotion, I decided to love books as well.

3 I can remember picking up my father's books before I could read. The words themselves were mostly foreign, but I still remember the exact moment when I first understood, with a sudden clarity, the purpose of a paragraph. I didn't have the vocabulary to say "paragraph," but I realized that a paragraph was a fence that held words. The words inside a paragraph worked together for a common purpose. They had some specific reason for being inside the same fence. This knowledge delighted me. I began to think of everything in terms of paragraphs. Our reservation was a small paragraph within the United States. My family's house was a paragraph, distinct from the other paragraphs of the LeBrets to the north, the Fords to our south, and the Tribal School to the west. Inside our house, each family member existed as a separate paragraph, but still had genetics and common experiences to link us. Now, using this logic, I can see my changed family as an essay of seven paragraphs: mother, father, older brother, the deceased sister, my younger twin sisters, and our adopted little brother.

4 At the same time I was seeing the world in paragraphs, I also picked up that *Superman* comic book. Each panel, complete with picture, dialogue, and narrative, was a three-dimensional paragraph. In one panel, Superman breaks through a door. His suit is red, blue, and yellow. The brown door shatters into many pieces. I look at the narrative above the picture. I cannot read the words, but I assume it tells me that Superman is breaking down the door. Aloud, I pretend to read the words and say, "Superman is breaking down the door." Words, dialogue, also float out of Superman's mouth. Because he is breaking down the door, I assume he says, "I am breaking down the door." Once again, I pretend to read the words and say aloud, "I am breaking down the door." In this way, I learned to read.

5 This might be an interesting story all by itself. A little Indian boy teaches himself to read at an early age and advances quickly. He reads *Grapes of Wrath* in kindergarten when other children are struggling through Dick and Jane. If he'd been anything but an Indian boy living on the reservation, he might have been called a prodigy. But he is an Indian boy living on the reservation, and is simply an oddity. He grows into a man who often speaks of his childhood in the third person, as if it will somehow dull the pain and make him sound more modest about his talents.

6 A smart Indian is a dangerous person, widely feared and ridiculed by Indians and non-Indians alike. I fought with my classmates on a daily basis. They wanted me to stay quiet when the non-Indian teacher asked for answers, for volunteers, for help. We were Indian children who were expected to be stupid. Most lived up to those expectations inside the classroom, but subverted them on the outside. They struggled with basic reading in school, but could remember how to sing a few dozen powwow songs. They were monosyllabic in front of their non-Indian teachers, but could tell complicated stories and jokes at the dinner table. They submissively ducked their heads

when confronted by a non-Indian adult, but would slug it out with the Indian bully who was ten years older. As Indian children, we were expected to fail in the non-Indian world. Those who failed were ceremonially accepted by other Indians and appropriately pitied by non-Indians.

7 I refused to fail. I was smart. I was arrogant. I was lucky. I read books late into the night, until I could barely keep my eyes open. I read books at recess, then during lunch, and in the few minutes left after I had finished my classroom assignments. I read books in the car when my family traveled to powwows or basketball games. In shopping malls, I ran to the bookstores and read bits and pieces of as many books as I could. I read the books my father brought home from the pawnshops and secondhand stores. I read the books I borrowed from the library. I read the backs of cereal boxes. I read the newspaper. I read the bulletins posted on the walls of the school, the clinic, the tribal offices, the post office. I read junk mail. I read auto-repair manuals. I read magazines. I read anything that had words and paragraphs. I read with equal parts joy and desperation. I loved those books, but I also knew that love had only one purpose. I was trying to save my life.

8 Despite all the books I read, I am still surprised I became a writer. I was going to be a pediatrician. These days, I write novels, short stories, and poems. I visit schools and teach creative writing to Indian kids. In all my years in the reservation school system, I was never taught how to write poetry, short stories, or novels. I was certainly never taught that Indians wrote poetry, short stories, and novels. Writing was something beyond Indians. I cannot recall a single time that a guest teacher visited the reservation. There must have been visiting teachers. Who were they? Where are they now? Do they exist? I visit the schools as often as possible. The Indian kids crowd the classroom. Many are writing their own poems, short stories, and novels. They have read my books. They have read many other books. They look at me with bright eyes and arrogant wonder. They are trying to save their lives. Then there are the sullen and already defeated Indian kids who sit in the back rows and ignore me with theatrical precision. The pages of their notebooks are empty. They carry neither pencil nor pen. They stare out the window. They refuse and resist. "Books," I say to them. "Books," I say. I throw my weight against their locked doors. The door holds. I am smart. I am arrogant. I am lucky. I am trying to save our lives.

Comprehension Check

Directions: Answer the following questions about the selection you just read.

1. What is unusual about the author's reading of the *Superman* comic book? ______

____

2. The author of this story was raised

a. in a variety of homes as the family moved.

b. on a Spokane Indian Reservation in Washington State.

c. in a suburb of Washington, D.C.

d. in a wealthy family.

3. T/F His father's favorite books were westerns.

4. How was the author's love of books related to his love of his father? __________

____

5. When the author first understood the purpose of a paragraph, what did he compare it to? ____

____

6. His memory of reading in kindergarten involves reading
   a. *Dick and Jane* books.
   b. *Superman* comic books.
   c. a wide variety of books.
   d. *Grapes of Wrath.*

7. How did being an early and good reader affect his relationship with other Indian students?____

____

8. So many of the Indian children failed at school. Why does Alexie feel he didn't fail?____

____

9. Why does the author teach creative writing to Indian kids? ________________

____

____

10. In your opinion, how is the author's love of books related to his love of writing?

____

____

Vocabulary Check

Directions: Define the following underlined words from the selection.

1. My father was an <u>avid</u> reader of westerns, spy thrillers, murder mysteries, gangster epics, . . . and anything else he could find. ______________________________

____

2. I cannot recall which particular *Superman* comic book I read, nor can I remember which <u>villain</u> he fought in that issue. ______________________________

____

3. My father loved books, and since I loved my father with an <u>aching</u> devotion, I decided to love books as well. ______________________________

____

4. Each family member existed as a separate paragraph, but still had <u>genetics</u> and common experiences to link us. ______________________________

____

5. Each panel of the *Superman* comic book, complete with picture, dialogue, and <u>narrative</u>, was a three-dimensional paragraph. ______________________________

____

6. If he'd been anything but an Indian boy living on the reservation, he might have been called a <u>prodigy</u>. ______________________________

____

7. Most Indian children lived up to these expectations inside the classroom, but <u>subverted</u> them on the outside. ______________________________

____

8. They <u>submissively</u> ducked their heads when confronted by a non-Indian adult, but would slug it out with the Indian bully who was ten years older. ______________

____

9. I refused to fail. I was smart. I was <u>arrogant</u>. ______________________________

____

10. Then there are the <u>sullen</u> and already defeated Indian kids who sit in the back rows and ignore me with theatrical precision. ______________________________

____

Record the results of the comprehension check and vocabulary check on the Student Record Chart in the Appendix. Each answer for both checks is worth 10 percent for a total of 100 percent possible for comprehension and 100 percent for vocabulary.

Remember to make vocabulary cards for any words that gave you trouble.

PRACTICE E-2: Timed Reading

Directions: This is your first chance to see what your current reading rate is. Remember that your current rate is not as important as understanding why you are reading at that rate and how it helps or hinders you. If you read too slowly (approximately below 180 wpm), keeping your concentration on the reading will be difficult. If you read too quickly and can't answer the questions, you are reading fast but with no comprehension. You want to read this first timed reading at a rate that is fast enough to feel slightly forced but slow enough to understand what you read.

Begin timing: ____________

IN PRAISE OF THE F WORD

Mary Sherry

1 Tens of thousands of 18-year-olds will graduate this year and be handed meaningless diplomas. These diplomas won't look any different from those awarded their luckier classmates. Their validity will be questioned only when their employers discover that these graduates are semiliterate.

2 Eventually a fortunate few will find their way into educational-repair shops—adult-literacy programs, such as the one where I teach basic grammar and writing. There, high-school graduates and high-school dropouts pursuing graduate-equivalency

Reprinted by Permission of Mary Sherry, as published in *Newsweek*.

certificates will learn the skills they should have learned in school. They will also discover they have been cheated by our educational system.

3 As I teach, I learn a lot about our schools. Early in each session I ask my students to write about an unpleasant experience they had in school. No writers' block here! "I wish someone would have had made me stop doing drugs and made me study." "I liked to party and no one seemed to care." "I was a good kid and didn't cause any trouble, so they just passed me along even though I didn't read well and couldn't write." And so on.

4 I am your basic do-gooder, and prior to teaching this class I blamed the poor academic skills our kids have today on drugs, divorce, and other impediments to concentration necessary for doing well in school. But, as I rediscover each time I walk into the classroom, before a teacher can expect students to concentrate, he or she has to get their attention, no matter what distractions may be at hand. There are many ways to do this, and they have much to do with teaching style. However, if style alone won't do it, there is another way to show who holds the winning hand in the classroom. That is to reveal the trump card of failure.

5 I will never forget a teacher who played that card to get the attention of one of my children. Our youngest, a world-class charmer, did little to develop his intellectual talents but always got by. Until Mrs. Stifter.

6 Our son was a high-school senior when he had her for English. "He sits in the back of the room talking to his friends," she told me. "Why don't you move him to the front row?" I urged, believing the embarrassment would get him to settle down. Mrs. Stifter looked at me steely-eyed over her glasses. "I don't move seniors," she said. "I flunk them." I was flustered. Our son's academic life flashed before my eyes. No teacher had ever threatened him with that before. I regained my composure and managed to say that I thought she was right. By the time I got home I was feeling pretty good about this. It was a radical approach for these times, but, well, why not? "She's going to flunk you," I told my son. I did not discuss it any further. Suddenly English became a priority in his life. He finished out the semester with an A.

7 I know one example doesn't make a case, but at night I see a parade of students who are angry and resentful for having been passed along until they could no longer even pretend to keep up. Of average intelligence or better, they eventually quit school, concluding they were too dumb to finish. "I should have been held back" is a comment I hear frequently. Even sadder are those students who are high-school graduates who say to me after a few weeks of class, "I don't know how I ever got a high-school diploma."

8 Passing students who have not mastered the work cheats them and the employers who expect graduates to have basic skills. We excuse this dishonest behavior by saying kids can't learn if they come from terrible environments. No one seems to stop to think that—no matter what environments they come from—most kids don't put school first on their list unless they perceive something is at stake. They'd rather be sailing.

9 Many students I see at night could give expert testimony on unemployment, chemical dependency, abusive relationships. In spite of these difficulties, they have decided to make education a priority. They are motivated by the desire for a better job or the need to hang on to the one they've got. They have a healthy fear of failure.

10 People of all ages can rise above their problems, but they need to have a reason to do so. Young people generally don't have the maturity to value education in the same way my adult students value it. But fear of failure, whether economic or academic, can motivate both.

11 Flunking as a regular policy has just as much merit today as it did two generations ago. We must review the threat of flunking and see it as it really is—a positive teaching tool. It is an expression of confidence by both teachers and parents that the students have the ability to learn the material presented to them. However, making it work again would take a dedicated, caring conspiracy between teachers and parents.

It would mean facing the tough reality that passing kids who haven't learned the material—while it might save them grief for the short term—dooms them to long-term illiteracy. It would mean that teachers would have to follow through on their threats, and parents would have to stand behind them, knowing their children's best interests are indeed at stake. This means no more doing Scott's assignments for him because he might fail. No more passing Jodi because she's such a nice kid.

12 This is a policy that worked in the past and can work today. A wise teacher, with the support of his parents, gave our son the opportunity to succeed—or fail. It's time we return this choice to all students.

Finish timing. Record time here: ____________ and use the Timed Readings Conversion Chart in the Appendix to figure your rate: ____________ wpm.

Comprehension Check

Directions: Now answer the following questions:

1. What is the author's main point? ______________________________
____
____
____

2. What does the author mean by the term *educational-repair shops?* ____________
____
____

3. T/F The author is a high school English teacher.

4. Before teaching her present classes, on what things did she blame the poor academic skills of students? ______________________________
____
____

5. What does she now feel is a major cause of poor academic performance by students? ______________________________
____
____

6. What, according to the author, is wrong with passing students who have not mastered the course work? ______________________________
____
____

7. Most of the author's students have what she calls a "healthy fear of failure." What does she mean?______________________________
____
____
____

8. T/F The author feels that most young people generally don't have the maturity to value education the way adults do.

9. Why does the author believe flunking students as a regular policy has merit? ____

____

____

____

____

10. What does she feel it would take to make her policy work? ______________

____

____

For every question you missed, find the place in the article that contains the correct answer. Try to determine why you missed the questions you did. If you read faster than you normally do, a score of 60 percent correct is considered good. As you get used to faster speeds, you will discover your comprehension scores will improve.

Vocabulary Check

Part A

Directions: Define the following underlined words or phrases as they appear in the article.

1. their validity will be questioned (paragraph 1)

____

2. drugs, divorce, and other impediments to concentration (paragraph 4)

____

3. don't put school first on their list unless they perceive something is at stake (paragraph 8)

____

4. a dedicated, caring conspiracy between teachers and parents (paragraph 11)

____

5. testimony on unemployment, chemical dependency, abusive relationships (paragraph 9)

____

Part B

Directions: Select from the right-hand column the best definition for each word in the left-hand column. Write the letter of the correct definition by the word.

______	**6.** radical (paragraph 6)	**a.** calmness, tranquillity
______	**7.** priority (paragraph 9)	**b.** favoring extreme change
______	**8.** flustered (paragraph 6)	**c.** confused, befuddled

_______	**9.** steely-eyed (paragraph 6)	**d.**	something given attention over competing alternatives
_______	**10.** composure (paragraph 6)	**e.**	a hard or severe look

Record your rate (wpm), comprehension, and vocabulary scores for this article on the Student Record Chart in the Appendix. Each question counts 10 percent. An average score is around 250 wpm with 70 percent comprehension. Discuss any problems, concerns, or questions you have with your instructor.

Questions for Group Discussion

1. Now that you have finished the chapter on vocabulary, discuss the power of new vocabulary in your life. As a group, be specific about where you notice the effects of new vocabulary.
2. As a group, discuss the differences in the ways that Malcolm X and Sherman Alexie developed their vocabularies.
3. We have different vocabularies for listening, reading, writing, and speaking. Decide which is your largest vocabulary and arrange the others in descending order.
4. As a group, decide which method of vocabulary development helps the most for class terminology you are learning right now.
5. Discuss why, as a group, you agree with Mary Sherry's view that passing students who have not mastered the course work should receive a failing grade.

CHAPTER TWO

Developing Literal Recall

A. Finding the Topic, Main Idea, and Supporting Details

As you read, one of the keys to good comprehension is the ability to distinguish between the topic, the main idea, and the details used to support the main idea.

Finding the Topic

All good paragraphs are made up of sentences dealing with a particular subject or idea called a **topic.** The topic is simply what the paragraph is about. Notice in the following paragraph how each sentence deals with Indiana University's e-mail system.

> When Indiana University installed its new e-mail system in 2000, it spent $1.2 million on a network of nine computers to process e-mail for 115,000 students, faculty members, and researchers at its main campus and at satellite facilities throughout the state. It had expected the system to last at least through 2004, but the volume of mail is growing so fast, the university will need to buy more computers this year instead at a cost of $300,000. Why? Mainly, the rising volume of spam, which accounts for nearly 45 percent of the three million e-mail messages the university receives each day. (Saul Hansell, "Totaling up the Bill for Spam," *New York Times*, 28 June 2003.)

Each sentence says something about the e-mail system at Indiana University. In cases such as this one, the topic of the paragraph is easy to determine because the same word or phrase is repeated. Here, the word "e-mail" or "mail" is used four times.

Finding the Main Idea

After you recognize the topic of a paragraph or passage, you need to identify the **main idea.** The main idea is the point the author is trying to make about the topic. In the paragraph above, the author's point or main idea is that Indiana University's expensive e-mail system is no longer adequate. Why? Because of the rising volume of e-mail spam.

Here is another example. Ask yourself what the following paragraph is about (the topic) and what point (main idea) the author is making.

> Unfortunately, I can name only a few good U. S. history textbooks for students. *America: The Glorious Republic* by Henry Graff is comprehensive and well-written. Another is Boorstin and Kelly's *History of the United States,* probably the most comprehensive and well-balanced in its coverage. *American Journey* by Appleby, Brinkley, and McPherson, if taught along with Boorstin and Kelly, would show students that textbook editors' choices on content and "facts" often disagree.

As you can see, the topic of the paragraph is U.S. history textbooks. Each sentence says something about U.S history textbooks. The point or main idea the author is making is that there are not many good U.S. history textbooks for students. In this example, the author happens to state his main idea in the first sentence.

Recognizing a Topic Sentence

When an author states the main idea of a paragraph, as above, it is called a **topic sentence.** A topic sentence can appear anywhere in a paragraph depending on the writer's method of paragraph development. You'll learn more about paragraph patterns later on. For now, read the following paragraph, identify the topic, and see if the main idea appears in any one sentence.

> Irresponsible drinking on the part of college students is not new. But it has gotten even more serious among today's college students. A recent study at 113 colleges and universities reports that alcohol abuse is responsible for 64 percent of campus incidents of violent behavior, 42 percent of physical injuries, two-thirds of all property damage, and close to 40 percent of both emotional and academic difficulties.

What is the topic of the paragraph? ______________________________

____

What is the main idea of the paragraph? ___________________________

____

In what sentence is the main idea stated? __________________________

If you said the topic of the paragraph is college students, you're partly correct. More specifically, the topic is alcohol abuse among college students. The main idea is that alcohol abuse among college students has gotten worse. The topic sentence is the second sentence. The first sentence helps establish the topic, but it's the second sentence that best states the main idea regarding the growing seriousness of alcohol abuse among today's college students.

Here's another example. Read the following paragraph looking for the topic, the main idea, and the placement of the topic sentence.

> "The first time I applied to college," said Jeff Dinlay of Raleigh, North Carolina, "I figured that one place was as good as another. So I applied to three state universities because the applications were easy to fill out. I was accepted at only one of them, so that didn't give me much of a choice. Still, I went off with the unrealistic expectation that by just being in college, I'd become an educated person. I got an education, all right, but not the kind I was interested in. What I learned from experience was that I had to value myself, and I had to learn to value learning. When I transferred the following year, I chose my college with great care. I learned there are smart and dumb ways to choose a college." (From Bryna J. Fireside, *Choices: A Student Survival Guide,* Ferguson Publishing, 1997.)

What is the topic of the paragraph? ______________________________

____

What is the main idea of the paragraph? ___________________________

____

In what sentence is the main idea stated? __________________________

____

The topic is choosing a college, more specifically, Jeff Dinlay's way of choosing a college. The main idea is that there are smart ways and dumb ways to choose a college. In this case, the topic sentence is the last sentence. It summarizes Dinlay's experience in choosing a college. The rest of the paragraph supports that point by telling what was smart and what was not about the way the student applied for college.

Here's one more example. Carefully read the paragraph looking for the topic, main idea, and topic sentence.

> Computers have a place in our schools. They have the potential to accomplish great things. With the right software, they could help make science tangible or teach neglected topics like art and music. In practice, however, computers make our worst educational nightmares come true. Computers dismiss linear argument and promote fast, shallow romps across the information landscape. While we weep over the decline of literacy, computers discount words in favor of pictures and pictures in favor of video. While we worry about basic skills, we allow into the classroom software that will do a student's arithmetic and correct his spelling. (David Gelernter, "Computers Cannot Teach Children Basic Skills," *Computers and Society*, Greenhaven Press, 1997.)

What is the topic of the paragraph? ____________________

____

What is the main idea of the paragraph? ____________________

____

In what sentence is the main idea stated? ____________________

This paragraph requires careful reading. The topic has to do with computers in the schools. But what is the main idea? The author says computers should be in the schools and gives reasons why. But then he says, "Computers make our worst educational nightmares come true," showing their negative effects. In this case, the author does not state his main idea in any one sentence. Instead, it is **implied.** A careful reading shows that the author says computers in schools have potential with the use of the right software, but feels the way computers are being used is contributing to the decline in literacy. We can determine that the implied main idea is that computers are not being used correctly in our schools.

As you can see from these examples, a paragraph's main idea might be expressed in a topic sentence anywhere in a paragraph: in the beginning, at the end, in the middle, or not at all. When the main idea does not appear in a paragraph at all, it is called an implied main idea.

Recognizing Supporting Details

As you have noticed in the examples, the main idea in a paragraph or passage is the most general statement about the topic. The main idea stated in the topic sentence is then developed by **supporting details.** Being able to separate supporting details from the main idea is necessary for good comprehension.

Read the following paragraph looking for the topic, the main idea, and the details or statements that support the main idea.

> Some words are loaded with pleasant associations. Words such as *home, happiness, tenderness, contentment, baby,* and *mother* usually bring about favorable feelings or memories, provided the type of home life we've had. The word *mother,* for instance, makes many people think of home, safety, love, care, food, and security.

What is the topic of the paragraph? ______________________________

____

What is the main idea of the paragraph? ______________________________

____

In what sentence is the main idea stated? ______________________________

What are some supporting details used to make the main idea clear? ____________

____

The topic of this paragraph is words because every sentence in the paragraph is about words or examples of words. The main idea is the first sentence in the paragraph because it is the most general statement about the topic: Some words bring about favorable memories. Supporting details provided are examples of words that bring about favorable memories: *home, happiness, tenderness, mother, care, love,* and so on.

An outline of the paragraph might look something like this:

Topic:	words
Main idea:	Some words are loaded with pleasant associations.
Supporting details:	1. general word examples: home, happiness, tenderness, contentment, baby, mother 2. specific word example: mother (home, safety, love, care, food, security)

Here's another paragraph example. See if you can find the topic, main idea, and supporting details.

> A major part of our self-image is shaped by the work we do. Consider how we describe ourselves: "I'm just a janitor." "I'm only a housewife." "I'm senior vice president of the company." "I'm out of work right now." "I'm the boss here." Even our friends and fellow workers refer to us by our work or status (teacher, student, lawyer, doctor, pilot) and by what we do.

What is the topic of this paragraph? ______________________________

____

What is the main idea? ______________________________

____

What are the supporting details the author provides to give specifics about the main idea? ______________________________

____

The topic of this brief paragraph is work and our self-image. Notice how the topic is a phrase rather than just one word. The most general statement about work and our self-image (the main idea) is the first sentence. What two details are used to show how our work shapes our self-image? The writer talks first about self-descriptions or what we say about ourselves and, second, about how others refer to us by our status or work. All the rest of the paragraph consists of minor details or specifics about our own words or others' descriptions.

Once you have identified the main idea and supporting details, you can outline the paragraph or passage. In an outline, the main ideas are the first points written at the left margin and usually have Roman numerals I, II, III, and so on. Supporting details are indented about five spaces and numbered 1, 2, 3, and so on. The specifics or minor details are indented ten spaces and labeled with small letters a, b, c, d, and so on. An outline of a paragraph (or passage) looks like this:

I. (main idea)
- **1.** (first supporting detail)
  - **a.** (specific about the detail or minor detail)
  - **b.** (another specific example)
- **2.** (second supporting detail)
  - **a.** (specific about the detail or minor detail)
  - **b.** (another specific example)

When you can pick out the main idea and differentiate between supporting and specific details, an outline is one logical way of showing those relationships.

An outline of the preceding paragraph on work and self-image looks like this:

I. The work we do shapes a major part of our self-image.
- **1.** consider our self-description
  - **a.** just a janitor
  - **b.** only a housewife
  - **c.** senior vice president
  - **d.** out of work
  - **e.** boss
- **2.** Friends and fellow workers refer to us by our work or status.
  - **a.** teacher
  - **b.** student
  - **c.** lawyer
  - **d.** doctor
  - **e.** pilot

Again, the main idea is more general, with specific details supporting this main idea.

Find the topic, main idea, and supporting details in the following paragraph.

> A young college student is constantly discouraged, irritable, and unable to sleep. Frequent crying spells have ended, but she's still very unhappy. A middle-aged man has become increasingly indecisive in business affairs. He has strong feelings of

worthlessness and guilt, and has lost interest in sex. An elderly woman complains of fatigue and lack of appetite. Her weight has been dropping steadily. Three different problems? Not really. These people—and millions like them—suffer from the most common mental ailment in the book: depression. (From Maxine Abram, "Rx for Depression," *TWA Ambassador,* January 1987.)

Topic: ______________________________

Main idea: ______________________________

____

Three supporting details: ______________________________

____

The topic is depression, and the main idea comes in the last sentence. Everything up to this point is an example or specific about the main idea.

Here's a blank outline of the paragraph for you to practice your outlining skills. Cover up the answer as you try your hand at outlining.

I.

1.

a.

b.

c.

d.

e.

2.

a.

b.

c.

3.

a.

b.

c.

Does your outline look like the following? If not, analyze your mistakes and figure out how to do it right the next time. If it does look like this, congratulate yourself on your outlining skills.

I. These people—and millions like them—suffer from the most common mental ailment in the books: depression.

1. young college student's problems

a. discouraged

b. irritable

c. unable to sleep

d. frequent crying spells

e. unhappy

2. middle-aged man's problems
   a. indecisive
   b. feelings of worthlessness and guilt
   c. lost interest in sex
3. elderly woman's problems
   a. fatigue
   b. lack of appetite
   c. loss of weight

Now analyze the following paragraph.

> Distractibility is one symptom of Attention Deficit Disorder (ADD) in college students. ADD students become easily sidetracked and jump from topic to topic in conversation. Time-management problems are another symptom. Both procrastination and being unrealistic about how long a task will take are ADD issues. Organization is yet another symptom of ADD. ADD students tend to be messy, have trouble keeping up with several simultaneous projects, and have a difficult time prioritizing. Knowing these and other symptoms of ADD may help a college student gain better self-awareness.

Fill in the outline, stating the main idea and each of the major and minor details.

Main Idea:

1.
  a.
  b.

2.
  a.
  b.

3.
  a.
  b.
  c.

The topic is ADD and the main idea is the last sentence of the paragraph. The three symptoms are specifics about ADD and include distractibility, time management, and organization. Notice that this paragraph also contains quite a few specifics (or minor details) about the three symptoms.

Your outline should look something like this:

I. Knowing these and other symptoms of ADD may help a college student gain better self-awareness. (topic sentence stating main idea)

1. distractibility (major detail: one of the symptoms)
   a. sidetracked (minor detail)
   b. jump from topic to topic (minor detail)

2. time-management problems (major detail: a second symptom)
   a. procrastination (minor detail)
   b. being unrealistic about time (minor detail)
3. organization (major detail: a third symptom)
   a. tend to be messy (minor detail)
   b. trouble keeping up (minor detail)
   c. trouble prioritizing (minor detail)

The next two paragraphs are more complex and have implied main ideas. See if you can take the skills you've learned so far and apply it to these paragraphs from actual articles and texts.

> This is the story of a sturdy American symbol which has now spread throughout most of the world. The symbol is not the dollar. It is not even Coca-Cola. It is a simple pair of pants called blue jeans. . . . Blue jeans are favored equally by bureaucrats and cowboys; bankers and deadbeats; fashion designers and beer drinkers. They draw no distinctions and recognize no classes; they are merely American. Yet they are sought after almost everywhere in the world—including Russia, where authorities recently broke up a teenaged gang that was selling them on the black market for two hundred dollars a pair. They have been around for a long time, and it seems likely that they will outlive even the necktie. (From Carin Quinn, "The Jeaning of America—and the World," *American Heritage,* April 1978.)

Topic: ____

Main idea (in your own words): ______________________________

____

Three supporting details: ______________________________

____

The topic is blue jeans, even though the introductory statements about American symbols may have distracted you. The main idea is not stated in any one sentence. You must combine part of the first sentence and the fourth sentence to come up with the main idea. The main idea: blue jeans, an American symbol, are popular all around the world. The first supporting detail is that jeans are popular across classes and in a variety of groups. The second detail is that they are sought everywhere in the world. The third detail is that they've been around for a long time and will stay around for a long time. All the other details are specifics or minor details about these major details.

Here's one last paragraph example, taken from a history textbook. Don't try to remember all the facts and figures for this reading; just look for the main idea in it:

> In 1840, only one-twelfth of the American population lived in cities of 8,000 or more. By 1860, the proportion of city-dwellers had grown to one-sixth, and by 1900 to one-third of the population. In 1900, more than 25 million Americans were living in cities, most of them in the metropolises that had grown so lustily in the preceding 50 years. In 1850, New York City and independent Brooklyn

together had a population of 1,200,000. By 1900 (after official consolidation in 1898), their population had soared to over 3 million. In that same period, Philadelphia rose from 560,000 to 1,300,000. Most spectacular of all was Chicago. Starting out in 1831 as a muddy trading post on the prairie with 12 families and a meager garrison as its only inhabitants, Chicago had grown to 30,000 by 1850; 500,000 by 1880. In the next 20 years, its population soared to 1,700,000, a figure that placed it far ahead of Philadelphia and second only to New York in size. (From Hofstader, Miller, and Aaron, *The United States: The History of a Republic,* Prentice-Hall, 1987, p. 510.)

Topic: ______________________________

Implied main idea: ______________________________

____

Three supporting details: ______________________________

____

The topic is American population in cities. Note once again that a topic may be a phrase rather than a single word. You need to think about all the details and what they are saying in order to come up with a main idea. It isn't stated anywhere in the paragraph. The main idea: In the second half of the nineteenth century, Americans moved to cities in startling rates. The three main examples the historians use are New York City, Philadelphia, and Chicago.

Because the authors provide us with dates and statistics, we are able to infer the main idea. Notice that all of the dates provided are between 1850 and 1900, the late or latter part of the nineteenth century. All of the cities (New York, Philadelphia, and Chicago) are examples of fast population growth during these dates. Because of these details, we see for ourselves, without the authors telling us, that America urbanized very rapidly during the last half of the nineteenth century.

As you can see, sometimes it is easy to figure out an author's main idea and separate it from details, but sometimes we have to be more alert to what is being said. As you work through the following practices, become more conscious of how writers express their main points and provide details to support them.

PRACTICE A-1: Recognizing Topics, Main Ideas, and Supporting Details

Directions: Read the following paragraphs and in the appropriate blanks write the topic, the main idea, and the supporting details. The first one has been done for you.

Paragraph 1

Many of us impose unnecessary limitations on ourselves. We say, or think, we can't do something without checking. We hold ourselves back when we could move ahead. We assume that certain good occupations are closed to us when they're really not closed at all. We think we're not as good as the next person when we really are.

Topic: *limitations*

Main idea: *Many of us limit our potential unnecessarily*

Supporting details:

1. We say we can't without really knowing
2. We hold back
3. We think we're not good enough for certain jobs
4. We think we're not as good as others

Paragraph 2

Nature has provided natural means to soothe the mind and body. Herbal remedies for sleeplessness have been used successfully for centuries. Valerian root, for example, lessens irritability and excitement in the nervous system by rebuilding frayed nerve endings. Scullcap produces a peacefully drowsy feeling and restful sleep. A cup of chamomile tea is also a sleep producer and is a delicious break from stimulating hot caffeine drinks at night. Other valuable herbs for relaxing include hops, yellow jasmine, and lady slipper. Herbs also offer the advantage of containing important vitamins and minerals, which further increases their benefit to your general mental and physical health. (From Josie Knowles, "The Big Business of Falling Asleep," *Soma,* September/October 1980.)

Topic: ____________________

Main idea: ____________________

Supporting details: ____________________

Paragraph 3

Cocaine has a long history of use and misuse in the United States. At the turn of the century, dozens of nonprescription potions and cure-alls containing cocaine were sold. It was during this time that Coca-Cola was indeed the "real thing." From 1886, when it was first concocted, until 1906 when the Pure Food and Drug Act was passed, Coca-Cola contained cocaine (which has since been replaced with caffeine). In the 1930s, the popularity of cocaine declined when the cheaper synthetic amphetamines became available. This trend was reversed in the 1960s when a federal crackdown on amphetamine sales made this drug less available and more expensive. Today, cocaine is becoming one of the most widely abused illegal drugs.

Topic: ____________________

Main idea: ____________________

Supporting details: ____________________

Paragraph 4

Our studies on people also produced striking results. Because of the 21 minimum drinking age law, we studied people ages 21–29. Alcohol impaired learning much more in 21–24-year-olds than in those just a few years older at 25–29. During young adulthood, alcohol is a very potent drug, and it interferes with memory formation. The effects might be even more striking in teens. (From Scott Swartzwelder, "Alcohol and the Adolescent Brain," Opposing Viewpoints Resource Center.)

Topic: ______________________________

Main idea: ______________________________

Supporting details: ______________________________

____

____

____

____

Paragraph 5

The meanings of words change as their uses change. "Stout" at one time meant "valiant." Today it is used to characterize people who are portly. "Courtesan" once meant "lady at court" and "wench" meant any young girl. "Get off," according to Harper Barnes, "started as a drug term, became a sexual term and ending up meaning, more or less, to have a good time." "Sophomore" no longer means "person with the wisdom of a moron," and "professor" no longer means "person who has taken religious vows." Some words have no contemporary meaning at all, and if they are listed in the dictionary are labeled "archaic" or "obsolete." We usually find the word "prithee," but most dictionaries no longer include such splendid terms from the past as "snollygoster," "poop-noddy," "snodderclout," "bedswerver," and "mubblefubbles." (From Gerald Runkle, *Good Thinking: An Introduction to Logic,* 3rd edition, Holt, Rinehart and Winston, 1991, p. 14.)

Topic: ______________________________

Main idea: ______________________________

Supporting details: ______________________________

____

____

____

____

Paragraph 6

Caffeine speeds up the heart, promotes the release of stomach acid, and increases urine production; also, it dilates some blood vessels while narrowing others. In large amounts, caffeine may cause convulsions, but this is highly unlikely. It takes about ten grams of caffeine, the equivalent of one hundred cups of coffee, to run a serious risk of death. Caffeine has various effects on the body and mind. Psychologically, caffeine suppresses fatigue or drowsiness and increases feelings of alertness.

Topic: ______________________________

Main idea: ______________________________

Supporting details: ______________________________

____

____

____

____

____

Paragraph 7

Most of us are unaware that we use probably only a third of our lung capacity. Our breathing is shallow and occurs about fifteen to seventeen times a minute, taking in about a pint of air each time. Yet our lungs can hold eight times as much air. Therefore, shallow breathing provides only a limited amount of fresh oxygen and doesn't fully expel all the burnt gases, such as carbon dioxide. Despite the central role breathing plays in our lives as organisms, few of us have been taught to breathe. (From Richard Stein, "What Is the Best Form of Exercise?" John Gallagher Communications, p. 1.)

Topic: ______________________________

Main idea: ______________________________

Supporting details: ______________________________

____

____

____

____

Paragraph 8

Do people really need stress as a motivator? Apparently so, but perhaps many people confuse stress with goals. For example, getting through school is stressful, but the stress is not the reason for finishing school. Graduating and reaping the benefits of education are the motivation. This is an important distinction. The stress encountered while pursuing a goal, however, does seem to be less destructive when the goal is kept in mind. Stress that drives us seems to be more harmful than stress that results from our own interests. We suspect that the statement, "If it weren't for stress, I would be a vegetable," really means, "If I didn't have goals, I would be a vegetable." Even so, stress is not all bad. (From Judith Green and Robert Shellenberger, *The Dynamics of Health and Wellness,* Holt, Rinehart and Winston, 1991, p. 83.)

Topic: ______________________________

Main idea: ______________________________

Supporting details: ______________________________

____

____

____

____

Paragraph 9

Computers have not only changed the physical act of revising and editing but they have also changed the way we analyze our texts for revision. Most companies that publish word processing programs also publish *spell-checker* programs that analyze texts for misspelling of common words (and any words that you add to their vocabularies). More and more companies are publishing programs that can analyze texts for grammatical errors and that can make suggestions about the readability of your style. Such programs have (and perhaps always will have) serious flaws, but they can help your editing if you use them with caution. (From Christopher Thaiss, *Write to the Limit,* Holt, Rinehart and Winston, 1991, p. 341.)

Topic: ______________________________

Main idea: ______________________________

Supporting details: ______________________________

____

____

____

____

Paragraph 10

Why do American students remember so little of the history that they are taught? When the National Assessment of Educational Progress tested for knowledge of U.S. history in 1994 and 2001, more than half of high school seniors scored below basic, which is as low as one can score. In no other subject—not in mathematics or science or reading—do American seniors score as low as they do in U.S. history. Maybe it is because their textbooks are so dull; maybe it is because so many of their history teachers never studied history and can't argue with the textbooks' smug certainty. Maybe it is because the students don't know why they are supposed to remember the parade of facts that are so glamorously packaged between two covers. Or maybe it is because, with the teenager's usual ability to spot a scam, they know that much of what is taught to them is phony and isn't worth remembering. (Diane Ravitch, *The Language Police,* Knopf, 2003.)

Topic: ______________________________

Main idea: ______________________________

Supporting details: ______________________________

____

____

____

____

PRACTICE A-2: Separating Main Ideas from Supporting Details

Directions: For each of the paragraphs that follow, circle the topic and underline the main idea sentence. Then, in the space provided, write the major supporting details.

1. An unrealistically poor self-concept can also arise from the inaccurate feedback of others. Perhaps you are in an environment where you receive an excessive number of downer messages, many of which are undeserved, and a minimum of upper messages. We've known many housewives, for example, who have returned to college after many years spent in homemaking, where they received virtually no recognition for their intellectual strengths. It's amazing that these women have the courage to come to college at all, so low are their self-concepts; but come they do, and most are thrilled to find that they are much brighter and more competent intellectually than they suspected. In the same way, workers with overly critical supervisors, children with cruel "friends," and students with unsupportive teachers are all prone to low self-concepts owing to excessively negative feedback. (From Ronald B. Adler and Neil Towne, *Looking Out, Looking In,* 6th edition, Holt, Rinehart and Winston, 1990, p. 69.)

Supporting details: ______________________________

____

2. With digital television (DTV), benefits will include spectacular picture quality and better sound. The screen will be wider, so televisions will look quite different than they do today. Better reception is another plus; we'll no longer get poor reception when certain weather patterns hang over our area. Even more impressive will be the wider choices of programs and the interactivity. If the news anchor mentions problems in Malaysia, the viewer can click on Malaysia and find out background information about that country. DTV represents a major revolution in broadcasting technology with the potential to significantly change, for the better, the way televisions are used and viewed.

Supporting details: ______________________________

____

3. There is not one of us who is always a teacher or always a learner. In fact, the children often teach us to look at something differently—a story or picture, which they see more clearly than we do. The other day I came upon Tonia and a six-year-old friend sitting in her bedroom reading a simple comic book. He was teaching her what he learned in school—pointing out words, reading sentences, explaining the story. He remembered what he picked up in school and being just a first-grader saw nothing wrong with sharing that knowledge. (From Herbert Kohl, *Reading, How To.*)

Supporting details: ______________________________

____

4. In Chicago, a correspondence school took in more than $3 million a year from students enrolled in its law course, but not one graduate was able to qualify for the bar exam. A New York City nurses' training school collected $500 tuition fees for a course in nurse's aid, but not one graduate of the course could obtain a job in any New York hospital. A St. Louis school advertised an aircraft mechanics course that promised high pay and jobs at a time when the airlines were laying off mechanics.

These are only a few of the many examples of the widespread cheating of students that the Federal Trade Commission has discovered.

Supporting details: ____________________

____

5. A reader is not like a miner, recovering the meaning buried in the text, but more like a detective, reconstructing what happened by gathering bits of evidence and putting together a coherent picture, filling in the gaps. Both the reader and writer construct meaning. Similarly, a writer is not like a computer, merely printing out "data"; meaning is not somehow buried in the writer's mind. The writer constructs meaning, starting with some purpose (to get a job through a letter of application, to explain a complex process, to convince readers they should take certain actions). The writer then assembles the "data" he or she has gained through experience, education, and research and uses his or her skills with language to present that data to readers. (W. Ross Winterowd and Geoffrey R. Winterowd, *The Critical Reader, Thinker, and Writer,* 2nd edition, Mayfield, 1997, p. 1.)

   Supporting details: ____________________

   ____

6. Simply put, comprehension is the act of understanding or the capacity to understand. It can be divided into three levels: literal, critical, and affective. Literal comprehension is the basic level of understanding that entails the ability to identify main ideas and supporting details, to follow the sequence of events, to recognize cause-effect relationships, to interpret directions, and to perceive organizational patterns in various types of reading matter. Critical comprehension requires distinguishing opinion from fact; recognizing an author's intent, attitude, and bias; and making critical judgments. Affective comprehension is your intellectual and emotional response to what you read.

   Supporting details: ____________________

   ____

7. Yet the contrast between America's global position and its internal condition is painful. Just stroll through America's cities and consider the dark side of daily life. As someone who travels regularly to the U.S., who was partly educated there, whose vision of life has been transformed by the openness and dynamism of American society, and who cherishes the generosity of its political principles and respects the strength of its democratic creed, I can only witness the deterioration in American life with dismay and sorrow. A country that is bound to lead should not have cities whose centers look like Third World slums or sections of Beirut. It should not have a lackluster educational system or an infrastructure that is falling apart. It should not have people being turned away by hospitals because they lack insurance, or dying in the street of drug overdoses, or becoming victims of random crime because they were in the wrong place at the wrong time. (From Dominique Moisi, "Some Well-Wishing Advice from Europe," *TIME,* October 29, 1990, p. 116.)

   Supporting details: ____________________

   ____

8. The conditions of American pioneer life had fostered equality of the sexes, even to the franchise in New Jersey and Virginia. After the Revolution, however, the

dependent and protected status of women was emphasized. In a legal sense a woman was a perpetual minor, with her property and wages at the absolute disposal of her husband. Also, he had the right of chastisement: halfway through the century he had the legal right to beat his wife with a reasonable instrument, which in one case was adjudged to be a stick no thicker than a man's thumb. Widows and unmarried women had more extensive rights over their own property and their own actions, but courts were not inclined to favor them. (From Leland D. Baldwin, *The Stream of American History,* vol. 1, American Book Co., 1987, p. 618.)

Supporting details: ______________________________

____

Practice A-3: More on Main Ideas

Directions: Read the following article. At the end of each paragraph, write a one-sentence statement in the blank, stating what you think is the main idea of the paragraph.

Interviewing for a Job

1. One of the most important components of successful job hunting is the job interview. There are thousands of people entering new careers and searching for job placement. In order to give yourself an edge over others applying for the job you want, it is important to create a solid impression during the job interview.

Main idea: ______________________________

____

2. Because what you say during an interview is so important, there are two rules to remember. One is to present yourself in a favorable way and stress your areas of competence. However, don't exaggerate; tell the truth. Second, listen carefully and get involved in what the interviewer is saying. Notice the interviewer's interests and relate your comments to them.

Main idea: ______________________________

____

3. The job interview is the time to "sell" yourself by giving examples of experiences you've had related to the job and by revealing your good points. It's a good idea to have handy your job résumé or a list of school courses that prepared you for the job. Don't exaggerate the truth. Be honest, but show confidence in yourself and your ability to do the job.

Main idea: ______________________________

____

4. If you are not certain what the job will require of you, ask questions to see whether you do feel qualified. Do more listening than talking. Don't be afraid to ask for a second interview if you need time to gather information that will be more useful in the second interview. Most interviewers will appreciate your questions and your ability to listen and respond.

Main idea: ______________________________

____

5. Some people talk themselves out of a job by saying too much or by digressing. Although it's important to talk about your successful experiences, don't come on too strong and sound like a braggart.

Main idea: ____

____

6. Each of us has sensitive areas, and you might anticipate your responses in the event that you are asked about your own. Such questions could refer to your lack of an academic degree, a long period of unemployment, or your lack of work experience if you are entering a new field. Answer sensitive questions briefly and positively, because even one negative example can create doubt in the interviewer's mind. If you believe that this area presents a real obstacle to a job offer, you could be communicating this doubt to the interviewer. Many times, however, an interviewer will override these sensitive areas if you have a confident, positive attitude.

Main idea: ____

____

7. Making a favorable impression is especially important in light of recent estimates, which show that most hiring is done on an emotional rather than a factual basis. An interviewer who accepts you as a person and is emotionally on your side may consider you favorably for the job—even if you don't fit the preestablished qualifications.

Main idea: ____

____

8. The job interview is an important part of the job search because the attitude and impression you project can make the interviewer feel "with you" or "against you." Remember that you have the power to create a favorable impression. Interviewers have the intelligence to recognize genuine enthusiasm and interest.

Main idea: ____

____

Application I: Finding Main Ideas and Supporting Details

In a textbook for another class, select five paragraphs throughout the text and mark the main idea for each paragraph or write the implied main idea. List the supporting details for each paragraph. Bring your text to class and be prepared to justify your choice of main ideas with a class study partner.

B. Reading for Main Ideas: Paragraph Patterns

Another way to distinguish between an author's main ideas and supporting points is to pay attention to the writing patterns used frequently by authors. Authors use a variety of writing patterns to develop their ideas: illustration or example, definition of terms, comparison or contrast, sequence of events, cause and effect, description, or a combination of these. These patterns are called **rhetorical modes.** They are useful for better understanding paragraphs and entire reading passages. If you have taken an English composition course, you may already know the terms. They are frequently used to teach students how to write better. As a reader, your awareness of these patterns can help you more readily identify an author's main idea and supporting details. Let's examine each pattern.

Example

An easy writing pattern to spot is the use of an *example* (or examples) to support a main idea. Phrases, such as *for example, for instance,* and *to illustrate,* all signal or alert you that an example or examples are about to be given. It's a good guess that the example given is not the main idea of the paragraph. Instead, it is being used to support a main idea that has probably already been stated or will be stated.

Notice in the following paragraph how the topic sentence, the first one, is made clearer with the support of examples:

> It would seem the lesson to be gained from famous love stories is that passionate love and marriage do not mix. For instance, witness the ending to the stories of Antony and Cleopatra, Tristan and Isolde, Lancelot and Guinevere, Dante and Beatrice, and poor Cyrano and Roxanne. Even Romeo and Juliet ran into problems.

All of the names listed in the paragraph are given as examples to illustrate and support the main idea: Marriage and passionate love don't seem to go together. Even if you don't know who all the characters listed are, you can infer that they were all passionate lovers who never got married, or if they did, presumably the marriages didn't last. Otherwise, the author wouldn't use them as examples to support the main idea.

Here is another example showing how this writing pattern works:

> It's hard to believe, but in the ninth decade of the 20th Century, *The Catcher in the Rye, Of Mice and Men, Huckleberry Finn,* and *The Diary of Anne Frank,* among other books, are still the objects of censorship in the nation's public schools. And the incidence of book bannings is going up, according to a report by People for the American Way, the liberal watchdog group. In the last year, the study found, there were efforts to ban books in the schools in 46 of the 50 states, including California. Many of them succeeded. (Editorial, *Los Angeles Times*)

In this case, no signal words are given. But examples of books that have been and continue to be banned in public school are used to support the surprise of the author that such censorship is still happening.

You've probably noticed by now how we are using examples here to explain the use of this writing pattern and to illustrate how recognizing it can help you sort out main ideas from supporting details.

Definition

Another frequently used writing pattern is *definition,* or an attempt to explain what is being discussed through elaborate defining of terms. Here is an example:

> A word generally has two meanings: a denotative meaning and a connotative meaning. The denotative meaning of a word is its most direct or literal meaning as found in the dictionary. What the word suggests or implies beyond its literal definition is its connotative meaning.

The author's main point here is to define the terms denotative and connotative.

Frequently, when authors define a word or term, they also use examples. Notice in the following example how a definition of *inference* is provided, then an example of how we make inferences is given:

> An inference is a statement about the unknown made on the basis of the known. In other words, an inference is an educated guess. If a woman smiles when we see a man whisper something in her ear, we can infer or assume that she is pleased or amused. Because smiles generally mean pleasure and frowns generally mean displeasure, we can infer that she is pleased.

In this example, the definition of inference is given, then an example of how we make inferences is given, thus combining both the definition and illustration/example patterns.

Comparison/Contrast

The *comparison/contrast* writing pattern is also used with some frequency. With this pattern, authors attempt to develop the main point by either comparing or contrasting one thing or idea with another, or by using both. Here's an example of the use of comparison/contrast:

> Crime as presented on television is different from what it is in reality. On television, murder, assault, and armed robbery are the most common crimes. However, in reality, quiet burglaries, clever larcenies, unspectacular auto thefts, and drunkenness are the most common. Video detectives solve 90 percent of their cases. But in reality, the figure is much lower. On TV only 7 percent of violence occurs between relatives. In reality, this accounts for 25 to 30 percent of interpersonal violence.

Notice that what is being contrasted is crime as portrayed on television and what it is like in reality. The author's main idea is that television does not portray crime realistically. To prove this, the author contrasts three points: the most common crimes as portrayed on television with real crime, the difference in the number of cases detectives solve on television and in reality, and the percentage of family violence on television and in reality.

In the following paragraph, only a contrast is being drawn. See if you understand what is being contrasted.

> Sweden offers a unique and independent voice in today's international debates. With a tradition of social democracy, its society is influenced by a *multilateral* approach to international cooperation. In contrast, The United States is an uncontested world power and the September 11 attacks have served to strengthen the already *unilateralist* direction of its foreign policy. A recent survey of public opinion in 44 nations concluded that U.S. citizens' views on fundamental world problems

> differ greatly from public attitudes in the rest of the world. A serious joint discussion of critical world issues by students from each society could be exciting, timely, and educational. (Linda York, "Summer in Sweden," World 2003, University of California, 2003.)

Notice that the attitudes of Swedish citizens toward the way foreign problems should be handled is termed *multilateral,* or shared by all nations. In contrast, (the same words used in the paragraph) the U.S. policy toward handling foreign affairs is *unilateral,* or doing things alone. Another contrast is shown in the results of the poll mentioned, which reveals that public opinion of 44 nations holds views different from those of U.S. citizens. The main idea is that a serious joint discussion of these differences among students would be "exciting, timely, and educational."

As this example shows, sometimes signal words are used to alert you to a contrast or comparison, sometimes not. Still, be alert to signal words and phrases that show comparison, such as *in comparison, similar, like, also, too,* and *the same as.* Words and phrases that will reveal contrast are *in contrast, on the contrary, however, but, on the other hand,* and *even though.* When you see such a word or phrase being used, you know that you are being provided with supporting details or information, not the main idea. The main idea will be whatever the comparison or contrasting details are supporting.

Sequence of Events

A fourth writing pattern is *sequence of events.* This is a pattern used when directions are given, when there is a certain order to events, or when chronology is important. Sometimes certain key words, such as *first, second, third,* or the numbers themselves, are used. Words such as *then, later, finally,* and *thus* also serve as guides to a sequence of events. Notice the sequence of events in the following example:

> An algorithm is a step-by-step procedure for solving a problem in a finite amount of time. When you start your car, you go through a step-by-step procedure. First, you insert the key. Second, you make sure the transmission is in neutral or park. Third, you depress the gas pedal. Fourth, you turn the key to the start position. If the engine starts within a few seconds, you then release the key to the ignition position. If the engine doesn't start, you wait ten seconds and repeat steps three through six. Finally, if the car doesn't start, you call the garage. (From Nell Dale, *Programming in Pascal,* D.C. Heath, 1990, pp. 27–28.)

Notice how the author has related the sequence of events necessary in starting a car. Numbers and words such as *first, second, then,* and *finally* aid the reader. An awareness of this use of words provides a pattern for understanding as you read, as well as a way to remember the information.

Sometimes numbers or signal words are not used to make clear the sequence of events. See if you can recognize and follow the sequence of events in the following paragraph:

> When you receive an unexpected physical threat, what happens to your system during the first ten or fifteen seconds? The moment your stress response is triggered by a threat your heartbeat quickens to pump more blood into your vital organs. Part of this additional blood is taken from blood vessels under your skin, leaving you with cold, clammy hands. As your heartbeat quickens, raising your

> blood pressure, more blood is received by the muscles and brain enabling you to react more quickly. Sugar is poured into the system from the liver, supplying quick energy. The adrenal glands pump adrenaline for strength. The digestive system shuts down so there will be no wasted energy. In all, stress activates the body's entire mental and physical systems causing more than 1400 physiological changes. All this happens in a matter of seconds. (From David Danskin and Mark Crow, *Biofeedback: An Introduction And Guide*, Mayfield Publishing, 1981.)

The sequence of events described here shows what happens in a matter of seconds to your body when you are physically threatened. The paragraph lists step by step what happens:

- Your heartbeat quickens, pumping more blood into your vital organs.
- Part of this additional blood is taken from blood vessels under your skin, leaving you with cold, clammy hands.
- Your heartbeat quickens, raising your blood pressure.
- More blood is received by the muscles and brain, enabling you to react more quickly.
- Sugar is poured into the system from the liver, supplying quick energy.
- The adrenal glands pump adrenaline for strength.
- The digestive system shuts down so there will be no wasted energy.

Each of these steps provides the details of what happens when the body is physically threatened. The actual order in which events take place is important in understanding how the body reacts.

Cause and Effect

Still another writing pattern is the use of *cause and effect.* With this pattern, the author attempts to show how one action or a series of actions causes something to happen. For instance, tapping a raw egg on a skillet causes it to crack. In a cause/effect paragraph, the author links what causes an event with the effects it brings. Here is an example of cause/effect relationship in a paragraph:

> The permissive nature of society in the United States is notorious. With Dr. Benjamin Spock's books on child raising, the Bible of the last generation of parents, family life has become very democratic. In recent decades, many school teachers have urged children to express themselves, to give their opinions rather than to regurgitate the rote recitations that used to characterize—and still characterize elsewhere—much of what we call education. The point is not that there is no discipline or authoritarianism in the family or school, but that there is considerably less than in the American past or in the present of most other nations. (From John Gillingham, "Then and Now," *Radical Reader.*)

Notice that the point of the paragraph is that permissiveness in the United States is greater than ever (effect). The use of Dr. Spock's books in rearing children (cause) and the urging of children by teachers to give their opinions rather than to learn by rote (cause) explain why discipline in the family and school is less than in the past. Thus, the author of the preceding paragraph sees the effect of two causes.

Look for the cause and effect in the following paragraph:

> If you're within a few miles of a nuclear detonation, you'll be incinerated on the spot! And if you survive that blast, what does the future promise? The silent but deadly radiation, either directly or from fallout, in a dose of 400 rems could kill you within two weeks. Your hair would fall out, your skin would be covered with large ulcers, you would vomit and experience diarrhea and you would die from infection or massive bleeding as your white blood cells and platelets stopped working. (Ken Keyes, Jr., *The Hundredth Monkey*)

Here the *cause* is a nuclear detonation. The *effects* of such a detonation are everything from possibly being reduced to ashes on the spot, to the effects of radiation from fallout.

Description

Another pattern is the use of *description*. Usually the author is attempting to give you a visual picture or a feeling for something. Generally, but not always, there is no topic sentence. Notice this example:

> The old fire road runs through the pines for several miles, winding its way around the shoulders of the mountain. The footing is good, so I let my horse step up from a trot into a slow gallop. But once the fire in her blood is lit, the wind fans her flame and she stretches her legs and burns the miles. I am riding with only a bareback pad, and the faster she runs the easier it is to find the still point behind her withers where I can sit motionless and become one with her motion, horse and man a single centaur. The road dips and passes through a swampy place. Aspens replace the pines, the underbrush is thick, and the roadway is muddy. I rein my mare down to a walk. She doesn't like it, but once or twice I have seen bears eating berries in this thicket and I don't want to surprise one in the middle of a meal. (From Sam Keen, *Fire in the Belly,* Bantam, 1991, pp. 181–182.)

As you can see, there is no topic sentence. The whole paragraph is a description of horseback riding on an old fire road in the mountains.

Narration

When authors want to tell a story about something that has happened in their lives, they use narration. It is not always easy to spot a topic sentence in narrative paragraphs because a story is being told and events move from one paragraph to another. In the following example, the author uses first-person narration:

> I was saved from sin when I was going on thirteen. But not really saved. It happened like this. There was a big revival at my Auntie Reed's church. Every night for weeks there had been much preaching, singing, praying, and shouting, and some very hardened sinners had been brought to Christ, and the membership of the church had grown by leaps and bounds. Then just before the revival ended, they held a special meeting for children, "to bring the young lambs to the fold." . . . That night I was escorted to the front row and placed on the mourners' bench with all the other young sinners. (Langston Hughes, "Salvation")

The author reflects on an incident in his past, a time when he "was saved from sin . . . But not really saved." The paragraph sets us up for more of the story to come. You will see how this paragraph is developed when you read the entire story in a later reading practice.

Combination of Patterns

Some paragraphs use more than one pattern. What two patterns that you have learned are used in the following paragraph?

> One of the most controversial data collection practices on the Web involves the use of "cookies." A **cookie** is a file created by a Web server and stored on your host machine. It's a small file that patiently awaits your next visit to the Web. Any Web server can check to see if you have a cookie file and, if so, whether it has any useful information about you. For example, suppose that the last time you visited a particular site, you spent all your time on two particular pages. A cookie can record this information so that the next time you visit the site, the server might greet you with a page display that makes it especially easy to navigate to those pages again. (Wendy Lehnert, *Light on the Internet and the World Wide Web*, Longman, 1999.)

In this case, the author uses both the pattern of definition and example. A definition of a "cookie file" is given, and then an example of how a "cookie file" works.

Your ability to understand what you read can be enhanced by an awareness of these writing patterns. The patterns themselves are not important, but an awareness of how an author presents information can aid comprehension. To help you develop this ability, the next practices provide you with opportunities to work on identifying writing patterns.

As you progress through this section, keep in mind the fourth objective listed in the introduction to this unit. You should be able to identify the following writing patterns: illustration/example, definition, cause and effect, comparison/contrast, description, and sequence of events.

PRACTICE B-1: Finding Main Ideas through Paragraph Patterns

Directions: For each of the following paragraphs, write what you think are the main idea and key supporting details. As organizational patterns get more complex, main ideas are often implied. Then, identify which of the organizational patterns listed best describes the paragraph.

a. illustration/example
b. definition
c. comparison/contrast
d. sequence of events
e. cause/effect
f. description
g. combination (include the letters of the patterns)

Write the letter of the correct pattern in the blank before the paragraph.

______ **1.** College athletes ought to be paid a salary on top of any scholarships and allowances they receive. Major college athletics is a form of entertainment. As with other entertainments, talented people perform for audiences who pay to watch. What universities are doing is using performance for publicity purposes. College athletes should be paid for their part in this. Other people in the collegiate-sport industry—coaches, athletic directors, trainers—are making a good living. Why not the athletes, the actual producers of the event?

Main idea: ____

____

Supporting details: ____

____

____

____

_____ **2.** College athletes should not be paid a salary on top of any scholarships and allowances they receive. A student athlete is a part of a university family, along with other students, the faculty, and so on. Only a handful of students—a maximum of 110 in men's football and basketball—play sports that generate revenue. A school's resources, regardless of how they are generated, should be used to benefit the entire college. To pay athletes in football and basketball—most of whom already receive full tuition and room and board—the institution would have to cut some nonrevenue sports or reassign resources from some other academic area. How about other athletes, like wrestlers, swimmers, and softball players? They must train as rigorously and may receive only a partial grant or none at all.

Main idea: ____

____

Supporting details: ____

____

____

____

_____ **3.** Here is a four-step method to prevent your mind from wandering while reading. First, before you attempt to read anything, look over the length of the material to see whether you have time to read it all; if not, mark a spot where you intend to stop. Second, read the title and the first paragraph, looking for the main idea of the article. Next, read the boldface headings, if there are any, and the first sentence of each paragraph. Finally, read the last paragraph, which probably contains a summary of the material. These steps condition your mind to accept the material you want to read and keep it from wandering.

Main idea: ____

____

Supporting details: ____

____

____

____

______ **4.** Irony is a figure of speech whereby the writer or speaker says the opposite of what is meant; for the irony to be successful, however, the audience must understand the writer's true intent. For example, if you have slopped to school in a rainstorm and your drenched teacher enters the classroom saying, "Ah, nothing like this beautiful sunny weather," you know that your teacher is being ironic. Perhaps one of the most famous cases of irony occurred in 1938, when Sigmund Freud, the famous Viennese psychiatrist, was arrested by the Nazis. After being harassed by the Gestapo, he was released on the condition that he sign a statement swearing he had been treated well by the secret police. Freud signed it, but he added a few words after his signature: "I can heartily recommend the Gestapo to anyone." Looking back, we easily recognize Freud's jab at his captors; the Gestapo, however, apparently overlooked the irony and let him go. (From Jean Wyrick, *Steps to Writing Well,* 3rd edition, Holt, Rinehart and Winston, 1987, p. 112.)

Main idea: ____

____

Supporting details: __________________________________

____

____

____

____

______ **5.** In the U.S., the age-old problem of excessive drinking is taking a disturbing new turn and affecting new kinds of victims. On a New York subway train, a school-bound fifteen-year-old holds his books in one hand, a brown paper bag containing a beer bottle in the other. He takes a swig, then passes the bottle to a classmate. In a San Francisco suburb, several high school freshmen show up for class drunk every morning, while others sneak off for a nip or two of whiskey during the lunch recess. On the campuses, the beer bash is fashionable once again, and lowered drinking ages have made liquor the high without the hassle.

Main idea: ____

____

Supporting details: __________________________________

____

____

____

______ **6.** But Walnut Canyon offered the Sinagua more than cozy homesites. A dependable supply of water flowed along the streambed on the floor of the canyon. Fertile volcanic-cinder soil lay within about two miles of the canyon rim. A great variety of trees, for fuel and implements, grew within the canyon and on the mesa. Other wild plants, a source of food and medicines, lined the banks of the stream and blanketed the slope. Game, furred and feathered, abounded in the canyon and on the mesa top. (From *Walnut Canyon,* Superintendent of Documents, U.S. Government Printing Office, 1968.)

Main idea: ____

____

Supporting details: ____

____

____

____

______ **7.** The patients wandered aimlessly about, mumbling incoherently. Violent ones were wrapped in wet sheets with their arms pinned, or they wore straitjackets. Attendants, in danger of assault, peered at their charges through screens. The floor lay bare, because rugs would have quickly been soiled with excrement. The large mental institution of thirty years ago was a madhouse.

Main idea: ____

____

Supporting details: ____

____

____

____

______ **8.** Because of the way prime-time television portrays them, we have a distorted image of America's elderly. Only one out of every fifty fictional television characters is over sixty-five; in real life one out of every ten persons has passed that age. Studies show that, in 1,365 nighttime programs, older people are portrayed as stubborn, eccentric, ineffectual, sexually unattractive, and sometimes silly. Older women appear on television shows seldom and in roles with few romantic possibilities. Old men are shown as having evil powers. Because the largest group of people watching television is over 55, television could end up alienating its most faithful viewers.

Main idea: ____

____

Supporting details: ____

____

____

____

____

______ **9.** There are basically two different types of purchasers who respond to advertising. One type rushes out to buy 50 percent of all the products they see advertised. Such buyers help make advertising a highly successful, multibillion-dollar-a-year industry. People of the second type think they are immune to ads; they think most ads are silly, stupid, and "beneath their dignity." This type of purchaser believes ads are aimed at the "suckers" of the first type. Yet 90 percent of the nation's adults who believe themselves immune are responsible for about 90 percent of all purchases of advertised products.

Main idea: ______________________________

____

Supporting details: ______________________________

____

____

____

____

_______ **10.** Television is addictive. For example, when a set breaks, most families rush to have it repaired, often renting one if the repair process takes longer than a day or two. When "nothing's on TV," people experience boredom with their lives, not knowing what to do with themselves. Perhaps the best example of television addiction was an experiment in Germany where 184 volunteers were paid to go without television for a year. At first, most volunteers did well, reporting that they were spending more time with their children, reading, and visiting friends. Then, within a month, tension, restlessness, and quarreling increased. Not one volunteer lasted more than five months without a television set. Once the sets were on again, people lost their anxieties and returned to normal.

Main idea: ______________________________

____

Supporting details: ______________________________

____

____

____

____

Application 2: Finding Paragraph Patterns

In a textbook for another class, find an example of at least five different paragraph patterns. Label each one, put a line in the margin by the main idea sentence or sentences, and number the supporting details. Bring your paragraphs to class and be prepared to justify your paragraph patterns with a class study partner.

PRACTICE B-2: Main Ideas in Longer Passages

Directions: The following reading passages are longer than the ones in the previous drills. Read them and answer the questions that follow. Use what you have learned about main ideas, supporting details, and paragraph patterns.

Passage A

The two most popular aerobic exercises are jogging and swimming. The latter is more enthusiastically recommended because it avoids the trauma to the legs and spine of jogging and utilizes the arms and chest muscles as well as the legs. It is done with the help, or buoyancy, of water. The gravitational force on your joints is not nearly so great as when standing out of water. Your weight in the water (with only your head and neck exposed) is only one-tenth what it is out of water.

Since the water, and not your body, bears much of your weight, swimming is an excellent exercise for those suffering with arthritis. At the same time the buoyancy also spares your knees, ankles, and lower back from the constant pounding associated with jogging. In fact swimming is often prescribed for those people who have suffered joint injuries from other sports or exercise activities. It strengthens the muscles of your abdomen and has been prescribed as the one exercise program for those with chronic back problems. (From Richard Stein, "What Is the Best Form of Exercise?" John Gallagher Communications.)

1. Which statement best describes the main idea of the passage?

a. The two most popular aerobic exercises are jogging and swimming.

b. Jogging is better than swimming.

c. Swimming is more popular than jogging.

d. Swimming is recommended over jogging.

2. The writing pattern most used in this passage is

a. definition.

b. comparison/contrast.

c. cause/effect.

d. both b and c.

3. In the space provided, list some of the details given to support your answer to question 1.

____

____

____

____

Passage B

Race is a social concept that varies from one society to another, depending on how the people of that society feel about the importance of certain physical differences among human beings.

In biology, *race* refers to an in-breeding population that develops distinctive physical characteristics that are hereditary. But the choice of which physical characteristics to use in classifying people into races is arbitrary. Skin color, hair form, blood type, and facial features such as nose shape and eyefolds have been used by biologists in such efforts. In fact, however, there is a great deal of overlap among the so-called races in the distribution of these traits.

Of course these races exist. But they are not a set of distinct populations based on biological differences. The definitions of race used in different societies emerged from the interaction of various populations over long periods of human history. The specific physical characteristics that we use to assign people to different races are arbitrary and meaningless—people from the Indian subcontinent tend to have dark skin and straight hair; Africans from Ethiopia have dark skin and narrow facial features; American blacks have skin colors ranging from extremely dark to extremely light. There is no scientifically valid typology of human races; what counts is what people in a society define as meaningful. (From William Kornblum, *Sociology in a Changing World*, Harcourt Brace College Publishers, 1994, Chapter 13.)

1. Which is the basic pattern used in the above passage?

a. illustration/example
b. definition
c. cause/effect
d. comparison/contrast

2. Explain why you selected the writing pattern you circled.

____

____

____

3. While the basic pattern is one of the choices in question 1, what other method is also used to a lesser degree?

a. illustration/example
b. definition
c. cause/effect
d. comparison/contrast

4. Explain your answer to question 3.

____

____

____

5. What is the main idea of this passage?

____

____

____

Passage C

Modern unionism also concentrates power and control in industry and government. A union will attempt to establish uniform wage rates in all plants in which the majority of workers are members of that union. In competition with other unions for members and power, it cannot accept lower rates of pay than those secured by other unions, even in different industries. Union competition of this kind tends to equalize wage rates for comparable work throughout a given industry and ultimately narrows the spread between wages paid for similar skills in different industries. But it is the bigger and longer established companies which are in the best position to absorb added wage costs to production. A particular handicap is presented new companies, with limited capital, once they are caught in such a competitive wage spiral. The established corporation, with a quasi-controlled market, can invariably pass on added labor costs either to distributors or to consumers, which a new company is unable to do. The charge has been made that some big corporations welcome "another round" of wage increases that will eliminate newer companies from "free competition." (From Arnold Green, *Sociology: An Analysis of Life in Modern Society*, McGraw-Hill, 1984, p. 265.)

1. What writing pattern is used in this passage?
   - **a.** definition
   - **b.** sequence of events
   - **c.** comparison/contrast
   - **d.** cause/effect

2. There are two results that occur when a union attempts to establish uniform wage rates in all plants in which the majority of workers are union members. Name them.

   ____

   ____

3. State in your own words what you think the main idea of this passage is.

   ____

   ____

   ____

   ____

   ____

Passage D

An analogy is a figure of speech in which two things are asserted to be alike in many respects that are quite fundamental. Their structure, the relationships of their parts, or the essential purposes they serve are similar, although the two things are also greatly dissimilar. Roses and carnations are not analogous. They both have stems and leaves, and may both be red in color. But they exhibit these qualities in the same way; they are of the same genus. The comparison of the heart to a pump, however, is a genuine analogy. These are disparate things, but they share important qualities: mechanical apparatus, possession of valves, ability to increase and decrease pressures, and capacity to move fluids. And the heart and the pump exhibit these qualities in different ways and in different contexts.

In discussing a crowded city, we do not offer an analogy when we compare it with another city. We are *merely* making a comparison. But if we compare the crowded city to an ant colony, we are setting forth an analogy. The two cities are not analogs; the city and the ant colony are. A ship manned by officers and a crew and crossing a stormy sea is a common analogy for a political state passing through perilous times. This is a popular analogy, for it brings out the striking similarities between two things notably dissimilar.

Like all figures of speech, the analogy serves rhetorical purposes. It enlivens discourse and may be used to stir the emotions. An analogy may, in addition, serve the descriptive function of giving a concrete and vivid simile for a concept that is too abstract or remote from ordinary experience to be clearly grasped. (From Gerald Runkle, *Good Thinking,* 3rd edition, Holt, Rinehart and Winston, 1991, p. 242.)

1. What is an analogy?

   ____

   ____

2. Why can an analogy be made between a heart and a pump?

   ____

   ____

3. Why can't an analogy be made between roses and carnations?

4. Why is the comparison of a crowded city with an ant colony considered an analogy?

5. What is the purpose of an analogy?

Passage E

1 Perceptual differences make communication challenging enough between members of the same culture. But when communicators come from different backgrounds, the potential for misunderstandings is even greater. Culture provides a perceptual filter that influences the way we interpret even the most simple events. This fact was demonstrated in studies exploring the domination of vision in one eye over the other. Researchers used a binocular-like device that projects different images to each eye. The subjects were 12 Americans and 12 Mexicans. Each was presented with ten pairs of photographs, each pair containing one picture from U.S. culture (e.g., a baseball game) and one from Mexican culture (e.g., a bullfight). After viewing each pair of images, the subjects reported what they saw. The results clearly indicated the power of culture to influence perceptions: Subjects had a strong tendency to see the image from their own background.

2 The same principle causes people from different cultures to interpret the same event in different ways. Blinking while another person talks may be hardly noticeable to North Americans, but the same behavior is considered impolite in Taiwan. A "V" made with fingers means victory in most of the Western world . . . as long as the palm is facing out. But in some European countries the same sign with the palm facing in roughly means "shove it." The beckoning finger motion that is familiar to Americans is an insulting gesture in most Middle and Far Eastern countries.

3 Even beliefs about the very value of talk differ from one culture to another. North American culture views talk as desirable and uses it for social purposes as well as to perform tasks. Silence has a negative value in this culture. It is likely to be interpreted as lack of interest, unwillingness to communicate, hostility, anxiety, shyness, or a sign of interpersonal incompatibility. Westerners are uncomfortable with silence, which they find embarrassing and awkward. Furthermore, the *kind* of talk Westerners admire is characterized by straightforwardness and honesty. Being indirect or vague—"beating around the bush," it might be labeled—has a negative connotation.

4 On the other hand, most Asian cultures discourage the expression of thoughts and feelings. Silence is valued, as Taoist sayings indicate: "In much talk there is great weariness," or "One who speaks does not know, one who knows does not speak." Unlike Westerners who are uncomfortable with silence, Japanese and Chinese believe that remaining quiet is the proper state when there is nothing to be said. To Easterners a talkative person is often considered a show-off or insincere. And when an Asian does speak up on social matters, the message is likely to be phrased indirectly to "save face" for the recipient.

5 It is easy to see how these different views of speech and silence can lead to communication problems when people from different cultures meet. Both the talkative Westerner and the silent Asian are behaving in ways they believe are proper, yet each views the other with disapproval and mistrust. Only when they recognize the different standards of behavior can they adapt to one another, or at least understand and respect their differences. (From Ronald Adler and George Rodman, *Understanding Human Communication,* fourth edition, copyright © 1991 by Harcourt, Inc. Reprinted by permission of the publisher.)

1. What is the main idea of paragraph 1? ______________________________

____

____

2. What paragraph pattern is used in paragraph 2 and for what purpose? __________

____

____

3. What is being contrasted in paragraphs 3 and 4? ______________________

____

____

4. The topic of the passage is perception and culture. What is the main point being made? ____

____

C. Finding an Author's Thesis

Now is the time to put together all the skills you have learned and practiced in paragraphs. When you are reading essays or articles, you will need to follow many of the same steps used in reading individual paragraphs to increase your comprehension, but note that they often have slightly different terminology.

Every article or essay has a topic, or subject. The topic or subject is what the author is writing about, such as computers, good manners, horse racing, war, a country, and the like. The *thesis,* or main idea, is not the same as the topic or subject. A thesis is what the author wants to say about the subject or the author's feelings about the subject. Every well-written essay or article contains a thesis or a main idea about the subject that the author wants the reader to accept or think about.

Instead of finding the main idea in each paragraph, you will now want to look at the entire essay or article and figure out what the thesis of the whole piece is. Let's say you are reading an essay about grades and their value. That would be the subject or topic of the essay. But you need to understand the main point the author is making about grades. Is the author in favor of grades or against them? Is the author presenting a new concept about grading that she or he wants the reader to accept? A thesis, then, is what the author wants to say about that particular subject. Recognizing an author's thesis is basic to developing good literal comprehension.

A thesis of an article or essay is often near the beginning or end of the article. The thesis may not be the first or last paragraph, however, because authors often use introductory and concluding paragraphs to get the interest of the reader. Find the thesis in the same way you look for topics and main ideas in paragraphs. First, read through the article quickly to discover the subject or topic. Then, use headings or subheadings to get the big picture about what the author is saying about this subject. Now, look through the article for the most general statement about that topic. Don't forget that main ideas may be implied.

Finding the subject and thesis of an article is central to understanding the article. Poor readers often get bogged down in details and then have no idea what the article is about. Make this search for the author's subject and thesis the first priority of your reading.

The next few practices help you recognize an author's thesis.

PRACTICE C-1

Directions: As you read the following essay, look for the author's thesis and the major details used to develop the thesis.

CONGRESS MUST SEND SPAMMERS A MESSAGE

Jonathan Turley

1 If the Internet had existed when Moses came down from Mt. Sinai, there might have been an 11th Commandment: "Thou shalt not spam thy neighbor."

2 In fact, some faithful might have asked Moses whether the 10th might be better directed at spamming than coveting. Unlike some harmless fantasy featuring the neighbor's wife or goods, spamming imposes huge costs on the system and society.

3 America Online recently sued 12 individuals and companies that are clogging its subscribers with unwanted, unsolicited e-mail. AOL has reason to worry; those spammers alone are reportedly responsible for more than 1 billion such messages, and this new form of pollution threatens one of the greatest technological advances of this generation.

4 The five AOL lawsuits, files in federal court in Alexandria, Va., may lead to important insight into the workings of these shadowy operators. But, without congressional action, they may do little to stem the tide of spam.

5 Despite anti-spam software, spam is expanding exponentially. In 2001, according to one industry study, spam represented roughly 8% of all Internet e-mail. By last year, that percentage was at more than 40%. For some users, it can be as high as 90%.

6 Spam now costs American businesses about $9 billion a year in lost productivity and screening. Many users currently receive the equivalent of a discount catalog of junk mail with a single legitimate message buried within it. Few people have the time or inclination to sort through hundreds of spam messages to find the one e-mail that is not marketing discount Viagra or a Russian wife.

7 As a result, some people are abandoning e-mail and returning to conventional mail and telephone communications. This is already occurring in countries such as Japan, where people are giving up cell-phone services because 90% of text messages are now spam.

8 As the AOL lawsuit illustrates, spammers have changed subject lines, routed e-mails through foreign servers, adopted fictitious names and taken other deceptive measures to get through to computer users. One growing subset of spammers are called spoofers, who use subject lines that feign familiarity to trick users into opening spam messages.

9 When legislation has been threatened, spammers have cloaked themselves in the 1st Amendment, insisting that any prohibition on spam would violate guarantees of free speech.

Los Angeles Times, April 21, 2003, B13. Reprinted by permission of the author.

10 In the last year, however, both the practical and legal positions of spam have changed. Spam now is a real threat to the medium of Internet communications. In this sense, it is like virtual pollution. The Internet is a common resource that will be lost unless we protect it.

11 This is a situation analogous to Garrett Hardin's classic economic model, "The Tragedy of the Commons." Under this model, a group of people live around a commons green in which any individual can introduce cattle to graze. So each person brings more and more cattle until, finally, the commons area is destroyed.

12 The Internet is a type of virtual commons that is being destroyed by a small number of people who individually are acting rationally to maximize profits. Their collective actions, however, will ultimately kill the resource they are exploiting. Likewise, the first federal environmental statutes were enacted in the 1960s after a failure of private property interests and state laws in stemming pollution in common resources like air and water.

13 This is one area where a useful distinction can be drawn between commercial and political or religious speech. Commercial speech is protected, but it is not given the same range of protection as political or religious speech. Congress could prohibit forms of spam and impose criminal penalties on the worst of them: pornographic images that pop up without a user opening the e-mail, exposing children to the images.

14 Barring political spam ads would raise constitutional questions, but there is little need to do that: With spam less popular than the Ebola virus, savvy politicians aren't likely to use it.

15 For commercial spammers, however, the 98% rejection rate still allows a hefty profit on the 2% return. The U.S. government has sued a porn site spammer in Illinois who made $1 million a year on such a margin. The suit accuses the spammer of using innocuous subject lines like "Wanna Hear a Joke" to get users to open a link to his porn site.

16 One solution would be federal legislation that prohibits forms of spam and imposes heavy financial penalties on both spam operators and the advertised businesses. The European Union chose this course in May. In the U.S., lobbyists have effectively killed bills banning forms of spam in the last two sessions. Members of Congress need to be prodded to ban this virtual pollution.

17 Just remember to use the telephone; their e-mail inboxes are full.

Directions: Answer the following questions. You may need to reread portions of the article to answer all the questions.

1. What is the topic or subject of the article?

____

2. What is "spam" as discussed in the article?

____

3. What is the thesis or point the author makes about the topic?

____

4. In what paragraph, if any, is the thesis stated?

5. List at least three reasons the author offers to support his thesis.

____

____

____

6. According to the author, what is one solution to the problem? ______________________

____

Finding the thesis in a reading selection such as the one you just read is similar to finding the main idea in a paragraph. The difference is that in a longer selection, paragraphs are used to support the thesis whereas sentences are used to support the topic sentence in a paragraph. Of course, the longer the selection, the more difficult it is to separate supporting details from the thesis.

See how well you did on the questions above. The answer to the first question is e-mail spam. The word "spam" or references to it appear in nearly every paragraph and in the title.

Your answer to the second question should reflect the idea that the author refers to spam as pollution of the Internet, unwanted advertising e-mail that clogs people's e-mail.

The third question should have an answer that reflects the author's position: Spam is a threat to the Internet and requires some action be taken to stop it before it destroys e-mail communications.

Probably the best answer to this question is paragraph 10, where the author states, "Spam now is a real threat to the medium of Internet communications." That something should be done about it is more implied throughout the article than actually stated in so many words.

For question 5, you might have answered any of these:

- AOL is worried enough to bring lawsuits to stop spammers.
- Spamming use is expanding.
- There are huge costs to the system and society.
- Some people are abandoning e-mail.
- Time is wasted sorting through e-mail.

The answer to the last question appears both in the title and in paragraph 16, where he states what he feels would be "one solution."

Before going on to the next practice, make certain that you understand any mistakes or misinterpretations you may have made in answering the above questions.

Practice C-2

Directions: Follow the same directions as for the last practice; read carefully, looking for the subject, the thesis, and the supporting details in the essay. If you had any problems with the last practice, make certain you understand your mistakes before going on.

WAR ON PREJUDICE STARTS WITH OURSELVES

Michael Yachnik

1 All of us have prejudices. We might like to believe that we outgrow most of them. Unfortunately, a large number of prejudices begin early in life and linger until we confront and change them.

Los Angeles Times, March 28, 1994, B5. Reprinted by permission of Michael Yachnik, Ph.D.

2 That is because early life exposure to society's rejection of select groups is profound. Sadly, the attitudes of fear and loathing are often delivered to us by people we love and depend on. The messages of intolerance and mistrust of others are interwoven with messages of nurturing and affection for us.

3 When we were children and our caregivers expressed their affection by telling us about threats and promising to protect us from *them,* that made us feel loved and secure. But if those caregivers didn't differentiate between "real threats" (people who drive recklessly, push drugs or bully others) and "imagined threats" (people who have a different race, religion or sexual orientation), then we developed fears and dislikes of people who are merely different. Those fears, though irrational, were paired with early memories of love and security—and that makes them powerful and enduring.

4 As children, we weren't sophisticated enough to determine which messages were necessary for our survival and which reflected the prejudices of our caregivers. Unwittingly, we went along, reinforcing negative ideas about others because we trusted those who gave us those ideas in the first place. Many of us arrive at adulthood with some harmful baggage.

5 So what can we do about it now?

6 A lot. First, we can examine the many messages we have received and determine which we want to foster and which we want to change. It is possible to value the loving and nurturing messages we received from caregivers while acknowledging that they grew up with prejudices that may have been inadvertently passed along to us.

7 Next, we can educate ourselves and confront any false ideas we have about people who are different. The many cultural events in Los Angeles, including festivals, fairs, films and art exhibits, offer a great way to learn something new while having fun. If nothing new is allowed in, we're stuck with the information that created the prejudices in the first place.

8 Finally, we can put our learning into action. Do we let derogatory remarks about others pass without comment because we can remember hearing someone from our past say them? Or do we remind ourselves and others that we need to shed some of our old ideas and develop new ones? Do we structure our lives to avoid people who are different from us because "that's the way it's always been"? Or do we evaluate our behavior rationally and try to change it?

9 Examining old attitudes, seeking out information to form new ones and changing behavior—those are the key elements to winning the war on prejudice.

10 What is the most effective way to do these things on a regular basis? If, in our personal and professional lives, we reach out to meet and interact with people who are different from us, we will be able to confront old attitudes regularly. New friends can help educate us by sharing their life experiences and listening to ours. As the friendships grow, our motivation to change will also grow. And as the number of friendships and acquaintances increases, we will have more examples of people in our lives who reinforce new ideas about others who may be different.

Directions: Now answer the following questions. You may need to reread portions of the essay, especially when certain paragraphs are referred to.

1. Which of the following best states the main idea of the essay? ______________

a. All of us have prejudices, but they change as we grow older.

b. We are exposed to prejudices as children but can change them by examining our messages, educating ourselves, and changing our actions.

c. The way to win the war on prejudice is to meet and interact with a diverse group of people.

d. None of the above.

2. In paragraph 3, what does the author say about caregivers and threats that may then develop into prejudices? ______________________________

____

3. T/F We can infer from this essay that it is each person's responsibility to overcome prejudices that caregivers pass on. Explain why you think this inference is true or false. ______________________________

____

4. List details that show how people in Los Angeles can educate themselves and perhaps change their prejudices. ______________________________

____

5. List the three ways this essay gives us to overcome our prejudices. ______________

____

6. Give an example of how you have used one of the three elements to overcome a prejudice in your own life. ______________________________

____

D. Summarizing as a Way to Test Your Understanding

Now that you have practiced identifying main ideas and supporting details, recognizing basic patterns, and finding the thesis of longer articles, you have the skills to put all these together by learning how to summarize. You will need to use all the skills you've learned in this chapter in order to write a summary.

Frequently, instructors in your college classes will ask you to write summaries of reading assignments. In addition, many essay exams you will be required to take are really nothing more than a test of your ability to write summaries in answer to questions based on sections from your textbooks. What, then, *is* a summary, and how do you write one?

A summary is a brief statement in your own words of the main ideas and support used in a reading selection. Writing summaries requires that you include only the most vital information presented in a piece of writing. The practices you have been doing that require you to separate the main ideas from details provide the basis for writing summaries.

There are three basic things to keep in mind when you write a summary: Be brief, be complete, and be objective. This can sound easier than it is. If you are too brief, you may not be complete; if you try to be too complete, you may write too much; if you're not careful, you may slip into subjectivity, allowing your own feelings and opinions to creep in. A summary has no place for your views. As a guideline, a good rule of thumb in writing summaries is to make them no longer than one quarter of the length of the passage you are summarizing. But this may vary depending on the instructor's summary assignment.

Let's say you are asked to summarize the essay you just read in Practice C-2, "War on Prejudice Starts with Ourselves." The best way to get started is to begin with the author's thesis, which is reflected in his title. Yachnik believes that doing away with prejudice starts with each person. Why? What does he want us to do about these prejudices?

As we look over the essay paragraph by paragraph, we see that the first two paragraphs set up the idea that we all have prejudices and they start early in life.

The third and fourth paragraphs show how caregivers pass on prejudices, often unwittingly by failing to differentiate between real and imagined threats.

Paragraph 6 uses the signal word *first* so we clearly recognize it as a first major point that we need to examine the messages we received as children.

Paragraph 7 uses the signal word *next* to signal the next major point, that we can educate ourselves about people who are different from us.

Paragraph 8 uses the signal word *finally* to show the third major point, that we need to change our actions.

Paragraph 9 summarizes these three points as an extra assurance we will recognize their importance.

The last paragraph ends with specific ideas each of us can use on a daily basis to overcome prejudices, emphasizing the need to make friends with people who are different from us.

As we move through the paragraphs, we can list what the author suggests to recognize and overcome prejudices.

1. All of us have prejudices, which will stay the same unless we take steps to change them.
2. Our prejudices often started in childhood when our caregivers didn't differentiate between real and imagined threats, so we received some negative ideas.
3. The first thing we can do to overcome prejudice is examine the messages we have received.
4. The second thing we can do to overcome prejudice is educate ourselves and confront prejudices.
5. The third thing we can do to overcome prejudice is to put our plan into action, not allowing prejudice in others around us.
6. We can do this on a regular basis by developing friendships with people who are different from us.

Now, if we put all this together, we might have a summary that says something like this:

> In his essay "War on Prejudice Starts with Ourselves," Michael Yachnik states that each of us has prejudices and that doing away with them takes work. These prejudices, he feels, start in childhood when caregivers don't differentiate between real and imagined threats, so we receive some negative ideas. He says we can do three things to overcome these prejudices. The first step is to examine the messages we have received. The second step is to educate ourselves about people who are different. The third step is to change our actions, refusing to participate or encourage prejudice in others. Yachnik concludes we can do this on a daily basis by seeking out friendships with people who are different from us.

Obviously things have to be left out of a summary, but this example is brief, complete in presenting the thesis and support used by Yachnik, and objective.

In order to write this summary, it was necessary to go over Yachnik's essay very carefully. Summary writing requires using the skills necessary for separating main ideas from details and identifying the author's thesis, both skills that were taught in this unit. The practice of writing summaries of what you read can be of great benefit to your literal comprehension development.

PRACTICE D-1: Practice in Summarizing

Directions: In the space provided, write a summary of passage B on page 87–88 that you have already read. You may want to use the answers to your questions as a guide.

PRACTICE D-2: More Summarizing

Directions: In the space below, write a summary of passage E on pages 90–91 that you have already read. You may want to use your answers as a guide.

PRACTICE D-3: And Still More on Summarizing

Directions: On another sheet of paper, write a summary of the essay "Congress Must Send Spammers a Message" (page 92–93) and turn it in to your instructor.

Application 3: Summarizing Materials of Your Own Choice

Find a 750–1000-word article in a current magazine or a textbook and summarize it. Turn in a copy of the article and the summary.

E. Flexible Reading Rates

Another skill you will find essential is developing reading-rate versatility. How fast a person reads is irrelevant if good comprehension doesn't match the speed. Yet with a little training, most people can easily increase their reading rate without a loss in comprehension. Most people have never been trained in reading rate, yet college students are often hard pressed to keep up with assignments, and their concentration may wander when a textbook is open.

There are several factors to consider when discussing reading speed. First, not everything can be—or should be—read at the fastest rate. Your reading rate should depend on your *purpose* for reading. Surveying to get an idea of what you will be reading, looking for specific items, and reviewing for tests are purposes that allow fast reading rates. Some textbooks may be easy enough that faster rates are appropriate. But if you have been assigned to write an essay about a poem in your English textbook, you will probably need to read that poem several times before you can even begin to get an idea for your essay. You may need to look up the definitions of many of the words used, considering their connotative meanings. You may need to consider the rhyme schemes used and the form of the poem. With poetry, you will get more out of it if you read aloud. The reading and understanding of that poem may take longer than the reading of fifty pages in a psychology text. Reading rates vary with reading purposes.

A second factor in reading speed has to do with your *concentration* as you read. The most intense concentration in difficult school tasks occurs in about twenty-minute segments. This does *not* mean you can only study for twenty minutes, but it does mean you will concentrate better if you set short frequent study sessions and change study activities more often. Learn to take advantage of the short concentration span, especially with college assignments that do not automatically grab your interest and keep it. People who set long study periods ("I'll study all day Saturday") are usually deluding themselves. Are you aware when your concentration wanders? Is there a pattern to when you can and cannot concentrate? What is your shortest concentration span? your longest? The important point is *not* to sit with your book open while your mind drifts. Once you have allowed yourself to drift, just opening that book will often trigger daydreaming. The minute your mind wanders, turn away from that book immediately.

A third factor affecting reading speed is lack of knowledge about how to read faster. Old reading habits are hard to break. Since most people are never trained to read quickly, reading habits learned early in life are never broken. Training in four areas can help you speed up your reading rate with no loss in comprehension:

1. *Reading for ideas and detecting patterns.* Untrained readers read as if every word is equally important in every kind of reading. Instead, you should read for ideas and think about what you're reading.

a. The first exercise to help you read for ideas is *closure,* or the mind's ability to fill in blanks without seeing every detail. If I say, "Tom went to the __________ and bought a loaf of ____________," your mind closes on the blank spaces, and you know he went to the store or bakery and bought a loaf of bread.

Here is an exercise to help you understand how closure works. In the following paragraph from this section, twenty-five of the sixty-one words are crossed out, yet the meaning is still clear.

> Another study skill ~~you will find~~ essential ~~is developing~~ reading-rate versatility. How fast ~~a person reads is~~ irrelevant if good comprehension doesn't match ~~the~~ speed. ~~Yet,~~ with ~~a little~~ training, ~~most~~ people ~~can easily~~ increase ~~their~~ reading rate without ~~a~~ loss in comprehension. ~~Most~~ people read ~~as~~ slowly ~~as they do~~ because ~~they've~~ never ~~been~~ shown how to read faster.

With twenty-five words crossed out, the paragraph now reads:

> Another study skill essential reading-rate versatility. How fast irrelevant if good comprehension doesn't match speed. With training, people increase reading rate without loss in comprehension. People read slowly because never shown how to read faster.

Do you see how you can get full meaning without stopping at each word? You can practice closure in your textbooks.

b. The second exercise to help you read faster for ideas is to pick out main ideas, select supporting details, and detect paragraph patterns. These skills, which you learned in this chapter will enable you to read faster with better comprehension.

Practice reading for ideas by seeing how quickly you can pick out main ideas and figure out the pattern of details in the following paragraphs.

> As a technical writer, you need to remember these four ethical principles. First, don't leave out any vital information (such as safety hazards). Next, don't exaggerate (such as claims for absolute success). Third, create a clear understanding of what the information means. Finally, respect copyrighted information. Don't knowingly download or distribute copyrighted information.

Where is the main idea? ______________________________

How many supporting details are there? ______________________

> When interviewing for a job, don't ask about salary or bonuses during the first interview. Be prepared to ask questions that show your knowledge of the job or the company. Act as if you are determined to get the job. These are some of the tips to help you function most effectively in a job interview.

Where is the main idea? ______________________________

How many supporting details are there? ______________________

> Low-level concentration is characterized by an inability to settle on one activity or to discipline the mind to follow one track at a time. People who operate at this level are often very busy people who try to do two or three tasks at the same time. Dabblers, another group with low concentration, do a lot of different things but never seem to master any of them. A third group is daydreamers, who may have textbooks open but their minds are not engaged.

Where is the main idea? ______________________________

How many supporting details are there? ______________________

Here are the answers: In the first paragraph, the main idea in the first sentence and there are four major details (don't omit, don't exaggerate, be clear, respect copyrights). In the second paragraph, the main idea is the last sentence, and there are three major details (no salary questions, ask questions, be determined). In the third paragraph, the main idea is the first sentence, and there are three major details (busy people, dabblers, daydreamers).

2. *Increasing vocabulary.* If a page has three or more unfamiliar words on it, you will not be able to speed read it. You therefore need to continue the vocabulary strategies you learned in Chapter One. As your vocabulary increases, you will find more materials you can read quickly. If you want to read quickly, you need to learn the terminology first.

3. *Learning pacing strategies.* Untrained readers often find their minds wandering while they read. Training yourself to read at a forced rate with good concentration will take practice. Use an index card to cover each line as you read it, moving it down the page a little faster than you currently read. Another pacing strategy is to use your hand or a pen to keep you reading at a forced rate. Do not use your hand to trace each word or each line. Pull it straight down the page at a rate a little faster than your current rate.

4. *Practice fast reading rates.* The only way to learn flexible reading rates is to practice for a short time each day with fast rates. Find an easy, interesting book with no new vocabulary. Students have found it helpful to check out young juvenile literature from the library for this exercise. Work up to more difficult books as you feel more comfortable with fast rates.

Start with five to ten-minute practice sessions and work up to longer periods of time as your concentration and rate increase. If your concentration wanders, stop your practice session and turn away from your book.

Surveying

In order to increase your reading rate, you need to start surveying selections *before* you start reading. Surveying is defined as the ability to identify *main ideas* while very rapidly and selectively skipping over the reading material. Surveying is a technique used to find out how a news story, magazine article, or textbook chapter is organized and what it is generally about in a short time. You can learn more about the SQ3R method in the Appendix.

Contrary to what most readers think, surveying is not a sloppy, hit-or-miss technique. To survey a news story, you need to understand the organizational pattern of writing news stories. Usually each sentence or two is a paragraph in itself. This style prevents paragraphs from looking too long in the narrow columns that newspapers often use. The opening sentence to a news story often covers *who, what, where, when,* and sometime *why.* At the very least, most stories tell *who* and *what* in the opening line. Thus, when surveying a newspaper story, it is always advisable to concentrate on the opening sentence.

A magazine article or essay has a different organization. Titles are more reliable here then in newspaper stories, which can be misleading. Magazine titles tend to reveal a subject and sometimes a thesis or the author's attitude. This is an aid to surveying. For instance, if the title of a magazine article reads "Lake Havasu: A Fisherman's Paradise," you already have a clue to the article's content and the author's attitude or point of view. As you survey, you would then look for reasons the author feels the lake is a "paradise" for fisherman.

Some magazine articles are set up the same way as most textbook chapters. In addition to helpful titles, most contain headings and subheadings to alert the reader that a new idea related to the subject is being introduced. The word *alert* is the key to being a good surveyer.

Here is what to be alert to when you survey magazine articles:

1. Read the title and scan the opening paragraph or two, looking for the subject of the article and the author's thesis or point of view about the subject.

2. Read the first sentence or parts of the first sentence of each following paragraph, looking for ideas related to or supporting the author's thesis.

3. Read the last paragraph (of last two depending on the article), looking for a summary of conclusion about the subject.

4. If there are questions (as there are in the following selection), look at the questions during your survey.

This approach of a modification of it will help you get a preview of an article's contents. At least you will know whether you want or need to read the article more closely.

F. Putting It All Together

The next two practices give you the opportunity to use what you have learned about reading to find an author's thesis and use of main ideas and supporting details. Before you begin, it is recommended that you refer to the Student Record Chart and review your scores for the reading selections in Chapter One. Note your comprehension and vocabulary scores. Try either to match your scores or to do better this time. As you progress through this book, use these scores as a motivation and challenge to do better each time. Your only competition is yourself.

PRACTICE F-1

Directions: As you read the following essay, distinguish between the subject and the thesis and note what main ideas and supporting details are used to back up the author's thesis.

THINKING: A NEGLECTED ART

Carolyn Kane

1 It is generally agreed that the American educational system is in deep trouble. Everyone is aware of the horrible facts: school systems are running out of money, teachers can't spell.

2 Most of us know or think we know who is to blame: liberal courts, spineless school boards, government regulations. It is easy to select a villain.

3 But possibly the problem lies not so much in our institutions as in our attitudes. It is sad that although most of us profess to believe in education, we place no value on intellectual activity.

4 We Americans are a charitable and humane people: we have institutions devoted to every good cause from rescuing homeless cats to preventing World War III. But what have we done to promote the art of thinking? Certainly we make no room for thought in our daily lives. Suppose a man were to say to his friends, "I'm not going to PTA tonight (or choir practice or the baseball game) because I need some time to myself, some time to think"? Such a man would be shunned by his neighbors; his family would be ashamed of him. What if a teen-ager were to say, "I'm not going to the dance tonight because I need some time to think"? His parents would immediately start looking in the Yellow Pages for a psychiatrist. We are all too much like Julius Caesar: we fear and distrust people who think too much. We believe that almost anything is more important than thinking.

5 **Guilty**: Several years ago a college administrator told me that if he wanted to do any serious thinking, he had to get up at 5:30 in the morning—I suppose because that was the only time when no one would interrupt him. More recently I heard a professor remark that when his friends catch him in the act of reading a book, they say, "My, it must be nice to have so much free time." And even though I am an English teacher—a person who should know better—I find myself feeling vaguely guilty whenever I sneak off to the library to read. It is a common belief that if people are thinking or reading, they are doing nothing. Through our words and our actions, we express this attitude every day of our lives. Then we wonder why our children refuse to take their studies

seriously and why they say to their teachers, "This stuff won't do me any good because I'll never need to use it."

6 It is easy to understand the causes of this prejudice against thinking. One problem is that to most of us, thinking looks suspiciously like loafing. *Homo sapiens* in deep thought is an uninspiring sight. He leans back in his chair, props up his feet, puffs on his pipe and stares into space. He gives every appearance of wasting time; he reminds us more of Dagwood and Beetle Bailey than of Shakespeare and Einstein. We wish he would get up and *do* something; mow the lawn, maybe, or wash the car. Our resentment is natural.

7 But thinking is far different from laziness. Thinking is one of the most productive activities a human being can undertake. Every beautiful and useful thing we have created—including democratic government and freedom of religion—exists because somebody took the time and effort to think of it.

8 And thinking does require time and effort. It is a common misconception that if a person is "gifted" or "bright" or "talented," wonderful ideas will flash spontaneously into his mind. Unfortunately, the intellect does not work in this way. Even Einstein had to study and think for months before he could formulate his theory of relativity. Those of us who are less intelligent find it a struggle to conceive even a moderately good idea, let alone a brilliant one.

9 **Seclusion**: Another reason why we distrust thinking is that it seems unnatural. Human beings are a social species, but thinking is an activity that requires solitude. Consequently, we worry about people who like to think. It disturbs us to meet a person who deliberately chooses to sit alone and think instead of going to a party or a rodeo or a soccer match. We suspect that such a person needs counseling.

10 Our concern is misplaced. Intelligence is just as much a part of human nature as sociability. It would certainly be unnatural for a person to retreat into total seclusion. It would be equally unnatural for a person to allow his mind to die of neglect.

11 If Americans ever became convinced of the importance of thought, we would probably find ways to solve the problems of our schools, problems that now seem insurmountable. But how can we revive interest in the art of thinking? The best place to start would be in the homes and churches of our land. Ministers should admonish their congregations to do some purposeful procrastination every day, to put off one chore in order to have a few minutes to think. Family members should practice saying such things as, "I'll wash the dishes tonight because I know you want to catch up on your thinking."

12 This may sound un-American, possibly sacrilegious. But if we are to survive as a free people, we will have to take some such course of action as soon as possible, because regardless of what some advertisers have led us to believe, this country does not run on oil. It runs on ideas.

Comprehension Check

Directions: Answer the following questions without looking back.

1. What is the *subject* of the essay you just read? ______________________

____

2. What is the *thesis* of this essay? ______________________

____

3. According to the author, if someone is thinking or reading, that person is frequently thought of as

   a. weird.
   b. doing nothing.
   c. studying.
   d. not using his or her time wisely.

4. State two reasons the author gives for prejudice against thinking: __________

5. According to the author, thinking requires

   a. time.
   b. effort.
   c. solitude.
   d. all three.

6. The author uses Einstein as an example to support one of her main ideas. What point is she making? __________

7. If a person chooses to sit alone and think instead of going to a party or sports event, we tend to suspect that person

   a. is a nerd.
   b. is another Einstein.
   c. needs counseling.
   d. none of these.

8. How, according to the author, can we revive interest in the art of thinking? __________

9. T/F The author claims that while we profess to believe in education, we place no value on intellectual activity.

10. The author concludes that this country runs on __________

Vocabulary Check

Directions: Define the following underlined words used in the essay.

1. <u>spineless</u> school boards (paragraph 2)

2. will flash <u>spontaneously</u> into his mind (paragraph 8)

3. he could <u>formulate</u> his theory (paragraph 8)

4. problems that now seem <u>insurmountable</u> (paragraph 11)

5. should <u>admonish</u> their congregations (paragraph 11)

6. some purposeful <u>procrastination</u> (paragraph 11)

7. may sound . . . possibly sacrilegious (paragraph 12)

____

8. shunned by his neighbors (paragraph 4)

____

9. What is the suffix in spineless and what does it mean? (Chapter One, Practice C-7)

____

10. What is the first prefix in insurmountable and what does it mean? (Chapter One, Practice C-1) ______________________________

Record the results of the comprehension and vocabulary checks on the Student Record Chart. Make certain you understand any mistakes you may have made before going on. Use whatever method you are using to learn any words you missed.

PRACTICE F-2: TIMED READING

Directions: You have a lot of information about vocabulary and literal comprehension strategies now. The third—and most often overlooked—strategy to improve your reading is reading rate. The purpose is not to make you read faster and lose your comprehension but rather to read faster and increase your comprehension. Very slow readers (under 180 wpm) will often lose concentration and focus only on details or isolated words rather than understanding what the article or essay is saying. If you read too slowly, you also can't get through all your college assignments (unless you give up sleep!).

The first step to reading faster is to decide what rate you want to set, based on three factors. The first factor is how familiar you are with the topic in the first place. In this article, you can look at the title, "Putting Reading in Its Proper Place," and realize that it is about reading and what importance we give to it. This topic is familiar to all of us, even if we haven't actually thought about it before. If the topic is particle physics, on the other hand, you would probably not know much about it and would need to set a slower rate.

The second factor to help you set your rate is the difficulty of the material. Glance at any paragraph and see if you understand the vocabulary. If there are more than three unfamiliar words on a page, you will find the material more difficult and will need to set a slower rate. Can you figure out the unfamiliar words from context, or will it affect your comprehension if you don't know the words? If English is not your primary language, you may find that unfamiliar words are hampering your comprehension. If that is the case, practice the rate exercises and learn the skills, but make comprehension your primary goal.

The third factor is your purpose for reading the material. In this text, the purpose is to answer the comprehension questions accurately and well. In order to help you do this, you should look at the questions first—before you even start reading. This will help you decide what you need to get out of the reading. If there are questions at the end of your college textbook chapters, read them first. If the instructor asks questions in class, let those questions guide your reading. Now, look at the ten comprehension questions and read them before you actually start reading the article.

You should have now looked at the title and read the comprehension questions. Now you want to read this 460-word article at a faster rate. Try to read at least 50 wpm faster than you read the article in Chapter One. See if it helps your comprehension to push yourself as you read.

Begin timing: ____________

PUTTING READING IN ITS PROPER PLACE

Dominic F. Martia

1 As more and more Americans depend exclusively on television for information and ideas, the nation's reading proficiency suffers—and so does society.

2 It isn't hard to see why TV is so appealing. It offers the immediacy of real life. Yet, TV doesn't merely give us real life. Events in real life occur without commentary. In contrast, televised events are often delivered from prefabricated perspectives. In real life, we are forced to make up our own minds as to the meaning of events. When we see televised news events, the meaning often is supplied through selection, angle, emphasis, and accompanying narrative.

3 But the point isn't that TV may be biased. So may books, magazines or newspapers. The point is that television's seductive and misleading immediacy lulls our critical judgment. Watching TV requires much less effort than reading does. Our preference for TV as a source of information and ideas is a measure of intellectual laziness.

4 TV long ago won the battle for our attention. But the real loser has been our ability to read, which, like other learned abilities, needs regular practice to maintain its strength.

5 As we seek a better balance between our dependence on TV and our use of the print media, we will increase the time we spend reading. This will be a good start. If overreliance on TV has atrophied our reading skill, then reading more should help restore it. But besides reading more, we need to become more selective and more critical readers. Much of what we might read isn't worth reading. It panders to the same laziness that induces us to turn on the TV rather than open a book.

6 In a nation our size, it would be surprising if there weren't a persistent market for serious and high-quality publications. But the demise of many newspapers, the shaky economics of journals of opinion and the unprofitability of serious books indicate that the general level of reading taste has declined sharply since the '50s.

7 Our concern for providing basic literacy to adults seems to recognize the importance of reading. But let's also encourage people who are already literate to aspire to a higher level of reading skill and taste. It will take some thought, study and debate before we can decide exactly what should be done to achieve this goal. Schools, libraries and publishers would be the logical ones to begin the process, the guiding assumption of which is that reading is essential to education and to effective citizenship.

8 The issue is not a simple one of whether one source of information and ideas is better than another. We need them all. But intelligent use of our media requires the critical judgment that is best developed through reading. So let's put reading where it belongs—in first place.

Finish timing. Record time here: ____________ and use the Timed Readings Conversion Chart in the Appendix to figure your rate: ____________ wpm.

Comprehension Check

Directions: Answer the following questions without looking back.

1. What is the *subject* of the essay you just read? ______________________________

____

2. What is the *thesis* of this essay?______________________________

____

3. According to the author, TV, as opposed to reading, is appealing because

a. it forces us to make up our own minds.

b. the meaning to events is supplied.

c. we are intellectually lazy.

d. all of the above.

4. T/F The author believes TV is biased whereas reading books, newspapers, or magazines is not.

5. Because TV has won the battle for our attention, the author believes that the real loser is

a. our ability to read.

b. our desire to read.

c. our need to read.

d. our children.

6. In order to maintain a proper balance between our dependence on TV and our use of the print media, we need to increase the time we spend ______________________________

____

7. According to the author, our reading skills require regular ______________________________

____

8. Besides reading more, we need to become

a. more selective in our reading.

b. more critical readers.

c. both a and b.

d. none of the above.

9. What support does the author provide for his statement that the general level of reading taste has declined since the 1950s? ______________________________

____

10. The author believes that reading

a. is essential to education.

b. is essential to effective citizenship.

c. is essential to developing critical judgments.

d. all of the above.

Vocabulary Check

Directions: Define the following underlined words from the essay.

1. the nation's reading proficiency suffers (paragraph 1) ____________________
____
2. often delivered from prefabricated perspectives (paragraph 2) ____________________
____
3. it lulls our critical judgment (paragraph 3) ____________________
____
4. TV has atrophied our reading skill (paragraph 5) ____________________
____
5. it panders to the same laziness (paragraph 5) ____________________
____
6. the same laziness that induces us to turn on the TV (paragraph 5) ____________________
____
7. the demise of many newspapers (paragraph 6) ____________________
____
8. to aspire to a higher level of reading (paragraph 7) ____________________
____
9. the guiding assumption (paragraph 7) ____________________
____
10. intelligent use of our media (paragraph 8) ____________________
____

Record the results of the rate, comprehension, and vocabulary checks on the Student Record Chart.

Before you go on to the next chapter, make certain you understand any mistakes or problems you may have encountered in this one. It is important that you learn from mistakes, so don't despair when you make them. Accept mistakes as normal. Making mistakes is often the best way to discover what you do and don't know.

Questions for Group Discussion

1. As a group, come up with a summary of what this chapter taught you about how to improve your comprehension.
2. The last two selections deal with problems with thinking and reading in our culture today. Compare and contrast what Kane and Martia say.
3. Why do you think the first two chapters in this text deal first with vocabulary and second with comprehension? Can you think of other orders or other topics that should be covered first?
4. Have everyone in the group come up with at least one thing learned in this chapter which he or she didn't know before.

CHAPTER THREE

Developing Computer Reading Skills

A. Reading on the World Wide Web

In a relatively few years, the World Wide Web has become a major player in providing information on practically every subject. Daily, the number of homes and schools hooking up to the Internet grows. Many schools and colleges require students to buy computers and use the Internet as a matter of course, providing Internet hookups in libraries and dormitories. Even hotels now provide rooms with availability to the Internet. Many children in elementary schools are growing up learning how to read both print and electronic text. Some of us have to learn to read anew.

The fast-growing availability and use of computers and Web sites on the Internet have brought about changes in the way we read. As the sophistication of Web sites continues to grow, so must our skills in using them intelligently and correctly.

Right now you are reading traditional print, following along from the beginning of a passage to the end. You read in a single, familiar direction. Your eyes can glance over a whole page, noting titles, headings, and paragraph forms and lengths. You can quickly flip pages back and forth. You have been taught to read printed matter that conforms to an understood pattern.

Reading Web sites is different. You've probably already experienced reading on the Internet. If so, you know that data on many Web sites are not presented in a traditional way, varying widely in the way information is presented on the screen. The computer screen limits the amount of text you can see at one time, often surrounded by color, sounds, or animation. The information may not appear as a typical paragraph with topic sentence and supporting detail. Each sentence may itself be a topic needing further support provided on yet another screen page.

In most cases, reading on a computer screen is slower than reading printed text. Information is not presented in a linear fashion, but divided up into links. It becomes a matter of moving from link to link.

Web Site Links

Most Web sites lead you in many directions. You are offered choices, called links, which take you to other pages on the site. For instance, **Figure 3.1** shows the home page (or first page) of a Web site for the University of California, Davis. Notice all the links on both sides of the photos, serving as a Table of Contents for the Web site. For information on any one of those topics, you click on it and wait while the site loads the page you want. How fast the page comes up depends on the computer's speed. Once you get to that page, you may have other link choices for more detailed information. Sometimes you will click on a subject link and discover it does not contain the information you want. You then have to go back to the home page and start over. Some Web sites, as in Figure 3.1, will retain a list of the major links on one side of the screen so you can move from link to link.

An Example of Reading a Web Site

As an example of reading on the Internet, let's say you wanted to attend the University of California, Davis. You want to know their admissions requirements. On the home page in Figure 3.1, you click on "Admissions." After it loads the page on your screen, it loads **Figure 3.2** on your screen. Notice the various links provided in Figure 3.2. As an undergraduate, you click on "Undergraduate Admissions: all you need to know about UC Davis."

This brings up **Figure 3.3**. Now you have another batch of links to choose from. You want to learn when and how to apply to UC Davis and their requirements, so you click on "Admissions" and get what you see in **Figure 3.4**. Once again, choices for various links are provided. Notice in the upper right-hand corner even more links for selection depending on whether or not you're applying as a freshman, transfer student, or international student.

At this point you can see how different reading on the Web is compared with traditional printed text. While you may be clicking on one link, another user may

[Text-only version] MyUCDAVIS

News | Find Info/People | Calendar | Help

Quick Links

Find: GO

UCDAVIS
University of California, Davis

About UC Davis
Admissions
Schools & Colleges
Arts & Entertainment
Libraries & Exhibits
Administration
Teaching
Research
Public Service
Students
Faculty
Staff
Alumni, Friends & Visitors
Principles of Community
Mission Statement

UC Davis has some of the world's strongest programs in environmental education and research.

Spotlight

UC Davis historian Eric Rauchway helps boost skills and knowledge of teachers as part of the UC Davis' Area 3 History and Cultures Project. With the help of grants from the U.S. Department of Education, including $940,000 just this month, the campus is leading a regional effort to raise student literacy and achievement in history.

Headlines

UC's new president, Robert Dynes, begins his new job this week.

Clean living and spirituality lead to long life, UC Davis aging specialists say.

Dick Lewis, beloved Aggie athletic trainer, dies.

Vintners are finding a tough market for selling wine, UC Davis survey shows.

[More news...]

Campus Issues

About 30,000 students arrive for the fall quarter. The campus is planning for their arrival and future growth.

Regents view options for '04-05 budget. More budget news is on our special report site.

The campus waits to hear this month who the National Institutes of Health will choose to build biocontainment laboratories for the study of infectious diseases.

News | Find Info/People | Calendar | Help

About UC Davis | Admissions | Schools & Colleges | Arts & Entertainment | Libraries & Exhibits | Administration | Teaching | Research | Public Service | Students | Faculty | Staff | Alumni, Friends & Visitors | Principles of Community | Mission Statement

Figure 3.1

be clicking on other links for different information. There is a skill in learning to follow multiple links or paths that contain what you want.

Many Web sites follow this UC Davis example: a home page with various links for you to follow. Clicking on the links provided serves as turning the pages in a book.

Web Reading Tips

Here are a few tips to help you get the most from reading on the Internet:

1. Be patient. Computers vary in speed, in screen size, and in the way they are linked to the Internet. Going from one link to another may take time, because the Web page may contain colored pictures, sound, or animation that can distract as well as aid. These all take time to load on to the computer screen. Sometimes a Web site may be "down" for some technical reasons, and you may need to try

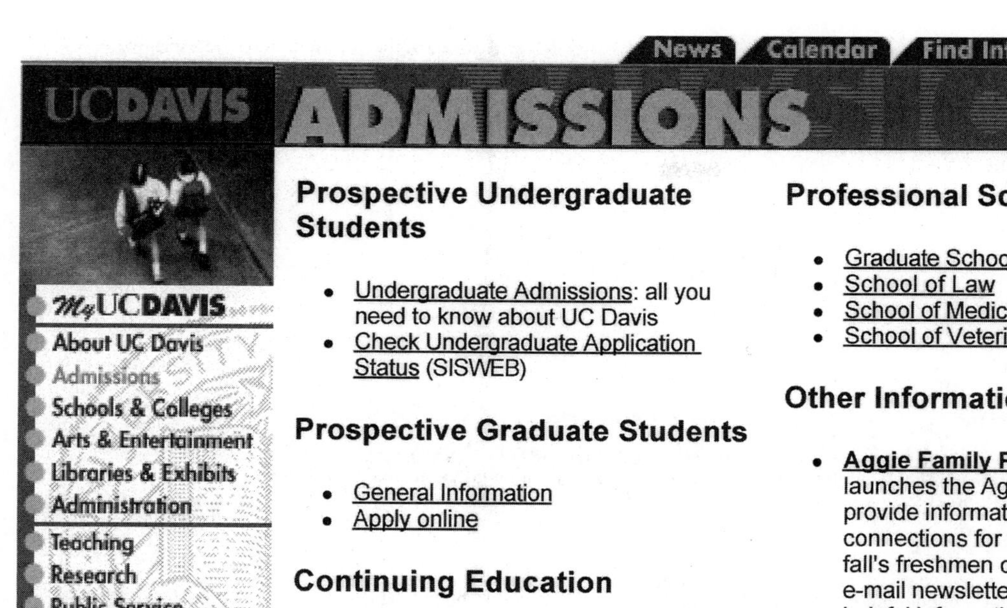

Figure 3.2

loading the site later. It's also possible the site no longer exists. Many Web sites come and go.

2. Expect little of the information you are seeking on the first page of a Web site. Home pages are usually "grabbers." Sounds, movement, and flashing colors are often used to get your attention. Unlike reading traditional print, you are often required to respond to these sights and sounds in order for any action to take place. Advertisements often pop up and intrude on your reading. This usually occurs only when a Web site has something to sell, but it's also a good way to question the legitimacy of the Web site.
3. Read a Web site's home page carefully. Make certain the Web site contains the information you need. Notice the way the information is arranged on the screen. Look again at Figure 3.1. Notice that in the upper right-hand corner is a small box labeled "Find." This box may also be labeled "Search." If you don't see exactly what you want on the Web page itself, you can type in a key word, such as "tuition costs," and click "Go." The Web site will bring up any information it contains on tuition costs. Some Web sites, however, don't have this feature.
4. As you move from link to link, bookmark the beginning site's home page. At the top of your Internet browser, you'll see a function called Bookmarks or Favorites. You can save the Web site and open it up again later by clicking on the site's name.
5. Before you start clicking on different links, determine which ones will lead you to what you want to know. You could spend a long time going from link to link

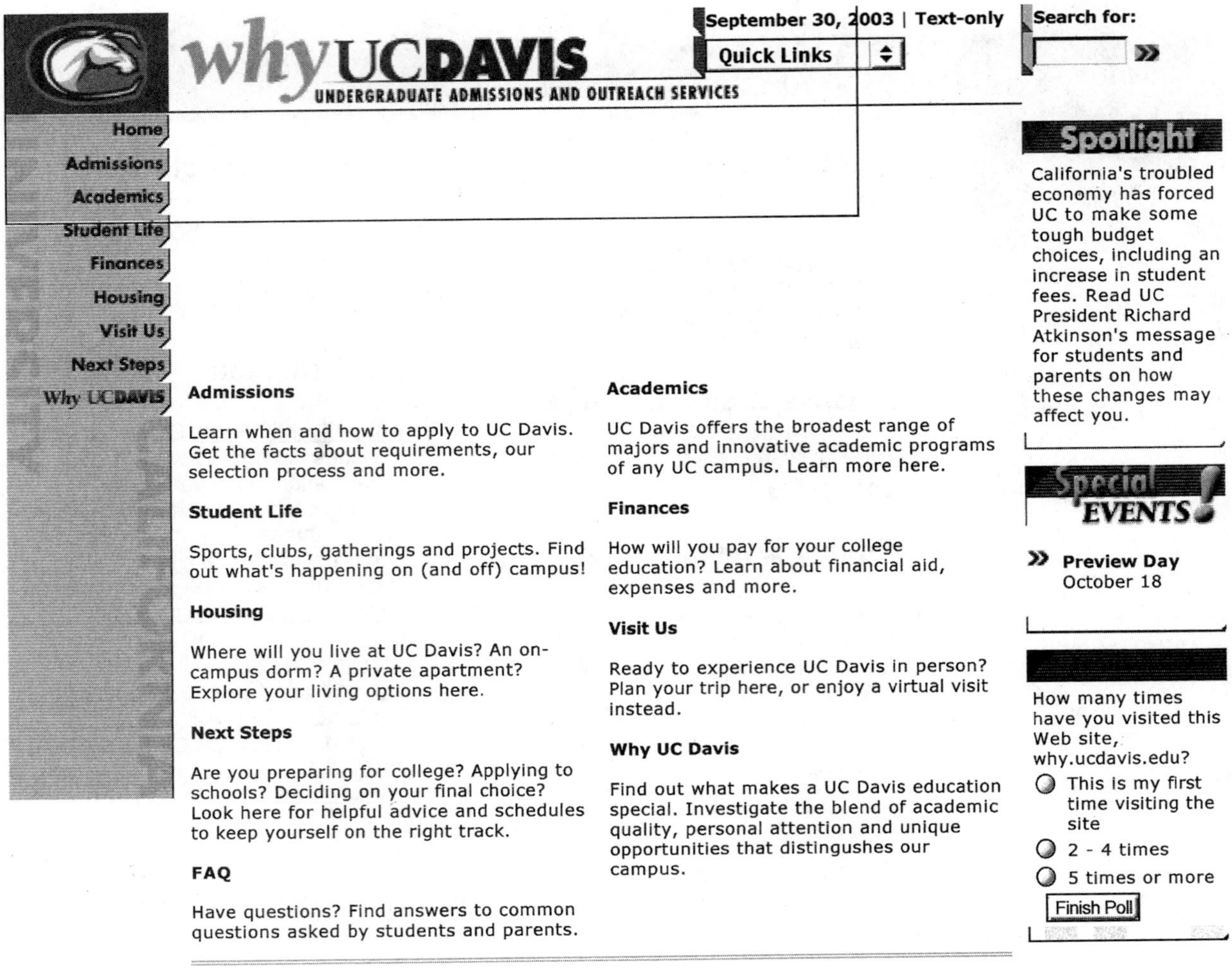

whyUCDAVIS
UNDERGRADUATE ADMISSIONS AND OUTREACH SERVICES

September 30, 2003 | Text-only
Quick Links
Search for:

Home
Admissions
Academics
Student Life
Finances
Housing
Visit Us
Next Steps
Why UCDAVIS

Admissions

Learn when and how to apply to UC Davis. Get the facts about requirements, our selection process and more.

Student Life

Sports, clubs, gatherings and projects. Find out what's happening on (and off) campus!

Housing

Where will you live at UC Davis? An on-campus dorm? A private apartment? Explore your living options here.

Next Steps

Are you preparing for college? Applying to schools? Deciding on your final choice? Look here for helpful advice and schedules to keep yourself on the right track.

FAQ

Have questions? Find answers to common questions asked by students and parents.

Academics

UC Davis offers the broadest range of majors and innovative academic programs of any UC campus. Learn more here.

Finances

How will you pay for your college education? Learn about financial aid, expenses and more.

Visit Us

Ready to experience UC Davis in person? Plan your trip here, or enjoy a virtual visit instead.

Why UC Davis

Find out what makes a UC Davis education special. Investigate the blend of academic quality, personal attention and unique opportunities that distingushes our campus.

Spotlight

California's troubled economy has forced UC to make some tough budget choices, including an increase in student fees. Read UC President Richard Atkinson's message for students and parents on how these changes may affect you.

Special EVENTS!

» **Preview Day**
October 18

How many times have you visited this Web site, why.ucdavis.edu?

- This is my first time visiting the site
- 2 - 4 times
- 5 times or more

Finish Poll

Figure 3.3

without obtaining what you are looking for. It may be that the Web site isn't worth your investigating and you need to select another Web site.

6. Print out any material you want to save to read later. It's advisable to take notes as you move from link to link, because some pages may not be printable, or you may need to return to that link at a later date.
7. Don't trust everything you read on the Internet. Anyone can create a Web site. Check to see who provided the information. Is it a trustworthy source? Is the information dated? What is the purpose of the Web site: to sell something or to provide knowledgeable information? Don't accept what is presented just because it is on the Internet.

Internet Language

The Internet contains millions of Web sites. A Web site address is known as the URL, or uniform resource locator. The Web address for the University of California, Davis, for instance, is: http://www.ucdavis.edu. The "http" stands for hypertext transport protocol, the language of the Web. The "www" refers to the World Wide Web. The last parts of the address are called the domain name and end with ".com"

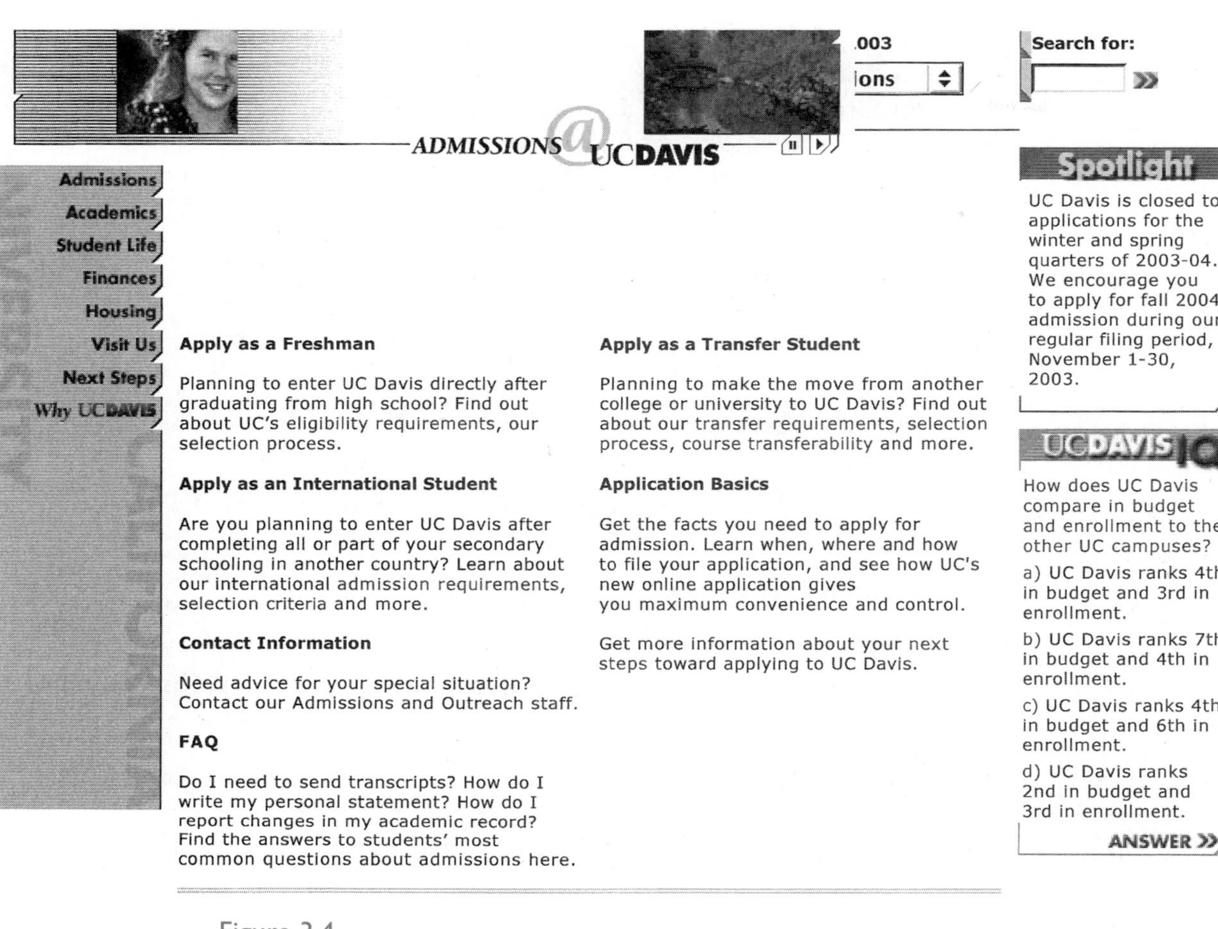

Figure 3.4

for commercial sites, ".edu" for educational sites, ".gov" for government sites, and ".org" for nonprofit organizations. These can sometimes help in determining the legitimacy of some sites.

Search Engines

If you didn't already know the domain name of UC Davis mentioned above, you could use one of many search engines on the Internet to find it. A search engine is like a directory for the Web. Some useful search engines are:

Search Engine Name	URL
Google	http://www.google.com
Yahoo!	http://www.yahoo.com
Alta Vista	http://www.altavista.com
WebCrawler	http://www.webcrawler.com
Infoseek	http://www.infoseek.com
Excite	http://www.excite.com

To reach a search engine, type in a search engine address from the above list. Once you log on to one of these search engines, you will see a search box. Type in the keywords for a topic or person you may want to research, and the search engine will list all its Internet sites for that topic. Make certain your keywords aren't too broad or you will get thousands of useless listings. Narrow your keywords down to specific rather than broad areas.

Try different search engines. Some have better listings than others.

PRACTICE A-1: Reading on the World Wide Web

Directions: Place a T in the blank for any of the following statements that are true.

_______ **1.** The Internet has become a major source for obtaining information on practically every subject.

_______ **2.** Reading on the Internet requires a different approach from the way we read printed text.

_______ **3.** A link is another term for the home page of a Web site.

_______ **4.** A Web site's address is known as a URL.

_______ **5.** A search engine can take you directly to the information you want on the Internet.

PRACTICE A-2: Understanding Web Sites

Directions: Answer the following questions in the spaces provided using the figures indicated.

Using Figure 3.1:

1. You are interested in finding out more about the students who attend UC Davis. What link would you click on? _______________

2. If you did not see a link for the information you wanted, what aids are provided to help your search? _______________

3. How would you find the university's calendar of events? _______________

____

Using Figure 3.2:

4. How would you find information on financial aid? _______________

____

5. Is it possible to do off-campus coursework at the university? How do you know?

____

Using Figure 3.3:

6. What information would you receive if you clicked on "Spotlight"? _______________

____

7. What information would you get if you clicked on "FAQ"? _______________

____

Using Figure 3.4:

8. What three requirements must be met to be eligible for UC admission?__________

____

9. What criteria does the UC system use to select their freshman students? __________

____

10. If you discovered you were on the wrong page, where would you click to start your search over? ____

____

B. Reviewing Summarizing

A summary, as you remember from Chapter 2, is a brief statement in your own words of the main ideas and support used in a reading selection. The three basic things to keep in mind when you write a summary are to be brief, be complete, and be objective. Review pages 96–99 if you feel the need before doing the following practices.

PRACTICE B-1: Summarizing "Web Reading Tips"

Directions: In the space below, summarize the "Web Reading Tips" on pages 110–112.

____

____

____

____

____

____

____

PRACTICE B-2: Summarizing "You've Got Mail! Oh, No!!"

Directions: The Internet has brought with it another feature: e-mail. It, too, presents us with another way of reading. E-mail often is abbreviated, sometimes using visual symbols for words, such as:

:-) used as a smile
;-) used as a smile and a wink
:-(used to express sadness
8-) used as a smile from a person with glasses

These symbols and others are known as *emoticons* or icons that express emotion. As the use on the Internet expands, so must our ability to read "Internet talk."

Read the following newspaper article that expresses one person's reaction to e-mail.

"YOU'VE GOT MAIL! OH, NO!!"

Lenore Skenazy

1 Me, three years ago: Why on Earth do I need e-mail?

2 Me, three months ago: Oh, goody—got some e-mail!

3 Me, three minutes ago: Ugh. More e-mail.

4 Delete, delete, delete.

5 If you live a wired life at work or home, chances are you have experienced a similar e-mail evolution. What was once a gimmick for geeks quickly became an incredible convenience and then, just as quickly, a new source of irritation.

6 The reason? Too many ads.

7 If this keeps up, e-mail may soon go the way of the ringing phone at dinnertime: snarled at and unanswered.

8 The problem is that unscrupulous marketers are flooding the world's inboxes with offers of everything stupid, suspicious, or sick. When I log on, my inbox looks like the National Enquirer's classifieds. Do I want a new diet? Boyfriend? Bust? Click here!

9 Collectively, the stuff is called spam. And because sending a million spams is even cheaper than taking out one measly classified—in fact, it's practically free—the practice is exploding exponentially.

10 Already, spam accounts for about 50 percent of all e-mail—up from just 8 percent in 2001. Back in December, America Online boasted that it had blocked half a billion spams from its members in one day.

11 Now, it routinely blocks a billion. And still, an annoying number get through. On Tuesday, AOL announced yet another lawsuit against spammers—its 100th—proof of the difficulty of spam slamming.

12 "I'm going crazy wondering why I get all these e-mails about how to get a bigger penis," says Lonnie (a guy). "Why me? It is clearly going to ruin e-mail if it is not dealt with. I'm going back to carrier pigeons."

13 Pigeons might not be the answer, but he's right: e-mail cannot go on this way.

14 Just as Americans eventually learned to slam the door on Fuller Brush salesmen, toss out junk mail and mute commercials, they will parry this assault as well. It's just a question of how.

15 It could be that legislation will be passed to outlaw spam. Or technology may come along that effectively filters it out. But then again, it could be we who change.

16 Already, legislation has been enacted in California that requires all advertisers to announce themselves by putting "ADV" in the subject heading. But since many spammers operate offshore or can't be traced, it's unclear how effective this law—or any law—will be.

17 Meanwhile, techies are hard at work devising ever newer filters to scan e-mail before it gets to the inbox. But so far, these don't work perfectly. Some legitimate e-mails get spiked while some sleazy ones get through. "I check my junk folder three times a day to make sure no good ones have gone in there," says April Mason, a twenty-something businesswoman in Manhattan. And sometimes they have. So the filters have a way to go.

18 That leaves it to us to change—and we just might. Some folks already have started using two e-mail addresses: One for their inner circle, the other for all their online searches and purchases. That way, they can ignore any messages sent to the second address.

19 Or it also could be that more and more of us will start accepting e-mails only from friends we have pre-approved, the same way some people program their phones to accept calls only from a select list of buddies.

20 But maybe—just maybe—we will opt out of e-mail entirely. Spam will spoil the medium the way sewage can spoil a lake. We'll regard the inbox with disgust.

21 If so, a new technology could spring up to replace e-mail. Or we just may go back to those incredibly hokey methods of communication we'd been so ready to mothball: The phone. The letter. The knock on the door.

In the space below, summarize the article, stating the thesis and support given.

C. Practices Using the Internet

The following practices require that you have access to a computer. If you do not have a personal computer, your school will have computer services available in the library or learning center that you can use.

PRACTICE C-1: Using Search Engines

Directions: Find the following Web sites by using one of the search engines mentioned on page 113 and write in the domain address.

1. *The Washington Post* ____________________

2. *Biography* ____________________

3. *One Look Dictionaries* ____________________

4. *Women in Sports* ____________________

5. *Information Please Almanac* ____________________

6. *Rock and Roll Hall of Fame and Museum, Cleveland* ____________________

7. *Museum of Modern Art, New York* ______________________

____

8. *The Internet Public Library* ______________________

____

PRACTICE C-2: On Your Own: An Internet Training Guide

Directions: As a way to learn more about using the Internet, you may want to work through the RDN Virtual Training Guide offered by the University of Bristol in England. While the site is geared toward British students, it can be a useful tool in learning how to use the Internet to help you with coursework, literature searching, teaching, and research. The site can be found at: http://www.vts.rdn.ac.uk/

PRACTICE C-3: Visiting Sites on the Internet

Directions: Practice reading from the following Web sites to see how different Web pages are designed. Notice the various uses of color, sounds, text sizes, and fonts. Apply to each Web site the three questions in the directions to Practice D–1, "Case Study: The State of the Onion" on page 121. In some cases, you will need to type the preface "http://" at the beginning of the following domain addresses:

www.ed.gov

www.peacecorps.gov

promo.net/pg/history.html

www.yahoo.com/News_and_Media/Journals

www.nytimes.com

www.house.gov

www.rairarubia.com

www.onion.com

www.wadsworth.com

After you have found and evaluated some of the Web sites, pick one. Then, on another sheet of paper, write a summary of your experience of reading the Web site and turn it in to your instructor.

D. Putting It All Together

In Chapter 2, you learned how to read better at the literal level of comprehension. You learned how to separate main ideas from details, how to use paragraph patterns to find main ideas, and how to determine an author's thesis. Use those skills as you read the following selections dealing with reading on the Internet.

PRACTICE D-1: Reading about Internet Literacy

Directions: The following selection is taken from the book *Literacy in the Cyberage: Composing Ourselves on Line* by R. W. Burniske. The author feels there are three basic questions students should ask when they read any Web site. These three questions are referred to as a "rhetorical triangle of *ethos*, *logos*, and *pathos*":

Ethos: Who or what organization created the Web document?
Logos: Is the document's argument or position logical and coherent?
Pathos: What emotional appeals are used (visual, sound, textual) to persuade the reader?

If you need to, feel free to return to these definitions for clarity as they appear in the selection.

CASE STUDY: THE STATE OF THE ONION

R. W. Burniske

1 Mr. Bellamy, the instructor of a rhetoric and composition seminar for undergraduates, had repeatedly admonished his charges to pay close attention to sources they selected from the Internet. All too often, he thought, students would browse the Web looking for something "cool" to put into their essays without considering the source of the information they borrowed. To exacerbate matters, they often failed to provide proper documentation, revealing a scholarly approach that was as casual as it was careless. In the most celebrated instance, one student's citation for a Web site said nothing more than "Internet." Now, as his students prepared for their final essay of the semester, a proposal argument, Mr. Bellamy felt obliged to teach them a lesson in a most unusual manner.

2 He would pull an April Fools' Day prank.

3 If successful, it would teach his students the value of visual literacy and the dangers of virtual gullibility. More than anything, he wanted to teach them how to read a Web document with a more critical eye, examining information through the filters of ethos, logos, and pathos. By now, they knew enough about the rhetorical triangle to apply it to written words. They seemed quite capable of analyzing newspaper editorials and short essays that had served as the topic of class discussions. However, something happened when they turned to online sources featuring colorful graphics, animated icons, motion pictures, and sound. To practice what he preached as a composition teacher—"show, don't tell"—Mr. Bellamy wondered how he might demonstrate the consequences of weak visual and textual literacy skills. He wanted to present his students with a document that looked real, even sounded real, but came from an unreliable source or delivered misinformation.

4 So he went online and used a search engine to locate satirical Web sites. He didn't know where to begin, because he had never before looked for online, satirical publications. He was surprised to find so many but finally settled upon an article in *The Onion*, a weekly publication that specializes in satire (http://www.theonion.com). The article, "America Online to Build Three Million Home Pages for the Homeless," claimed that one of the largest Internet service providers in the United States had announced ambitious plans for a unique social service. Beneath its bold headline, the article featured America Online's (AOL) logo, a picture of Steve Case, the chief executive officer of AOL, and the image of a homeless man pushing a shopping cart full of

From "Case Study: The State of the Onion," p. 141–151 in Literacy in the Cyberage by R.W. Burniske. Reprinted by permission.

belongings through snowy streets. Among other things, the article claimed that Mr. Case said "there is room enough for everyone in cyberspace," and that this new program was inspired by the belief that "no American should be without an address."

5 Mr. Bellamy liked this very much. It was just believable enough to fool gullible readers. The bold headlines, standard journalistic features, and details of the bogus social program established enough ethos to persuade some students that this was an authentic report; the photos of a smiling Steve Case and the man with his shopping cart would capture them through the emotional appeal of pathos; finally, the argument, though clearly flawed, was just persuasive enough to make less critical readers think it a sensible proposal. Would his students see right through this, or would they fall into this satirical web of deceit? Would the seductions of visual imagery overwhelm their ability to critique faulty logic ("Give a person a homepage, and you have given that person dignity")? Would they notice how this satire played with words, combining the ideas of a "home" and an "address" to create its humor? Mr. Bellamy honestly wasn't sure what would happen, but he decided to give this a try, typing up a brief prompt for an online discussion, one that would help "show" students what he had tried to "tell" them throughout the semester.

6 On April Fools' Day, Mr. Bellamy greeted his students as he would any other day, then announced that he wanted to hold a synchronous, online discussion to examine a "proposal argument" in preparation for the final essay assignment of the semester. The focus of the discussion would be a proposal he had discovered while reading an online article. He then divided the class of 21 students into three discussion groups, with students numbering off so that the members of the respective groups were not seated beside each other. Students were given five minutes to individually read and study the one-page article on the Internet. They were not allowed to discuss it with their classmates before joining their online groups, which would have approximately ten minutes for their synchronized discussion.

7 Much to his delight, the groups conducted an extremely animated debate over this proposal. In fact, it was one of the liveliest synchronous, online discussions Mr. Bellamy had ever witnessed. Despite a deliberate prompt, however, the students failed to consider all three points of the rhetorical triangle. To his amazement and alarm, he watched 21 of 22 students fall victim to the prank, engaging in a heated argument over this most foolish proposal. Not until Mr. Bellamy interrupted to ask a question about ethos did 1 student out of 22 pause to consider the source of the information.

STUDENT REFLECTIONS

8 What did the students learn from this exercise? Following the synchronous discussions and the revelation that this had been an April Fools' prank, Mr. Bellamy asked each student to read the transcript of the synchronous discussions, which he posted on the class Web site, and then type a brief reflection on what caused them to fall for this foolish prank. In the first of these, Jennifer B. offers one of the most common reactions, lamenting her failure to consider the source and pay attention to the ethos of the Web document.

> I fell for this April Fool's trick because I assumed it was from a legitimate source. Being in a classroom setting, I did not think that the exercise would be fake. I was concentrating more on the assignment than I was on the source. In reading the Interchange that took place after reading the article, I noticed only one person in the classroom said anything about The Onion as the source. Even after it was posted that the document was fake, no one responded. It was as if no one cared and that they were more concerned with the other aspects of the exer-

> cise. I fell into the same trap as the rest of the class. It has taught the class and myself to always begin with the legitimacy of the source.

9 Jennifer B.'s comments reveal a disturbing tendency, which one might describe as the "transferal of ethos" from one source to another. In this instance, Jennifer and her classmates transferred the teacher's ethos, and their expectations for the kind of article their teacher would choose, to the Web document they encountered. Based on informal surveys of students, this seems a common phenomenon. In the following reflection, Brent S. reinforces this notion. He explains his misreading as a consequence of blind faith in the professor and susceptibility to the pathos of the text and images he encountered, which resulted from a preoccupation with the article's appearance.

> Why did I fall for this article? Well, first of all, I guess I believed it because Mr. B. told us to read it. It was something he had found and gave to us. That gave it some credibility in my mind. I thought, "Well, Mr. B. gave it to us, it's most likely not a joke." Why would he give us something to discuss if it weren't real? Now I know why he did it, but that is the main reason why I thought it was real. I also believed it because it looked real. It looked like any other article you would find in an on-line newspaper. It had pictures. It just looked authentic. This experience has hopefully taught me to be more critical of the things I read, especially when they are on the Internet.

10 There is also the matter of the message. Where the first two reactions stress ethos and pathos, Kara W.'s reflection touches the third point on the rhetorical triangle. She notes the way in which preoccupation with an item's logos—and the heated debates it inspires—can blunt one's attention to other points on the triangle.

> I bought into the article simply because I did not check out the source or author. In fact, it seems that the entire group focused on the logos of his argument, and a little on the pathos. But no one gave a single thought on his ethos. We all overlooked the fact that there was no author, no credentials, and no justification as to why this guy has any authority to write the article. Strange, seeing as how this class emphasizes all THREE parts of the rhetorical triangle, and we manage to totally ignore one. In the future, we must all be more wary of where the information is coming from.

11 Obviously, statements like these are cause for hope, suggesting that this student has learned a valuable lesson about the rhetorical analysis of Web sites. As this final reflection indicates, an exercise such as this helps students learn a good deal about visual literacy and their own skills. Kelly, the author of the following reflection, had already created her own Web pages and used the Internet extensively for research, yet she couldn't resist the seductions of this satirical presentation. Rather than attempt to explain or excuse her misreading of the document, she seizes this opportunity to look upon her own mistakes and learn from them. Much to her credit, she draws valuable lessons from the exercise, recognizing her own tendencies and realizing the actions she must take in order to prevent future misreadings.

> It is interesting to see the discussion others had about the subject. It seems I was not the only one who was duped into thinking AOL was actually going to implement this program. It just shows how people are incredibly vulnerable. It is a little bit scary to think that I can be tricked so easily. This was a harmless joke,

but if I believe everything I read than I could be giving people false information and perhaps harming myself and others. In the future, I need to look at the source more carefully. If I would have just looked at the address I would have seen that this did not come from AOL. It is important to examine the address. Who is writing it? Why are they writing it? What audience are they writing to? And what message are they trying to portray? These are some of the questions I need to start asking myself instead of immediately divulging into the article.

SEEING IS BELIEVING (AND OTHER SATIRICAL LESSONS)

12 There are many lessons to be learned from this exercise, but perhaps one of the most important echoes John Berger's earlier observation: "The way we see things is affected by what we know or what we believe." These students, who in many ways are fairly typical undergraduates at a public university, fell for this prank because of what their eyes told them they were seeing. Aesthetically, this item looked like something they might find in the online version of a newspaper or magazine. The bold font style, the color photos, and the AOL logo made them believe they were looking at an authentic document. However, the key to this exercise, and one that Mr. Bellamy understood intuitively, is the manner in which the item is presented. Had the teacher prefaced the exercise by saying, "I thought we'd have some fun on April Fools' Day by looking at some satirical Web sites," students would have brought that expectation—that "belief system"—to their reading of the document. However, since the teacher tied the exercise to the students' assignment—a proposal argument—they brought different expectations with them, expectations that influenced what they saw and how they intepreted it. This speaks volumes about the importance of teaching visual literacy skills. Although educators may not think in these terms yet, the exponential growth of the World Wide Web and Internet connectivity in schools compels them to find ways to teach visual literacy. Exercises like Mr. Bellamy's may help students resist the seductions of fancy graphics and overcome the visual cues that excite the passion of pathos and overwhelm judgment of the author's credibility and logos.

Comprehension Check

Directions: Answer the following questions about the selection you just read. Try to answer using complete sentences.

1. What is the author's thesis or main idea? ____________________________

2. Why did Mr. Bellamy, the instructor, conduct his April Fools' Day prank on his students? ____________________________

3. What Web site did Mr. Bellamy use in his experimental prank? ____________________________

4. What features did the Web site have that made Mr. Bellamy think it would be useful in his teaching? ____

____

____

5. What did the Web site claim that AOL was going to do? ____________________

____

____

6. How much time were students given to read and study the Web page? __________

7. How many of the twenty-two students in his class fell victim to the prank? ______

____

8. John Berger is quoted as saying, "The way we see things is affected by what we know or what we believe." Explain what this has to do with reading on the Internet. ____

____

____

9. Circle any of the following that are lessons for reading on the Internet that students learned from Mr. Bellamy's assignment.____________________

   a. Begin by checking the legitimacy of the Web source.
   b. Don't believe what's on a Web site just because it looks "real."
   c. Don't be taken in by the visuals on a page; examine them.
   d. Don't believe everything you read, even if it's assigned by an instructor.

10. Do you think you would have been fooled by Mr. Bellamy's prank? Why or why not?____

____

____

Vocabulary Check

Directions: Define the underlined words used in the selection.

1. He had repeatedly admonished his charges to pay close attention to sources they selected from the Internet.
2. To exacerbate matters, they often failed to provide proper documentation.
3. One student's citation for a Web site said nothing more than "Internet."
4. It would teach his students the value of visual literacy and the dangers of gullibility.
5. He went on line and used a search engine to locate satirical Web sites.
6. There is room enough for everyone in cyberspace.
7. Would the seductions of visual imagery overwhelm their ability to critique faulty logic?
8. He wanted to hold a synchronous, online discussion to examine a "proposal argument."

9. She offers one of the most common reactions, lamenting her failure to consider the source.

10. Aesthetically, this item looked like something they might find in the online version of a newspaper or magazine.

Record the results of the Comprehension Check and the Vocabulary Check on the Student Record Chart in the Appendix. Each answer for both checks is worth 10 percent for a total of 100 percent possible for each check.

Remember to make vocabulary cards for any words that gave you trouble.

PRACTICE D-2: Timed Reading

Directions: The following selection can be used as a Timed Reading if so assigned. You may want to review the comments about timing your reading on page 103 before you begin. Check your reading-rate score from the last timed reading you did and try to read at least 50 wpm faster.

The article appeared in the *New York Times* in 1997. As you read for the author's thesis and main ideas, determine if the information is dated or if it still has value for today's Internet usage.

Begin Timing: ____________

HOW STUDENTS GET LOST IN CYBERSPACE

Steven R. Knowlton

1 When Adam Pasick, a political science major at the University of Wisconsin at Madison, started working on his senior honors thesis this fall, he began where the nation's more than 14 million college students increasingly do: not at the campus library, but at his computer terminal.

2 As he roamed the World Wide Web, he found journal articles, abstracts, indexes, and other pieces of useful information. But it wasn't until he sought help from his professor, Charles H. Franklin, that he found the mother lode.

3 Dr. Franklin steered Mr. Pasick to thousands of pages of raw data of a long-term study of political attitudes, information crucial to Mr. Pasick's inquiry into how family structure affects political thinking.

4 The Web site containing all this data is no secret to political scientists, Dr. Franklin said, but can be hard for students to find.

5 "It is barely possible that if you did a Web search, you would show it up," he said. "Whether the average undergraduate could is another question." It would be even harder for the uninitiated to find their way around the site, he said. "One of the things you're missing on the Web is a reference librarian."

6 It is just such difficulties that worry many educators. They are concerned that the Internet makes readily available so much information, much of it unreliable, that students think research is far easier than it really is. As a result, educators say, students are producing superficial research papers, full of data—some of it suspect—and little thought. Many of the best sources on the Web are hard to find with conventional

search engines or make their information available only at a steep price, which is usually borne by universities that pay annual fees for access to the data.

7 Mr. Pasick, 21, of Ann Arbor, Mich., whose conversation is filled with computer and Web search terms, admits that he would never have found the site, much less the data, on his own.

8 "All the search engines are so imprecise," Mr. Pasick said. "Whenever I have tried to find something precise that I was reasonably sure is out there, I have had trouble."

9 Dr. David B. Rothenberg, a philosophy professor at the New Jersey Institute of Technology, in Newark, said his students' papers had declined in quality since they began using the Web for research.

10 "There are these strange references that don't quite connect," he said. "There's not much sense of intelligence. We're indexing, but we're not thinking about things."

11 One way to improve the quality of student's research is to insist that students be more thorough, said Elliot King, a professor of mass communication at Loyola College of Maryland and author of "The Online Student," a textbook for on-line searching.

12 "Because information is so accessible, students stop far too quickly," he said. If a research paper should have 15 sources, he said, the professor should insist students find, say, 50 sources and use the best 15. When Dr. King assigns research papers in his own classes, he insists that students submit all the sources they did not use, along with those they finally selected.

13 The jumble in Web-based student papers mirrors the information jumble that is found on line, said Gerald M. Santoro, the lead research programmer at the Pennsylvania State University's Center for Academic Computing in State College, Pa.

14 The Internet, he said, is commonly thought of as a library, although a poorly catalogued one, given the limitations of the search engines available. But he prefers another analogy.

15 "In fact, it is like a bookstore," Dr. Santoro said, explaining that Web sites exist because someone wants them there, not because any independent judge has determined them worthy of inclusion.

16 Dr. William Miller, dean of libraries at Florida Atlantic University in Boca Raton, and the immediate past president of the Association of College and Research Libraries, cautioned that free Web sites were often constructed "because somebody has an ax to grind or a company wants to crow about its own products." And he said that the creators of many sites neglect to keep them up to date, so much information on the Web may be obsolete.

17 "For the average person looking for what is the cheapest flight to Chicago this weekend, or what is the weather like in Brazil, the Web is good," Dr. Miller said. But much of its material, he added, is simply not useful to scholars.

18 Yet despite the Web's limitations, educators like Dr. King still see it as a way to "blast your way out of the limitations of your own library."

19 Some of the most valuable information comes from home pages set up by the government and universities. One example, said Dr. King, was research conducted by a student trying to find information on cuts in financing for the Corporation of Public Broadcasting. The relevant books in the college's library were few and outdated, he said, but, with his help, the student found full texts of Congressional hearings about public broadcasting's budget.

20 "Her essay no longer consisted of relying on books or magazines," he said, "but in getting raw data on which the books and magazines are based."

21 On the Web, students can also find electronic versions of the most popular academic journals, the mainstay of research for faculty and advanced students. Most

university libraries now have electronic subscriptions to a few hundred journals. Dr. Miller warned, however, that while that may be a tenth of the journals in the library of a small liberal arts college, it is a tiny fraction of the journals subscribed to by a large research university, which may order more than 100,000. The trend is clearly toward electronic versions of academic journals, he added, but most are still not on line and the ones that are tend to be expensive. On-line subscriptions, for instance, can often run into thousands of dollars a year.

22 The time will surely come, Dr. Miller said, when most academic journals are on line, "but you'll need either a credit card number or a password" from an institution that has bought an electronic subscription. "And if you don't have one or the other, you won't get in," he said.

23 When Mr. Pasick turned to Dr. Franklin for help, the professor's expertise was only one of the necessary ingredients for success. The other was the University of Wisconsin's access to the Web site, as one of 450 research institutions that pay up to $10,000 a year for the privilege. (The site is operated by the Interuniversity Consortium for Political and Social Research, at http://www.icpsr.umich.edu.)

24 Even at an institution with the resources to take full advantage of cyberspace, there are some forms of assistance that the Web will never provide, some educators say.

25 Dr. Santoro describes academic research as a three-step process: finding the relevant information, assessing the quality of that information, and then using that information "either to try to conclude something, to uncover something, to prove something or to argue something." At its best, he explained, the Internet, like a library, provides only data.

26 In the research process, he said, "the Internet is only useful for that first part, and also a little bit for the second. It is not useful at all in the third."

Finish timing. Record time here: ____________ and use the Timed Readings Conversion Chart in the Appendix to figure your rate: ____________ wpm.

Comprehension Check

Directions: Answer the following questions about the selection you just read without looking back. Try to answer using complete sentences.

1. What is the author's thesis or main idea? ____________

____

2. Why do some students think that research using the Internet is easier than it is?

____

____

3. Why are many of the best sources on the Web hard to find or to obtain? ____________

____

4. What does one professor suggest doing that would improve the quality of a student's research on the Web? ____________

____

____

5. One person quoted in the article believes that the Internet should not be thought of as a library but as a bookstore. What does he mean? ____________

6. Why, according to one interviewer, are many free Web sites not reliable?

7. Who creates some of the most valuable home pages?

8. What is the mainstay of research on the Web for faculty and advanced students?

9. Dr. Santoro describes academic research as a three-step process. What are the three steps?

10. Why do you think the information in this article is or is not relevant today?

Vocabulary Check

Directions: Define the following underlined words from the selection.

1. . . . not at the campus library, but at his computer terminal.

2. As he roamed the World Wide Web, he found journal articles, abstracts, indexes, and other pieces of useful information.

3. Dr. Franklin steered Mr. Pasick to . . . information crucial to Mr. Pasick's inquiry.

4. It would be even harder for the uninitiated to find their way around the site.

5. Many of the best sources on the Web are hard to find with conventional search engines.

6. All the search engines are so imprecise.

7. Because information is so accessible, students stop far too quickly.

8. Web sites were often constructed because somebody has an ax to grind.

9. . . . or a company wants to crow about its own products.

10. Creators of many sites neglect to keep them up to date, so much information on the Web may be obsolete.

____

Record the results of the rate, comprehension, and vocabulary checks on the Student Record Chart in the Appendix. Each answer for both checks is worth 10 percent for a total of 100 percent possible for each check.

Before you go on to the next chapter, make certain you understand any mistakes or problems you may have encountered in this chapter. It is important that you learn from mistakes, so don't despair when you make them. Accept mistakes as normal. Making mistakes is often the best way to discover what you do and don't know.

Remember to make vocabulary cards for any words that gave you trouble.

Questions for Group Discussion

1. As a group, discuss your various experiences using the Internet. How do your experiences differ and compare? For what reasons have most of you made use of the Internet?

2. Discuss what each of you has learned from reading this chapter. Each one should state something he or she didn't know about the Internet before reading this chapter. Who in your group has had the most experience on the Web and is willing to help those with less experience?

3. Referring back to "Case Study: The State of the Onion" (pp. 121–124), discuss the three fundamental questions referred to as *ethos*, *logos*, and *pathos*. How helpful will knowing these fundamental questions be as you read more Web sites?

4. Discuss how useful the Internet is or will be to each of you as students.

UNIT TWO

CRITICAL COMPREHENSION

Unit Two builds on what you learned in Unit One. A look at the comprehension triangle on the next page shows what you learned about literal comprehension and what you will learn about critical comprehension in this unit. As you work through this unit, you will continue to develop your ability to read at the literal level while learning to develop your ability to read critically.

What Is Critical Comprehension?

Critical comprehension is that level of understanding that entails the distinguishing of fact from opinion; the recognition of an author's intent, attitude, or bias; the drawing of inferences; and the making of critical judgments. It's the second branch on the comprehension triangle explained in Unit One. Critical comprehension is a more sophisticated level of understanding than literal comprehension. A well-known reading expert, Dr. Francis Triggs, says, "Critical reading requires a contribution by both the author and the reader and an interplay which usually results in a new understanding." For instance, Jonathan Swift's *Gulliver's Travels* appeals to young people because at the literal level it reads like a fairy-tale adventure story

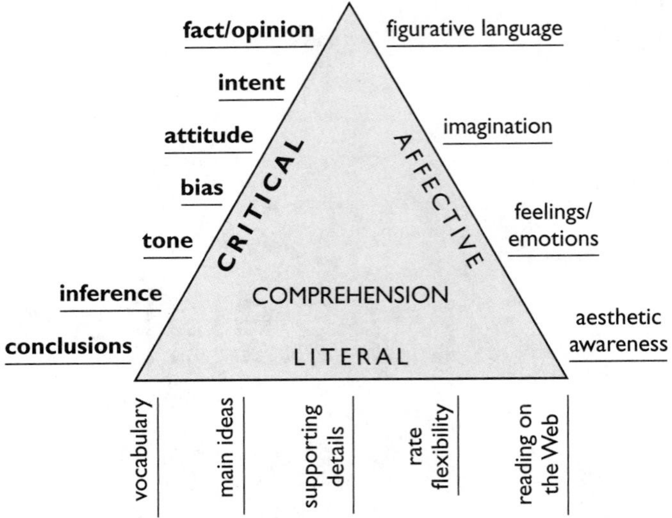

about a man who lives with giants and miniature people. However, when the story is read at a more critical level of understanding, it is a very bitter satire on mankind. In other words, an understanding beyond the literal level is necessary for thorough comprehension.

What Does This Unit Cover?

There are three chapters in this unit, each one covering a different facet of critical comprehension. Chapter Four deals with separating fact from opinion. Exercises will call your attention to how we think we are dealing with fact when often we are accepting opinion.

Chapter Five provides exercises for developing the ability to recognize an author's intent or real purpose in writing. Sometimes authors "disguise" their true purpose or thesis by the use of metaphor, satire, irony, or humor. Other times, authors use propaganda or present their evidence in a biased way. Chapter Five should help you analyze an author's actual intention and evaluate bias.

Chapter Six contains practices for discovering how both the author and the reader often draw inferences. Rather than coming right out and saying what they mean, authors sometimes imply or suggest what they want the reader to understand. Likewise, readers often draw inferences about what an author says. When you hear students talking about the "hidden meaning" of a work, or when you hear the statement "Read between the lines," drawing inferences is what is meant. This chapter also provides an opportunity to react to quoted statements, advertisements, and short articles, using what you learned in previous chapters to help you make critical judgments and draw conclusions.

A comment regarding reading rate is in order here. As you learned in Unit One, speed of reading is not as important as good comprehension. By now you should have realized that although you can increase your overall speed, your reading rate fluctuates with your interest in the topic, the length of the reading selection, your knowledge of the subject, the level of difficulty, and even how you feel on a certain day. That is natural. Some reading selections in this section of the book are timed, mostly for your own concern. Most students developing their reading versatility like to have some idea of how fast they are reading. That's fine. Go ahead and practice reading faster. Just remember not to let speed be your goal. As you get to be a better reader, your reading speed also will increase.

What Should You Know after Completing This Unit?

Here are six objectives to work toward in this unit. By the time you complete this unit, you should be able to:

1. Distinguish fact from opinion.
2. Recognize an author's intent, attitude, and tone.
3. Recognize an author's bias and use of propaganda.
4. Recognize inferences being made by an author and make your own inferences from what you read.
5. Make critical judgments and draw conclusions by analyzing the author's diction, style, and use of figurative language.
6. Write a definition of critical comprehension.

If you have any objectives of your own, write them down below and share them with your instructor.

Personal reading objectives for Unit Two:

____

____

____

____

____

____

____

____

For now, concentrate on objective 1, distinguishing fact from opinion, which is covered in the next chapter.

CHAPTER FOUR

Distinguishing Fact from Opinion

Distinguishing fact from opinion is not always easy. A fact is usually defined as a truth, something that can be tested by experimentation, observation, or research and shown to be real. But even that is an elusive definition. For example, in 1930 it was generally accepted as fact that the atom was the smallest particle of an element and could not be split. With the advent of atomic power in the 1940s, scientists split the atom, making what was once thought to be a fact a fallacy. Today, physicists are just beginning to understand subatomic particles and refer to many of their findings as theory rather than fact. The point is that facts are sometimes "slippery."

An opinion, on the other hand, is often easier to distinguish. Your belief, feeling, or judgment about something is an opinion. It is a subjective or value judgment, not something that can be objectively verified. Even though you base your opinion on fact, others may not agree; an opinion cannot be proven to everyone's satisfaction. For instance, you may be of the opinion that Martin Sheen is the greatest actor of our time, but there is no way to make your opinion fact. Others have their own favorite actors, while still others do not know who Martin Sheen is. The only fact that you can prove is that Martin Sheen is an actor.

Test your skill in recognizing fact from opinion by placing an *F* in the blank in front of any of the following statements you believe to be fact.

______ **1.** Harry S. Truman was the president of the United States.

______ **2.** Truman was one of the best presidents the United States has had.

______ **3.** Generally speaking, movies are more entertaining than books.

______ **4.** *Time* is a better magazine than *Reader's Digest.*

______ **5.** Columbus, in 1492, was the first person to discover America.

Now see how well you did. You should have marked the first one. It is a fact that can be verified objectively. The second statement, however, is not a fact. It is a subjective statement claiming "Truman was one of the best." This claim is a value judgment; although we can prove that Truman was a president, historians may never agree that he was one of the best, even though he might have been. Words that give something value, such as *great, wonderful, beautiful, ugly, intelligent,* or *stupid,* make statements subjective opinions, not verifiable facts.

The third statement is not fact; it is a value judgment. To say something is "more entertaining" or "better" or "worse" is to place a personal value on something. Value judgments may be based on facts, but they are opinions nonetheless.

Number 4 is not a fact. You may believe one magazine is better than another; but *Reader's Digest* has a much larger circulation than *Time,* so many readers disagree. However; the fact—and it *is* a fact—that *Reader's Digest* has a larger circulation than *Time* does not mean it is any better either. The use of the word "better" needs clarification. Better in what way? Paper? Size? Cost? Contents? Again, "better" implies a value judgment.

The fifth statement is one of those "slippery" facts. According to many sources, Columbus did discover America in 1492. Yet, factually, he never actually landed on the continent; Vikings are said to have explored America long before Columbus, and evidence indicates that Native Americans inhabited America over 25,000 years or more before Columbus. Obviously, he wasn't the first person to discover America. It is a European viewpoint that many history books continue to express, yet many textbooks are now changing wording to clarify this historical point. As stated, number 5 is not an opinion; it is more an erroneous statement than anything else.

On the other hand, if someone were to claim that Columbus sailed to the New World in 1592 rather than 1492, it would be easy enough to consult historical records to show the correct date was 1492. Knowledge that we share and agree upon as a society is called *shared knowledge*. Agreed-upon facts, then, are generally referred to as objective. If we argue that Columbus was a better sailor than Magellan, we get into the subjective realm of opinion. Unless we can find objective evidence that one was better than the other, we can't speak factually.

Which of the following statements are based on objective evidence?

1. Coca-Cola tastes better than Pepsi-Cola.
2. The capital of Illinois is Springfield.
3. The moon revolves around the earth.
4. Italians make great lovers.

Both statements 1 and 4 are based on subjective evidence. You might get fifty people to say Coke tastes better than Pepsi, but you can get another fifty to say the opposite. The same goes for Italians as great lovers. These statements are opinions, not facts. Items 2 and 3 can be verified by checking agreed-upon information; thus they are facts based on objective evidence until such time as Springfield is no longer the capital and the moon quits revolving around the earth.

Just as our purpose for reading affects our speed and comprehension needs, so does it affect the degree to which we must be aware of the differences in objective and subjective statements. When we read the paper for the news of the day, we want facts based on objective reporting. If we want to read someone's interpretation of the facts and what implications that news may have for us, we read editorials and columnists' opinions to see how they subjectively interpret the news. When we read a recipe, we want factual measurements, not opinions on how the finished product will taste. When we read an encyclopedia, we want the facts. But when we read a critic's opinion or interpretation of the importance of those facts, we are looking for a subjective reaction, an opinion.

As a critical reader of all kinds of writing, you need to be able to discern between objective and subjective statements and then draw your own conclusions. The following drills will help you develop your ability to distinguish facts, opinions, and erroneous-sounding statements. If some of the answers seem "picky," just remember that the point is to sharpen your reading versatility.

A. Fact-Finding

PRACTICE A-1: Fact-Finding

Directions: Read each of the following statements and place an *F* in the blanks of those statements that you feel are *mostly* fact and an *O* in the blanks of those statements that are *mostly* opinion.

______ **1.** A world auction record for a single piece of furniture—$415,800 for a Louis XVI table—was set today at a sale of the French furniture collection of the late Mrs. Anna Thomson Dodge of the Detroit auto fortune. (From a United Press release.)

______ **2.** The junior college is a better place to attend school for the first two years than is a university or four-year school. This is so primarily because classes are smaller at a junior college and more individualized attention can be given to students.

______ **3.** Medsker and Trent found that four-year colleges draw approximately three-fourths of their freshmen from the upper 40 percent of the high school graduating class, whereas about half the junior college transfer students were in the upper

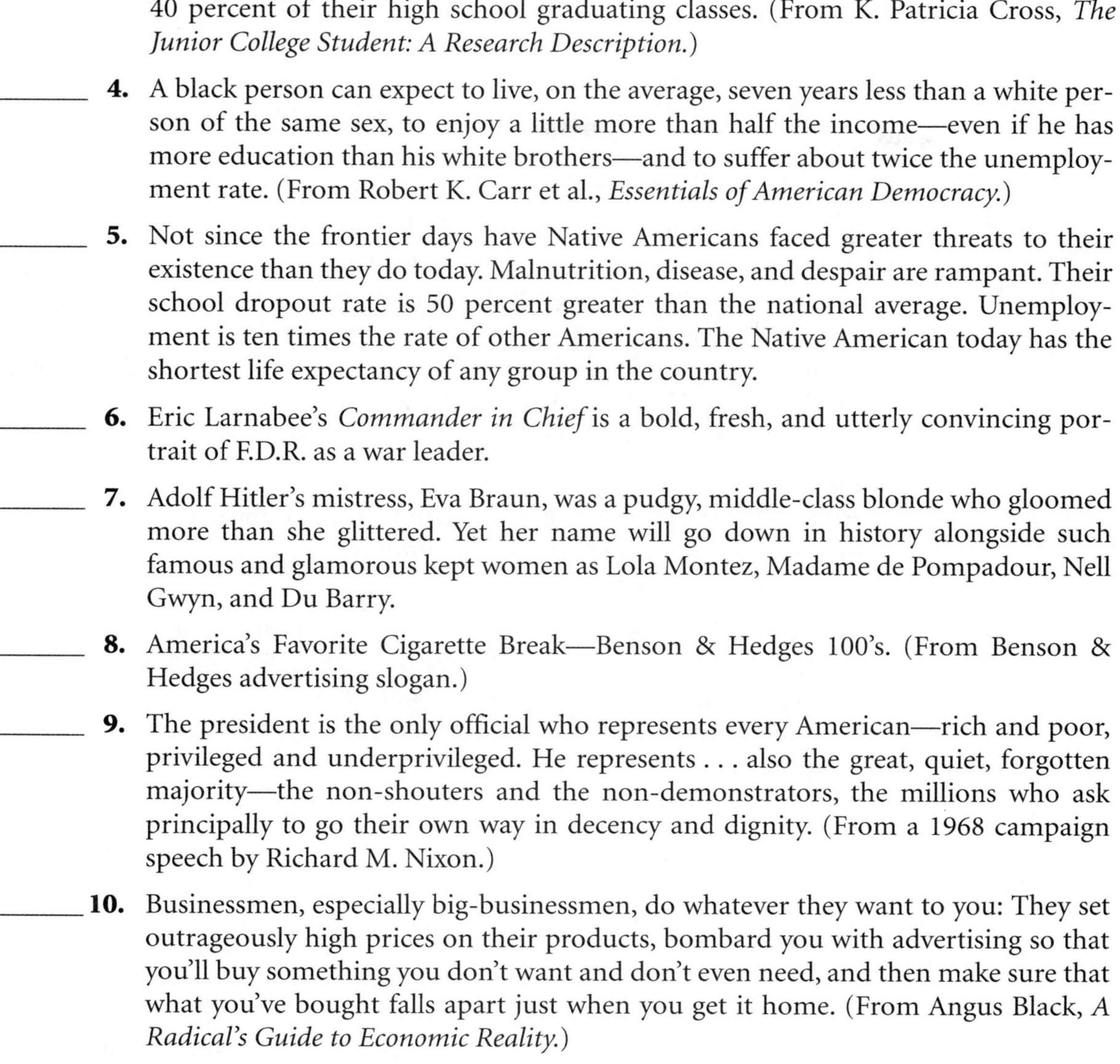

40 percent of their high school graduating classes. (From K. Patricia Cross, *The Junior College Student: A Research Description.*)

_______ **4.** A black person can expect to live, on the average, seven years less than a white person of the same sex, to enjoy a little more than half the income—even if he has more education than his white brothers—and to suffer about twice the unemployment rate. (From Robert K. Carr et al., *Essentials of American Democracy.*)

_______ **5.** Not since the frontier days have Native Americans faced greater threats to their existence than they do today. Malnutrition, disease, and despair are rampant. Their school dropout rate is 50 percent greater than the national average. Unemployment is ten times the rate of other Americans. The Native American today has the shortest life expectancy of any group in the country.

_______ **6.** Eric Larnabee's *Commander in Chief* is a bold, fresh, and utterly convincing portrait of F.D.R. as a war leader.

_______ **7.** Adolf Hitler's mistress, Eva Braun, was a pudgy, middle-class blonde who gloomed more than she glittered. Yet her name will go down in history alongside such famous and glamorous kept women as Lola Montez, Madame de Pompadour, Nell Gwyn, and Du Barry.

_______ **8.** America's Favorite Cigarette Break—Benson & Hedges 100's. (From Benson & Hedges advertising slogan.)

_______ **9.** The president is the only official who represents every American—rich and poor, privileged and underprivileged. He represents . . . also the great, quiet, forgotten majority—the non-shouters and the non-demonstrators, the millions who ask principally to go their own way in decency and dignity. (From a 1968 campaign speech by Richard M. Nixon.)

_______ **10.** Businessmen, especially big-businessmen, do whatever they want to you: They set outrageously high prices on their products, bombard you with advertising so that you'll buy something you don't want and don't even need, and then make sure that what you've bought falls apart just when you get it home. (From Angus Black, *A Radical's Guide to Economic Reality.*)

Practice A-2: More Fact-Finding

Directions: Read each of the following statements. Circle the number of any that you think are primarily factual or can be objectively proven. Then underline any words in the statements that you feel are too subjective to be verified as factual.

1. In the first seven months of 1988, once-private companies raised $17.4 billion through initial public offerings, or two-thirds more than in the same period of 1987.

2. There are still young persons who read for pleasure and who do well in school, but their number dwindles. The middle range of children muddles through high school and some go through college, but the general level of their academic achievement is significantly below what it was thirty years ago.

3. In the presidential election of 1828, Andrew Jackson defeated John Quincy Adams with a popular vote of 647,286 votes over 508,064 for Adams.

4. Take the plunge into the splashiest resort on the most spectacular beach on the most exquisite island in Hawaii—the new Willoughby Maui Hotel. Join in the dreamlike atmosphere of waterfalls, tropical lagoons, and lush tiered gardens—or simply soak up the sun.

5. While grammar usage offers the most immediate clues to a person's educational background, another important clue is vocabulary. The writer or speaker who uses words appropriately and accurately is probably well educated. One who often misuses words or phrases is not soundly educated, because a major purpose of education is to teach people to use their native tongue with accuracy.

6. Since 1957, writes Ben J. Wattenberg in his *The Birth Dearth,* the average American woman's fertility rate has dropped from 3.77 children to 1.8—below the 2.1 size needed to maintain the present population level. Meanwhile, he argues, Communist-bloc countries are producing at a rate of 2.3 children per mother, while the Third World rate is rising so fast that within fifty years its population may be ten times that of the West.

7. But specific challenges to Wattenberg's data have been raised. Some demographers question his projections, since he gathered his information from population trends with little or no regard for such unpredictable factors as wars, epidemics, famines, and baby booms.

8. Scientific data show that, although the Sahara desert did move south between 1980 to 1984, it went north in 1985 and 1986. In 1987 the Sahara's border shifted south, north in 1988, and south again in 1989 and 1990. To find any long-term trends in these annual fluctuations, the researchers say, data would have to be taken for several decades.

Practice A-3: Fact versus Opinion

Directions: Each sentence is lettered in the following statements. On the line below each statement, write the letter of each sentence you think can be accepted as a statement of fact. The first one has been done for you.

1. (a) The last great Greek astronomer of antiquity was Claudius Ptolemy (or Ptolemeus), who flourished about A.D. 140. (b) He compiled a series of thirteen volumes on astronomy known as the *Almagest.* (c) All of the *Almagest* does not deal with Ptolemy's own work, for it includes a compilation of the astronomical achievements of the past, principally of Hipparchus. (d) In fact, it is our main source of information about Greek astronomy. (e) The *Almagest* also contains accounts of the contributions of Ptolemy himself. (From George Abell, *Exploration of the Universe,* 1982.)

   a, although the phase "last great" may not be fact: b, c, d, e

2. (a) The July 1987 Almanac states that there are four West Coast species of salmon. This is incorrect. (b) There are five species. (c) The West Coast species belong to the genus *Oncorhynchus.* (d) Their common names are chinook, also called the spring or king salmon; the chum or dog salmon; the coho or silver salmon; the pink salmon; and the sockeye or red salmon.

   ____

3. We hold these truths to be self-evident, (a) that all men are created equal; (b) that they are endowed by their Creator with certain unalienable rights; (c) that among these are life, liberty, and the pursuit of happiness; (d) that to secure these rights, governments are instituted among men. (From the Declaration of Independence.)

   ____

4. (a) If the American political system is to survive without repression, it will be because of positive political leadership that faces up to the problems and convinces both private citizens and public officials that these problems are serious and interrelated; (b) that they must be attacked, attacked immediately, and attacked together by coordinated and probably expensive programs. (c) As we have said so many times . . . if there is to be positive leadership in American politics, it can only come from the president. (d) Even then the Madisonian system may stalemate. (e) But without presidential leadership there is no hope that the system can move with any speed or controlled direction.

____

5. (a) *The Glass Bead Game* by Hermann Hesse appeared in Switzerland in 1943. (b) It was his last major work of any importance. (c) It is also the best of all his novels, an "act of mental synthesis through which the spiritual values of all ages are perceived as simultaneously present and vitally alive." (d) It was with full artistic consciousness that Hesse created this classic work.

____

6. (a) Although over 500 ruins are recorded within the Grand Canyon National Park, we know only the outline of this area's prehistory. (b) Most ruins are small surface pueblos in and along the north and south rims of the canyon. (c) No large communal centers have been found. (d) Small cliff dwellings and numerous granaries occupy caves and niches in the canyon walls. (e) A few early pit houses, some ruins of late Havasupai houses, and occasional hogans and sweat lodges left by the Navajos complete the roster. (From Joe Ben Wheat, *Prehistoric People.*)

____

Practice A-4: Interpreting "Facts"

Directions: Read the two paragraphs below. They are accounts of the same historical event written by two different historians. Notice how they both use facts and how they interpret these facts.

When anarchy visited Nicaragua, Coolidge had no choice but to act unilaterally. First, in 1925, he withdrew a token force of marines from that nation, which then seemed capable of servicing its foreign debt and preserving its internal stability. But the appearance was deceptive. Almost at once revolution broke out, and Coolidge again landed the marines, in time some five thousand. Regrettably, in its quest for order, the United States chose to support the reactionary faction, whose identification with large landowners and foreign investors had helped provoke the revolution in the first place. (From John Blum et al., *The National Experience,* Harcourt Brace Jovanovich, 1963, p. 617.)

The United States, despite the current anti-war sentiment, was reluctantly forced to adopt warlike measures in Latin America. Disorders in Nicaragua, perilously close to the Panama Canal jugular vein, had jeopardized American lives and property and in 1927 President Coolidge felt compelled to dispatch over 5,000 troops to this troubled banana land. His political foes, decrying mailed-fist tactics, accused him of waging a "private war," while critics south of the Rio Grande loudly assailed *Yanqui* imperialism. (From Thomas A. Bailey, *The American Pageant,* 2nd edition, D. C. Heath, 1961, p. 503.)

1. Underline the main idea in each paragraph, and be ready to justify your answer.
2. List two supporting details that support the main idea in *each* of the paragraphs.

____

____

____

3. What facts reported in the first passage are also reported in the second one? Are there any differences in the reporting of facts? ____________________

____

____

4. Explain whether or not the two authors agree on the reason Coolidge sent troops to Nicaragua. ____________________

____

5. Do the two authors agree on the reactions to Coolidge's action? Explain.

____

____

PRACTICE A-5: Comparing "Facts"

Directions: In 2003, the U. S. Court of Appeals for the Ninth Circuit in California declared unconstitutional the phrase "one nation under God" in the Pledge of Allegiance. At the time of this writing, the ruling has been sent to the Supreme Court on appeal. Two essays on the issue are presented here. One author believes the phrase should not be in the pledge; the other author believes it belongs there.

Before you read the essays, check one of the following statements:

_______ **1.** I believe the phrase "one nation under God" belongs in the pledge.

_______ **2.** I believe the phrase "one nation under God" does not belong in the pledge.

_______ **3.** I don't know.

Now read both of the following essays. As you read them, underline any statements you think are factual. Then answer the questions that follow each selection.

DO WE NEED GOD IN THE PLEDGE?

Jay Sekulow

IT'S A STATEMENT OF PATRIOTISM, NOT RELIGION

1 As our nation battles terrorism—at home and abroad—there is a very real threat that millions of students in the western United States will no longer have an opportunity to express their patriotism by voluntarily reciting the Pledge of Allegiance with the phrase "one nation under God."

From "Do We Need God in the Pledge" by Jay Sekulow, Santa Barbara Press News, May 18, 2003. Reprinted by permission of the American Center for Law and Justice, Virginia Beach, VA 23467.

2 That phrase has been declared unconstitutional by the U.S. Court of Appeals for the 9th Circuit in California. The full appeals court refused to reconsider an earlier ruling by a three-judge panel of the appeals court that determined the phrase "one nation under God" violates the separation of church and state. Now, the only recourse rests with the Supreme Court.

3 The Supreme Court is being asked to take the case and ultimately uphold the constitutionality of a phrase that has become a time-honored tradition—an integral part of the Pledge for nearly 50 years.

4 The Pledge first appeared in print in 1892 as a patriotic exercise expressing loyalty to our nation. Congress added the phrase "under God" in 1954. That phrase first appeared in President Lincoln's Gettysburg Address, which concluded that "this nation, under God, shall have a new birth of freedom—and that the government of the people, by the people, shall not perish from the earth."

5 While the Supreme Court has never ruled directly on the constitutionality of the Pledge, there are numerous cases over the years where justices concluded that the phrase "one nation under God" is not an establishment of religion, but merely a way for the government to acknowledge our religious heritage.

6 In 1962, in Engel v. Vitale, Justice Potter Stewart referred to the Pledge of Allegiance as an example of governmental recognition when he quoted a 1952 finding by the court (Zorach v. Clauson) that Americans " . . . are a religious people whose institutions presuppose a Supreme Being."

7 In Abington v. Schempp, Justice Willan Brennan wrote in 1963 that such patriotic exercises like the Pledge do not violate Establishment Clause of the First Amendment because such a reference, as he put it, "may merely recognize historical fact that our nation was believed to have been founded 'under God.' Thus reciting the pledge may be no more of a religious exercise than the reading aloud of Lincoln's Gettysburg Address."

8 In 1984, the court in Lynch v. Donnelly recognized "there is an unbroken history of official acknowledgement by all three branches of government of the role of religion in American life." Among the many examples of our government's acknowledgement of our religious heritage, according to the court, is the phrase "one nation, under God."

9 And in 1985, Justice Sandra Day O'Connor, quoting herself from Lynch v. Donnelly, argued in Wallace v. Jaffree that the inclusion of the words "under God" in the Pledge is not unconstitutional because they "serve as an acknowledgement of religion with 'the legitimate secular purpose of solemnizing public occasions, and expressing confidence in the future.'"

10 The California appeals court relied on faulty legal reasoning in reaching a troubling conclusion that can now only be overturned by the Supreme Court. There is no guarantee that the high court will hear the case. But it should. The Pledge is a patriotic expression—not an affirmation of a particular faith.

11 As the Supreme Court considers what to do, it's important to note that the decision will not be made in a vacuum. After all, the court has its own time-honored tradition at stake. Each session begins with the sound of a gavel—and a dramatic call to order that concludes with these words: "God save the United States and this honorable court."

12 The Supreme Court should take the case and keep the Pledge intact.

Now answer the following questions:

1. Is this essay mostly fact or opinion? ______________________________

____

2. What is the author's thesis or main idea? ______________________________

____

3. Is the thesis or main argument based on facts? Explain.

____

____

4. Did the author convince you of his position? ______________________

____

The following essay offers the opposite opinion regarding the pledge. As you read, underline any statements you feel are factual. Then answer the questions that follow the selection.

GOVERNMENT SHOULDN'T IMPOSE RELIGION ON CITIZENS

Barry W. Lynn

1 A federal appeals court decision declaring school-sponsored recitation of the Pledge of Allegiance unconstitutional has generated tremendous confusion, to say nothing of downright hysteria.

2 Contrary to popular belief, the use of the phrase "under God" in the Pledge does not have a long history in America. The Pledge was written in 1892 by a clergyman, and it was originally secular. "Under God" was inserted by Congress in 1954 at the behest of conservative religious pressure groups.

3 To hear some tell it, removing "under God" from the Pledge would all but ensure America's downfall. In fact, the United States won two world wars, survived the Great Depression, and became a world economic and military powerhouse with a non-religious Pledge.

4 Under the Constitution, our laws are supposed to have a secular purpose. What is the secular purpose of having schoolchildren recite a pledge with religious content everyday? It can't be to foster love of country and respect for democracy. Those goals could be—and in the past were—met with a non-religious pledge.

5 No, the politicians who altered the Pledge in 1954 by adding "under God" knew exactly what they were doing. They wanted to make a religious statement. They wanted to send the message that belief in God is an essential part of being a good American. "God and country" was their motto.

6 The problem with this is that not everyone believes in God. Some Americans believe in no God, others believe in many gods.

7 For them, "under God" in the Pledge and "In God We Trust" on our money are a constant slap in the face, a daily reminder that they are different, that they are indeed not full members of the American experiment. That they're out of step—and wrong.

8 But it isn't just atheists and polytheists who are offended by government's use of generic religiosity. Many devoutly religious people are offended by the emptiness of such "God and Country" rhetoric. Real devotion to God, they argue, is not enhanced by the endless repetition of a phrase.

9 Some courts have upheld government's use of generic religious language, calling it "ceremonial deism." It's all right for the government to employ ceremonial deism, the argument goes, because it's not really that religious, and the government's constant use of a phrase like "under God" drains it of religious meaning.

10 As a minister, I find this argument bizarre and offensive. Religious terminology does not lose its sacred meaning just because people use it a lot, no more so than a prayer becomes non-religious through frequent repetition.

11 If that argument were true, it should be all the more alarming to the devout because it suggests that the state may promote religion as long as it first drains it of all meaning and power. In other words, we can have an official, government-supported religion in the United States—as long as it is bland, watered-down, generic, and ultimately meaningless.

12 In fact, the U.S. Constitution allows for no establishment of religion, specific or generic. The U.S. Congress lost sight of that fact in 1954 when it altered the Pledge of Allegiance. It has taken nearly 50 years for a federal court to recognize Congress' mistake. It shouldn't take another 50 for people to realize that "ceremonial deism" is a fraudulent myth that offends both church and state.

Now answer the following questions:

1. Is this essay mostly fact or opinion? ______________________________

____

2. What is the author's thesis or main idea? ______________________________

____

____

3. Is the thesis or main argument based on facts? Explain. ______________________________

____

____

4. Did the author convince you of his position? ______________________________

____

5. Have you changed your opinion after reading these two essays? Explain why or why not? ______________________________

____

____

B. Reading Opinions of Others

PRACTICE B-1

Directions: Take a few seconds to survey the following selection. Referring to the title, the headings, and your brief survey, write in the space below what you think the article will cover.

Probable coverage: ______________________________

Now read the article, underlining factual statements. Then answer the questions that follow.

HOW GOOD ARE YOUR OPINIONS?

Vincent Ryan Ruggiero

1 "Opinion" is a word that is often used carelessly today. It is used to refer to matters of taste, belief, and judgment. This casual use would probably cause little confusion if people didn't attach too much importance to opinion. Unfortunately, most do attach great importance to it. "I have as much right to my opinion as you to yours" and "Everyone's entitled to his opinion" are common expressions. In fact, anyone who would challenge another's opinion is likely to be branded intolerant.

2 Is that label accurate? Is it intolerant to challenge another's opinion? It depends on what definition of opinion you have in mind. For example, you may ask a friend "What do you think of the new Buicks?" And he may reply, "In my opinion, they're ugly." In this case, it would not only be intolerant to challenge his statement, but foolish. For it's obvious that by opinion he means his *personal preference,* a matter of taste. And as the old saying goes, "It's pointless to argue about matters of taste."

3 But consider this very different use of the term. A newspaper reports that the Supreme Court has delivered its opinion in a controversial case. Obviously the justices did not state their personal preferences, their mere likes and dislikes. They stated their *considered judgment,* painstakingly arrived at after thorough inquiry and deliberation.

4 Most of what is referred to as opinion falls somewhere between these two extremes. It is not an expression of taste. Nor is it careful judgment. Yet it may contain elements of both. It is a view or belief more or less casually arrived at, with or without examining the evidence.

5 Is everyone entitled to his opinion? Of course. In a free country this is not only permitted, but guaranteed. In Great Britain, for example, there is still a Flat Earth Society. As the name implies, the members of this organization believe that the earth is not spherical, but flat. In this country, too, each of us is free to take as creative a position as we please about any matter we choose. When the telephone operator announces "That'll be 95¢ for the first three minutes," you may respond, "No, it won't—it'll be 28¢." When the service station attendant notifies you "Your oil is down a quart," you may reply "Wrong—it's up three."

6 Being free to hold an opinion and express it does not, of course, guarantee you favorable consequences. The operator may hang up on you. The service station attendant may threaten you with violence.

7 Acting on our opinions carries even less assurance. Some time ago in California a couple took their eleven-year-old diabetic son to a faith healer. Secure in their opinion that the man had cured the boy, they threw away his insulin. Three days later the boy died. They remained unshaken in their belief, expressing the opinion that God would raise the boy from the dead. The police arrested them, charging them with manslaughter. The law in such matters is both clear and reasonable. We are free to act on our opinions only so long as, in doing so, we do not harm others.

OPINIONS CAN BE MISTAKEN

8 It is tempting to conclude that, if we are free to believe something, it must have some validity. But that is not so. Free societies are based on the wise observation that since knowledge often comes through mistakes and truth is elusive, every person must

be allowed to make his own path to wisdom. So in a way, free societies are based on the realization that opinions can be wrong.

9 In 1972 a British farmer was hoeing his sugar beet field when he uncovered a tiny statue. It looked to him like the figure of a man listening to a transistor radio. In his opinion, it was a piece of junk. Yet it turned out to be a work of art made of gilt bronze in the twelfth century and worth more than $85,000. He was free to have his opinion. But his opinion was wrong.

10 For scores of years millions of people lit up billions of cigarettes, firm in their opinion that their habit was messy and expensive, but harmless. Yet now we know that smoking is a significant factor in numerous diseases and even does harm to nonsmokers who breathe smoke-polluted air and to unborn babies in the wombs of cigarette addicts. Those millions of people were free to believe smoking harmless. But that didn't make them right. Nor did it protect their bodies from harm.

KINDS OF ERROR

11 There are four general kinds of error that can corrupt anyone's beliefs. Francis Bacon classified them as follows: (1) errors or tendencies to error common among all people by virtue of their being human; (2) errors that come from human communication and the limitations of language; (3) errors in the general fashion or attitude of an age; (4) errors posed to an individual by a particular situation.

12 Some people, of course, are more prone to errors than others. John Locke observed that these people fall into three groups. He described them as follows:

a. Those who seldom reason at all, but do and think according to the example of others, whether parents, neighbors, ministers, or whoever else they choose or have implicit faith in, to save themselves the pain and trouble of thinking and examining for themselves.

b. Those who are determined to let passion rather than reason govern their actions and arguments, and therefore rely on their own or other people's reasoning only so far as it suits them.

c. Those who sincerely follow reason, but lack sound, overall good sense, and so do not have a full view of everything that relates to the issue. They talk with only one type of person, read only one type of book, and so are exposed to only one viewpoint.

INFORMED VERSUS UNINFORMED OPINION

13 In forming our opinions it helps to seek out the views of those who know more than we do about the subject. By examining the views of informed people, we broaden our perspective, see details we could not see by ourselves, consider facts we were unaware of. No one can know everything about everything. It is not a mark of inferiority but of good sense to consult those who have given their special attention to the field of knowledge at issue.

14 Each of us knows something about food and food preparation. After all, most of us have eaten three meals a day all our lives. But that experience doesn't make us experts on running a restaurant or on the food packaging industry. Many of us have played varsity sports in high school. But it takes more than that experience to make us authorities on a particular sport.

15 Some years ago the inmates of Attica prison in New York State overpowered their guards and gained control of the prison. They took a number of hostages and threatened to kill them if their demands were not met. Negotiations proceeded for a

time. Then they were at an impasse. The situation grew tense. Finally lawmen stormed the prison and, before order was restored, a number of the hostages were killed. In the wake of the tragedy were two difficult questions: Had the prisoners' demands been reasonable? And who was responsible for the breakdown in negotiations?

16 A number of people in public and private life offered their opinions. One newspaper editorial stated that the main fault lay with the prisoners, that they had refused to negotiate reasonably. A letter to the editor explained that the prisoners were unquestionably in the wrong simply because they were prisoners, and thus had forfeited all rights and privileges. A U.S. senator from another state declared that the blame lay with American life in general. "We must ask," he said, "why some men would rather die than live another day in America."

17 The governor of New York State issued this statement: "The tragedy was brought on by the highly-organized, revolutionary tactics of militants who rejected all efforts at a peaceful settlement, forcing a confrontation, and carried out cold-blooded killings they had threatened from the outset."

18 In a much less publicized statement, a professor at a small liberal arts college, an expert in penology (the study of prison systems), expressed sympathy with the prisoners, criticized the terrible conditions in the nation's prisons, agreed fully with many of the prisoners' demands, rejected a few as absurd, and explained some of the underlying causes of prison unrest.

19 Now all those opinions deserved some consideration. But which was most helpful in coming to an understanding of the issue in all its considerable complexity? Certainly the most informed opinion. The opinion of the expert in penology.

20 For all of us, whether experts or amateurs, it is natural to form opinions. We are constantly receiving sensory impressions and responding to them first on the level of simple likes and dislikes, then on the level of thought. Even if we wanted to escape having opinions, we couldn't. Nor should we want to. One of the things that makes human beings vastly more complex and interesting than trees or cows is their ability to form opinions.

21 This ability has two sides, though. If it can lift man to the heights of understanding, it can also topple him to the depths of ludicrousness. Both the wise man and the fool have opinions. The difference is, the wise man forms his with care, and as time increases his understanding, refines them to fit even more precisely the reality they interpret.

Comprehension Check

Part A

Directions: Answer the following questions. Don't look back unless you are referred to a particular paragraph for an answer.

1. Circle the letter of the statement that best expresses the thesis of the article:

a. We need to form our opinions with care.

b. It is natural to form opinions.

c. The word "opinion" is used carelessly today.

d. Everyone has a right to his or her own opinion.

2. T/F The statement "Being free to hold an opinion and express it does not, of course, guarantee you favorable consequences" is a fact.

3. T/F Paragraph 9 is mostly factual in content.

4. Which of the following are mentioned as the kinds of error that can corrupt anyone's beliefs?

   a. Errors posed to an individual by a particular situation

   b. Errors or tendencies to error common among all people by virtue of being human

   c. Errors in the general fashion or attitude of an age

   d. Errors that come from limitations of language

5. T/F In forming our opinions, it helps to seek out the views of those who do not know more than we do about the subject.

6. T/F "No one can know everything about everything" is an opinion.

7. In paragraph 19, the author claims the expert in penology was the most helpful in coming to an understanding of the prison riot issue. Why would this opinion be better than the others mentioned? ____

   ____

   ____

8. What is the difference between personal preference and considered judgment?

   ____

   ____

   ____

   ____

9. "One of the things that makes human beings vastly more complex and interesting than trees or cows is their ability to form opinions," says the author. Is this a statement of fact or opinion?____________________ Explain. __________________

   ____

10. Is the article mostly fact or opinion?__________________ Explain. ___________

   ____

   ____

Part B

Directions: The preceding questions can be answered objectively. The following questions require subjective responses. Be ready to explain your answers in class discussion.

1. "We are free to act on our opinions only as long as, in doing so, we do not harm others," says the author. Is this a good rule to follow? ________________ Explain.

   ____

   ____

   ____

   ____

2. The author refers to a couple who took their diabetic son to a faith healer as an example of how acting on our opinions can be dangerous. Give an example of an opinion you hold or held at one time that could be dangerous in certain circumstances. ____________________

3. Reread paragraph 12. In your opinion, do you fit any one of the three groups? Explain. ____________________

4. Give an example of an opinion you once held but no longer do. Explain why you changed your viewpoint. ____________________

Vocabulary Check

Part A

Directions: Write a definition for each underlined word in the blank following each statement.

1. their <u>considered</u> judgment

2. it must have some <u>validity</u>

3. errors <u>posed</u> to an individual

4. some are more <u>prone</u> to errors

5. they have <u>implicit</u> faith in themselves

Part B

Directions: Using the words from the list below, write the correct word in the appropriate blank.

overpowered	inmates	tense
impasse	proceeded	

"Some years ago the **(6)** __________ of Attica prison in New York State (7) __________ their guards and gained control of the prison. Negotiations

(8) ____________ for a time. Then they were at an **(9)** ____________. The situation grew **(10)** ____________."

Record the results of the comprehension (Part A only) and vocabulary checks on the Student Record Chart in the Appendix. Discuss any problems or questions with your instructor before you continue.

PRACTICE B-2: Evaluating Differing Opinions

Part A

Directions: It is the opinion of some people that the execution of convicted criminals should be made public via television. Others are opposed. Following are two different arguments on the subject of publicizing criminal execution. Before you read them, use the space below to write why you do or do not support showing criminal executions on television.

YOUR OPINION ON TELEVISING CRIMINAL EXECUTIONS: ____________________________

____

____

____

Now read the selection, separating facts from opinions.

SHOULD EXECUTIONS BE TELEVISED?

Richard Moran

1 A publicly supported TV station in San Francisco, KQED, has filed a federal civil lawsuit asking for permission to televise a California execution. The request should be granted, for it would spark a national debate on the death penalty and provide a much-needed test of the deterrent effect of capital punishment.

2 Since 1977, when executions were resumed in the United States, 142 men and one woman have been put to death. Much attention was given to the first few executions, but news reports of executions no longer occupy a prominent place in the national media. Press coverage has become so scant that even interested scholars find it difficult to catalogue the steady procession of condemned prisoners into our nation's death chambers.

3 A terrible paradox has resulted. As executions have become more numerous, they have become less visible. For executions to function as a deterrent, they must be visible: Potential criminals must know about them. The more public the execution, the more effective the deterrent. By executing condemned criminals in private, and by barring television cameras, photo equipment, and tape recorders from the death chamber, we have robbed the execution ceremony of any possible deterrent value. And in doing so, we have undercut the basis of its moral justification.

4 Research published in 1987 by sociologist Steven Stack (then at Auburn University, now at Wayne State) suggests that a highly publicized execution is associated with an average drop nationwide of 30 homicides in the month following the execution.

This appears to be good news for those who support the death penalty. But between 1950 and 1980, only 16 of the 600 executions that occurred in America were given national media coverage. Even if we eliminate the 10 years in which no one was executed (1967–77), publicized executions still average less than one a year, hardly enough to produce a deterrent effect, especially when one considers that each year there are more than 20,000 homicides in the United States.

5 For policy-makers interested in fashioning a death penalty that saves lives, the question becomes how to increase the publicity given to executions by the national media. The answer is as disturbing as it is obvious: Make executions public once again. At minimum, let TV broadcast executions live. We view plane crashes and auto accidents, burn victims and mutilated bodies on the evening news. Even if these acts of violence are news, the viewing of them is generally devoid of social or moral purpose. Why protect our sensibilities when it comes to state-imposed executions, especially if there is a moral lesson to be learned and a legitimate social policy goal to be achieved?

6 There is a shocking and even barbaric quality of KQED's proposal; I am aware of that. But right now we have the worst of both worlds. People are being executed each month and only those who read the middle pages of our newspapers are made aware of this fact. The televising of executions would allow us to test the deterrence argument for the first time this century—to find out if the imposition of the death penalty can save the lives of innocent people by deterring potential murderers.

7 Televised or public executions would have two additional positive effects. First, they would ignite a much-needed national debate on the death penalty. Second, the new information on deterrence would help us evaluate the moral foundation of the death penalty. If Stack's research is correct and publicized executions can save lives, then this fact alters the moral equation.

8 We have to balance the saving of lives against the taking of lives. A 30–1 ratio of lives saved to lives taken should prove enormously persuasive to all but the most hardened opponents of capital punishment. On the other hand, if the death penalty proved not to deter, then proponents would be forced to rely on the morally questionable motives of retribution and revenge.

9 If we are ever to resolve the disturbing paradox of people being executed and no one being deterred, then we ought to make executions public once again. Those who believe in the deterrent value of the death penalty should welcome the chance to demonstrate it. Its opponents should welcome the opportunity to expose the death penalty for the morally bankrupt social policy it has become.

10 At the very least, public executions would force all of us to face directly the consequences of our decision to kill those who have killed.

Now answer the following questions:

1. What is the main idea of the essay? ______________________________

____

2. Is the essay mostly fact or opinion? ______________________________

3. What is the author's main argument in favor of televising the executions of convicted criminals?______________________________

____

____

4. Is the main argument based mostly on facts? __________ Explain. ____________

____

____

5. Did the author convince you of his argument? _________ Explain. ____________

____

____

Part B

Directions: The next essay offers the opposite view on publicly televising executions. As you read, separate fact from opinions. Then answer the questions that follow the reading selection.

THE VICTIM WILL NOT GET EQUAL TIME

Harriet Salarno

1 America's last public execution took place in Galena, Mo., on May 21, 1937. Since that time, all executions in the United States have been conducted inside prison grounds, sparing the families of both the victim and the criminal unnecessary pain and suffering.

2 Now, after more than half a century, public TV station KQED in San Francisco is trying to revive the practice of public executions by suing for the right to take cameras into the gas chamber. KQED's lawyer, William Turner, said, "It is appropriate in a democratic society for citizens to be able to see virtually firsthand . . . the ultimate sanction of our criminal-justice system."

3 A federal judge must decide the questions of law in this case. But for most of us, it is not a question of law but of decency. Public execution has drawn opposition from both supporters and opponents of the death penalty because it violates commonly held standards of decency.

4 Letting cameras into prisons to record executions will not serve the public good. Instead, it will compound the tragedy of violent crime by focusing attention on the method of punishment rather than the nature of the crime.

5 The terrible events that prompt the state to deal out its harshest penalty cannot be captured on videotape for live broadcast on the nightly news. The victims of these crimes are not available for comment because they are long dead. Their stories will be left untold.

6 This is just the latest example of how the rights of victims and their families are too often ignored. KQED argues that it has a right to film executions. What gives it this right? Cameras are not allowed in the Supreme Court and federal courtrooms. Why should they be permitted in the gas chamber?

7 The news director for KQED contends that the television camera is the "only neutral witness," implying that newspaper reporters are incapable of objectivity at such an event. Have television journalists grown so arrogant that they feel the camera has replaced the written word? Do they think that an event has meaning only if a camera is there to record it?

8 It does not trouble KQED that their "neutral witness" was not present when the crime was committed. And that the terrible acts of brutality committed by the individual sentenced to death will not be broadcast on a split screen along with the execution. The victim will not receive equal time.

9 An execution is not a media event or photo opportunity. It is the method of punishment the people of California have chosen for individuals convicted of the most vicious crimes.

10 As such, it should not be sensationalized or used as a forum to advance a particular political agenda. Live broadcast of an execution would only tell us what we already know—that an execution is a grim proceeding. And it would give those who oppose capital punishment an opportunity to garner sympathy for the criminal.

11 In a very real sense, reviving public executions would give criminals the last word.

Now answer the following questions:

1. What is the main idea of the essay? ______________________________

____

2. Is the essay mostly fact or opinion? ______________________________

3. What is the author's main argument against televising the executions of convicted criminals? ______________________________

____

____

4. Is the main argument based mostly on facts? __________ Explain. __________

____

____

5. Did the author convince you of her argument? ________ Explain. __________

____

____

6. Reread your stated opinion on the subject (page 149). Then explain why you have or have not changed your mind after reading these two essays. ______________

____

____

____

____

7. What would it take to change your opinion? ______________________________

____

____

____

____

PRACTICE B-3: Quick Quiz on Fact/Opinion

Part A

Directions: In the space provided, explain the differences between fact and opinion.

____

____

____

____

____

____

____

____

____

____

____

Part B

Directions: Place an *O* in the blank in front of all statements of opinion, an *F* if a statement is fact or can be verified.

_______ **1.** There are fifty-seven items in the L. L. Bean Women's Outdoor Catalog offered in various shades of pink.

_______ **2.** We can no longer get along in our present society without telephones.

_______ **3.** It is important for college students to have good study skills if they are to succeed in the academic world.

_______ **4.** The Tobacco Institute donated $70,000 to help underwrite the antidrug booklet *Helping Youth Say No.*

_______ **5.** The two most interesting things in the world, for our species, are ideas and the individual human body, two elements that poetry uniquely joins together.

_______ **6.** Last year, as a result of the worldwide collapse of oil prices, the Mexican economy shrank 5 percent, and underemployment reached 50 percent. Things are worse in El Salvador.

_______ **7.** The United States is a nation of immigrants, and of immigration policies—policies designed to facilitate the orderly entry of people into the country, but also to keep them out.

_______ **8.** War against the Plains Indians in the early nineteenth century was a hopeless proposition for Europeans armed with swords, single-shot pistols, and breech-loading rifles. The Indians were infinitely better horsemen and could loose a continuous fusillade of arrows from beneath the neck of a pony going at full tilt.

_______ **9.** Mark Hunter's comments on the lack of spirit and spontaneity found in contemporary rock music are accurate. But his attack on MTV is misguided and his assertion that rock music is no longer worth listening to is absurd.

______ **10.** Your jeweler is the expert where diamonds are concerned. His knowledge can help make the acquisition of a quality diamond of a carat or more a beautiful, rewarding experience.

Part C

Directions: In the space provided, explain what kind of evidence you would have to gather to prove the following statements as facts.

1. The viewing of violence on television has created a more violent society.________

____

____

____

____

2. City slums breed crime. ______________________________________

____

____

____

____

3. Solar energy is the most efficient way to heat homes in some parts of the United States. ______________________________________

____

____

____

____

4. A college education provides better job opportunities. ______________

____

____

____

____

5. If you are rich, you probably won't get convicted of a crime as easily as you will if you are poor. ______________________________________

____

____

____

Turn in the quiz to your instructor.

Name ______________________________ Section __________ Date __________

C. Detecting Propaganda

Before you begin this section on propaganda, answer the following questions.

1. Define *propaganda.* ______________________________

2. Does the word *propaganda* have a positive or negative connotation for you? Explain. ______________________________

3. Give some examples of the use of propaganda. ______________________________

4. Do you think you are always aware of propaganda when it is being used? Explain. ______________________________

Now read the following information, comparing your definition and examples of propaganda with those provided here.

Propaganda is the deliberate attempt on the part of a group or an individual to sway our opinions in their favor. Contrary to what some think, propaganda is not merely a tool used by dictatorial governments. We are exposed to various propaganda techniques nearly every day of our lives. Politicians use propaganda, along with other devices, to get us to accept their opinions and vote for them. Newspapers and magazines use propaganda techniques to influence our opinions on political and social issues. Religious leaders use propaganda to influence our opinions on morality. Advertisers, through television, radio, newspapers, and magazines, use propaganda techniques to get us to buy things we often don't need or to change the brand of soap we use.

Propaganda techniques usually appeal to our emotions or our desires rather than to our reason. They cause us to believe or do things we might not believe or do if we thought and reasoned more carefully. When we are too lazy to think for ourselves, we often become victims of propaganda. Propagandists are usually not concerned with good or bad, right or wrong. They are more concerned with getting us to believe what they want us to believe. The techniques they use can range from outright lies to subtle truths.

The power of propaganda cannot be overrated. While some propaganda may be socially beneficial, it can also be harmful. Through propaganda techniques, our opinions can be changed to be "for" or "against" certain nations, political rulers, races, moral values, and religions. What we must guard against is having our opinions formed for us by others. We must not let ourselves be used or fooled, even for good causes.

Those who investigate the way propagandists work have identified seven basic techniques that are used frequently:

1. *Name calling:* using names that appeal to our hatred or fears; if the propagandists know a group fears communism, they might call an opponent a "commie" or a "red" to get the group to distrust the opponent.
2. *Glittering generalities:* using words that appeal to our emotions such as *justice, founding fathers, freedom fighters, love, loyalty,* or *the American way* are vague but have positive connotations that appeal to us; they are often used because propagandists know we are touched by such words.
3. *Transfer:* linking something we like or respect to some person, cause, or product; if we respect the flag or the Christian cross, our respect for the symbol is transferred to whatever use it is being associated with.
4. *Testimonial:* using well-known people to testify that a certain person, idea, or product is "the best"; if we admire Robert Redford and we see him in advertising for a particular product or politician, we then buy the product or vote for the person because of our respect for Redford, even though he may not be an authority on the subject.
5. *Plain folks:* a device used by politicians, labor leaders, businesspeople, ministers, educators, and advertisers to win our confidence by appearing to be just plain folks like ourselves; the good-old-boy image.
6. *Card stacking:* stacking the evidence against the truth by lying, omitting, or evading facts; underplaying or overemphasizing issues; telling half-truths; or stating things out of context; advertisers might say their product "helps stop bad breath," leading us to think it *does* stop it.
7. *The bandwagon:* appealing to our desire to be on the winning side, to be like or better than everyone else, and to follow the crowd or be one of the gang "in on the latest fad."

Most of these devices work because they appeal to our emotions, our fears, our ignorance, or our desire to do the "right thing." But by sorting facts from opinions, and by recognizing these propaganda techniques when used, we won't become victims, but rather thoughtful readers and thinkers.

Practice C-1: Detecting Propaganda Techniques

Directions: Read each of the following items and in the space provided write in which propaganda technique is being used and why you think so.

1. "My opponent, Senator Glick, has a record of being soft on crime at a time when we need to be strong." ______________________________

____

____

2. "Senator Cluck cares what happens to the farmers; he cares for the future of the American tradition of prosperity. He'll put this country back on track!" __________

____

____

3. "Jerry Seinfeld. Cardmember since 1986" (American Express ad). ____________

____

____

4. "M Lotion helps skin keep its moisture . . . discourages tired-looking lines under eyes." ____

____

5. "Over 8,000,000 sold! Why would anyone want to buy anything else?" __________

____

____

6. "Buy Banhead. It contains twice as much pain reliever." ____________________

____

____

7. "Mayor Naste has shown time and again he's for the little guy. You don't see him driving a big limo or wearing fancy suits. No, sir. You'll find him out talking to us folks to see how he can serve us better." ____________________________

____

____

8. "Buy the Sportsman's Shaving System, appointed the exclusive skin care system for the Winter Olympics." ____

____

____

9. "Yes, I lied. But I did it for my country. As God is my witness, I felt in my heart—and still do—that what I did was right, and the people of this country who want to preserve its freedom will thank me some day." ________________________

____

____

10. "Drive to class reunions in the new Hummer 3 and even Mr. Most-Likely-to-Succeed will be envious." ____

____

____

Practice C-2

Directions: Survey the following passage from a textbook entitled *Preface to Critical Reading* by reading the opening paragraph, some of the first sentences in selected paragraphs, and the questions that follow the reading. Then use the information from the survey to read the selection, marking key points. When finished, answer the questions that follow the reading.

DETECTING PROPAGANDA

Richard D. Altick and Andrea A. Lunsford

1 All of us, whether we admit it or not, are prejudiced. We dislike certain people, certain activities, certain ideas—in many cases, not because we have reasoned things out and found a logical basis for our dislike, but rather because those people or activities or ideas affect our less generous instincts. Of course we also have positive prejudices, by which we approve of people or things—perhaps because they give us pleasure or perhaps because we have always been taught that they are "good" and never stopped to reason why. In either case, these biases, irrational and unfair though they may be, are aroused by words, principally by name-calling and the use of the glittering generality. Both of these techniques depend on the process of association, by which an idea (the specific person, group, proposal, or situation being discussed) takes on emotional coloration from the language employed.

2 *Name-calling* is the device of arousing an unfavorable response by such an association. A speaker or writer who wishes to sway an audience against a person, group, or principle will often use this device.

> The bleeding-heart liberals are responsible for the current economic crisis.
> The labor union radicals keep honest people from honest work.
> Environmental extremists can bankrupt hard-pressed companies with their fanatical demands for unnecessary and expensive pollution controls such as chimney-scrubbers.

Name-calling is found in many arguments in which emotion plays a major role. It rarely is part of the logic of an argument but instead is directed at personalities. Note how the speakers here depend on verbal rock throwing in their attempt to win the day:

> He's no coach, but a foul-mouthed, cigar-chomping bully who bribes high-school stars to play for him.
> The Bible-thumping bigots who want to censor our books and our television shows represent the worst of the anti-intellectual lunatic fringe.
> Mayor Leech has sold the city out to vested interests and syndicates of racketeers. City Hall stinks of graft and payola.

The negative emotional associations of the "loaded" words in these sentences have the planned effect of spilling over onto, and hiding, the real points at issue, which demand—but fail to receive—fair, analytical, objective judgment. Generating a thick emotional haze is, therefore, an affective way for glib writers and speakers to convince many of the unthinking or the credulous among their audience.

3 The *glittering generality* involves the equally illogical use of connotative words. In contrast to name-calling, the glittering generality draws on traditionally positive associations. Here, as in name-calling, the trouble is that the words used have been applied too freely and thus are easily misapplied. Many writers and speakers take advantage of the glitter of these words to blind readers to real issues at hand. *Patriot, freedom, democracy, national honor, Constitution, God-given rights, peace, liberty, property rights, international cooperation, brotherhood, equal opportunity, prosperity, decent standard of living:* words or phrases like these sound pleasant to the listener's ear, but they can also divert attention from the

ideas the speaker is discussing, ideas which are usually too complex to be fairly labeled by a single word.

> The progressive, forward-looking liberal party will make certain that we enjoy a stable and healthy economy.
>
> The practical idealists of the labor movement are united in supporting the right of every person to earn an honest living.
>
> Dedicated environmentalists perform an indispensable patriotic service for us all by keeping air-polluting industries' feet to the fire.
>
> He's a coach who is a shining light to our youth. He believes that football helps to build the character, stamina, and discipline needed for the leaders of tomorrow.
>
> The decent, God-fearing people who want to protect us from the violence and depravity depicted in books and on television represent the best of a moral society.
>
> Mayor Leech has stood for progress, leadership, and vision at a time when most cities have fallen into the hands of the corrupt political hacks.

4 The effectiveness of name-calling and the glittering generality depends on stock responses. Just as the scientist Pavlov, in a classic experiment, conditioned dogs to increase their production of saliva every time he rang a bell, so the calculating persuader expects readers to react automatically to language that appeals to their prejudices.

5 The abuse of authority is one of the *transfer devices* which exploit readers' willingness to link one idea or person with another, even though the two may not be logically connected. The familiar *testimonials* of present-day advertising provide an instance of this device. In some cases, the "authority" who testifies has some connection with the product advertised. The problem to settle here is, when we try to decide which brand of sunburn cream is best, how much weight may we reasonably attach to the enthusiastic statements of certain nurses? When we are thinking of buying a tennis racket, should we accept the say-so of a champion who, after all, is well paid for telling us that a certain make is the best? In other cases, the testifying authorities may have no formal, professional connection with the products they recommend. An actor, who may very well be a master of his particular art, praises a whiskey, a coffee, or an airline. He likes it, he says. But, we may ask, does the fact that he is a successful actor make him better qualified than any person who is not an actor to judge a whiskey, a coffee, or an airline? Competence in one field does not necessarily "transfer" to competence in another.

6 Furthermore, advertisers often borrow the prestige of science and medicine to enhance the reputation of their products. Many people have come to feel for the laboratory scientist and the physician an awe once reserved for bishops or statesmen. The alleged approval of such people thus carries great weight in selling something or inducing someone to believe something. Phrases such as "leading medical authorities say . . . " or "independent laboratory tests show . . . " are designed simply to transfer the prestige of science to a toothpaste or deodorant. Seldom are the precise "medical authorities" or "independent laboratories" named. But the mere phrases carry weight with uncritical listeners or readers. Similarly, the title "Dr." or "Professor" implies that the person quoted speaks with all the authority of which learned people are capable—when, as a matter of fact, doctoral degrees can be bought from mail-order colleges. Therefore, whenever a writer or speaker appeals to the prestige that surrounds the learned, the reader should demand credentials. Just *what* "medical authorities" say this? Can they be trusted? What independent laboratories made the tests—and what did the tests actually reveal? Who are the people who speak as expert educators,

psychologists, or economists? Regardless of the fact that they are "doctors," do they know what they are talking about?

7 Another closely related form of transfer is the borrowing of prestige from a highly respected institution (country, religion, education) or individual (world leader, philosopher, scientist) for the sake of enhancing something else. Political speakers sometimes work into their speeches quotations from the Bible or from secular "sacred writings" (such as a national constitution). Such quotations usually arouse favorable emotions in listeners, emotions which are then transferred to the speaker's policy or subject. When analyzing an appeal that uses quotations from men and women who have achieved renown in one field or another, the chief question is whether the quotation is appropriate in context. Does it have real relevance to the point at issue? It is all very well to quote George Washington or Abraham Lincoln in support of one's political stand. But circumstances have changed immensely since those statements were first uttered, and their applicability to a new situation may be dubious indeed. The implication is, "This person, who we agree was great and wise, said certain things which 'prove' the justice of my own stand. Therefore, you should believe I am right." But to have a valid argument, the writer must prove that the word of the authorities is really applicable to the present issue. If that is true, then the speaker is borrowing not so much their prestige as their wisdom—which is perfectly justifiable.

8 Another version of the transfer device is one which gains prestige not through quotations or testimonials of authorities but from linking one idea to another. Here is an advertisement that illustrates how this device works.

THE TELEPHONE POLE THAT BECAME A MEMORIAL

9 The cottage on Lincoln Street in Portland, Oregon, is shaded by graceful trees and covered with ivy.

10 Many years ago, A. H. Feldman and his wife remodeled the house to fit their dreams . . . and set out slips of ivy around it. And when their son, Danny, came along, he, too, liked to watch things grow. One day, when he was only nine, he took a handful of ivy slips and planted them at the base of the telephone pole in front of the house.

11 Time passed . . . and the ivy grew, climbing to the top of the pole. Like the ivy, Danny grew too. He finished high school, went to college. The war came along before he finished—and Danny went overseas. And there he gave his life for his country.

12 Not very long ago the overhead telephone lines were being removed from the poles on Lincoln Street. The ivy-covered telephone pole in front of the Feldman home was about to be taken down. Its work was done.

13 But, when the telephone crew arrived, Mrs. Feldman came out to meet them. "Couldn't it be left standing?" she asked. And then she told them about her son.

14 So the pole, although no longer needed, wasn't touched at all. At the request of the telephone company, the Portland City Council passed a special ordinance permitting the company to leave it standing. And there it is today, mantled in ivy, a living memorial to Sergeant Danny Feldman.

15 What did the telephone company wish to accomplish by this ad? Readers are not urged to install a telephone, equip their homes with extra telephones, or use any of the various new services the company has developed. Nor are they told how inexpensive and efficient the telephone company thinks those services are. Instead, this is what is known as an "institutional" advertisement. Its purpose is to inspire public esteem, even affection, for the company.

16 How do such advertisements inspire esteem and respect? Simply by telling an anecdote, without a single word to point up the moral. In this ad, every detail is carefully chosen for its emotional appeal: the cottage ("home, sweet home" theme), the ivy

(symbol of endurance through the years; often combined, as here, with the idea of the family home), the little boy (evoking all the feelings associated with childhood), the young man dying in the war (evoking patriotic sentiment). Thus at least four symbols are combined—all of them with great power to touch the emotions. Then the climax: Will the company cut down the ivy-covered pole? To many people, *company* has a connotation of hardheartedness, impersonality, coldness, which is the very impression this particular company, one of the biggest in the world, wants to erase. So the company modestly reports that it went to the trouble of getting special permission to leave this one pole standing, "mantled in ivy, a living memorial."

17 The writer of this advertisement has, in effect, urged readers to transfer to the telephone company the sympathies aroused by the story. The ivy-covered pole aptly symbolizes what the writer wanted to do—"mantle" the pole (symbolizing the company) with the ivy that is associated with home, childhood, and heroic death. If it is possible to make one feel sentimental about a giant corporation, an advertisement like this one—arousing certain feelings by means of one set of objects and then transferring those feelings to another object—will do it. But the story, although true enough, is after all only one incident, and a sound generalization about the character of a vast company cannot be formed from a single anecdote. The company may well be as "human" as the advertisement implies, but readers are led to that belief through an appeal to their sympathies, not their reason.

18 A third kind of fallacy involves *mudslinging,* attacking a person rather than a principle. Mudslingers make personal attacks on an opponent (formally known as *ad hominem* arguments, those "against the man"), not merely by calling names, but often by presenting what they offer as damaging evidence against the opponent's motives, character, and private life. Thus the audience's attention is diverted from the argument itself to a subject which is more likely to stir up prejudices. If, for example, in denouncing an opponent's position on reducing the national debt, a candidate refers to X's connection with certain well-known gamblers, then the candidate ceases to argue the case on its merits and casts doubt on the opponent's personal character. The object is not to hurt X's feelings but to arouse bias against that person in the hearer's mind. Critical readers or listeners must train themselves to detect and reject these irrelevant aspersions. It may be, indeed, that X has shady connections with underworld gamblers. But that may have nothing to do with the abstract right or wrong of his stand on the national debt. Issues should be discussed apart from character and motives. Both character and motives are important, of course, since they bear on any candidate's fitness for public office and on whether we can give him or her our support. But they call for a separate discussion.

19 A somewhat more subtle kind of personal attack is the *innuendo,* which differs from direct accusation roughly as a hint differs from a plain statement. Innuendo is chiefly useful where no facts exist to give even a semblance of support to a direct charge. The writer or speaker therefore slyly plants seeds of doubt or suspicion in the reader's or listener's mind, as the villainous Iago does in the mind of Shakespeare's Othello. Innuendo is a trick that is safe, effective—and unfair. "They were in the office with the door locked for four hours after closing time." The statement, in itself, may be entirely true. But what counts is the implication it is meant to convey. The unfairness increases when the doubts that the innuendo raises concern matters that have nothing to do with the issue anyway. An example of the irrelevant innuendo is found in the writings of the historian Charles A. Beard. In assailing the ideas of another historian, Admiral Alfred T. Mahan, Beard called him "the son of a professor and swivel-chair tactician at West Point," who "served respectably, but without distinction, for a time in the navy" and "found an easy berth at the Naval War College." Actually, the occupation of Mahan's father has nothing to do with the validity of the son's

arguments. But observe the sneer—which is meant to be transferred from father to son—in "professor" and "swivel-chair tactician." Beard's reference to Mahan's naval record is a good elementary instance of damning with faint praise. And whether or not Mahan's was "an easy berth" at the Naval War College (a matter of opinion), it too has no place in a discussion of the man's ideas or intellectual capacities.

20 Newspapers often use this device to imply more than they can state without risking a libel suit. In reporting the latest bit of gossip about celebrated members of the "jet set" or the "beautiful people" (what do the terms suggest about the habits and tastes of the people referred to?), a paper may mention the fact that "gorgeous movie actress A is a frequent companion of thrice-divorced playboy B" or that they "are seen constantly together at the Vegas night spots" or that they are "flitting from the Riviera to Sun Valley together." The inference suggested, however unfounded it may be, is that their relationship is not just that of good friends who happen to be in the same place at the same time. Similarly, newspapers which value sensationalism more than responsibility may describe an accused "child slayer" or "woman molester" as "dirty and bearded" (implication: he is a suspicious-looking bum). His face may, in addition, be "scarred" (implication: he is physically violent). Such literal details may be true enough. But how much have they to do with the guilt or innocence of the person in this particular case? The effect on the reader is what courts of law term "prejudicial" and therefore inadmissible. Unfortunately the law does not extend to slanted writing, however powerfully it may sway public opinion.

21 Another instance of the way in which emotionally loaded language can be combined with unproved evidence to stir up prejudice may be taken from the field of art. A modern critic condemned certain paintings as "a conventional rehash of cubist patterns born among the wastrels of Paris forty years ago." In so doing, the critic attacked the art through the artist. The artistic merit of paintings has nothing to do with the private lives of the people who paint them. The painters referred to may well have been wastrels. But that fact—if it is a fact—has no bearing on the point at issue. The assumed connection between the personal virtues or shortcomings of artists and the artistic value of their productions has resulted in a great deal of confused thinking about literature, music, and the other arts.

22 Another diversionary tactic which introduces an irrelevant issue into a debate is the *red herring*. It too may involve shifting attention from principles to personalities, but without necessarily slinging mud or calling names. Since neither relaxing at a disco nor having a taste for serious books is yet sinful or criminal, a political party slings no mud when it portrays the other party's candidate as a playboy or an intellectual. Still, such matters are largely irrelevant to the main argument, which is whether one or the other candidate will better serve the interests of the people. The red-herring device need not involve personalities at all; it may take the form simply of substituting one issue for another. If a large corporation is under fire for alleged monopolistic practices, its public relations people may start an elaborate advertising campaign to show how well the company's workers are treated. Thus, if the campaign succeeds, the bad publicity suffered because of the assertions that the company has been trying to corner the market may be counteracted by the public's approval of its allegedly fine labor policy.

23 Unfortunately, most of us are eager to view questions in their simplest terms and to make our decisions on the basis of only a few of the many elements the problem may involve. The problem of minority groups in North America, for instance, is not simply one of abstract justice, as many would like to think. Rather, it involves complex and by no means easily resolvable issues of economics, sociology, politics, and psychology. Nor can one say with easy assurance, "The federal government should guarantee every farmer a decent income, even if the money comes from the pocketbooks of the citizens

who are the farmer's own customers" or "It is the obligation of every educational institution to purge its faculty of all who hold radical sympathies." Perhaps each of these propositions is sound; perhaps neither is. But before either is adopted as a conviction, intelligent readers must canvass their full implications . . . . After the implications have been explored, more evidence may be found *against* the proposition than in support of it.

24 Countless reductive generalizations concerning parties, races, religions, and nations, to say nothing of individuals, are the result of the deep-seated human desire to reduce complicated ideas to their simplest terms. We saw the process working when we touched on stereotypes in Chapter One and in our discussion of rhetorical induction in this chapter. Unfortunately, condemning with a few quick, perhaps indefensible assumptions is easier than recognizing the actual diversity in any social group. But every man and woman has an urgent obligation to analyze the basis of each judgment he or she makes: "Am I examining every aspect of the issue that needs to be examined? Do I understand the problem sufficiently to be able to make a fair decision? Or am I taking the easiest and simplest way out?"

Directions: Now answer the following questions. You may look back if necessary.

1. According to the authors, what two propaganda devices are used to stir up our prejudices? ______

2. What part do our emotions play in the effectiveness of some propaganda techniques? ______

3. What do the authors mean when they say that "advertisers often borrow the prestige of science and medicine to enhance the reputation of their products"?

______

4. What is meant by the term "transfer device"? Give some examples. ______

5. Name the three devices or methods frequently used to attack a person rather than a principle. ______

6. Define the following terms: ______

a. transfer devices ______

b. testimonials ______________________________

____

c. mudslinging ______________________________

____

d. innuendo ______________________________

____

e. red herring ______________________________

____

f. oversimplification ______________________________

____

7. Why is it important to recognize and understand how propaganda is used?______

____

____

____

____

Application I: Recognizing Propaganda at Work

Find an example of one of the seven propaganda techniques used in a current magazine or newspaper advertisement. Write a brief explanation of how the technique is being used, attach it to the ad, and share it in class.

D. Putting It All Together

The next two practices give you the opportunity to use what you have learned about critical comprehension to distinguish fact from opinion, read opinions of others, and detect propaganda. Review your scores on the Student Record Sheet in the Appendix and try to match or do better than your scores for the previous reading selections. If you make mistakes, analyze errors and figure out how to improve the next time. The first practice follows an introduction to the author Ishmael Reed; the second practice is timed.

Now, read about the following author, Ishmael Reed, to understand more about how an author's life affects his opinions. His views on reading and literacy may inspire you to develop different views. Another way to find current information, quotations, or pictures of this author is to use the World Wide Web. Using a search engine such as Google or AltaVista, type the author's name under "Search."

Introducing Ishmael Reed

Ishmael Reed has been called one of the most innovative and outspoken voices in contemporary literature. His work embodies seven novels, four books of poetry, three plays, several collections of essays, and book reviews. In addition to these

works, Reed is a songwriter, television producer, and magazine editor. Reed has taught at Harvard, Yale, Dartmouth, and the University of California, Berkeley.

Reed is a strong advocate of literacy and its power. In an essay that first appeared in the *San Francisco Examiner* and was later reprinted in his collection *Writin' Is Fightin'*, Reed spoke out against illiteracy:

> If you're illiterate, people can do anything they want to you. Take your house through equity scams, cheat you, lie to you, bunko you, take your money, even take your life. . . .
>
> As you go through life X-ing documents, unable to defend yourself against forces hostile to you, people can deprive you of your voting rights through gerrymandering schemes, build a freeway next to your apartment building or open a retail crack operation on your block, with people coming and going as though you lived next door to Burger King—because you're not articulate enough to fight back, because you don't have sense enough to know what is happening to you, and so you're shoveled under at each turn in your life; you might as well be dead.
>
> One of the joys of reading is the ability to plug into the shared wisdom of mankind. One of my favorite passages from the Bible is "Come, and let us reason together"—Isaiah 1:18. Being illiterate means that you often resort to violence, during the most trivial dispute . . . because you don't have the verbal skills to talk things out. . . .
>
> I'm also convinced that illiteracy is a factor contributing to suicide becoming one of the leading causes of death among white middle-class youngsters, who allow their souls to atrophy from the steady diet of spiritual Wonder Bread: bad music and bad film, and the outrageous cheapness of superficial culture. When was the last time you saw a movie or TV program that was as good as the best book you've read, and I don't mean what imitation elitists call the classics. I'd settle for Truman Capote, John A. Williams, Cecil Brown, Lawson Inada, Paule Marshall, Xam Wilson Cartier, Victor Cruz, Howard Numerov, William Kennedy, Paula Gunn Allen, Margaret Atwood, Diane Johnson, Edward Field, Frank Chin, Rudolfo Anaya, Wesley Brown, Lucille Clifton, Al Young, Amiri Baraka, Simon Ortiz, Bob Callahan, David Metzer, Anna Castillo, Joyce Carol Oates and Harryette Mullen, a group of writers as good as any you'd find anywhere. . . . (From Ishmael Reed, "Killer Illiteracy," *Writin' Is Fightin'*, Atheneum, 1988, pp. 185–186.)

Reed's essay "America: The Multinational Society" offers his reasons for disagreeing with those who believe the United States "is part of Western civilization because our 'system of government' is derived from Europe."

Practice D-1

Directions: Read the following article. As you read, look for the main argument, underline facts, and be aware of opinions.

AMERICA: THE MULTINATIONAL SOCIETY

Ishmael Reed

At the annual Lower East Side Jewish Festival yesterday, a Chinese woman ate a pizza slice in front of Ty Thuan Duc's Vietnamese grocery store. Beside her a Spanish-speaking family patronized a cart with two signs: "Italian Ices" and "Kosher by Rabbi Alper." And after the pastrami ran out, everybody ate knishes.

(*New York Times*, 23 June 1983)

1 On the day before Memorial Day, 1983, a poet called me to describe a city he had just visited. He said that one section included mosques, built by the Islamic people who dwelled there. Attending his reading, he said, were large numbers of Hispanic people, forty thousand of whom lived in the same city. He was not talking about a fabled city located in some mysterious region of the world. The city he'd visited was Detroit.

2 A few months before, as I was leaving Houston, Texas, I heard it announced on the radio that Texas's largest minority was Mexican American, and though a foundation recently issued a report critical of bilingual education, the taped voice used to guide the passengers on the air trams connecting terminals in Dallas Airport is in both Spanish and English. If the trend continues, a day will come when it will be difficult to travel through some sections of the country without hearing commands in both English and Spanish; after all, for some western states, Spanish was the first written language and the Spanish style lives on in the western way of life.

3 Shortly after my Texas trip, I sat in an auditorium located on the campus of the University of Wisconsin at Milwaukee as a Yale professor—whose original work on the influence of African cultures upon those of the Americas has led to his ostracism from some monocultural intellectual circles—walked up and down the aisle, like an old-time southern evangelist, dancing and drumming the top of the lectern, illustrating his points before some serious Afro-American intellectuals and artists who cheered and applauded his performance and his mastery of information. The professor was "white." After his lecture, he joined a group of Milwaukeeans in a conversation. All of the participants spoke Yoruban, though only the professor had ever traveled to Africa.

4 One of the artists told me that his paintings, which included African and Afro-American mythological symbols and imagery, were hanging in the local McDonald's restaurant. The next day I went to McDonald's and snapped pictures of smiling youngsters eating hamburgers below paintings that could grace the walls of any of the country's leading museums. The manager of the local McDonald's said, "I don't know what you boys are doing, but I like it," as he commissioned the local painters to exhibit in his restaurant.

5 Such blurring of cultural styles occurs in everyday life in the United States to a greater extent than anyone can imagine and is probably more prevalent than the sensational conflict between people of different backgrounds that is played up and often encouraged by the media. The result is what the Yale professor, Robert Thompson, referred to as a cultural bouillabaisse, yet members of the nation's present educational and cultural Elect still cling to the notion that the United States belongs to some vaguely defined entity they refer to as "Western civilization," by which they mean, presumably, a civilization created by the people of Europe, as if Europe can be viewed in monolithic terms. Is Beethoven's Ninth Symphony, which includes Turkish marches, a part of Western civilization, or the late nineteenth- and twentieth-century French paintings, whose creators were influenced by Japanese art? And what of the cubists, through whom the influence of African art changed modern painting, or the surrealists, who were so impressed with the art of the Pacific Northwest Indians that, in their map of North America, Alaska dwarfs the lower forty-eight in size?

6 Are the Russians, who are often criticized for their adoption of "Western" ways by Tsarist dissidents in exile, members of Western civilization? And what of the millions of Europeans who have black African and Asian ancestry, black Africans having occupied several countries for hundreds of years? Are these "Europeans" members of Western civilization, or the Hungarians, who originated across the Urals in a place called Greater Hungary, or the Irish, who came from the Iberian Peninsula?

7 Even the notion that North America is part of Western civilization because our "system of government" is derived from Europe is being challenged by Native American historians who say that the founding fathers, Benjamin Franklin especially, were actually influenced by the system of government that had been adopted by the Iroquois hundreds of years prior to the arrival of large numbers of Europeans.

8 Western civilization, then, becomes another confusing category like Third World, or Judeo-Christian culture, as man attempts to impose his small-screen view of political and cultural reality upon a complex world. Our most publicized novelist recently said that Western civilization was the greatest achievement of mankind, an attitude that flourishes on the street level as scribbles in public restrooms: "White Power," "Niggers and Spics Suck," or "Hitler was a prophet," the latter being the most telling for wasn't Adolph Hitler the archetypal monoculturalist who, in his pigheaded arrogance, believed that one way and one blood was so pure that it had to be protected from alien strains at all costs? Where did such an attitude, which has caused so much misery and depression in our national life, which has tainted even our noblest achievements, begin? An attitude that caused the incarceration of Japanese-American citizens during World War II, the persecution of Chicanos and Chinese Americans, the near-extermination of the Indians, and the murder and lynchings of thousands of Afro-Americans.

9 Virtuous, hardworking, pious, even though they occasionally would wander off after some fancy clothes, or rendezvous in the woods with the town prostitute, the Puritans are idealized in our schoolbooks as "a hardy band" of no-nonsense patriarchs whose discipline razed the forest and brought order to the New World (a term that annoys Native American historians). Industrious, responsible, it was their "Yankee ingenuity" and practicality that created the work ethic. They were simple folk who produced a number of good poets, and they set the tone for the American writing style, of lean and spare lines, long before Hemingway. They worshiped in churches whose colors blended in with the New England snow, churches with simple structures and ornate lecterns.

10 The Puritans were a daring lot, but they had a mean streak. They hated the theater and banned Christmas. They punished people in a cruel and inhuman manner. They

killed children who disobeyed their parents. When they came in contact with those whom they considered heathens or aliens, they behaved in such a bizarre and irrational manner that this chapter in the American history comes down to us as a late-movie horror film. They exterminated the Indians, who taught them how to survive in a world unknown to them, and their encounter with the calypso culture of Barbados resulted in what the tourist guide in Salem's Witches' House refers to as the Witchcraft Hysteria.

11 The Puritan legacy of hard work and meticulous accounting led to the establishment of a great industrial society; it is no wonder that the American industrial revolution began in Lowell, Massachusetts, but there was the other side, the strange and paranoid attitudes toward those different from the Elect.

12 The cultural attitudes of that early Elect continue to be voiced in everyday life in the United States: the president of a distinguished university, writing a letter to the *Times,* belittling the study of African civilizations; the television network that promoted its show on the Vatican art with the boast that this art represented "the finest achievements of the human spirit." A modern up-tempo state of complex rhythms that depends upon contacts with an international community can no longer behave as if it dwelled in a "Zion Wilderness" surrounded by beasts and pagans.

13 When I heard a schoolteacher warn the other night about the invasion of the American educational system by foreign curriculums, I wanted to yell at the television set, "Lady, they're already here." It has already begun because the world is here. The world has been arriving at these shores for at least ten thousand years from Europe, Africa, and Asia. In the late nineteenth and early twentieth centuries, large numbers of Europeans arrived, adding their cultures to those of the European, African, and Asian settlers who were already here, and recently millions have been entering the country from South America and the Caribbean, making Yale Professor Bob Thompson's bouillabaisse richer and thicker.

14 One of our most visionary politicians said that he envisioned a time when the United States could become the brain of the world, by which he meant the repository of all of the latest advanced information systems. I thought of that remark when an enterprising poet friend of mine called to say that he had just sold a poem to a computer magazine and that the editors were delighted to get it because they didn't carry fiction or poetry. Is that the kind of world we desire? A humdrum, homogeneous world of all brains but no heart, no fiction, no poetry; a world of robots with human attendants bereft of imagination, of culture? Or does North America deserve a more exciting destiny? To become a place where the cultures of the world crisscross. This is possible because the United States is unique in the world: The world is here.

Comprehension Check

Directions: Now answer the following questions.

1. List one fact about Detroit. ______________________________

____

2. Is the following statement fact or opinion? "If the trend continues, a day will come when it will be difficult to travel through some sections of the country without hearing commands in both English and Spanish." ______________________________

____

3. What is Reed's main argument about "Western civilization"? ______

4. List one of the facts he gives to support his argument. ______

5. List another fact he gives to support his argument. ______

6. According to Reed, what are some of the problems in the United States because of the attitude that Western civilization is the greatest achievement of mankind? ______

7. What is Reed's overall opinion of the Puritans? ______

8. List one or two of the facts he uses to support this opinion. ______

9. Are Reed's arguments in this article based more on fact or opinion? Explain. ______

10. Did the author convince you of his argument? Explain. ______

Vocabulary Check

Directions: Define the following underlined words.

1. has led to his ostracism (paragraph 3) ______

2. from some monocultural intellectual circles (paragraph 3) ______

3. Afro-American mythological symbols (paragraph 4) ______

4. referred to as a cultural bouillabaisse (paragraph 5) ______

5. as if Europe can be viewed in <u>monolithic</u> terms (paragraph 5) ________________

____

6. and what of the <u>cubists</u> (paragraph 5) ________________

____

7. Hitler, the <u>archetypal</u> monoculturist (paragraph 8) ________________

____

8. the <u>incarceration</u> of Japanese-American citizens (paragraph 8) ________________

____

9. simple structures and <u>ornate</u> lecterns (paragraph 9) ________________

____

10. those whom they considered <u>heathens</u> (paragraph 10) ________________

____

Record your comprehension and vocabulary scores on the Student Record Chart in the Appendix.

PRACTICE D-2: Timed Reading

Directions: Before reading the following article, take a minute to survey it and the questions. Then time yourself as you begin to read the article. As you read, notice the author's opinion on cloning.

Begin timing: ____________

CLONING COULD HALT HUMAN EVOLUTION

Michael Mautner

1 Cloning is not only less fun than sex, it would freeze evolution and destroy our chances for survival in the future.

2 The cloning of the first mammal brings the prospects of human cloning closer to reality. Now the public should ponder the implications. Among these, the most important is the effect on our future evolution.

THE NEED FOR DIVERSITY

3 Cloning will be attractive because of some medical uses. Genetic replicas of geniuses might also benefit society. On the other hand, ruthless and egocentric despots may replicate themselves millions of times over. Cloning on a large scale would also reduce biological diversity, and the entire human species could be wiped out by some new epidemic to which a genetically uniform population was susceptible.

4 Beyond these important but obvious results, cloning raises problems that go to the core of human existence and purpose. One important fact to recognize is that cloning is asexual reproduction. It therefore bypasses both the biological benefits of normal reproduction and the emotional, psychological, and social aspects that surround it: courtship, love, marriage, family structure. Even more importantly, if cloning became the main mode of reproduction, human evolution would stop in its tracks.

5 In sexual reproduction, some of the genetic material from each parent undergoes mutations that can leads to entirely new biological properties. Vast numbers of individual combinations become possible, and the requirements of survival—and choices of partners by the opposite sex—then gradually select which features will be passed on to the following generations.

6 Cloning will, in contrast, reproduce the same genetic makeup of an existing individual. There is no room for new traits to arise by mutation and no room for desirable features to compete and win by appeal to the judgement of the opposite sex. The result: Human evolution is halted.

EVOLVING IN NEW WORLDS

7 Is it necessary for the human species to evolve further? Absolutely! We are certainly far from achieving perfection. We are prone to diseases, and the capacity of our intelligence is limited. Most importantly, human survival will depend on our ability to adapt to environments beyond Earth—that is, in the rich new worlds of outer space.

8 Some people question whether we can save ourselves from manmade environmental disasters on Earth, whose resources are already pressured by human population growth. And limiting the population to one planet puts us at risk for extinction from all-out nuclear or biological warfare, climate change, and catastrophic meteorite impacts.

9 Humanity could vastly expand its chances for survival by moving into space, where we would encounter worlds with diverse environments. To live in space, we will have to increase our tolerance to radiation, to extremes of heat and cold, and to vacuum. We will also need more intelligence to construct habitats. Our social skills will need to advance so that billions of humans can work together in the grand projects that will be needed.

10 If we are to expand into space, we surely cannot freeze human evolution. The natural (and possibly designed) mechanisms of evolution must therefore be allowed to continue.

PRESERVING LIFE

11 Socially, the relations between the sexes underlie most aspects of human behavior. The rituals of dancing, mating, and marriage and the family structures that surround sexual reproduction are the most basic emotional and social factors that make our lives human. Without the satisfactions of love and sex, of dating and of families, will cloned generations even care to propagate further?

12 Cloning therefore raises fundamental questions about the human future: Have we arrived yet at perfection? Where should we aim future human evolution? What is the ultimate human purpose? The prospect of human cloning means that these once-philosophical questions have become urgent practical issues.

13 As living beings, our primary human purpose is to safeguard, propagate, and advance life. This objective must guide our ethical judgments, including those on cloning.

14 Our best guide to this purpose is the love of life common to most humans, which is therefore reflected in our communal judgement. All individuals who sustain the present and build the future should have the right to participate equally in these basic decisions. Our shared future may be best secured by the practice of debating and voting on such biotechnology issues in an informed "biodemocracy."

Finish timing: Record time here: ____________ and use the Timed Readings Conversion Chart in the Appendix to figure your rate: ____________ wpm.

Comprehension Check

Directions: Answer the following questions. Try to use complete sentences:

1. What is Mautner's thesis or main point about the subject of cloning? ______

2. What is the main reason the author feels the public should consider the implications of cloning humans? ______

3. How does cloning differ genetically from sexual reproduction? ______

4. Cloning on a large scale would reduce biological diversity. Why, according to Mautner, is that good or bad? ______

5. The author says cloning will stop human evolution. Why, in his opinion, would this be wrong? ______

6. Why does the author believe that humanity may have to move into space in the future? ______

7. According to the author, in what ways would humans need to evolve in order to exist in space? ______

8. The author says the prospect of cloning means that once-philosophical questions have become urgent practical issues. What does he mean? ______

9. How would courtship, love, marriage, and family structure be affected by human cloning? ______

10. Is Mautner's thesis supported mostly by facts or opinions?

For every question you missed, find the place in the article that contains the correct answer. Try to determine why you missed the questions you did. If you read faster than you normally do, a score of 60 percent correct is considered good. As you get used to faster speeds, you will discover that your comprehension scores will improve.

Vocabulary Check

Directions: Explain what the underlined words or phrases mean as they are used in the article.

1. it [cloning] would freeze evolution (1)

   ____

2. the public should ponder the implications (2) ______________

   ____

3. ruthless and egocentric despots may replicate themselves (3)

   ____

4. ruthless and egocentric despots may replicate themselves (3)

   ____

5. cloning is asexual reproduction (4)

   ____

6. genetic material from each parent undergoes mutations (5)

   ____

7. relations between the sexes underlie most aspects of human behavior (11)

   ____

8. will cloned generations even care to propagate further (11)

   ____

9. must guide our ethical judgments (13)

   ____

10. All individuals who sustain the present (14)

    ____

Record your rate (wpm), comprehension, and vocabulary scores for this article on the Student Record Chart in the Appendix. Each question counts as 10 percent. An average score is around 250 wpm with 70 percent comprehension. Discuss any problems, concerns, or questions you have with your instructor.

Questions for Group Discussion

1. As a group, discuss Michael Mautner's opinions about cloning. Can your group think of any one living who should be cloned? If so, who and why?
2. Divide your group in two, one group arguing for cloning, the other group against. How much of each argument is based on facts and opinion?
3. If your group has access, use the online Opposing Viewpoints Resource Center and read an article that supports human cloning. Does the author support his or her points with mostly facts or opinions? With which author do you agree? Why?

CHAPTER FIVE

Recognizing Tone, Figurative Language, and Point of View

A. Recognizing Intent, Attitude, and Tone

In addition to distinguishing fact from opinion, critical reading requires an awareness of an author's *intent, attitude,* and *tone.*

An author's **intent** is not always easy to recognize. Let's say, for instance, that you are reading Jonathan Swift's essay "A Modest Proposal," an essay that appears frequently in English literature anthologies. At the time he wrote this essay in the eighteenth century, many Irish people were dying from famine. To read his essay at the literal level, Swift would seem to be in favor of taking the profusion of children in Ireland and treating them as cattle, fattening up some for slaughter, exporting some to boost the economy, and raising some strictly for breeding. However, to accept his essay on the literal level would be to miss his intent. His essay is a satire, and his intent was to make his readers more aware of a social problem that existed in his day. His real purpose was to ridicule the people in power at the time. He intentionally wrote in a rather cold, uncompassionate way to shock his readers into action. Yet, if you were not perceptive enough to understand Swift's intent, you could completely miss his point.

An author's intent may be to satirize a problem or condition; to amuse readers; to make them cry by arousing sympathy, pity, or fear; to argue a point that another writer has made; or to accuse someone of something. But whatever an author's intent may be, you, as a critical reader, need to be absolutely certain that you understand what it is.

An author's treatment of a subject reflects an **attitude** toward it. Swift, for instance, in the essay mentioned here, uses satire, but his attitude is serious. He is not serious about using children as an economic commodity, even though he provides a detailed plan for doing so. He was angry at the people of his day for allowing such deplorable conditions to exist. He was serious about wanting to change these conditions. An author's attitude, then, is the author's personal feeling about a subject. Attitudes can range from sad to happy, angry to delighted, sympathetic to unsympathetic, tolerant to furious.

The language an author uses is frequently a clue to that writer's attitude both to his or her subject and to the reader. In his book *Preface to Critical Reading,* Richard Altick provides a good example of how paying attention to the language a writer uses can reflect intent and attitude:

> Compare the two ways in which a person could express the desire [intent] to borrow some money: (1) "Hey, good buddy, how about loaning me a ten for a few days? I'm in a bind. You'll get it back on Friday." (2) "I'm very sorry to impose on you, but I'm in a bit of a predicament, and I need ten dollars just until payday. I'd be extremely grateful." The language of the first appeal suggests that slang is the normal means of expression for this speaker. The meaning of the second appeal is identical, and the general approach is the same. But whereas the first speaker is forthright and unembarrassed, the other seems hesitant and apologetic. The personalities of the two seem as different as the connotations of *bind* and *predicament.*
>
> Richard Altick, *Preface to Critical Reading,* Fifth Edition,
> Holt, Rinehart, and Winston, 1960, p. 90.

In other words, the intent of both the appeals in the example is the same; they want to borrow money. But the attitudes are different. Critical reading requires an ability to distinguish such differences.

How an author uses language creates what is called a **tone.** Tone in writing is similar to what we call a tone of voice. For instance, the phrase "Thanks a lot!" can have different meanings based on the tone of voice used to express it. If we are truly grateful, we will say it one way; if we want to be sarcastic, we'll say it another way; and if we are angry or disgusted, we'll say it still another way. When reading, however, we can't hear an author's tone of voice. But as critical readers, we must be able to recognize the true tone intended by the author.

The following practices will help you learn to recognize intent, attitude, and tone in various types of writing.

PRACTICE A-1

Directions: Read the following magazine article, looking for fact, opinion, intent, attitude, and tone. Then answer the questions that follow it.

HOW MUCH IS ENOUGH?

Alan Durning

1 In the days after World War II, a retailing analyst named Victor Lebow prophetically set the tone for the coming era: "Our enormously productive economy . . . demands that we make consumption our way of life, that we convert the buying and use of goods into rituals, that we seek our spiritual satisfaction, our ego satisfaction, in consumption. We need things consumed, burned up, worn out, replaced, and discarded at an ever-increasing rate." Americans have risen to Mr. Lebow's call, and much of the world has followed.

2 Since 1950, American consumption has soared. Per capita, energy use climbed 60 percent, car travel more than doubled, plastics use multiplied 20-fold, and air travel jumped 25-fold. We are wealthy beyond the wildest dreams of our ancestors.

3 But all this abundance—while taking a terrible toll on the environment—has not made people terribly happy. In the United States, repeated opinion polls of people's sense of well-being conducted by the University of Chicago's National Opinion Research Center show that Americans are no more satisfied with their lot now than they were in 1957. Despite phenomenal growth in consumption, the list of wants has grown faster still.

4 Psychological data from several nations confirm that the satisfaction derived from money does not come from simply having it. It comes from having more of it than others do and from having more this year than last. Thus, the bulk of survey data reveals that the upper classes in any society are more satisfied with their lives than the lower classes are, but they are no more satisfied than the upper classes of much poorer countries—nor than the upper classes were in the less-affluent past.

5 More striking, perhaps, most psychological data show that the main determinants of happiness in life are not related to consumption at all: Prominent among them are satisfaction with family life, especially marriage, followed by satisfaction with work, leisure, and friendships. Indeed, in a comprehensive inquiry into the relationship between affluence and satisfaction, social commentator Jonathan Freedman notes, "Above the poverty level, the relationship between income and happiness is remarkably small."

Now answer these questions.

1. T/F The opinions in this article are mostly based on fact.

2. Which of the following is the best statement regarding the article's intent?

- **a.** To report facts about consumption
- **b.** To question psychological data
- **c.** To prove that consumption doesn't bring contentment
- **d.** To objectively report facts on consumption and contentment

3. Which of the following best describes the author's attitude toward income and happiness?

- **a.** Concerned
- **b.** Open-minded
- **c.** Humorous
- **d.** Sarcastic

4. The tone of the article is

- **a.** objective.
- **b.** apologetic.
- **c.** humorous.
- **d.** bitter.

5. Based on what is presented in the article, do you believe consumption does not equal contentment? Explain. ______________________________

____

____

PRACTICE A-2

Directions: Read the following newspaper article, also about consumerism. As you read, consider the author's opinion, attitude, intent, and tone. You will also want to be thinking about how this article on consumerism compares and contrasts with the previous article.

IT'S AN EMBARRASSMENT OF STUFF, NOT RICHES

Suzan Nightingale

1 We've been dealing with stuff at our house—getting rid of old stuff to make room for new stuff; returning new stuff for other new stuff; packing away Christmas stuff; packing away wrapping stuff; calculating the logistics of where to put the rest of the new stuff.

2 It's a January tradition that always ignites my house-burning-down fantasy. In this particular fantasy, no one gets hurt and all the sentimental stuff gets saved but everything else burns to the ground. This gives us a chance to start fresh with no excess stuff.

3 Something tells me I'm not alone—like all those ads for closet organizers, stacking storage units, under-the-bed organizers and even professional storage advisors that pop up like ravens around a take-out dumpster this time of year. I even heard of one woman who joined a group whose sole purpose was to battle stuff. Every week, she

Reprinted by permission of the author: From *Anchorage Daily News,* January 14, 1996.

had to bring a trash bag full of stuff to a meeting to throw away. No one was allowed to look in anyone else's bag; it had to be thrown out, unopened.

4 It's hard to say when the stuff problem started in this country. Maybe with post-war foreign trade. Cheap labor meant cheap goods. Made it easier to afford more stuff, extra stuff, newer stuff.

5 Of course, Christmas has become the centerpiece of all this. The prevailing wisdom is that people will buy as much stuff as they can, year in and year out. This season, early as November, one of the credit card companies was singing the blues because people weren't whipping out their plastic at the same pace as previous years. "Crisis of confidence!" the company lamented. At that point, no one said people weren't buying; they just said people weren't charging.

6 Then, during the Monday morning quarterbacking earlier this month, retailers picked up the cry again, saying consumers had been too spooked about the economy to buy. Sales were down. The end was nigh.

7 Well, if you're a furloughed federal employee, it makes sense that you didn't shoot the wad in a big way this year. But most of us aren't furloughed federal employees. Most of us did the forced march on the malls the same as always.

8 Except for one thing. We bought less.

9 At our house, the decision was a conscious one. We looked around at the wrapping paper and the rubble last year and decided that wasn't the point of the exercise. It wasn't a question of economics as much as values. All those geegaws and cheap toys with 60-second warranties, well, cheapened the whole day. Judging from conversations I've had with other parents, plenty of people have reached the same conclusion.

10 Yet on Wall Street, the assumption continues to be that people will mindlessly buy stuff, lots of stuff, as much stuff as they can afford—or charge. Anything less is viewed as the portent of a nervous herd getting ready to stampede all the way to Alan Greenspan's house.

11 I think these guys have missed the message here. For most of middle-class America, the last thing we need is more stuff. And if there's anything we need less than more stuff, it's more cheap, disposable stuff with the life expectancy of a souffle.

Now answer these questions.

1. T/F The opinions in this article are mostly based on factual studies and reports.

2. What is the author's opinion about "stuff" at her house this year? ______________

____

3. Which of the following best describes the author's attitude toward stuff?

a. Concerned **c.** Humorous

b. Open-minded **d.** Sarcastic

4. Give at least one example from this article that shows the author's humorous tone.

____

5. Based on what is presented in the article, do you believe middle-class America is cutting down on consumption? Explain. ______________________________

____

Questions for Group Discussion

1. Explain some of the differences in these two articles and their approach to consumerism.
2. Which article did you find more convincing? Why?
3. Do you believe you have become more or less of a consumer in the last year? Why?

B. Recognizing Figurative Language

Frequently, writers use **figurative language** to express their tone. Figurative language is used in an imaginative way rather than in a literal sense. For instance, when a writer says, "her eyes flashed fire," the intent is not for us to imagine real fire coming from someone's eyes but to realize that the character is angry. Or, when we read that a lawyer "dropped his client like a hot potato," we are given to understand that the lawyer's actions were quick, just as we'd be quick to drop a hot potato.

Figurative language is familiar to everyone. A great deal of our slang and ordinary speech is based on figurative language, as well as a great many works in literature. Without figures of speech, our language would be dull and mechanical. It becomes, therefore, important in developing reading comprehension to know the difference between literal and figurative language. It also becomes important to know the difference between literal and figurative language in developing your aesthetic understanding of what you read.

One form of figurative language is the **metaphor.** A metaphor is a comparison of two things without the use of the words "like" or "as." For instance, when you say someone "clammed up and wouldn't talk," you are comparing the person's closed mouth with the tightness of a closed clam. When you say someone has a "stone face," you are comparing the unchanging expression with the immobility of stone.

Dead metaphors are metaphors that have been used so frequently that we accept them almost literally. Terms such as "a tenderfoot," "hands" on a watch, the "head" of a cane, a "run" in a stocking, or an engine "knocking" are all dead metaphors, yet they help us convey meaning that is seldom misunderstood. S. I. Hayakawa says that metaphors are probably the most important of all the means by which language develops, changes, grows, and adapts itself to our changing needs.

A **simile** is another form of figurative language. It, like a metaphor, compares one thing with another but uses the word "like" or "as." Examples of similes are: "out like a light," "sparkles like a lake," "sounds like a machine gun," "cool as spring water," and "phony as a three-dollar bill."

When metaphors and similes are overused, they turn into **clichés.** Clichés are worn-out figures of speech such as "a blanket of snow covered the hill," or "the silence was broken," or "my old lady." Such terms have been used so often in speech and writing that they lose their real effectiveness and seem stale.

Still another type of figurative language is **hyperbole.** Hyperbole is a deliberate exaggeration or overstatement used to emphasize a point being made. For instance, if a friend tells you she can't go to the movies because she has "mountains of homework" to do, she is using hyperbole. If someone tells you that the story was "so funny he almost died laughing," he's using hyperbole. If you "love someone to pieces," know someone who "talked your ear off," or couldn't get your work done because "the phone rang ten thousand times," then you have been dealing with hyperbole. Like overused similes and metaphors that have become clichés, it can happen with hyperbole, too.

Recognizing how authors use figurative language helps us clarify whether or not an author's attitude is serious, playful, sympathetic, outraged, sarcastic, bitter, humorous, and so on. Thus, attitude and tone are closely allied through the use of figures of speech.

PRACTICE B-1: Identifying Literal versus Figurative Language

Directions: The following statements are either literal or figurative. Place an *F* in the blank next to each statement that uses figurative speech. If you want more practice with the identification of figurative language, see Chapter Eight, Practice A-2.

_______ **1.** Mr. Timpkin went through the ceiling when his son told him that he had wrecked the car.

_______ **2.** Alyce waited eagerly for the show to start.

_______ **3.** Doreen's checks are bouncing all over town.

_______ **4.** The crowd was getting increasingly angry waiting for the musicians to show up.

_______ **5.** The battery is dead as a doornail.

_______ **6.** Prices are being slashed to rock bottom.

_______ **7.** Mom really stuck her neck out for you this time.

_______ **8.** I find myself out on a limb.

_______ **9.** When Jimmy screamed, her hair stood on end.

_______ **10.** The Giants were defeated 18–4 in the last game.

PRACTICE B-2: Recognizing Tone through Figurative Language

Directions: Read the following paragraphs and answer the questions that follow them.

1. There is an appalling cloud of illiteracy shadowing America's pride. We would do well to attack some basic causes for the lack of literacy facing us. Instead, we seem to throw more money down the drain for more grants and studies.

a. The expression "cloud of illiteracy shadowing America's pride" means _______

____

b. T/F The literary term for the phrase in question *a* is simile.

c. T/F Using the phrase "money down the drain" lets us know the author is happy with what efforts are taking place.

d. The tone of this passage is best described as

_______ serious concern. _______ concerned displeasure.

_______ humorous concern. _______ sarcastic.

2. My job was really starting to get to me. It seemed a dead end, a treadmill taking me nowhere. If I was to keep from blowing a fuse, I had to somehow shatter my negativity toward my work or go for broke and resign. After what seemed like centuries of indecisiveness, one day I plunked myself down at the typewriter, quickly tossed off my resignation, and boldly signed it with great flair. So I wouldn't chicken out at the last minute, I sailed into my boss's office and slapped it down on her desk.

a. The tone of this passage is best described as

______ one of relief. ______ frustration.

______ fear of losing a job. ______ indecision.

b. The phrase "go for broke" here means ______________________________

____

c. T/F "My treadmill job was a dead end" is an example of a metaphor.

d. T/F It is possible to literally shatter a negative attitude.

3. Out deeper, in cooler water, where trout live, floating on one's back is a kind of free ride, like being fifteen again, like being afloat upon another sky. Perhaps there is a bit of Tom Sawyer's pleasure at watching his own bogus funeral in this, but before we get overly morbid, a fish begins nibbling our toes. Floating on one's back is like riding between two skies. (From Edward Hoagland, "Summer Pond," *New York Times.*)

a. T/F The author mostly uses similes in the above passage.

b. The tone of the paragraph is best described as

______ lazy. ______ morbid.

______ pleasant. ______ sad.

c. T/F The intent of the passage is to relive the joys of swimming in a pond or lake.

4. "C'mon, we're supposed to be having fun," snaps her companion, a clone. In razor-crease jeans and stiletto heels they stamp into the ladies room, flounce around the corner past the polished washbasins and disappear into the two long rows of toilet stalls. They are the kind of girls who obey their mothers' warnings never to sit on strange toilet seats. Attendants have to nip in after that type, making sure the next woman will have no unpleasant surprises. (From Jane O'Reilly, "In Las Vegas: Working Hard for the Money," *Time,* January 9, 1984.)

a. T/F The phrase "razor-crease jeans and stiletto heels" reflects a negative attitude toward the girls.

b. T/F The intent of the passage is to gain sympathy for the two girls.

c. The tone of the passage can best be described as

______ humorous. ______ sweet.

______ sarcastic. ______ apathetic.

PRACTICE B-3

Directions: Read the following essay, looking for intent, attitude, tone, and figurative language.

THIRST FOR A HERO CAN GET US IN HOT WATER

Philadelphia Inquirer

1 At a low point of the Iraq war, when unexpected Iraqi opposition seemed to threaten U.S. troops with a morass, America badly needed a hero.

2 And it found one.

3 This was the story, and a compelling one it was. Pfc. Jessica Lynch, a fresh-faced, 19-year-old Army supply clerk from West Virginia, was miraculously rescued from a hospital in Nasiriyah where, gravely injured, she was being held captive.

4 The Washington Post quoted unnamed U.S. officials recounting that Ms. Lynch had engaged in a "fierce" firefight after her unit was ambushed following a wrong turn. She shot several enemy soldiers before her ammo ran out and she was captured.

5 "She was fighting to the death" and has multiple gunshot wounds, said an unnamed U.S. official in the story.

6 The most exciting part of the tale came next: Ms. Lynch's rescue.

7 The defense sources described for the Post a classic Special Operations raid, with commandos in Black Hawk helicopters engaging Iraqi forces on their way into and out of Ms. Lynch's medical compound.

8 The commandos had been directed there by a heroic Iraqi lawyer who was appalled to see the bedridden Ms. Lynch slapped twice in the face by one of her captors. This account was trumpeted by U.S. print and broadcast outlets far and wide.

9 The story was a balm to American hearts.

10 Except that much of it now appears to be untrue. The British Broadcasting Corp. cast cold water on the tale two weeks ago:

11 Ms. Lynch's injuries were probably caused by a road crash; she had received good treatment at the hospital; there wasn't a single armed opposition soldier in the hospital when the U.S. troops burst in, John Wayne style.

12 Later—too much later—the American media have begun examining the story they had so eagerly swallowed in April.

13 Thursday, a lengthy Chicago Tribune story quoted Iraqis on the scene who said that much of the Lynch hero/rescue story was, basically, bunk. (Ms. Lynch herself has no memory of events.)

14 Now this glorious tale must be traded for some complicated questions about the sticky entanglements of a rah-rah Pentagon, a thirsty press, and a public desperate for good news.

15 Those questions don't just concern the story of Jessica Lynch.

16 Early reports of her rescue were, as the saying goes, the first, rough-draft history. But, then, so too are all the accounts so far of this fast-moving war.

17 Stay tuned—perhaps decades from now—for the real story. What really did become of those weapons of mass destruction, if they existed at all? Where is Saddam Hussein? Exactly how many Iraqi civilians suffered and died?

18 It's too easy just to blame a sloppy press for overdramatizing the Jessica Lynch story initially. In the fog of war, most reporting is quick and dirty, with virtually no chance for outside corroboration. Clearly, in this case, at least some in the military

were eager to peddle the more heroic narrative. And, to journalism's credit, the original, faulty stories usually get revised when facts finally become clear.

19 Is Pfc. Lynch indeed a hero?

20 For volunteering to serve the way she did, and enduring the way she did, she is. There are no doubt thousands more untold stories about the heroism of individual American and British soldiers in Iraq.

21 But a search for the perfect heroic story—and eager acceptance of any "facts" that enhance the tale—does a disservice to both heroes and the truth.

Comprehension Check

Directions: Answer the following questions.

1. What is the intent of this article? ______________________________

____

2. Which of the following best describes the author's attitude toward the media's coverage of the Jessica Lynch story?

a. Sympathetic

b. Tolerant

c. Furious

d. Alarmed

3. Which of the following best describes the author's attitude toward the U.S. official who gave the story to the press?

a. Praise

b. Disturbing

c. Accepting

d. Can't tell

4. The tone of the essay is mostly

a. humorous.

b. nasty.

c. sarcastic.

d. troublesome.

5. The tone of paragraph 14 can best be described as:

a. mean.

b. sarcastic.

c. serious.

d. ecstatic.

6. Rewrite paragraph 12 without using any figurative language.

____

____

7. T/F ___The phrases "a rah-rah Pentagon" and "a thirsty press" in paragraph 14 are examples of figurative language.
8. Reread paragraph 10. What, if any, figurative language is being used?___________

____
9. What examples of figurative language are used in paragraph 18?

____

____
10. Why does the author believe the press reported the Jessica Lynch story without checking on the "unnamed U.S. official"?

____

____

Vocabulary Check

Directions: Define the following underlined words from the essay. The number in parenthesis refers to the paragraph where the word appears.

1. opposition seemed to threaten troops with a <u>morass</u> (1)

____
2. and a <u>compelling</u> one it was (3)

____
3. was <u>appalled</u> to see (7)

____
4. this account was <u>trumpeted</u> by U.S. print and broadcast outlets

____
5. perhaps <u>decades</u> from now (17)

____
6. about the sticky <u>entanglements</u> (14)

____
7. no chance for outside <u>corroboration</u> (18)

____
8. <u>enduring</u> the way she did (20)

____
9. "facts" that <u>enhance</u> the tale (21)

____
10. a <u>disservice</u> to both heroes and the truth (21)

____

Record the results of the comprehension and vocabulary checks on the Student Record Chart in the Appendix.

PRACTICE B-4

Directions: Read the following essay, looking for intent, attitude, tone, and figurative language.

HOLLYWOOD PLAYS TO THE PIMPLY

Frank Pierson

About the author: *Frank Pierson, who wrote Cat Ballou, Cool Hand Luke, and Dog Day Afternoon, among others, was president of the Academy of Motion Picture Arts and Sciences when he gave this adapted speech to a graduating class of University of Southern California's film school.*

1 Hollywood was once a small company town, where everybody knew everybody, and if you dropped your pants at a party or punched a reporter or danced with a prostitute in the parking lot, it wasn't on "Entertainment Tonight" tonight.

2 It was even hard to get arrested. Every studio had a publicity department that paid the Los Angeles cops to stay away from show-business people. The police didn't arrest movie people. They drove them home.

3 We all went down to the film factories every day (at Warner Bros. even actors, directors and writers punched a time clock until the mid-1940s). We ate in the studio commissary, where the writer's table was preferred seating because the jokes were better there. If the New York writers were in town, slumming—sneering at the movies and cashing big, fat paychecks—you found yourself sitting next to Dorothy Parker or F. Scott Fitzgerald.

4 You could wander off to a sound stage and watch John Huston or Willy Wyler shooting a scene with Bogart or Hepburn or Peck. No security. We all knew each other.

5 It was up close, and personal.

6 Harry Cohn, the head of Columbia, was a legendary bully who admired Mussolini and had his office designed to resemble Mussolini's—with a long approach into blinding lights and himself behind a desk, raised a foot above the floor, ranks of Oscars his studio had won behind him. He said he made only pictures that he wanted to see, and once the public stopped wanting to see what he liked, he'd quit. Not for him delegating decisions to demographers, pollsters and marketing experts. Nobody knew what a demographer was in those days.

7 It was up close, and personal.

8 Then, in the 1960s, when the glove salesmen and carnival touts who built the studios began to grow old and retire, their grip on the business loosened. For a while, independent producers flourished. New companies, new writers and directors burst the bonds of studio-imposed style.

9 The '60s and the '70s produced movies now looked upon as a golden age: "The Godfather," "One Flew Over the Cuckoo's Nest," "Dr. Strangelove," "Taxi Driver," "Chinatown," "Clockwork Orange," "Annie Hall," "Midnight Cowboy," "MASH," "Bonnie and Clyde," and a couple I like, "Dog Day Afternoon" and "Cool Hand Luke." Even "Easy Rider," which symbolized the anarchistic spirit of that drug-ridden time, was a Columbia release.

10 Then, on Wall Street, it began to be noticed that a single blockbuster movie could make in a weekend what a substantial business made in a year.

11 Warner Bros. was bought by Seven Arts, Seven Arts was bought by Kinney Shoes, and the whole mess is now owned by AOL Time Warner (as are HBO, Warner Books, Turner networks, and CNN). Viacom owns Paramount, CBS, Showtime cable, and Blockbuster. Of the 100-odd prime-time shows that will premier on the four networks this fall and winter, more than 30—including CBS newsmagazines—will be made by companies owned by Viacom. An additional 25 or so will be made by Rupert Murdoch's News Corp., which owns the Fox network.

12 We had been having too much fun to notice: The barbarians were inside the gate. The polo games, the writers' table, Jack Warner's lunchtime tennis matches with Errol Flynn, the cops as our friends, all were a thing of the past.

13 We began to see Harvard Business School MBAs sit in on story conferences. Lawyers multiplied.

14 As the huge debt created by mergers was added to the rising costs of making little but blockbusters, the risks of making a film forced the businessmen to be risk-averse, to play to the least critical audience: teenage boys with disposable income.

15 The problem is how to keep this "average" moviegoer, male, 16 to 25, high school education at best, doesn't read books, gets his news from the 11 o'clock news if he bothers at all, never heard of Mussolini and thinks Korea is another part of downtown L.A. This pimply, oversexed slob with the attention span of a chicken, how do we keep him awake and interested while staying awake and interested ourselves?

16 It's not just Hollywood. What has happened here has happened to us all because the focus of international business has shifted from production to distribution. Whoever controls distribution shapes what is produced—to what will fit under the seat or in the overhead compartment. Today, agribusinesses have researchers trying to produce cube-shaped tomatoes that will be easier to pack in boxes (and that probably will taste like the boxes). Watch the odd, the old, the personal, the traditional, the idiosyncratic, the family-made, or the regional disappear from supermarket shelves that are rented by the foot to international companies that then stock them with their own water and sugar products.

17 As the movie business has changed, liberal critics have raised the alarm over corporate censorship. But the danger of censorship in the United States of America is less from business or the religious right or the self-righteous left than from self-censorship by artists themselves, who simply give up. If we can't see a way to get our story told, what is the point of trying? I wonder how many fine, inspiring ideas are strangled in the womb of the imagination because there's no way past the gates of commerce.

18 To the studios today, the art of film and TV is a byproduct of their main business, a side effect, and like most side effects, more likely to be a noxious nuisance than a benefit.

19 But movies are more than a commodity. Movies are to our civilization what dreams and ideals are to individual lives: They express the mystery and help define the nature of who we are and what we are becoming.

20 We need writers with ideas and passion, who write with force and conviction; directors who have minds enriched by their lives and not a library of stunts and special effects. They must be centered in their feelings and ideas in the culture and society, not in comparing grosses and applauding computer-generated ballets of violence.

21 We need it like we need clean drinking water and roads, green parks and libraries; it is as important as the breath of democratic life. Somehow we need to keep alive in our hearts the vision of community, shared interests and understanding of our neighbors' needs, the sense of connection this fractionated society is losing.

22 We need to recapture the spirit of Main Street. Up close. And personal.

Comprehension Check

Directions: Answer the following questions.

1. What does the author's title mean? ____

____

2. Which of the following best describes Pierson's attitude toward those in control of making movies and television programs?

a. Pleased

b. Shocked

c. Favorable

d. Disapproving

3. Pierson's intent is to

a. compare the old days of movie making with the present.

b. criticize Harvard Business School MBAs.

c. show how business mergers have changed the art of film and television into a byproduct of the corporation's main business.

d. praise the era of the 1960s and 1970s for producing the movies now looked upon as a golden age.

4. The tone of paragraph 1 is

a. serious.

b. playful.

c. wry.

d. bitter.

5. In paragraph 9, what pattern is used and for what purpose?

____

____

6. Several times, Pierson uses the phrase "Up close, and personal." What does he mean? (See paragraphs 5, 7, and 22.)

____

____

7. T/F When Pierson says in paragraph 12, "The barbarians were inside the gate," he is referring to the business conglomerates.

8. Reread the last sentence in paragraph 17. What does the author mean when he says he wonders "how many fine, inspiring ideas are strangled in the womb of the imagination"?____

____

____

9. T/F Pierson uses a metaphor when he says the average moviegoer has the attention span of a chicken.

10. What does Pierson mean in paragraph 20 when he calls for directors not to compare grosses or applaud "computer-generated ballets of violence"?______________

____

____

Class discussion question: Name a movie you have seen recently that relies more on computer-generated action than on human dialogue trying to recapture "the spirit of Main Street."

Vocabulary Check

Directions: Develop your own vocabulary test for this practice by selecting ten words you don't know and writing them on vocabulary cards. After you have had a chance to write the definitions, have a classmate test you on them. Share your cards with another classmate and see if they know the answers to your words.

Turn in your words to your instructor and record the results of your comprehension on the Student Record Chart in the Appendix.

> ***Application I: Finding Figurative Language in Other Materials***
>
> In magazines, newspapers, or textbooks, find at least two examples of metaphors or similes and underline them. Write a sentence about how the figurative language shows the author's tone and attitude.

C. Comparing Biased Points of View

A writer's attitude toward a subject may not be ours. However, as critical readers, it is important not to let either the author's **bias** or our own interfere with critical comprehension. Being biased means being prejudiced about or having a special leaning toward something. For instance, you may be biased about the type of music you listen to. Maybe you have no patience with classical music and prefer hard rock. That is a bias. Perhaps you are biased when it comes to food and would rather eat vegetables than meat. Everyone is biased about something, whether it's music, food, religion, politics, or people. Many of our biases are unconsciously learned from parents, friends, people we admire, or teachers. Reading critically can help us examine our own biases for their value.

While we are free to make up our own minds about a subject, we must still examine carefully the arguments and reasons of an author with opinions different from ours. We must recognize those biases of the author and not allow our own biases to interfere or shut out those of the author. Once we critically examine what we read, we should reflect on its worth before accepting or rejecting it.

Most of us tend to accept readily the ideas of writers who have the same biases we do, and we tend to reject the views of those we have biases against. To do so is to be closed minded. As critical readers, we must be willing to make critical judgments based on reason rather than emotion.

As you learn to read critically, you need to recognize bias in writing. If you don't, you may become the victim of an author's propaganda. You may miss seeing how an author takes facts and misrepresents them. You may not see that an author is being more subjective (using personal opinions) than objective (using undistorted facts). Or you may be unaware of how one-sided some writing is.

Sometimes recognizing an author's bias is easy; at other times it isn't. Bias is apt to be present in advertisements, newspaper and magazine editorials, and religious and political pamphlets. You generally pay little attention to an author's bias when it matches your own. When you don't agree with an author, the reverse is true. To read critically requires real involvement in the text and in thinking through what is being read. In effect, critical reading *is* thinking.

The following passage appeared in *Consumer Reports,* a publication of Consumers Union, a nonprofit organization. Read it and then answer the questions that follow.

> The letter, marked "confidential," was from the R.I. Research Special Human Being Laboratory in New York City and was signed by one Dr. Roger Grimstone. It informed the recipient that, based on the date and hour of her birth, she was an extraordinary individual, "apart from the rest of humanity," a "Beyonder."
>
> "Owing to some cosmic quirk," the letter went on, "your destiny operates independently of any stars. . . . Why have you suffered so much? *Why has true happiness, true love, wealth, a happy home always been out of your reach?* Why have the things you've yearned for most been snatched away?"
>
> Simple. According to the good Dr. Grimstone, it's because the recipient has yet to send him 20 bucks for something entitled "The Guide."
>
> The reader who sent us Dr. Grimstone's solicitation has a different theory, however. He believes that his daughter, the recipient of the letter, has yet to find happiness, companionship, and financial security because she is only four months old. (From "Selling It" copyright © 1987 by Consumers Union of U.S., Inc., Yonkers, NY 10703-1057, a nonprofit organization. Reprinted with permission from the September 1987 issue of *Consumer Reports* for educational purposes only. No commercial use or photocopying permitted. Log onto: *www.ConsumerReports.org.*)

1. What is the intent of the "confidential" letter sent by the R.I. Research Special Human Being Laboratory? ____________________

____

____

____

2. What is the intent of the article from *Consumer Reports?* ____________________

____

____

____

3. What attitude toward the recipient is implied by the originators of the letter?

____

____

4. What is *Consumer Reports's* attitude toward the laboratory? ____________________

____

____

____

5. What is the tone of the letter sent by Dr. Grimstone? ____________________

____

____

6. What is the tone of the passage from *Consumer Reports?* ________________

____

____

Your answers to the questions may be worded differently from the following, but see if they don't match up. The answer to the first question is to sell "The Guide" for twenty dollars by appealing to the recipient's "uniqueness" and desire for more wealth, happiness, and health, things most all of us want more of. The intent of *Consumer Reports,* the second question, is to expose the "Laboratory" as a fraud.

The third question can be answered by looking at such phrases as "apart from the rest of humanity," "owing to some cosmic quirk," and "Beyonder." The laboratory believes there are enough people (suckers?) who believe in astrology and who are dissatisfied enough with their lives (or curious enough) that they are willing to spend twenty dollars to find "the answer." *Consumer Reports's* attitude is that the whole thing is phony.

The tone of the letter is tied in with attitude. The letter's tone, based on what quotes are given, seems serious about wanting to help. Even the "doctor's" name is serious sounding—Grimstone (or is it a subtle touch of humor on the sender's part?). *Consumer Reports's* tone is humorous. Waiting until the end of the passage to let us know that the "confidential" letter was sent to a four-month-old makes us chuckle. We realize that phrases such as "the good Dr. Grimstone" and "20 bucks" provide a light, playful tone to it.

Critical reading requires identifying an author's point of view and motives. Nearly all controversial subjects are written from a particular point of view or bias. By their very nature, such controversial subjects cannot be written about with complete objectivity. For instance, if a Catholic priest were to write about abortion, chances are his point of view would reflect opposition by the very nature of his training and religious beliefs. On the other hand, a social worker who has seen many teenage lives destroyed because of unwanted pregnancies might very well speak in favor of abortion. Even though the priest and the social worker have different points of view, their motives are the same—to convince us their particular viewpoint is the correct one. As critical readers—and thinkers—we need to be alert to as many points of view as possible before making up our own minds on controversial issues. Then we need to examine the reasoning used to support those viewpoints.

Here are a few guides to follow so that you don't fall victim to poor reasoning. Watch out for:

1. Statements that oversimplify or distort the issue being discussed
2. Irrelevant or unsupported evidence
3. Left-out or suppressed information or evidence
4. Appeals to the emotions rather than reasonable evidence
5. Mudslinging, or attacks on people or groups rather than the issue itself

6. References to or quotations from the Bible or historical figures even though there is no connection to the issue

These are the most frequent, although not all, of the devices used to sway people to accept a particular point of view. They appear in advertisements, political campaigns, newspaper and magazine columns, editorials, and television commentaries.

The next reading is a syndicated column from the *Boston Globe* newspaper that appeared in hundreds of newspapers around the country. The subject has to do with the censorship of movies, videocassettes, television programs, and rock music. Before you read it, answer the following questions about your own biases regarding censorship.

1. Do you believe in censorship of any kind? ____________ Explain.____________

____

____

____

2. Do you believe that the electronic media (TV, videocassettes, records, radio) are generally responsible for the rise in drug addiction, adolescent suicides, and a decline in Scholastic Aptitude Test (SAT) scores? _________ Explain. _________

____

____

____

____

Now read the following essay, using the six previously listed guidelines that outlined what you should watch for when reading about controversial issues. Then answer the questions that follow the essay.

SHIELD OUR YOUTH WITH CENSORSHIP

William Shannon

1 The United States today has a popular culture at war against the nation's children and youth. Movies, video cassettes, television programs, and rock music have produced what the late Harvard sociologist Pitirim Sorokin called a "sensate culture." The message of this popular culture is "Feel good." What one thinks hardly matters.

2 These media bombard young people with sounds and images for several hours each day. The two dominant themes are sexual pleasure and sadistic violence. The indescribable "highs" and mysterious charms of using drugs also lurk as subsidiary themes.

3 The effect of this non-stop sensual assault is anti-intellectual and anti-academic. It is difficult for any classroom teacher to compete with the exciting images projected by television and films. Serious use of the mind requires patience, self-discipline, and the ability to defer present gratification in favor of future achievement. Very little in our culture supports these serious values. On the contrary, the fast pace and pounding rhythms of rock music and violent films tell impressionable youngsters "Go, go, go . . . now, now, now."

4 Parents are engaged in an uneven battle against this popular culture. There are still young persons who read for pleasure and who do well in school, but their number dwindles. The middle range of children muddles through high school and some go through college, but the general level of their academic achievement is significantly below what it was 30 years ago. The number of vulnerable youngsters cruelly damaged or destroyed by this culture grows. Victims are at every level of intelligence and family income. Their vulnerability is a matter of temperament, family history, and perhaps genetic endowment.

5 The casualty figures in this uneven battle between conscientious parents and the popular culture appear in the form of a rising number of adolescent suicides and drug addicts and in the Scholastic Aptitude Test scores, which have fallen significantly from their levels of 20 years ago. Parents try various expedients. Wealthy families send their children to private boarding schools in the hope that tight scheduling of time and close supervision by teachers will reduce the risks.

6 Other families—some of them non-Catholic—turn to the Catholic schools, in the hope that the schools' traditionally stricter discipline and the greater respect for authority that they inculcate will save their children.

7 No place in this society is a sanctuary, however, from the brutal and corrupting pressures of our popular culture. Schools of every kind, public and private, secular and religious, struggle valiantly to instill good work habits and encourage intellectual values, but the opposing cultural pressures are too pervasive.

8 The film industry makes much of ratings such as "R" for restricted to adults, and "PG" for parental guidance suggested, but these ratings are close to useless.

9 The only solution is to restore prior censorship over the electronic media. Everyone older than 50 grew up in a time when Hollywood films were strictly censored by the industry itself to exclude explicit sexual scenes, gruesome violence, and vulgar language. The Supreme Court in the 1950s struck down movie censorship. It extended to film makers the First Amendment protection traditionally enjoyed by newspapers and book publishers. The court also redefined the anti-pornography and anti-obscenity statutes into meaninglessness.

10 Those decisions were praised as liberal advances, but their consequences were unforeseen and disastrous. It would require a constitutional amendment to reverse those decisions. Unless they are reversed, the coarsening and corrupting of the nation's youth will continue.

Now answer the following questions:

1. What is the author's point of view toward censorship? ______________________

____

2. What is his attitude toward movies, videocassettes, and rock music? ___________

____

3. What is his intent in writing this essay? ______________________________

____

4. The statements made in paragraph 3 are factual.

   a. True because ______________________________________

   b. False because ______________________________________

5. The statements made in paragraph 3 are supported with evidence.

a. True because____

b. False because____

6. Statements such as "The only solution is to restore prior censorship over the electronic media" oversimplify the issue being discussed.

a. True because____

b. False because____

7. By blaming today's problems on the Supreme Court of the 1950s, the author is mudslinging rather than dealing rationally with the issue.

a. True because____

b. False because____

8. Circle any of the following that you feel the author does:

a. Makes irrelevant or unsupported statements

b. Oversimplifies the problem and solution

c. Refers to the Bible for support

d. Appeals to the emotions rather than providing reasonable evidence

9. For each of the items you circled in question 8, find a passage in the essay that serves as an example. ____

____

____

It's not too difficult to answer the first question. The title of the essay provides us with our first clue: "Shield Our Youth with Censorship." As we read through the essay, the author makes it clear he blames the electronic media as the corrupting pressure on today's youth. Thus, his attitude is negative. His intent seems to be to push for censorship of some kind, to bring a constitutional amendment that would reverse the Supreme Court's earlier decision. Otherwise, he says in the last paragraph, "the coarsening and corrupting of the nation's youth will continue."

Both questions 4 and 5 are false. The author makes three statements in paragraph 3, each one an opinion as stated. Though he may be correct, he needs facts to support his opinions. But instead of providing facts, he moves on to "the effects of this non-stop sensual assault."

Questions 6 and 7 are both true. The issue is too complex for such a simple solution. When he blames the Supreme Court of the 1950s for today's problems, he not only simplifies the issue again but also enters into what is called "mudslinging," attacking the Court rather than the problem he claims the electronic media are causing.

As to questions 8 and 9, he uses all but *c*. We've already seen that paragraph 3 is full of unsupported statements. Another example is the last sentence in paragraph 3. The last three sentences in paragraph 4 are also unsupported. Then in paragraph 5, he links adolescent suicides, drug addiction, and a decline in SAT scores together as though all of these are related to the electronic media. Admittedly, he could be correct, but his argument is not very convincing. His tone is frequently emotional. Wording and phrases such as "vulnerable youngsters cruelly damaged," "no place is a sanctuary," and "a popular culture at war against the nation's children" all appeal to our emotions. Censorship of any type is a serious matter. To accept the author's premise and solution as written is to do so without solid facts or rational reasoning.

It's important to remember that Shannon may be right. What we as critical readers must do is recognize his point of view or bias, then see what facts he provides to support his thesis. If his facts or supporting arguments are valid, then we should consider his point of view before making up our minds, especially if we disagree with him. If we already agree with him, but have no more facts or reasons to support our point of view than he has, then we need to critically evaluate our own reasons for having the views we do. One of the primary reasons for reading a wide range of viewpoints is to acquire, broaden, and strengthen intelligent views of our own.

Too often we tend to accept the views of others we trust or admire without examining the logic or reasoning behind them. Many people practice the religion they do not because they have truly examined the creeds but because parents or friends are members of that religion. Many politicians have been elected to office not because they are the best qualified but because they make a good impression in public. Many countries have gone to war not because it was the right thing to do but because people were led to believe it was the only solution to a problem.

The next set of practices will help you develop your critical reading skills in these areas.

PRACTICE C-1: Comparing Two Authors

Directions: Skim back over "How Much Is Enough?" on page 176 and "It's an Embarrassment of Stuff, Not Riches" on page 177. You may want to look over the answers to the questions that follow the two essays. Then answer the following questions:

1. Do you think the two authors would agree on the subject of consumerism? _____

Explain. ______________________________

____

____

2. Which essay has more facts to support its thesis? Explain. ______________

____

____

____

3. With which author do you agree? ______________________

Why?______________________________

____

____

4. Which essay is the most convincing? Explain. ______________________

____

____

____

____

5. Upon what is your bias based? ______________________________

____

____

____

____

PRACTICE C-2: Are We Overemphasizing the Importance of a Four-Year College Degree?

Directions: Before reading the next selection, answer the following questions.

1. I believe that a four-year college degree is

a. important because ______________________________

____

b. unimportant because ______________________________

____

2. I believe that our society overemphasizes the importance of a four-year college degree.

a. True because ______________________________

____

b. False because ______________________________

____

3. I personally have the following educational goals ______________________________

because ______________________________

____

You are about to read in this practice and Practice C-3 an exchange of two essays published in an American Federation of Teachers *On Campus* newsletter. This essay was written by Kenneth Gray, a professor of education at Pennsylvania State University and the author of *Getting Real: Helping Teens Find Their Future.* The other author, Susan J. Kaufman, is a professor of journalism at Eastern Illinois University and president of the EIU chapter of the University Professionals of Illinois. Both were asked to respond to the topic: Are we overemphasizing the importance of a four-year college degree?

Read the following essay by Kenneth Gray. Look for his stand on college degrees and his supporting points, intent, attitude, and bias.

THERE ARE OTHER WAYS TO WIN

Kenneth Gray

1 Today's teens, and seemingly everyone else, have concluded that getting a four-year college degree is the only sure path to economic security. In national studies, 85 percent of teens say they plan to get a university degree; 77 percent say in order to get "a good job." Yet, as college faculty know, too few of these students are academically prepared, and even fewer have pondered the details regarding what they want to study.

2 A baccalaureate education has become the default decision for many teens and their parents as well. Not knowing what else to do, these students enroll. Worse still, those who pursue postsecondary technical education, who consider waiting out a year, or who choose not go to college at all are labeled "weird."

3 Today, 72 percent of teens try college within two years of graduation. Of these, two-thirds are working toward a university degree. Should we celebrate how much opportunity we provided? I don't think so. Why? Because, the majority fail. Only half graduate in six years. And for about half of these students, the reward is underemployment.

4 Yes, university grads make more money, but for this generation, there are more grads each year than college level jobs. A four-year degree used to be a ticket to the professional ranks; today it is analogous to a ticket for an oversold airplane. For example, it has been estimated that for every 100 graduates, the economy annually will generate only 57 job openings that require a four-year degree. Indicative of the situation, 43 percent of recent university grads polled in a new national study said they held jobs that did not require a degree.

5 But there are other ways to win. Unlike the demand for four-year college graduates, there is a national shortage of technicians trained at the secondary and postsecondary pre-baccalaureate level. The second highest paying occupational group in the economy is craft/precision manufacturing/specialized repair. Those trained at the journeymen/associate degree level in these occupations have, as a group, higher annual earnings than four-year college grads.

6 The "one way to win" paradigm is great for some teens, but does the same plan make sense for all? In my view there is an unwarranted preoccupation with baccalaureate education; few find the promised opportunity. All students should go on to higher education, but only when: (1) they know why, (2) have the pre-requisite academic skills, and (3) have considered all the alternatives including one- and two-year technical education. Most important, it is time to stop looking down at those who do not go to college. After all, someday one of them could be your boss.

Now answer the following questions.

1. Circle the best statement of the *main point* being made in Gray's essay.

a. Most students should go on to higher education.

b. A university degree is still the best path to a good job.

c. Technical education is a better choice for most students today.

d. Most teens conclude that a four-year college degree is essential, but there are other ways to win.

2. The author's basic intent is

a. to convince students that a university degree is not the only path to jobs and financial security.

b. to maintain that most students who get a university degree still find it helpful.

c. to show that a university degree is a ticket to a professional job.

d. to change our view on technical education.

3. The author's attitude is

a. sarcastic. **c.** condescending.

b. sincere. **d.** humorous.

4. The author's tone is one of

a. anger. **c.** sadness.

b. concern. **d.** sympathy.

5. The section of the essay about technical education is mostly factual.

a. True

b. False because______________________________

6. This author is biased toward the value of one- and two-year technical education programs.

a. True

b. False because______________________________

7. Is this essay mostly objective or subjective? Explain. ____________________

____

____

8. Explain how your own bias toward college degrees may have an effect on your reaction to this essay. ______________________________

____

____

PRACTICE C-3

Directions: The following essay is a response to the essay you read in Practice C-2. Look for the author's stand on four-year degrees and her supporting points, intent, attitude, and bias.

IT'S ABOUT EMPOWERMENT, NOT JOBS

Susan J. Kaufman

1 Scratch the surface of the question and issues of gender, race, and class come into view. W.E.B. Du Bois knew that a century ago. His support of liberal arts education

drew the line in the sand that separated him from Booker T. Washington, champion of vocational-technical education.

2 "Never make the mistake of thinking that the object of being a man is to make a carpenter," Du Bois told a Boston audience in 1891. "The object of being a carpenter is to be a man." Higher education is about more than jobs. Du Bois knew that higher education is the third leg of the tripod of empowerment. Joining higher education with civil rights and political power creates a solid base from which to guarantee equal opportunity for people of every economic level.

3 In 1997, a Rand Institute report, "The Fiscal Crisis of Higher Education," called for community colleges to develop school-to-work programs with high schools, local governments, and business. The report recommended stripping the liberal arts mission from public undergraduate institutions and shifting it to the enclaves of independent (private) colleges and universities. (Today, voucher advocates stalk the corridors of the nation's state houses seeking a similar outcome, that is, a shift of public funds that benefit many to private entities for the benefit of the few.) The Rand report authors tossed public institutions two well-gnawed bones: teacher training and research/technical assistance for regional economic development. Federal research funding was to be given to the nation's top-ranked research universities, emptying the coffers of 800 or so universities and laboratories. The suggested changes were to be made cost-effective by using new technology.

4 Rand researchers spoke not a word in support of preserving the fundamentals of the Jeffersonian ideal of education: freedom of mind, equality of opportunity, establishment and maintenance of a classless nation. Their silence contrasts with the words of as unlikely a liberal arts booster as Alan Greenspan, chairman of the Federal Reserve Board. "A liberal arts education encourages an appreciation for life experiences," he told educators at a meeting of the American Council of Education, adding that "the challenge for our institutions of higher education is to successfully blend the exposure to all aspects of human intellectual activity, especially our artistic propensities and our technical skills."

5 If anything, we are underemphasizing the importance of public four-year education. The public must understand the consequences if one of the legs of the empowerment tripod collapses. The people of this nation need to know that public education is not merely another market. The nature of a university is far more complex and cannot be measured by the corporate bottom line.

Now answer the following questions.

1. Circle the best statement of the *main idea* of the essay.

a. The Rand Institute report wrongly favors private over public universities.

b. A liberal arts education encourages an appreciation for life experiences.

c. Higher education is the third leg of the tripod of empowerment.

d. The corporate bottom line is not a good way to measure education.

2. The author's main intent is

a. to show agreement on basic principles with the previous essay.

b. to persuade the public of the importance of liberal arts degrees in public institutions.

c. to convince students that technical education provides equal opportunity for people of every economic level.

d. to dispute the Rand report findings.

3. The author's attitude toward a four-year degree is

a. neutral.
b. negative.
c. positive.
d. not apparent.

4. The author's tone is

a. sarcastic.
b. silly.
c. humorous.
d. intellectual.

5. The author is biased against which of the following? (Select all that apply.)

a. Vocational-technical education
b. Public universities
c. Private universities
d. The Rand Institute report

6. Explain why this essay is mostly subjective or objective. ____________________

____

____

7. Explain what Kaufman means when she concludes her essay by saying, "The nature of a university is far more complex and cannot be measured by the corporate bottom line." ____________________

____

____

8. Explain which of the two essays is most convincing in their point of view.

____

____

____

Questions for Group Discussion

1. Discuss what Kaufman means by "empowerment," and why she considers it important.
2. Gray says people should go to college if they have followed three criteria (know why, have prerequisite academic skills, and explored alternatives). Does your group agree with these? Should there be other criteria?
3. Gray talks primarily about jobs and Kaufman talks primarily about empowerment. As a group, come up with an educational goal that would fulfill both these concepts.

D. Putting It All Together

The next two reading selections provide practice in what you have learned in this chapter and previous ones. First, read the following essay by Randy Alcorn, a newspaper editor. To find current information, quotations, or pictures of this author use the World Wide Web. Using a search engine such as Google or AltaVista, type the author's name under "Search."

PRACTICE D-1

Directions: Read the following selection by Randy Alcorn. Look for his thesis, supporting points, opinions, intent, attitude, and tone.

GODS ARE CREATED IN OUR OWN IMAGE

Randy Alcorn

1 Because religion has been an essential part of man's psychology, priests historically have wielded tremendous influence in affairs of state. The principle of keeping religion separate from government is a rather recent development in human history, and some folks haven't quite caught up yet.

2 There is growing pressure from some Americans to involve religion more deeply and directly into secular policy. Recently, we have seen Catholic bishops threatening to excommunicate Catholic politicians who, when conducting governmental duties, do not adhere to the tenets of their faith. We have seen an Alabama Supreme Court justice lose his job over his insistence on keeping the Biblical Ten Commandments displayed in stone in the lobby of that state's courthouse. We have seen the president of the United States exercising executive fiat to draw the church and government closer together to affect public policy.

3 Perhaps this atavistic behavior is to be expected. As soon as human creatures developed self-awareness they developed religions. Religion is man's way of explaining the mystery of his own existence, and reflects his own hopes and fears. The prehistoric talismans of plumply pregnant women represented the importance of female fertility and mirrored the overwhelming concern prehistoric man had for survival of his species. The gods of ancient Egypt ruled over the annual cycle of Nile flooding so vital to food production. Matters of life and death have long been considered the province of the divine, so why shouldn't the divine be dictating the affairs of men on earth?

4 There are those who staunchly believe this should be so, and while it is the right of every human to believe in the religion of his or her choice, it's not the right of any human to dictate religious beliefs to, or interfere with the harmless behavior of, others. The consequences of governing with or through religion include such horrors as human sacrifice, mass murder, torture, and a variety of state-sanctioned persecutions and confiscations.

5 One of the vexing problems with religion is there are so many of them, and the followers of all these mythical explanations of existence unquestionably believe in the absolute truth of their particular explanation. Even within a particular religion, like Islam or Christianity, there can be a multitude of denominations and sects all devoted to a unique version of the "truth" that makes all others "infidels."

6 Christianity and Islam are founded on remarkably malleable, if not inconsistent, ancient documents. The Christian Bible has a curious capacity for contradiction frequently condoning and condemning the same behavior. Its variety of interpretations has not only provided the genesis of a multitude of sects and denominations, but has also proved useful in supporting conflicting positions on many issues. Quoting the Bible to support one's position becomes a form of verbal fencing that can even be amusing, except when it enters the arena of public policy: then it can become oppressive, even deadly.

Reprinted by permission of Don Addis

7 The debate on marriage rights for homosexuals now swirls in the swill cooked up when religion becomes a primary ingredient in public policy. Christians in politics assert that their Bible clearly labels homosexuality as sin and an affront to God. Therefore government should not recognize or even permit legal matrimony between same-sex couples. Some good Christians don't want same-sex couples adopting and raising children for fear that the "unholy perversion" of homosexuality will be propagated among the innocent young. Have children been any safer in the care of Catholic clerics?

8 When religion infects government a nation can suffer some weirdly irresponsible public policy. Recall James Watt, interior secretary under President Reagan, who when questioned about the alarming depletion of natural resources, including clean water, forests, and topsoil, cavalierly responded that it didn't matter because Jesus is coming back soon anyway. Coming back to what?

9 Perverse notions of morality based on religion certainly are not peculiar to Christianity. Muslim terrorists interpret their religion's doctrine in a way that justifies mass murder and suicide, even of children. Nations ruled by theocracies or "holy" laws, such as Iran and Saudi Arabia, can in good conscience punish, persecute, even murder in the name of God. In nations brainwashed by religious dogma, what greater claim to legitimacy can those in power have than to be enforcing the will of God?

10 Why would the omnipotent creator of the universe require that fallible mortals record and enforce Its will? Why wouldn't God just come grab us by the lapels and say, "Listen buddy, this is what I want you to understand"? That would quickly silence the cacophony of religious opinions and eliminate the interpreters.

11 At the least, Christianity ought to retire the Bible as its doctrinal document and replace it with a primer, "The Essential Jesus Christ," containing only the profound fundamentals of moral behavior as Christ taught them. Then, there might be fewer opportunities for conveniently idiosyncratic interpretations of God's will.

12 Too many Christians are better at preaching what Christ practiced, than practicing what he preached. Christian doctrine affords an excuse for this failure—Christ,

after all, was not mortal; he was a god divinely capable of perfect moral behavior. Mere mortals can never be. What an accommodating abrogation of responsibility.

13 But then, the Christian god has a divine plan that allows Its flawed human creatures to freely decide which myth is the correct one. Guess wrong and the loving Christian god condemns Its creatures to eternal torment. The notion that the creator of the vast infinite universe, with all its miraculous interconnectivity and perfect balance, now amuses Itself by playing a deadly game of cosmic Jeopardy with sentient creatures on some speck of a planet is accepted as reality by many folks, including some who hold power in our government.

14 The human capacity for mass delusion can never be underestimated. Five centuries ago, most people, following the dictates of religion, believed the Earth was the center of the universe. What nonsense passes as divine truth these days?

15 Gods are created in man's own image, not the other way around. Responsibility for determining morality is ultimately our own, not derived from or deflected to mythical deities. Religious beliefs are personal, and all the conversions to faith, forced or voluntary, do not make a myth a fact. In a free, rational nation with impartial justice for all, religious myths should not determine public policy.

Comprehension Check

Directions: Answer the following questions. Use complete sentences where applicable.

1. Alcorn's thesis or main point is ____________________________________

____

____

2. The author's attitude toward those who wish to inject religious beliefs into governmental policy can best be described as

a. tolerant.

b. bitter.

c. angry.

d. cautionary.

e. negative.

3. T/F Alcorn's intent is to show how religion is humankind's way of explaining the mystery of its own existence.

4. T/F Alcorn asks, "Matters of life and death have long been considered the province of the divine, so why shouldn't the divine be dictating the affairs of men on earth?" How would he answer his own question? ____________________________

____

5. Which of the following reasons does Alcorn offer as a way of showing the growing pressure from some Americans to involve religion more deeply into civil policy?

a. Catholic bishops threatening to excommunicate Catholic politicians who do not conduct their governmental duties according to Catholic beliefs

b. An Alabama Supreme Court justice losing his job because he insisted on keeping the biblical Ten Commandments displayed in stone in the lobby of the state's courthouse

c. The president of the United States using executive powers to pull the church and government closer together to affect public policy

d. All of the above

e. None of the above

6. What is Alcorn's opinion of the Christian Bible? On what does he base his opinion?

____

____

7. Reread paragraph 9. What is the intent of this paragraph?

____

____

8. Reread paragraph 14. What is the intent of this paragraph?

____

____

9. According to Alcorn, what are some of the consequences of governing with or through religion? ____

____

____

10. Alcorn says, "Gods are created in our own image, not the other way around." Explain what he means. ____

____

____

Vocabulary Check

Directions: Define the following underlined words. The number in parentheses refers to the paragraph where the word is used.

1. priests historically have wielded tremendous influence (1)

____

2. secular policy (2)

____

3. this atavistic behavior is to be expected (3)

____

4. founded on remarkably malleable . . . ancient documents (6)

____

5. a form of verbal fencing (6)

____

6. will be propagated among the innocent (7)

____

7. silence the cacophony of religious opinions (10)

8. might be fewer . . . idiosyncratic interpretations (11)

9. abrogation or responsibility (12)

10. playing cosmic Jeopardy with sentient creatures (13)

Record the results of both checks on the Student Record Chart in the Appendix. Make certain you understand any reading or comprehension problems you may have had before going on.

PRACTICE D-2: Timed Reading

Directions: Read the following newspaper commentary. Because this selection appeared in a newspaper, you will notice many one- and two-sentence paragraphs. Apply what you have learned about reading, looking for the author's thesis, intent, attitude, tone, facts, and opinions. This is a timed reading. Try to read faster than your last timed reading rate without a loss in comprehension. Record your starting time and your finishing time.

Begin timing: ____________

PRESS FREEDOM UNDER ASSAULT AT HOME AND ABROAD

Jim Ottaway Jr.

Jim Ottaway Jr. is a former executive with Dow Jones and chairman of the World Press Freedom Committee.

1 One of the most damaging unintended consequences of terrorism, accentuated by the attacks on America on Sept. 11, 2001, is the crackdown on press freedom, and increased censorship of public information, all over the world.

2 At home and abroad, press freedom is under attack by elected democrats and military dictators, by legitimate governments and fanatic terrorists.

3 Governments everywhere are using the worldwide war against terrorism as a new excuse for controlling the press and its basic role in a free society as reporter and analyst of facts, and platform for public opinion, debate and criticism of the state.

4 Throughout the modern history of democracy, there has always been conflict between freedom and security, particularly in times of war.

5 Free people want public safety and personal security. We are not free if we are not safe. But free people also want freedom from unnecessary government interference in their private lives. We are not safe if we are not free.

6 The difficulty of finding the right balance between security and freedom is dramatically illustrated in the first two titles of The Patriot Act, a 346-page Congressional reaction to 9/11, which took only 45 days to enact.

7 We all agree with the purpose of Title I—"Enhancing Domestic Security Against Terrorism." But many Americans and some journalists are very concerned about possible abuses of new government powers granted in Title II—"Enhanced Surveillance Procedures."

8 Abuses such as U.S. Customs agents intercepting and confiscating a Federal Express package of research for an AP story on terrorism sent by an AP reporter in the Philippines to the Washington AP bureau in March.

9 It is the role and responsibility of a free press, as watchdog of government for the people, to report and criticize abuses of old and new immigration and terrorism laws.

10 We can be critical of rogue officials misusing The Patriot Act, without being "unpatriotic." It is our duty to protect the rule of law and to protest its abuses.

11 American journalists in time of war should oppose vigorously any attempts of U.S. and foreign governments to silence dissent or censor the news, as Attorney General John Ashcroft did when he told the Senate Judiciary Committee on Dec. 6, 2001:

12 "To those who scare peace-loving people with phantoms of lost liberty, my message is this, 'Your tactics only aid terrorists, they erode our national unity and diminish our resolve. They give ammunition to America's enemies, and pause to America's friends."

13 While U.S. foreign correspondents, and brave journalists in many nations, risk and lose their lives in daily struggles to tell the truth, too many American reporters and editors are too accepting of government press conference statements and news bite spin control.

14 Journalists across America should take courage from the bravery and commitment to telling the truth about difficult stories exhibited by the nine journalists who have died covering the war in Iraq, and the eight who died a year ago covering the war in Afghanistan.

15 The life and death of Danny Pearl, Wall Street Journal Southeast Asia correspondent, who was kidnapped and beheaded in Karachi a year ago, should inspire more journalists at home and abroad "to shine the light of truth in the dark corners of the world," as he described his mission.

16 As annual reports on world press freedom and human rights were published this spring, all condemned governments that used the war on terrorism as justification for new controls and censorship of their national media.

17 The International Press Institute in Vienna said in its 2002 World Press Freedom Review that "Under the pretext of fighting terrorism, several governments have rolled back progress made in the fields of democracy and human rights."

18 The Committee to Protect Journalists in New York City in its annual report, "Attacks on the Free Press 2002," listed 500 cases of media repression in 120 countries, including assassinations, assaults, imprisonments, censorship and increased legal harassment.

19 The committee also reported 19 journalists killed on duty in 2002, down from 37 in 2001, but 136 journalists in jail, up 15 percent in 2002, and up 68 percent since 2000, when "only 81" journalists were in jail. Censorship is global.

20 CPJ condemned Communist China as the world's leading jailer of journalists for the fourth consecutive year, with 39 journalists incarcerated at year's end.

21 In most of Africa, independent media have been censored or shut down by one-party rulers who allow no democratic dissent or debate.

22 President Robert Mugabe of Zimbabwe is guilty of the worst attacks on press freedom with his draconian licensing of journalists laws, and state censorship of all media, enforced by police torture and gang attacks on newspapers.

23 In Latin America, independent and aggressive journalists and news media are under attack from a wave of lawsuits filed by politicians and governments in compliant courts, trying to censor or stop any critical reporting.

24 Hundreds of criminal defamation, insult, or libel lawsuits all over Latin America have been called "the damages industry." Good business for lawyers; bad business for independent media and a free press.

25 Compared to the life-threatening struggles of journalists outside the U.S., to tell the truth, journalists' work in America, protected by our special First Amendment rights, is relatively safe and easy. We have no excuse for not doing a better job, for not fully exercising our press freedoms.

Comprehension Check

Directions: Answer the following questions without looking back at the reading selection.

1. Which best states the author's subject?

- **a.** The Patriot Act
- **b.** American journalists
- **c.** Foreign journalists
- **d.** Freedom of the press
- **e.** Responsibility of the press

2. Which best states the author's thesis or main idea about his topic?

- **a.** Journalists are concerned with abuses of power that may come from the enactment of the Patriot Act.
- **b.** It is the journalist's duty to be a watchdog of the government.
- **c.** Incidents of foreign journalists being killed are on the rise.
- **d.** Since September 11th, 2001, crackdowns on press freedom and increased censorship are on the rise around the world.
- **e.** American journalists in time of war should oppose any attempts of the U.S. government to silence dissent or censor the news.

3. What is the author's attitude toward the powers granted to the government in Title II of the Patriot Act?

- **a.** Favorable
- **b.** Unfavorable

4. Which best describes the author's tone?

- **a.** Humorous
- **b.** Sarcastic
- **c.** Serious

   d. Playful

   e. Angry

5. T/F The article is based mostly on supporting facts.
6. What is the author's opinion of Attorney General John Ashcroft's statement that statements of dissent of government actions "give ammunition to America's enemies?"

   a. Agrees

   b. Disagrees

7. T/F Annual reports on world press freedom and human rights in the spring of 2003 all condemned governments that used the war on terrorism as justification for new controls and censorship of their national media.
8. T/F The author believes that the deaths of journalists who have died covering the war in Afghanistan and Iraq have been in vain.
9. T/F The intent of the author is to urge journalists not to fall victim to government press conference statements and news bite spins, but rather to fully exercise the press freedoms afforded in this country.
10. T/F According to the author, it is easier for journalists to tell the truth in the United States than it is in many other countries.

Record finishing time here: ________________ and use the Timed Readings Conversion Chart in the Appendix to figure your rate: ____________ wpm.

Vocabulary Check

Directions: Define the following words. The number in parentheses refers to the paragraph where the word is used.

1. <u>enhancing</u> domestic security (7)

   ____

2. enhanced <u>surveillance</u> procedures (7)

   ____

3. intercepting and <u>confiscating</u> a Federal Express package (8)

   ____

4. critical of <u>rogue</u> officials (10)

   ____

5. <u>news bite spin</u> control (13)

   ____

6. journalists <u>incarcerated</u> at year's end (20)

   ____

7. his <u>draconian</u> licensing of journalists laws (22)

   ____

8. under attack from a wave of lawsuits (23)

____

9. governments in compliant courts (23)

____

10. The Patriot Act (6)

____

Be sure to record your rate and comprehension and vocabulary scores on the Student Record Sheet in the Appendix. Understand any errors before you go on.

Questions for Group Discussion

1. Discuss what the reading selections by Shannon (pp. 191–192) and Ottaway (pp. 204–206) have in common. How do they differ?
2. Underline facts in the last two essays and discuss the impact these facts have on each member of the group.
3. Discuss as a group your opinions about censorship. Is there a case for censorship? If so, under what circumstances?
4. Discuss Alcorn's essay (p. 200). On what issues does your group agree or disagree with Alcorn? Argue the pros and cons of Alcorn's last sentence.
5. If you or a member of your group has access to the Opposing Viewpoints Resource Center online, read the essay "Censorship Is Essential to an Open Society." Compare what this author says with what you have read in this chapter. Do you agree or disagree with this author? Why or why not?

CHAPTER SIX

Recognizing Inferences, Drawing Conclusions, and Evaluating Arguments

A. Recognizing Inferences

All the skills you have been practicing in this unit are a basis for making critical judgments. You have been learning to recognize an author's attitude, intent, tone, and bias. Here's another important aspect of reading critically: recognizing **inferences**. An inference is a conclusion or an opinion drawn from reasoning based on known facts or events. For instance, when people smile we infer that they are happy. We base our inference on the fact that most smiles are from happiness or pleasure. A frown, we know from experience, generally means displeasure or pain. Thus, when someone frowns, we infer that person is displeased. Our inferences are based on experience and/or knowledge. In his famous book *Language in Thought and Action,* S. I. Hayakawa defines an inference as "a statement about the unknown made on the basis of the known."

Drawing inferences is something we do everyday. For instance, if you met a woman wearing a large diamond necklace and three platinum rings with rubies and pearls, you would no doubt infer that she is wealthy. You may not be right; the jewelry could belong to someone else or it could be fake. But because we know from experience that the type of jewelry she is wearing is expensive, it is natural to assume she is wealthy. It's a good educated guess based on experience and knowledge. Without experience or knowledge, however, any inferences we make are based on shaky ground.

Complete the following statements by drawing inferences from what is known in each case:

1. We may infer from the boy's crying and a melting ice cream cone on the ground that the boy ____

   ____
2. We may infer from a woman's grease-stained hands and fingernails that she probably has been ____

   ____
3. We may infer from the many whitecaps on the ocean that sailing would be ______

   ____
4. We may infer from the way the man threw his food on the floor and refused to pay the restaurant bill that he was ______________________________

   ____
5. We may infer from an F grade on a test that we______________________________

   ____

Let's look now at some of the possible inferences. As to the first item, we can assume the boy dropped his ice cream cone; however, we don't know for a fact that is what happened. Someone may have knocked it out of his hands, or even thrown it at him. But based on the circumstances described, a good inference to draw is that he dropped it and is unhappy.

In the second item, we can infer that the woman has been working on something mechanical, such as an oily engine. Since we know that our hands and fingernails get greasy from such work, it's a good inference to make.

The circumstances in item 3 lead us to believe that sailing conditions might be rough, since whitecaps are caused by strong winds. However, a good sailor might like the conditions and think of it as a challenge. Of course, if you have never been around the sea, whitecaps might provide no information for drawing any kind of inference.

The man in item 4 might be angry, drunk, or "high" on something. We might further infer that he didn't like the food, didn't get what he ordered, or hated the service. Most of us don't make a habit of throwing our food on the floor and making a scene, so we can infer that something is greatly upsetting him to act this way.

In the last item, we probably infer that we failed. But is that technically an inference? The F grade is a symbol for failure. No inference need be drawn. But *why* did we fail? Maybe we didn't study hard enough, misunderstood the directions, or studied the wrong material; the test was a poor one; or the instructor made a mistake.

Drawing inferences while we read critically is no different from the kind of thinking done in the preceding examples. For example, read the following passage and then answer the questions that follow.

> If we compare college textbooks of just two decades ago with those of today, we see a dramatic decrease in the number of words, vocabulary level, and specificity of detail, but a sharp increase of graphics and, particularly, illustrations. Such textbook pictures can scarcely convey as well as words the subtle distinctions that emerge from scholarly or scientific work.

1. What is being compared in this paragraph? ______________________

____

2. What inference can be drawn about the author's attitude toward college textbooks today? ______________________

____

3. What inference can be drawn about today's college students? ______________________

____

Notice that the first question has nothing to do with inference, but it serves to remind you that in order to read critically you also have to put to use literal comprehension skills. The paragraph contrasts college textbooks of today with those published twenty years ago. In order to draw inferences, you have to understand that first. The answer to question 2 is that the author's attitude is negative. We can infer that because of the last sentence of the paragraph. The answer to question 3 is that today's college students' reading levels are probably lower than they were twenty years ago. Because of the decrease in words, lower vocabulary level, and more pictures, we can infer that today's students don't read as well. However, we could also infer that publishers are merely changing their way of publishing, but chances are that's not the author's intent here.

Here's a passage taken from a short story. Read it and answer the questions that follow.

> In walks these three girls in nothing but bathing suits. I'm in the third checkout slot, with my back to the door, so I don't see them until they're over by the bread. The one that caught my eye first was the one in the plaid green two-piece. She was a chunky kid, with a good tan and a sweet broad soft-looking can with those two crescents of white just under it, where the sun never seems to hit, at the top of the back of her legs. I stood there with my hand on a box of HiHo crackers trying to remember if I rang it up or not. I ring it up again and the customer starts

giving me hell. She's one of those cash-register-watchers, a witch about fifty with rouge on her cheekbones and no eyebrows, and I know it made her day to trip me up. She'd been watching cash registers for fifty years and probably never seen a mistake before. (John Updike, "A & P" from *Pigeon Feathers and Other Stories*. Reprinted by permission of the author and Alfred A. Knopf, a Division of Random House, Inc., Copyright © 1962.)

Based on the information provided, answer the following questions by drawing inferences:

1. How old and what sex is the narrator or person telling the story? What makes you think so? ____________________

____

2. Where is the story taking place? ____________________

____

3. People in bathing suits coming into the place where the narrator is working is not an everyday occurrence. ____________________

a. True because ____________________

____

b. False because ____________________

____

4. The narrator is not distracted by the girls.

a. True because ____________________

____

b. False because ____________________

____

5. The narrator is very observant. ____________________

a. True because ____________________

____

b. False because ____________________

____

As we find out later in the story, the answer to the first question is a nineteen-year-old male. But we can guess from the passage that the narrator is male because of his reaction to the girls, because of the language he uses, and because of his comments about the "witch about fifty" who catches his mistake. The tone has a youthful, informal quality about it.

It's not too difficult to infer that the story is taking place in a supermarket of some type, probably a grocery store. He is working at a checkout slot ringing up HiHo crackers, and he comments that the girls were "over by the bread" before he saw them. These are clues to us.

Question 3 is probably true, making question 4 false. He is distracted by the girls. No doubt girls come into the store all the time, but in this case they are wearing "nothing but bathing suits," making this an unusual event. It causes him to forget whether he has already rung up the crackers.

Question 5 is true; he is very observant. His description of the one girl and the "cash-register-watcher" are full of details, reflecting an observant person.

The word *critical* often connotes finding fault with something. But making valid critical judgments, in its strictest sense, implies an attempt at objective judging so as to determine both merits and faults. Critical reading is thoughtful reading because it requires that the reader not only recognize what is being said at the literal level but also distinguish facts from opinions; recognize an author's intent, attitude, and biases; and draw inferences. A reader who is not actively involved is not reading critically.

PRACTICE A-1: Drawing Inferences

Part A

Directions: An inference, remember, is "a statement about the unknown made on the basis of the known." Complete the following statements drawing inferences from what is known.

1. We may infer from the smile on the professor's face as he passed back the exams that ____

____

2. We may infer from the large turnout at our college orientation session that______

____

3. We may infer from the fact that a student in a college English class is consistently late for class that________________________________

____

4. We may infer from the number of Academy Awards a movie won that__________

____

5. We may infer from the extreme thinness of some current models and actresses that

____

Part B

Directions: Read the following passages and answer the questions that follow them.

1. The word *concerto* originally meant a group of performers playing or singing together, as "in concert" or making a "concerted effort" of entertaining. The Gabrielis of sixteenth-century Venice called their motets, scored for choir and organ, *concerti ecclesiastici.* Heinrich Schultz, a seventeenth-century German composer, titled his similar works *Kleine geistliche Konzerte.*

a. What is the intent of this paragraph? ________________________________

____

b. T/F The German word *Konzerte* probably means concerto.

c. T/F We can infer that the author probably knows some history of music.

2. He had a direct and unassuming manner and a candid way of speaking in a soft Minnesota voice. The interviewer rushed right in with questions, but he turned all the questions around and wanted first to know some things about the interviewer. She had a hard time getting the conversation centered on him-until he was ready. He was a bright, insightful man who seemed oblivious to his genius.

a. What words best describe the man in the preceding passage? ________________

____

b. T/F The man is important or famous.

c. T/F The interviewer was impressed with this man.

d. T/F We can infer that the man is talkative and open.

3. Infer as much as you can from each of the following statements:

a. The evening has proved to be most entertaining. I extend my deepest appreciation. ________________

____

b. Tonight's been a real blast! Thanks a bunch. ________________

____

c. Like, I mean, funwise, this night has blown me away, babe. ________________

____

4. There are all kinds of rumors about Ed Cantrell. Some say he can ride a horse for days without eating and still bring down a man at a thousand yards with a rifle. Some say he is almost deaf from practicing every day with a .38. Others say he can quote long passages from Hemingway's novels. And still others claim he has the eyes of a rattlesnake and faster hands. Most all who know him claim he is the last of the hired guns.

a. What is Ed Cantrell's occupation? ________________

____

b. T/F Based on the rumors, most people seem to admire him.

c. T/F Cantrell probably lives somewhere in the Western states.

d. What can we infer about Cantrell if it is true that he can quote long passages from Hemingway's works? ________________

____

e. Why would a man such as Cantrell be interested in Hemingway's works?

____

5. During the Middle Ages, many scholars regarded printed books with apprehension. They felt that books would destroy the monopoly on knowledge. Books would permit the masses to learn to improve their lives and to realize that no man is better than another. And not too long ago, slaves were strictly forbidden to learn to read and had to pretend that they were illiterate if they had learned how. Societies based on ignorance or repression cannot tolerate general education.

a. T/F The first sentence is fact.

b. What is the author's attitude toward education? ________________

____

c. What is the intent of the statement? ______________________

____

PRACTICE A-2: Recognizing Inferences

Directions: Read the following passages and answer the questions that follow them.

1. "Social science" in cold print gives rise to images of some robot in a statistics laboratory reducing human activity to bloodless digits and simplified formulas. Research reports filled with mechanical sounding words like "empirical," "quantitative," "operational," "inverse," and "correlative" aren't very poetic. Yet the stereotypes of social science created by these images are, I will try to show, wrong.

Like any other mode of knowing, social science can be used for perverse ends; however, it can also be used for humane personal understanding. By testing thoughts against reality, science helps liberate inquiry from bias, prejudice, and just plain muddleheadedness. So it is unwise to be put off by simple stereotypes—too many people accept these stereotypes and deny themselves the power of social scientific understanding. (From Rodney Stark, *Sociology,* 2nd edition, Wadsworth Publishing Co., 1987, p. 28.)

a. The author's intent in this passage is to ______________________

____

b. T/F We can infer that the author feels some of his readers have a negative attitude toward social science.

c. T/F The author believes strongly in the scientific method of inquiry.

d. T/F The author is probably a social science teacher.

2. On July 10, 1985, the following events worth reporting occurred around the world:

— An Israeli court convicted fifteen Jewish terrorists of murder and violence against the Arabs.

— Bishop Desmond Tutu, Nobel laureate, pushed himself through an angry mob to save an alleged police informer from being burned alive.

— An Iraqi missile struck and heavily damaged a Turkish supertanker.

— A ship photographer was killed when a Greenpeace protest ship was blown up in New Zealand.

— The Nuclear Regulatory Commission (NRC) was accused of not properly considering earthquake hazards at the Diablo Canyon, California, atomic energy plant.

— Numerous major fires in Northern California burned over 300,000 acres of forests and destroyed many homes.

Yet the lead story of the day on two of the three major American television news broadcasts that evening had to do with the Coca-Cola Company's decision to return to its original formula after experimenting with a new taste that few seemed to like. Even the country's major newspapers featured the Coke story on their front pages at the expense of more newsworthy events. The headline of the *Denver Post,* for example, stated "'The Real Thing' Is Back." In addition, a six-square-inch picture of a can of Coke in two colors appeared next to the column.

a. The intent of the passage is to ______________________________

____

b. T/F The passage is mostly opinion.

c. T/F The author feels that the type of news reporting described reflects an erosion of values in our society.

d. T/F The author of the passage would probably agree with this statement: Coca-Cola has become a national institution of sorts and what it does is of interest to almost all Americans.

e. State the author's attitude toward the reporting he describes. ______________

____

3. The United States Atomic Energy Commission, created by Congress in 1946, grew into a uniquely powerful, mission-oriented bureaucracy. One of its main goals, which it pursued with exceptional zeal, was the creation of a flourishing commercial nuclear power program.

By the late 1950s, the AEC began to acquire frightening data about the potential hazards of nuclear technology. It decided, nevertheless, to push ahead with ambitious plans to make nuclear energy the dominant source of the nation's electric power by the end of the century. The AEC proceeded to authorize the construction of larger and larger nuclear reactors all around the country, the dangers notwithstanding.

The AEC gambled that its scientists would, in time, find deft solutions to all the complex safety difficulties. The answers were slow in coming, however. According to the AEC secret files [obtained through the Freedom of Information Act], government experts continued to find additional problems rather than the safety assurances the agency wanted. There were potential flaws in the plants being built, AEC experts said, that could lead to "catastrophic" nuclear-radiation accidents—peacetime disasters that could dwarf any the nation had ever experienced.

Senior officials at the AEC responded to the warnings from their own scientists by suppressing the alarming reports and pressuring the authors to keep quiet. Meanwhile, the agency continued to license mammoth nuclear power stations and to offer the public soothing reassurances about safety. (Copyright © 1982, 1984 by Daniel Ford. Reprinted by permission of Simon & Schuster, Inc.)

a. The intent of the passage is to ______________________________

____

b. Describe the author's attitude toward the AEC. ______________________

____

c. T/F The passage is mostly opinion rather than factual.

d. T/F We can infer from the passage that the author is probably not worried about the number of atomic energy plants built and being built.

e. T/F The author implies that the AEC placed its own commercial desires over the safety of the American people.

f. What is your reaction to this passage and why? ______________________

____

4. Futurists generally assume that twenty-first-century medicine will include new and more powerful drugs and technologies to fight diseases. They tend to forget, however, the serious problems presently arising from conventional medication prescribed by the average doctor. According to 1987 statistics, the average American receives 7.5 prescriptions per year. This is even more frightening when we realize that many people have not been prescribed any medication at all. This means that someone else is getting *their* 7.5 medications.

Most drugs have serious side effects, some quite serious. Since the sick person is often prescribed several drugs at the same time, there is often unfavorable reaction or illness from the drugs themselves. Studies also show that 25 to 90 percent of the time, patients make errors when taking their prescribed drug dosage. Despite the respect that people generally have for present-day doctors, there doesn't seem to be equal confidence in the treatments they prescribe because 50 percent of the time people do not even get their prescriptions filled.

Homeopathic medicine (using natural means to help the body build immune systems) offers an alternative. Instead of giving a person one medicine for headache, one for constipation, one for irritability, and so on, the homeopathic physician prescribes one medicine at a time to stimulate the person's immune system and defense capacity to bring about overall improvement in health. The procedure by which the homeopath finds the precise substance is the very science and art of homeopathy. (From Dana Ullman, "Royal Medicine," *New Age Journal,* September/October 1987, p. 46.)

a. The intent of the passage is to

____

b. T/F The author's attitude toward conventional doctors and homeopathic doctors is equal.

c. T/F The passage is mostly opinion.

d. T/F We can infer from the passage that the author is biased against homeopathic medicine.

e. T/F The author implies that many patients do not trust or want to take the medications prescribed by their doctors.

f. Would you be willing to go to a homeopathic doctor rather than a conventionally trained physician?__________

Explain. ______________________________________

____

____

____

____

B. Recognizing Inferences and Facts

When inferences are based on facts, much useful information can be obtained. Scientists and historians, to name a few, have been able to infer from facts and observation most of the knowledge we have today. Below is a passage based on fact with many inferences that are probably true. As you read, note the inferences and the facts.

1 Nine hundred years ago, in what is now north-central Arizona, a volcano erupted and spewed fine cinders and ash over an area of about 800 square miles. The porous cinder layer formed a moisture-retaining agent that transformed the marginal farmland into a country of rich farmland.

2 Word of this new oasis spread among the Indians of the Southwest, setting off a prehistoric land rush that brought together the Pueblo dry farmers from the east and north, the Hohokam irrigation farmers from the south, and probably Mogollon groups from the south and east and Cohonino groups from the west. Focal points of the immigrants were the stretches of land lying some 15 miles northeast and southeast of the volcano, bordering territory already occupied by the Sinagua Indians.

3 Nudged out of their now-crowded corner by the newcomers, some of the Sinagua moved to the south of the volcano to a canyon that offered building sites and a means of livelihood. Here they made their homes.

4 Remains of the Sinagua's new homes, built in the early 1100s, are now preserved in Walnut Canyon National Monument; the cone of the benevolent volcano, in Sunset Crater National Monument; and part of the focal points of the immigrants, in Wupatki National Monument. (From the brochure *Walnut Canyon,* 1968-306-122/97, revised 1982, Superintendent of Documents, Washington, D.C.)

Now answer these questions.

1. T/F The first paragraph is mainly fact rather than inference.
2. T/F The first sentence of paragraph 2 is inference.
3. T/F The information in the last sentence of paragraph 2 is based on inference.
4. T/F Paragraph 3 is mostly inference.
5. T/F The last paragraph is mostly inference.
6. T/F Chances are that someday this information will prove to be in error.

The answer to question 1 is false; it's mainly inference based on facts or evidence that when put together leads scientists to believe the events described happened eight hundred years ago. We have no way to prove the eruption occurred as stated, yet scientists basically agree that this is what did happen.

Questions 2 and 3 are true. Again, no one was around to verify these statements, but the inference that it happened can be made from present-day evidence.

While question 4 is basically true, at least the first part, the last part is fact because the remains are still there to see. Question 5 is false since all statements can be verified by visiting those places mentioned.

Question 6 is false; it's possible, but highly unlikely because of present-day facts and remains. However, in the future, this might be a "slippery fact," like the atom being thought of as the smallest particle at one time. But based on all the known facts we have at present, the best answer is false.

You can see that much of what we call "fact" today is based on inferences. When scientists agree on inferences that are drawn from what is known, we tend to accept as fact their conclusions until such time that more evidence can show the inferences drawn were wrong.

The following practices will help you recognize the difference between facts and inferences.

PRACTICE B-1: Drawing Inferences from Facts

Directions: Read the following passages and answer the questions that follow them.

1.

The unit that is used to measure the absorption of energy from radiation in biological materials is the rem, usually abbreviated R. It stands for "Radiation Equivalent in Man." There is a unit called the rad, which corresponds to an amount of radiation that deposits 100 ergs of energy in one gram of material. The rem is defined as the radiation dose to biological tissue that will cause the same amount of energy to be deposited as would one rad of X rays.

A millirem (abbreviated mR) is one thousandth of a rem. To give some idea of the size of the things we are discussing, you get about 20 mR of radiation from a dental X-ray, about 150 mR of radiation from a chest X-ray. Since the average dose of radiation to the average American is about 130 mR, it is not hard to see that it would be very easy to absorb in medical and dental X-rays more radiation than one absorbs from natural causes.

The "average" dose of radiation, of course, varies as much as 150 or so mRs per year depending on where one lives. For example, in Colorado and Wyoming the average mR dose is about 250 per year, while in Texas the average dose is 100 mR. It is higher in the mountains because there is less air to shield us from cosmic rays and because there are more radioactive elements in the soil.

According to federal requirements in effect, the radiation dose at the fence of a nuclear plant can be no more than 5 mR per year. We can see that based on the average dose most of us receive, living near a nuclear plant offers relatively little dosage risk.

a. The intent of this passage is to ____

____

b. T/F The first paragraph is mostly factual.

c. T/F Living in higher altitudes is safer from radiation doses than living at sea level, based on the information in the passage.

d. T/F We can infer that the author is opposed to nuclear power plants.

e. T/F The last sentence in the passage is factual.

2.

In the 1980s, in an ebullient bid to curtail drunk driving by teenagers, the government imposed a nationwide minimum drinking age of 21. It was kind of second Prohibition, albeit for young adults only. The law's goal, of course, was to make young people happier, healthier, and safer.

By now it is obvious that the law has not succeeded in preventing the under-21 group from drinking. The popular press and higher-education media are filled with reports of high-visibility, alcohol-related troubles on our campuses. Serious riots by students who want to do their boozing unhindered have broken out at many institutions. Some of the melees, such as those at Ohio University, the University of Colorado, and Pennsylvania State University, have involved significant injuries and many arrests.

Reports of binge drinking come from all types of campuses across the country. In 1992, researchers reported that more college students were drinking to get drunk than their counterparts a decade earlier, and one recent study reported an increase, just since 1994, in the number of students who drink deliberately to get drunk. Of particular pertinence, in another national study, Ruth Engs and Beth Diebold of Indiana University and David Hanson of the State University of New York at Potsdam reported in 1996 in the *Journal of Alcohol and Drug Education* that, compared with those of legal age, a significantly higher percentage of students under age 21 were heavy drinkers.

Worst of all are the reports of drinking-related deaths. In 1997, at least two fraternity pledges died of alcohol poisoning, and in 1995 a third choked to death on his own vomit, all after initiation-night parties. One informal survey of alcohol-related deaths among college students during 1997 turned up 11 more fatalities: Three students fell from dormitory windows, one darted into the path of a motorcycle, one fell through a greenhouse roof, another was asphyxiated, and five died in highway crashes. At Frostburg State University, seven students were charged with manslaughter in 1997 in connection with the death of a freshman who guzzled beer and 12 to 14 shots of vodka in two hours at a fraternity party.

American's second experiment with Prohibition seems to have been no more effective than the first one. (From Document X3010 2152230, Opposing Viewpoints Resource Center, Gale Group, 2003. http://www.galenet.com/servlet/OVCR.)

a. The intent of this passage is to ____

____

b. T/F The passage is mostly factual.

c. T/F We can infer that the author believes the legal drinking age should be lowered from twenty-one.

d. T/F We can infer that the author believes the drinking age of 21 has driven college students to partying less in public and into more dangerous places.

3.

To understand the debate over global warming, it is important to understand the scientific concept known as the greenhouse effect. The greenhouse effect is a natural phenomenon involving the interaction of the sun's energy with atmospheric gases. After the sun's energy, or solar radiation, enters the atmosphere, the earth absorbs most of it while the rest is reflected back into space. Atmospheric gases, known as greenhouse gases, absorb a portion of this reflected energy. The energy trapped by these gases warms the planet's surface, creating the greenhouse effect. This natural process keeps Earth's atmosphere warm enough to support life. However, as the amount of greenhouse gases in the atmosphere increases, so too does the amount of heat they absorb: Global warming is the result.

The atmospheric concentrations of greenhouse gases have increased dramatically in the past century. Concentrations of carbon dioxide (CO_2), the primary greenhouse gas, have increased 30 percent, according to the Intergovernmental panel on Climate Change (IPCC), a group of about 2,000 scientists from 116 countries assembled to address the problem of climate change. Concentrations of the other main culprits, methane and nitrous oxide, have risen 145 percent and 15 percent, respectively. At the same time, the average atmospheric temperature has also risen between 0.3 and 0.6 degrees Celsius. Most scientists agree that human activity is the cause of the rise in greenhouse gases, which are in turn responsible for global warming. Thus, in its definitive 1995 report, the IPCC concluded, "The balance of evidence suggests that there is a discernible human influence on global climate. (From Document X3010101223, Opposing Viewpoints Resource Center, Gale Group, 2003. http://www.galenet.com/servlet/OVCR.)

a. The intent of this passage is to ______________________________

____

b. T/F The passage is mostly factual.

c. T/F We can infer that the author is concerned with the increase of greenhouse gases in the atmosphere.

d. T/F We can infer that the author agrees with the scientists who claim human activity is the cause for the increase of global warming.

4. From the seller's viewpoint advertising is persuasion; from the buyer's viewpoint it is education. No single group of people spends as much time or money per lesson to educate the masses as do the creators of ads.

Ads participate in a feedback loop. They reflect a society they have helped to educate, and part of the advertising reflection is the effect of the advertising itself. Every ad that exploits a personality hole educates the audience toward using a particular product to fill that hole. Just as drug ads teach a crude and sometimes dangerous form of self-medication, psychosell ads teach a form of self-analysis and cure for psychological problems.

An ad that stirs a hidden doubt, that causes a person to ask, "Why does no one love me?"; "Why don't I have more friends?"; "Why am I lonely?" invariably goes on to suggest a partial cure—use our product. If an announcer for Pepsi would appear on screen and say:

> Are you lonely? Do you feel left out? Do you sometimes feel that everybody else has all the fun in life? Are you bored and isolated? Well, if you are, drink Pepsi and find yourself instantly a part of all those energetic, joyful, young-at-heart people who also drink Pepsi.

Such an ad would be greeted as either laughable or insulting by the viewing audience. Yet the old "Pepsi generation" campaign used pictures and a jingle to make exactly such a point.

> The danger in psychosell techniques is not that people might switch from Coke to Pepsi in soft-drink loyalties or abandon Scope for Listerine. The danger is that millions learn (especially if the message is repeated often enough, as ads are) that problems in self-acceptance and boredom can be alleviated by corporate products. Which brand to buy is secondary to ads as education; the primary lesson is that the product itself satisfies psychological needs. (From Jeffrey Schrank, *Snap, Crackle and Popular Taste: The Illusion of Free Choice in America,* Delacorte Press, 1977.)

a. What is the intent of the author? ______________________________

____

b. Is the passage primarily fact or opinion? ______________________

Explain.______________________________________

____

c. T/F The author thinks ads may be silly and repetitive, but basically harmless. Explain.____

____

d. T/F The author believes that some advertising is a dangerous form of education because it brainwashes us into thinking we can solve many of our personal problems by buying corporate products.

Explain.____

____

e. T/F The author's bias is easy to identify.

Explain.____

____

PRACTICE B-2: Drawing Inferences from Descriptive Passages

Directions: Read the following passages and answer the questions that follow them.

1.

Daddy's genial voice sometimes traveled slowly through sentences, shaping each syllable correctly. He was polishing the skin of a second language. He would come to speak it much more eloquently than most people who grew up speaking only English. Sometimes he slipped Arabic words into our days like secret gift coins into a pocket, but we didn't learn his first language because we were too busy learning our own. I regret that now.

When someone else who spoke Arabic came to visit us, their language ignited the air of our living room, dancing, dipping and whirling. I would realize: all those sounds had been waiting inside our father! He carried a whole different world of sounds—only now did they get to come out! (From Naomi Shihab Nye, "Wealthy with Words," *The Most Wonderful Books,* Milkweed Editions, 1997, 193.)

a. T/F We can infer that the author's father's first language was Arabic.

b. T/F We can infer that her father learned to speak English well.

c. T/F We can infer that the author did not like the sound of Arabic being spoken.

d. T/F The author is bilingual.

e. What do you infer about the author's view of language? ____________________

2.

My van (and the passage of nearly 200 years) had made my journey both faster and easier than theirs. For much of their journey west—as they fought the Missouri's relentless current for its entire 2,400-mile length, then trudged through the snowy Bitterroot Range—Lewis and Clark would have defined substantial progress as making 12 miles a day. Shooting down the Snake and Columbia Rivers in their dugout canoes for the final stretch must have seemed like hyperdrive, although in fact it only increased their speed to 30 or 40 miles per day. No wonder it took them a year and a half to reach Cape Disappointment. Allowing plenty of time for unhurried stops and side trips, my camper covered the same distance in 60 days.

Needless to say, I also hadn't suffered the hardships the Corps of Discovery routinely faced: backbreaking toil, loss of a comrade to illness, encounters with enraged grizzlies, near-starvation in the ordeal across the Bitterroots, demoralizing coastal rains that rotted the clothes on their backs, and so much more. They had been making history; I was merely retracing it. (From Dayton Duncan, "American Odyssey," *Land's End Catalogue,* July/August, 2003.)

a. T/F We can infer that the author followed the same route as the Louis and Clark expedition in the early 1800s.

b. T/F We can infer that the author admires what the Corps of Discovery went through.

c. T/F The author feels proud of himself for having retraced the Corps of Discovery's route in only sixty days.

d. What do you infer about the author, based on this passage? ________________

____

3.

With that thought in mind, I raised my head, squared my shoulders, and set off in the direction of my dorm, glancing twice (and then ever so discreetly) at the campus map clutched in my hand. It took everything I had not to stare when I caught my first glimpse of a real live football player. What confidence, what reserve, what muscles! I only hoped his attention was drawn to my air if assurance rather than to my shaking knees. I spent the afternoon seeking out each of my classrooms so that I could make a perfectly timed entrance before each lecture without having to ask dumb questions about its whereabouts.

The next morning I found my first class and marched in. Once I was in the room, however, another problem awaited me. Where to sit? . . . After much deliberation I chose a seat in the first row and to the side. I was in the foreground (as advised), but out of the professor's direct line of vision.

I cracked my anthology of American literature and scribbled the date on the top of the crisp ruled page. "Welcome to Biology 101," the professor began. A cold sweat broke out at the back of my neck. (From Evelyn Herald, "Fresh Start," *Nutshell* magazine.)

a. Where can we infer that the event described in the passage is taking place?

____

How can you tell? ____

____

b. T/F The narrator telling the story is female. Explain. ________________________

____

c. T/F We can infer from the author's tone that the author has a sense of humor. Explain. ____

____

d. Why did the author break out in a cold sweat when the professor greeted the class? ____

____

e. T/F We can infer that the author is trying not to conceal his or her true feelings. Explain.____

____

C. Drawing Conclusions Using Induction and Deduction

A big part of critical reading is being able to draw conclusions based on the information authors provide. Once you understand the thesis or main idea of a reading selection, recognize fact from opinion, and understand intent, attitude, and inference, you almost automatically draw conclusions of your own. In fact, some of the questions you have been answering in the last practices require drawing conclusions based on the evidence provided.

Drawing conclusions is based on making **reasoned judgments.** Reasoned judgments usually come from two basic methods of reasoning: **deductive reasoning** and **inductive reasoning.** Deductive reasoning occurs when you begin with a general statement of truth and infer a conclusion about a particular specific. For instance, the old standby definition of deductive reasoning is shown through a **syllogism,** a three-step statement that begins with a general statement recognized as a truth and moves to a specific statement:

All humans are mortal.
Britney Spears is a human.
Therefore, Britney Spears is mortal.

Deductive reasoning is the subject of formal logic courses and involves a process of stating a series of carefully worded statements, such as the example just given, each related to the other statements. Deductive reasoning begins with a generalization:

*All dogs are animals. *or* *Athletes are physically strong.

The next statement identifies something as belonging (or not belonging) to that class:

__________________ is a dog.

What would be a second statement for the athlete generalization?

____

For the first example, you should have given the name of a dog you know or a famous dog. For example, Lassie is a dog. For the second statement, you should have named an athlete. "John Elway is an athlete" would be one example.

The third statement of deductive reasoning is the inference you arrive at if the first two statements are true:

All dogs are animals.	Athletes are physically strong.
Lassie is a dog.	John Elway is an athlete.
Lassie is an animal.	John Elway is physically strong.

Fully understanding deductive reasoning takes a lot of study but, for the purpose of this introduction, you should be aware that you start with a generalization and use a careful reasoning process to arrive at a conclusion.

You can make errors with deductive reasoning if you start with faulty generalizations or premises. If you started with the generalization that "all college students have high IQs," you would be starting with a false premise. Some college students have high IQs; others may be conscientious workers with average IQs.

Inductive reasoning works in the opposite way of deductive reasoning. With inductive reasoning, you begin with observing specifics and draw a general conclusion. You might move to a new town and notice that every time you see police officers they are wearing bright green uniforms. After seeing no police officer wearing anything other than this color, you might inductively reason that in this particular town the official police uniform is bright green.

Inductive reasoning is often used when you can't examine all the data but need to come to conclusions based on what you know. Political polls do this when they look at some voters and base conclusions on what "the people" want by that sample. You may come to inductive conclusions based on sensory observations (what you see or hear), lists or groups, cause-effect thinking, or pattern recognition.

**Sensory observation:* Using your eyes, ears, taste, or smell involves sensory observation. The police uniform example in the previous paragraph is an example of sensory observation.

**Lists or enumeration:* Often we look at lists of items and come to conclusions based on those lists. You may look at lists of what prevents heart problems and conclude you will not smoke and will exercise every day.

**Cause-effect:* When two events happen, we may decide that the first one was the cause of the second one (effect). Historians use this kind of reasoning. Cause-effect thinking means you notice that every time you run a red light, you are almost in an accident. The cause (running the red light) has a certain effect (near accident).

**Pattern recognition:* Pattern recognition involves looking at parts and drawing conclusions. A professor may notice one student who is rarely in class, doesn't turn in work, and flunks the midterm. That professor is likely to conclude that the student is a poor college student.

The conclusion you draw in inductive reasoning is usually called a hypothesis. Scientists use this method all the time.

As with deductive reasoning, you can make many errors with inductive reasoning. Some of these are listed in Practice C-4 of this chapter and include such obvious errors as oversimplification and using the wrong facts to come to your conclusion.

Perhaps the best way to explain these two types of reasoning is to quote Robert M. Pirsig in a passage from his book *Zen and the Art of Motorcycle Maintenance:*

> If the cycle goes over a bump and the engine misfires, and then goes over another bump and the engine misfires, and then goes over another bump and the engine misfires, and then goes over a long smooth stretch of road and there is no misfiring, and then goes over a fourth bump and the engine misfires again, one can logically conclude that the misfiring is caused by the bumps. That is induction: reasoning from particular experiences to general truths.
>
> Deductive inferences do the reverse. They start with general knowledge and predict a specific observation. For example if, from reading the hierarchy of facts about the machine, the mechanic knows the horn on the cycle is powered exclusively by electricity from the battery, then he can logically infer that if the battery is dead the horn will not work. That is deduction. (Robert M. Pirsig, *Zen and the Art of Motorcycle Maintenance,* William Morrow, 1974, 107).

We use these two types of reasoning every day, often without even knowing it.

To look more closely at how we draw conclusions, read the following passage and then answer the questions that follow.

> In 1832, a twenty-four-old Englishman named Charles Darwin, aboard the HMS *Beagle* on a surveying expedition around the world, was collecting beetles in a rain forest near Rio de Janeiro. In one day, in one small area, he found over sixty-eight different species of small beetles. That there could be such a variety of species of one kind of creature astounded him. In his journal he wrote that such a find "...is sufficient to disturb the composure of an entomologist's mind...." The conventional view of his day was that all species were unchangeable and that each had been individually and separately created by God. Far from being an atheist, Darwin had taken a degree in divinity in Cambridge. But he was deeply puzzled by his find. (Adapted from James Burke, *The Day the Universe Changed,* Little, Brown & Co., 1985, p. 267.)

1. T/F We can draw the conclusion that Darwin was not actually out searching for what he found.

2. T/F The evidence provided for our conclusion is based partly on Darwin's journal.

3. T/F What Darwin discovered was contrary to the beliefs of his day.

4. T/F Darwin's later "theory of evolution," that species were not fixed forever, probably began with his discovery about the beetle.

All of the answers to these questions are true. Based on his journal statement that the find was "sufficient to disturb" his composure, the statement that he was "deeply puzzled," and the fact that what he found was contrary to what he had been taught to believe all provide evidence to support our conclusions that he was not looking for what he found.

Even though no one living today was with Darwin in 1832, his journal notes leave evidence to help answer question 2 as true. As to question 3, if Darwin had a degree in divinity from Cambridge, he would have been taught to believe what was accepted as "fact" in his day: that God individually and separately created all species. The fact that he found sixty-eight different species is contrary to such a belief.

Question 4 is true, but unless you have knowledge of what Charles Darwin's "theory of evolution" is, you might have difficulty drawing such a conclusion. If you know that he continued to pursue the suspicion in his mind that all species were not fixed forever, and that he eventually wrote *On the Origin of Species by Means of Natural Selection,* then there's no problem in answering this question as true.

The following practices are designed to help you develop your ability to draw conclusions from what you read.

PRACTICE C-1: Drawing Conclusions from Paragraphs

Directions: Read the following paragraphs and answer the questions that follow them.

1. Look for a moment at the situation in those nations that most of us prefer to label with the euphemism "underdeveloped," but which might just as accurately be described as "hungry." In general, underdeveloped countries (UDCs) differ from developed countries (DCs) in a number of ways. UDCs are not industrialized.

They tend to have inefficient, usually subsistence agricultural systems, extremely low gross national products and per capita incomes, high illiteracy rates, and incredibly high rates of population growth. . . . Most of these countries will never, under conceivable circumstance, be "developed" in the sense in which the United States is today. They could accurately be called "never-to-be-developed" countries. (From Paul and Anne Ehrlich, *Population, Resources and Environment.*)

a. The intent of the passage is to ____________________________________

____

b. T/F The authors of the passage have drawn the conclusion that UDCs exist because they are not industrialized and have poor agricultural systems, high illiteracy rates, low incomes, and too much population growth.

c. T/F If a UDC has a population growth that is too high for its agricultural system, we can draw the conclusion that it will never become a DC.

d. T/F We can draw the conclusion from the information in the passage that the authors feel UDCs can eventually become DCs.

e. Identify what kind of reasoning (inductive or deductive) is required to answer *d.*____

____

2. Science is sometimes confused with technology, which is the application of science to various tasks. Grade-school texts that caption pictures of rockets on the moon with the title, "Science Marches On!" aid such confusion. The technology that makes landing on the moon possible emerged from the use of scientific strategies in the study of propulsion, electronics, and numerous other fields. It is the mode of inquiry that is scientific; the rocket is a piece of technology.

Just as science is not technology, neither is it some specific body of knowledge. The popular phrase "Science tells us that smoking is bad for your health" really misleads. "Science" doesn't tell us anything; people tell us things, in this case people who have used scientific strategies to investigate the relationship of smoking to health. Science, as a way of thought and investigation, is best conceived of as existing not in books, or in machinery, or in reports containing numbers, but rather in that invisible world of the mind. Science has to do with the way questions are formulated and answered; it is a set of rules and forms for inquiry created by people who want reliable answers. (From Kenneth R. Hoover, *The Elements of Social Scientific Thinking,* 3rd edition, St. Martin's Press, 1984, pp. 4–5.)

a. The intent of the passage is to ____________________________________

____

b. T/F According to the author, some grade-school textbooks contribute to the confusion between science and technology.

c. T/F The author does not think there is much difference between the terms *science* and *technology.*

d. T/F The author does not believe that science is something that cannot be written down.

e. T/F The author would agree with the statement, "Science has proven that too much sun causes skin cancer."

f. T/F The author has respect for scientific thinking.

g. What kind of reasoning (inductive or deductive) did you use to answer *f*?

---

3. Some years ago, I ran into an economist friend at the University of Michigan in Ann Arbor who told me, with concern bordering on shock, that assembly-line workers at the nearby Ford plant in Dearborn were making more money than an assistant professor at the University. It occurred to me that quite a few at Ford might prefer the more leisured life of a young professor: Certainly there seemed no need to fear any major movement of academic talent from Ann Arbor to the noisome shops in Dearborn. (From John Kenneth Galbraith, "When Work Isn't Work," *Parade* Magazine, February 10, 1985.)

a. T/F The author's economist friend believes that a university professor should be paid more than an assembly-line worker.

b. T/F The author agrees with his friend.

c. T/F The author feels that a university professor's work is easier than factory work.

d. T/F Because the pay is better for factory work, many professors will probably leave the university to seek factory jobs.

e. T/F The author probably believes the usual definition for "work" can be misleading when comparing various types of jobs.

4. Almost everyone in the middle class has a college degree, and most have an advanced degree of some kind. Those of us who can look back to the humble stations of our parents or grandparents, who never saw the inside of an institution of higher learning, can have cause for self-congratulation. But—inevitably but—the impression that our general populace is better educated depends on an ambiguity in the meaning of the word education, or fudging of the distinction between liberal and technical education. A highly trained computer specialist need not have any more learning about morals, politics or religion than the most ignorant of persons . . . . It is not evident to me that someone whose regular reading consists of *Time, Playboy* and *Scientific American* has any profounder wisdom about the world than the rural schoolboy of yore with his McGuffey's reader. (From Allan Bloom, *The Closing of the American Mind,* Simon & Schuster, 1987, p. 59.)

a. T/F The author believes that the general public today is better educated than before.

b. T/F The "McGuffey reader" must have been a widely used textbook in schools at one time.

c. T/F The author believes that learning about morals, politics, and religion is not the function of institutions of higher learning.

d. T/F The author favors a technical education over a liberal one.

e. T/F The passage suggests that the author is pleased with the direction education is taking and thinks it is much better than it was in his grandparents' day.

f. Identify the type of reasoning (inductive or deductive) the author uses to come to his conclusion.

PRACTICE C-2: Arguments and Responses

Directions: The legal drinking age in the United States is twenty-one. Some people want to lower the age, in most cases to age eighteen. Presented here are some argumentative statements or claims as reasons for lowering the legal age to twenty-one. Responses to those arguments follow. Read each argument and response, then answer the questions that follow.

1.

Argument
Lowering the drinking age will reduce the allure of alcohol as a "forbidden fruit" for minors.

Response
Lowering the drinking age will make alcohol more available to an even younger population, replacing "forbidden fruit" with "low-hanging fruit."

The practices and behaviors of 18 year-olds are particularly influential on 15–17 year-olds. If 18 year-olds get the OK to drink, they will be modeling drinking for younger teens. Legal access to alcohol for 18 year-olds will provide more opportunities for younger teens to obtain it illegally from older peers.

Age-21 has resulted in decreases, not increases in youth drinking, an outcome inconsistent with an increased allure of alcohol. In 1983, one year before the National Minimum Purchase Age Act was passed, 88% of high school seniors reported any alcohol use in the past year and 41% reported binge drinking. By 1997, alcohol use by seniors had dropped to 75% and the percentage of binge drinkers had fallen to 31%. (From Opposing Viewpoints Resource Center, document X3010084223, http://www.galenet.galegroup.com/servlet/OVRC.)

a. The argument for lowering the drinking age uses the term "forbidden fruit." Explain what is meant. ____

____

b. T/F The argument is based mostly on fact.

c. T/F The response to the argument is based mostly on facts.

d. Draw your own reasoned conclusion on the argument. If you support the argument, what reasons do you have? ____

____

____

2.

Argument
At 18, kids can vote, join the military, sign contracts, and even smoke. Why shouldn't they be able to drink?

Response
Ages of initiation vary—one may vote at 18, drink at 21, rent a car at 25, and run for president at 35. These ages may appear arbitrary, but they take into account the requirements, risks, and benefits of each act.

When age-21 was challenged in Louisiana's State Supreme Court, the Court upheld the law, ruling that "statutes establishing the minimum drinking age at a higher level than the age of majority are not arbitrary because they substantially further the appropriate governmental purpose of improving highway safety, and thus are constitutional."

Age-21 laws help keep kids healthy by postponing the onset of alcohol use. Deferred drinking reduces the risks of:

- developing alcohol dependence or abuse later in life.
- harming the developing brain.
- engaging in current and adult drug use.
- suffering alcohol-related problems, such as trouble at work, with friends, family, and police. (From Opposing Viewpoints Resource Center, document X3010084223, http://www.galenet.galegroup.com/servlet/OVRC.)

a. T/F As stated, the argument is mostly opinion.

b. Explain why you agree or disagree with the argument. ____________________

____

c. T/F The response uses more facts than opinions.

d. State your own conclusion regarding the argument and what reasoning you used. ____

____

3.

Argument
Minors still drink, so age-21 laws clearly don't work.

Response
Age-21 laws work. Young people drink less in response. The laws have saved an estimated 17,000 lives since states began implementing them in 1975, and they've decreased the number of alcohol-related youth fatalities among drivers by 63% since 1982.

Stricter enforcement of age-21 laws against commercial sellers would make those laws even more effective at reducing youth access to alcohol. The ease with which young people acquire alcohol—three-quarters of 8th graders say that it is "fairly easy" or "very easy" to get—indicates that more must be done. Current laws against sales to minors need stiff penalties to deter violations. Better education and prevention-oriented laws are needed to reduce the commercial pressures on kids to drink. (From Opposing Viewpoints Resource Center, document X3010084223, http://www.galenet.galegroup.com/servlet/OVRC.)

a. T/F As stated, the argument is mostly opinion, but true.

b. Explain why you agree or disagree with the argument. ____________________

____

c. T/F The response uses more facts than opinions.

d. State your own conclusion regarding the argument and what reasoning you used. ____

____

Questions for Group Discussion

1. As a group, discuss your views on lowering the drinking age. Are your views and conclusions based on reasoned judgment? Review pages 224–226 on reasoning.
2. Of late, "binge drinking" on college campuses has received widespread coverage. Does this occur on your campus? Why does drinking seem to attract many students?
3. If you or anyone in your group has access to the Opposing Viewpoints Research Center, read the article "The Drinking Age Should Be Lowered" by Michael Clay Smith and compare it with what you just read. Is it mostly facts or opinions? Is the argument based on reasoned judgments?

Logical Fallacies

Of course, we can make mistakes in our reasoning. Sometimes we make statements that draw the wrong conclusions. There are called **logical fallacies.** Here are some of the more common fallacies that you should avoid making and that you should look for when you are reading:

1. *Either-or thinking* or *oversimplification* occurs when a simplistic answer is given to a large problem: "You want to get rid of abortion clinics? Let's blow them up." Either-or thinking is also oversimplifying issues: "Let's either get rid of all the nuclear weapons in the world, or learn to live with the bomb." Such thinking ignores or covers up other possible answers to a problem.
2. *Stereotyping* ignores individuality. There are stereotypes about political parties (Republicans are pro-rich people; Democrats are pro-poor people), stereotypes about Jews (they always look for bargains), stereotypes about blacks (they are better athletes), and so on. Stereotyping disallows looking at people, groups, or ideas on individual merit.
3. *Attacking a person's character* (the Latin term is *ad hominem*) to discredit someone's views is also a faulty way to reason: "Sure, Senator Nicely favors a bill to stop acid rain from being carried to Canada. Why shouldn't he? He owns a big farm in Canada and probably plans to retire there."
4. *Non sequiturs* (just a fancy Latin name for "it does not follow") occur when a logical reason is not provided for the argument being made. It's a contradiction when a person says, "Clint Eastwood would make a good president; his Dirty Harry movies show you how tough he'd be on crime." The two assertions don't logically follow, since one has nothing to do with the other.
5. *Arguments because of doubtful sources* occur when an unknown source or a source lacking authority is cited: "The government doesn't want us to know about UFOs, but the *National Enquirer* has been providing a lot of evidence that proves contrary." While it might be true that the government is hiding something, the *National Enquirer*'s reputation for sensationalism does not make it a good source to use as a convincing argument. Also, be careful when you read that a story comes from an unnamed "high-level official."
6. *Begging the question* occurs when something that has already been proven as a truth is used to argue a point. Arguing that drunken drivers are a menace is begging the question since it's already been proven that they are.

7. *Irrational appeal* occurs when appeals to our emotions, to our religious faith, or to authority are made rather than appeals or reasons based on logic. "Of course you'll vote Republican; our family always has." "I'll get even. The Bible says 'an eye for an eye.'" "My country, right or wrong."
8. *Mistaking the reason for an occurrence* happens when we fail to see there may be other causes or we are misled. "John is a naturally brilliant student." (Is John brilliant, or does he do well in school because his parents make him study more than others? Maybe he's trying to impress a girl in his class.) "Karla is absent from class again. She must not be a serious student." (Maybe Karla has a health problem, or a small child to attend, or lacks transportation to campus on certain days.)

If you have already read Chapter Three, you might want to review Practice D-3. If you haven't read that part of the book yet, you may want to read it now and compare these examples with the ones in Practice D-3. That practice is based on a chapter from a textbook that deals with logical fallacies.

There are many kinds of faulty reasoning, but the ones described in this chapter are some of the more common ones you should begin to look for and avoid using when you draw conclusions or make inferences.

PRACTICE C-3: Identifying Logical Fallacies

Directions: Read the following dialogues and determine which of the following logical fallacies or errors in reasoning appear in the argument. There may be more than one type in a dialogue.

a. either-or thinking (oversimplification)
b. stereotyping
c. attacking character
d. non sequitur (contradiction)
e. doubtful sources
f. begging the question
g. irrational appeal
h. mistaking the reason

1. SAM: There's only one real aim of education—to learn all you can while going to school.

GEORGE: Nonsense. Today, the only real reason to go to college is to get the skills necessary for a good job.

Error in reasoning: ____________________

Explain: ____________________

____

2. PAULA: Let's go hear the Nicaraguan ambassador at Fraley Hall tonight. It should be interesting to hear his views.

SUE: There's nothing that little commie's got to say that I want to hear.

Error in reasoning: ____________________

Explain: ____________________

____

3. HARRY: George is forming an organization to protest the dumping of toxic waste near the bird wildlife sanctuary. He really seems concerned about this. Quite a few people I know are joining with him. I think I will, too.

SALLY: Don't be a sucker: George's just doing it to bring attention to himself. He plans to run for president of the student body next term and wants to look good. Anyway, I dated him once and he came on too strong for me.

Error in reasoning: ______________________________

Explain: ______________________________

____

4. KIP: You going to vote for Sally? She'd make a good school representative on the board of education. She gets A's in all her classes.

PIP: You kidding? What does she know about politics? Anyway, a female's place is in the home, not running for office.

Error in reasoning: ______________________________

Explain: ______________________________

____

5. DALE: Did you hear that Sue is moving to the Midwest? She's convinced a major earthquake is going to hit us any day now.

FRED: She may be right. Have you been reading that series on natural disasters in the local newspaper? They predict an 8.8 earthquake will occur here in the next two years. The Midwest is a lot safer, that's for sure.

Error in reasoning: ______________________________

Explain: ______________________________

____

6. RAUL: Did you read about the junior high kid who stabbed and killed his friend after they watched the movie *Friday the 13th* on TV?

PAM: Isn't that terrible? Maybe now they'll stop showing that worthless junk on television. Everybody knows what a big influence TV viewing has on kids.

RAUL: But how will this incident change anything?

PAM: Now there's proof of the harm.

Error in reasoning: ______________________________

Explain: ______________________________

____

PRACTICE C-4: Evaluating Pros and Cons of an Argument

Directions: The next two reading selections argue the question, "Is school violence caused by gun availability?" One argues yes, the other argues no. Apply all the reading skills you have learned as you read each one. Answer the questions that follow.

1. Pro Argument:

"SCHOOL VIOLENCE IS CAUSED BY GUN AVAILABILITY"

1 *Bethel, Alaska, February 19, 1997:* A high-school student shoots and kills the school principal and a student in the school's commons area. *Paducah, Kentucky, December 1, 1997:* A fourteen-year-old boy opens fire on a before-school student prayer group, wounding five and killing two students. *Jonesboro, Arkansas, March 24, 1998:* Two boys, ages eleven and thirteen, shoot and kill four students and a teacher and wound ten other students. *Littleton, Colorado, April 20, 1999:* Worst of all, fourteen students and one teacher are shot and killed and another twenty students are wounded when two students open fire.

2 These are only four of the numerous high-profile school shootings that have occurred in recent years. And these bare statistics tell only part of the story. They don't tell anything about the thousands of students and families whose lives are changed forever, who spend years jumping at popping sounds, who never again feel safe in the place that, besides their home, they should feel safest.

3 All of these traumas occurred for one reason: The young shooters had access to guns.

GUNS IN SCHOOLS

4 Accoring to FBI statistics, each year around six thousand gun-related incidents in the nation's schools come to the attention of law enforcement officials. There are uncounted numbers of other incidents that are not officially reported. No wonder many students tell pollsters that they "fear violent attacks traveling to and from school as well as within school itself."[1]

5 According to a 1997 survey by the Centers for Disease Control and Prevention, 8 percent of high-school students—that's 1 in 12—admitted carrying a gun to school in the month before the survey. The FBI reported that in 1995, 43,211 juveniles were arrested for weapons violations. That's a lot of students with a lot of guns—and it doesn't count the young people who carried guns but were not arrested.

6 Numbers like these prove that teenagers have easy access to guns. In fact, in many states it's legal for young people to own guns. In the states where hunting is a strong part of the people's heritage, children as young as eight, nine, and ten routinely handle guns and own their own hunting rifles. This is insanity. Children don't have sound enough judgment to be handling these lethal weapons. And when they become teenagers, the dangers become even greater.

7 Mature teens may exercise judgment as strong as that of any adult. But for most teens, the adolescent years are a roller coaster of emotional turmoil. Their bodies and lives change so dramatically during these years that they often have a hard time dealing with the changes. They are deeply depressed one moment, manically excited the next, and burning with anger a moment later—and they have little control over these emotions. They have energy to burn, and they often act out their emotions in physical ways: They dance wildly, weep or giggle for hours, throw themselves into athletic encounters—and fight. Psychiatrist Sabine Hack says, "One thing we know about adolescents is that when something bad happens, they often get tunnel vision and see it as the only thing . . . They feel stuck and desperate, and they don't see any way out." She adds, "All adolescents want to be like other adolescents . . . . Seeing that someone else has done something, even something horrific like shooting people at school, may

give kids the idea, and make them feel that this is their escape."[2] Toss a gun into this emotional mix and you often get murder or suicide.

8 Teens' anger and depression are not only worrisome, they are also dangerous. Teens and guns are simply a volatile combination. The Center to Prevent Handgun Violence reports that nearly three thousand teens use guns to commit suicide every year. In its 1991 report "Juvenile Offenders and Victims," the U.S. Department of Justice's Office of Juvenile Justice and Delinquency Prevention reports that 78 percent of murders committed by juveniles involved a gun.

WHERE DO THEY GET THEM?

9 Where do teens and children get all these guns? Not surprisingly, most get them at home: "School security experts and law enforcement officials estimate that 80% of the firearms students bring to school come from home, while students estimated that 40% of their peers who bring guns to school buy them on the street,"[3] states one writer. The most highly publicized school shootings fit this pattern:

- Jonesboro, Arkansas, March 24, 1998. The two cousins stole guns from their grandfather's home.
- Littleton, Colorado, April 20, 1999. The two students purchased their guns illegally.
- Conyers, Georgia, May 20, 1999. A fifteen-year-old used guns taken from his stepfather's gun cabinet to shoot and wound six schoolmates.

10 Twenty, thirty, forty years ago, these types of incidents were all but unheard-of. Children and teens were just as emotional in those days as they are today. The difference is that today more than 240 million guns circulate in American society. A report in the *Journal of the American Medical Association* stated that "an estimated 1.2 million elementary-aged, latchkey children have access to guns in their homes."[4] Nearly anyone who wants to obtain a gun can, even child who doesn't truly understand a gun's lethality or an emotionally unstable teen who is angry with his or her parents, classmates, and teachers.

END EASY ACCESS

11 The fact is, if young people did not have such easy access to guns, they would not take them to school and intimidate, injure, and kill teachers and students. It is essential that society find a way to prevent guns from getting into young people's hands. Congress restricts gun dealers from selling handguns to persons under twenty-one, but in many states minors may still purchase guns at unregulated venues such as flea markets. Furthermore, although Congress has set limits on the gun-*buying* age, many states allow children to *own* guns they have received as gifts. Congress must close these loopholes in the law.

12 Another effort is to require that adults who own guns store them in such a way that young people cannot get them. Kathy Kauffer Christoffel is the founder of the Handgun Epidemic Lowering Plan, a medical network in Chicago. She says, "We need to start recognizing that when a child gets a gun, an adult somewhere is responsible, maybe the parent or neighbor who didn't lock it up, or the unscrupulous person who sold it to them."[5] If the adult fails to safeguard his or her firearms or, worse yet, gives or sells a gun to a youngster, he or she should be prosecuted as a negligent criminal. This kind of law would have prevented the Jonesboro killings. If the two boys had not been able to get the grandfather's guns, they would not have killed.

13 The American people must support efforts like these and any others that will safeguard children from school violence.

14 Going beyond laws, the country must also look at schools and find ways to assure that no guns are on their premises. Some schools today have police guards or metal detectors that check students for weapons when they enter the school. Some critics say that precautions like these make schools feel more like prisons than joyful places of learning. But to save our children and make them know they are secure, perhaps that is a price worth paying.

CONCLUSION

15 America is a land of 240 million guns, any one of which could be used to cause another tragedy like that in Littleton, Colorado, or Paducah, Kentucky, or any of the other scenes of school violence. Americans must see to it that young people cannot get guns, and if they do, they cannot take them into our schools.

FOOTNOTES

1. Coalition to Stop Gun Violence, "Guns in Schools." www.gunfree.org/csgv/bsc_sch.htm.
2. Quoted in Tamar Lewin, "Bloodshed in a Schoolyard," *New York Times*, March 26, 1998, A23.
3. Donna Harrington-Loeuker, "Blown Away," *American School Board Journal*, May 1992, 22.
4. Quoted in Coalition to Stop Gun Violence, "Guns in Schools."
5. Quoted in Lewin, "Bloodshed in a Schoolyard," A23.

a. List the major evidence the author gives to support his argument. ____________

____

b. What does the author say needs to be done to stop school violence being caused by guns? ____________

____

c. Does the author anticipate a counterargument opposing his views? ____________

____

d. Are the sources the author uses and quotes from credible and balanced?

____

e. Do you believe the argument is logical and balanced? Explain. ____________

____

2. Con Argument:

"SCHOOL VIOLENCE IS NOT CAUSED BY GUN AVAILABILITY"

1 In recent years, there has been an alarming number of school shootings. Many people blame these tragedies on young people's ability to obtain guns. But that couldn't be further from the truth. There's an old saying that's very true: Guns don't kill; people do. If the young people who shot their classmates and teachers hadn't had guns, they

would have found another way to wreak their terrible violence. Only early, effective intervention in the lives of violent youth can prevent these tragedies.

SCHOOL SHOOTINGS ARE EXTREMEMLY RARE

2 While not belittling the seriousness and tragedy of school violence, it is important to note that these incidents happen very rarely. An article in the *Los Angeles Times* points out, "Of 20 million middle-school and high-school students, fewer than a dozen have been killed at school this year [1998]. Of 20,000 secondary schools [high schools] nationwide, only ten have reported a murder on campus."[1] Almost half of the nation's schools reported no crime of any sort in the 1996–1997 school year. Of the incidents that do occur, only a small number involve guns. School violence, while serious, is not an epidemic threatening all children.

3 In 1998 the Centers for Disease Control and Prevention reported that "less than one percent of all homicides among school-aged children (five to nineteen years of age) occur in or around school grounds or on the way to and from schools."[2] *Newsweek* magazine reports that in 1996 "only 10 percent of schools registered even one serious violent crime; on average a high-school senior is 200 times as likely to be admitted to Harvard as to be killed in his school."[3] Only a very few, seriously disturbed students bring guns to school with the intent to harm others-and carry out that intent.

4 Referring to a tragic event in Jonesboro, Arkansas, where two boys shot fourteen students and a teacher, killing five of them, psychologist and novelist Jonathan Kellerman writes, "The *world* didn't fire 134 bullets at innocent children and teachers; two individuals did. And we'd better pay close attention to them and others like them in order to learn what created them and how to handle them." He continues, "The sad truth is that there *are* bad people."[4]

COLD-BLOODED KILLERS

5 No one would deny that the acts committed by the young killers in Jonesboro in 1998, in Paducah, Kentucky, in 1997, and in Littleton, Colorado, in 1999 were bad acts. But most people shy away from the idea that the young shooters may have been bad people. Kellerman suggests that most of these school killers tend to be cold-blooded—what psychologists call psychopathic, sociopathic, or sufferers of antisocial personality disorder, the term currently in favor with mental health professionals. People identified in this way often have no real emotional ties to others, have patterns of cruel treatment of animals and people, lie without remorse, and get in trouble with authority—parents, school, and the law. These people know the difference between right and wrong, but they don't care. They are more concerned about wrongs they believe have been done against themselves. They often relish the power they feel they have over others because of their cruelty.

6 In most of the instances of school violence in which students have carefully planned and carried out mass shootings, the young people involved do exhibit these kinds of traits. As the fourteen-year-old from Springfield, Oregon, who first murdered his parents and then went to school and shot up the cafeteria, killing two students. Kinkel had a pattern of abusing animals, he bullied his parents, he had no close school friends, and he was often in trouble with school authorities.

7 In his years of practice as a child psychologist, Kellerman encountered a number of young people he believed could very well turn out to be mass killers like Kinkel or the boys at Jonesboro if their behavior did not turn around. These cases are rare, he said, but they were truly frightening because these children had no feeling about

hurting others. The fortunate thing is that there are almost always warnings. If people pay attention to these signs and act on them, school tragedies can be avoided.

KIDS WHO WANT GUNS GET THEM

8 Helen Smith, another psychologist, agrees with Kellerman's assessment. She says that people who think keeping guns away from kids would solve the problem make two wrong assumptions: first, that young people have easier access to guns that they did in the past, and second, that if young people could not obtain guns, they wouldn't kill.

9 She points out that while there are more guns in the United States now than there were twenty or thirty years ago, "the percentage of households having guns is about the same as it was decades ago."[5] She also points to the time of the Vietnam War, when young people were not only holding peaceful demonstrations but were listening to antiwar activists like Jerry Rubin, who was calling for young people to "burn plastic suburbia down,"[6] and to Black Panthers who were fighting for black Americans' rights and were urging their followers to use any means to achieve their goals.

10 "For the availability-of-guns explanation to make sense," she writes,

> it [would be] necessary to believe that [during Rubin's time] . . . groups of depraved teens sat around plotting killing sprees like that in Littleton and then gave up in dismay and slunk off to college when they realized that they would be unable to come up with any guns. How likely is that? The fact is, despite Rubin's exhortations, teens weren't thinking that way back then. If they had been, they could have gotten guns.[7]

11 Regarding the second assumption, Smith says,

> this assumes that in the absence of easily available guns, would-be killer teens wouldn't have done anything. The Littleton killers disproved that by producing an arsenal of explosive devices. . . . The availability-of-guns explanation assumes that otherwise harmless, even nearly normal, kids become dangerous only in the presence of guns. The truth is that these kids are dangerous anyway.[8]

12 Indeed, Smith quotes one of the jailed school shooters she counseled. This boy told her, "So let them take away my guns. I would just use a knife."[9] Smith warns that the problem lies not with guns, but kids today "reach the breaking point without adults even noticing."[10]

NO ONE NOTICED

13 And that's one of the keys to the problem. Over and over, we discover too late that killer kids have given plenty of warning before committing their terrible deeds. Kip Kinkel wrote in school papers that he was going to kill everyone. Eric Harris had a website saying the same thing, and he and Dylan Kiebold, the shooters in Littleton, Colorado, had made a movie for one of their classes in which they used real guns to pretend to kill the school's athletes. These kids told the people around them what they were going to do, but no one noticed.

14 Keeping guns out of kids' hands may make some people feel better and may even prevent a few acts of impulsive violence, but it won't solve the problem. Reducing teen access to guns is like putting a Band-Aid on a bear bite. Only by all of us working together—parents, schools, society as a whole—can we hope to end the threat of violence in our schools.

FOOTNOTES

1. Carol Tavris, "Violence is a Symptom, Not an Inevitability," *Los Angeles Times,* March 24, 1998.
2. Centers for Disease Control and Prevention, "Facts About Violence among Youth and Violence in Schools," May 21, 1998.
3. Jerry Adler and Karen Springen, "How to Fight Back," *Newsweek,* May 3, 1999, 37.
4. Jonathan Kellerman, *Savage Spawn: Reflections on Violent Children.* New York: Ballantine, 1999, 33.
5. Helen Smith, "It's Not the Guns," Nando Media, May 1999. www.nandotimes.com.
6. Smith, "It's Not the Guns."
7. Smith, "It's Not the Guns."
8. Smith, "It's Not the Guns."
9. Smith, "It's Not the Guns."
10. Smith, "It's Not the Guns."

a. List the major evidence the author gives to support his argument. ___________

____

____

____

____

b. What does the author believe is the cause of school violence? _____________

____

____

c. Does the author consider a counterargument opposing his views? ___________

____

d. Are the sources the author uses and quotes from credible and balanced?

____

e. Do you believe the argument is logical and balanced? Explain. ____________

____

____

____

3. Considering the Pros and Cons of Both Arguments

a. Both authors refer to the Centers for Disease Control and Prevention in their essays. How do they make use of the references to support their own arguments?______________________________________

____

b. Both authors refer to the same school killings in Paducah, Jonesboro, and Littleton. How do they differ on why these violent acts occurred? ____________

____

c. Which argument is most persuasive? Why? ______________________

____

Application I:
Recognizing Attitude, Bias, and Inference in Other Materials

From a magazine, newspaper, or textbook, choose a selection and come up with your own questions about attitude, bias, and inference (at least one question about each). Bring the selection and questions to class and exchange with a classmate. Each of you should answer the other's questions. Discuss what you learned from each article by using critical reading skills.

D. Putting It All Together

The word *critical* often connotes finding fault with something. But as you have seen in this unit, reading critically implies an attempt at objective judging so as to determine both merits and faults. Critical reading is thoughtful reading because it requires that the reader recognize not only what is being said at the literal level but also facts, opinions, attitudes, inferences, and bias. A reader who is not actively involved is not reading critically.

Knowingly or unknowingly, you make critical judgments all the time, from deciding on the type of toothpaste to buy to choosing a topic for an English theme. The trick is always to be aware of your critical judgments and to know the reasoning behind your decisions.

Making critical judgments is a two-way street. As a reader you must be aware of the judgments the author is making and you must also be aware of the judgments you make, based on evidence rather than bias. For instance, you may dislike the subject of history so much that you have a bias against anything you read before you even get started. Your mind is already partly closed to the author. On the other hand, you could be biased in favor of what you read and accept what is being said simply because you already agree with the author. True critical reading should leave you a little wiser, a little better informed, and less biased than before-both about the subject and yourself.

Use the following practices to help you develop the critical reading skills taught in this unit.

PRACTICE D-1:

Directions: Read the title and the first paragraph of the following essay. Then in the space provided, write what you think the essay will discuss.

____

____

Now, as you read the essay, apply all the reading techniques you have been learning. Then answer the questions that follow.

THE DEBATE OVER THE LEGALIZATION OF MARIJUANA: AN OVERVIEW

Paul Van Slambrouck

1 In a year when Woodstock makes headlines and Austin Powers does well at the box office, another 1960s phenomenon is attempting its own comeback: legalization of marijuana.

2 Even as the courts, law enforcement, and the federal government continue to wrestle with growing acceptance of marijuana for medicinal purposes, advocates have begun the first serious campaign in decades to erase penalties for its recreational use.

3 Billboards are sprouting up across San Francisco, laced with some humor, but carrying the tagline: "Stop arresting responsible pot smokers."

4 "We decided it was time to try and move the marijuana debate beyond the medicinal issue," says Keith Stroup, founder of the Washington-based National Organization for the Reform of Marijuana Laws, which is behind the new campaign.

5 While San Francisco, with its liberal reputation, was chosen as the launch site for the campaign, it is likely to spread to Los Angeles and other major cities in the coming months, Mr. Stroup says. The goal, he says, is to "introduce the concept of responsible marijuana use" by adults.

SENDING THE WRONG MESSAGE?

6 Opponents worry about a nascent softening of marijuana laws in general, and object in particular to the ripple effect of this newest campaign.

7 "This message is dangerous because it tells teens that marijuana is a benign drug," says Joseph Califano, president of the National Center on Addiction and Substance Abuse at Columbia University in New York. In reality, marijuana is a gateway drug that can lead to use of cocaine and other harder drugs, according to the center.

8 While backers of the new campaign favor legalization, they're attempting as a first step revival of the decriminalization trend that took hold from the late 1960s through 1978.

9 During that decade, 11 states passed laws reducing penalties, generally to a fine, for the private use of small amounts of marijuana. The movement was broad and embraced states as dissimilar as Nebraska, North Carolina, New York, Mississippi, Oregon, and California.

10 Then in the 1980s, the nation's political environment changed dramatically, with soaring public angst over crime and the general direction of the nation's youth. By the 1990s, the war on drugs was under way and marijuana advocates had shifted their strategy to focus more narrowly on legalizing the drug for medicinal purposes.

11 Now marijuana proponents think the nation's mood is shifting once again and that, for a variety of reasons, sentiment favoring liberalization is building anew. The Marijuana Policy Project, a Washington group involved in the effort to permit medical marijuana, predicts that the number of states allowing such use will double from four currently to eight or so over the next 18 months. Maine will vote in November 1999 on a medical marijuana initiative, with other states to follow in 2000 with ballot initiatives or legislation.

SHIFT IN FEDERAL RESEARCH

12 While the Clinton administration (1993-2001) has been a staunch opponent of loosening marijuana laws, the line of opposition was breached early in 1999 when the Institute of Medicine ruled, after assessing a wide range of scientific studies, that marijuana can be effective as medicine.

13 The study, requested by the White House, ran counter to the administration's previous insistence that there was no evidence marijuana had an beneficial role in treating the ill.

14 The Institute of Medicine finding has prompted new guidelines for scientific research on a number of remaining issues related to medical marijuana. Proponents consider the move a major step forward after years when the government basically blocked additional inquiry.

15 Still, the federal government has not softened its position that federal law prohibiting marijuana trumps state laws allowing medicinal use.

16 Early in August 1999, federal prosecutors won their first case against someone growing marijuana since California passed its medicinal marijuana initiative in 1996. A federal judge in Sacramento, disallowing any consideration of the state's voter-approved law, sentenced B. E. Smith to 27 months in prison for growing 87 pot plants.

17 Stroup says people are "fed up with the notion that we need to send everyone to prison for minor drug offenses," particularly for activities sanctioned by states. In fact, legislation in Congress would allow states to set medicinal-use policies without federal interference.

18 Most polls show strong public support of medical marijuana use, but most people do not favor legalization. Positions on decriminalization, where recreational use is punished with fines rather than jail, are less clear and depend on how the questions are phrased.

19 Decriminalization advocates say "prohibition" is a policy failure. The costs of funneling small-time marijuana users through the criminal courts far outweigh any discernible gains, they argue, particularly when penalties have not deterred the flood of marijuana on the streets. About 695,000 Americans were arrested in 1997 on marijuana charges, 83 percent for simple possession.

20 Still groups such as the Family Research Council say any easing of drug laws would send a dangerous signal, particularly to teens, that will only make a bad problem worse.

Comprehension Check

Directions: Answer the following questions.

1. What is the author's thesis? ____________________

____

2. What is the author's intent? ____________________

____

3. Describe the author's attitude toward marijuana. ____________________

____

4. The author's overall tone is one of:

a. indifference

b. concern

c. sarcasm

d. neutrality

e. accusation

5. T/F The essay is based mostly on the opinions of others.

6. T/F We can infer that the author feels that legalizing marijuana use would send the wrong message to young people.

7. T/F We can infer that advocates for legalizing the use of marijuana change their tactics as the nation's mood shifts in its attitudes.

8. T/F The author gives a balanced view of both the opponents' and advocates' views regarding the legalization of marijuana.

9. Reread paragraph 14. What can be inferred about the government's position on research into the effects of marijuana use?

____

10. What conclusion do you draw from this essay about the possibility of marijuana use ever being legalized?

____

Vocabulary Check

Directions: Define the following underlined words from the essay. The number in parentheses is the paragraph where the word is used.

1. continue to <u>wrestle</u> with growing acceptance (2)

____

2. <u>laced</u> with some humor (3)

____

3. worry about a <u>nascent</u> softening (6)

____

4. a <u>benign</u> drug (7)

____

5. the souring public <u>angst</u> (10)

____

6. a medical marijuana <u>initiative</u> (11)

____

7. the line of opposition was <u>breached</u> early in 1999 (12)

____

8. federal law <u>trumps</u> state laws (15)

____

9. activities <u>sanctioned</u> by states (17)

____

10. outweigh any <u>discernible</u> gains (19)

____

Record the results of both checks on the Student Record Chart in the Appendix. Make certain you understand any problems you may have had with any of the questions before going on.

The following three reading selections can be used to practice increasing your reading speed of comprehension. You may want to look at your Student Record Chart to review your rate and comprehension scores from the last timed readings you did. You may want to just use these as reading comprehension practices and not time yourself. It's up to you and your instructor.

Each of the next reading practices contains comprehension and vocabulary checks that require using all the skills taught in this and the first unit of the book. Remember that you are competing against yourself. Try to learn from any mistakes you may make so that you can do better on each consecutive practice.

PRACTICE D-2: Timed Reading

Directions: Practice speed-reading strategies on the following 745-word selection. Start with a one-minute survey, making sure you look at the questions during the survey too. Push yourself to read faster than before.

______________________**Begin timing:**

SELF-ESTEEM IS EARNED, NOT LEARNED

MIKE SCHMOKER

1 The word *self-esteem* has become an educational incantation. Every educational discussion, every stated school district goal and mission takes a bow in its direction. Its influence on academic and behavioral standards in our schools cannot be overstated. There is even an official California Task Force to Promote Self-Esteem and Social Responsibility, and the University of California recently published a book linking low self-esteem to societal problems.

2 At first, the word seems innocent enough and something about which we should be concerned. But if the meaning of a word is its use, we must look to pop psychology, which gave us this word, in order to fully understand its importance. Before it reached education, it had already taken on the fatuous implication that what is precious can be gotten cheaply. Self-esteem, as it is now used, isn't something earned but given. It isn't wrought but spontaneously realized. Such thinking is inimical to what schools should be trying to accomplish.

3 What disturbs me is that self-esteem has been sentimentalized. The new self-esteem has less to do with forging a connection between it and achievement and more to do with simply creating good feelings.

4 This is an understandable reaction to a difficult problem. So many young people are burdened with negative, defeatist feelings. We want to help them, and the quicker the better. But as time has passed, it is mystifying that we have not seen this impulse for what it is. I've seen whole auditoriums full of students being told, indiscriminately, to feel good about themselves, being asked at random to stand up and give testimonials on how swell they are, and being reassured that by clinging to this confidence they will succeed mightily.

5 This is a flimsy notion, and no one believes it. Not for very long anyway. Like it or not, self-esteem is very much a function of such unyielding realities as what we can do, what we've done with what we have and what we've made of ourselves. And so the school—with every effort toward sensitivity, compassion and encouragement—should reinforce this, while cultivating ability, talent, decency and the capacity for sustained effort, the belief that you get what you pay for.

6 Shortcuts, such as routinely heaping inordinate praise on shoddy work, or lowering academic standards, do not work. Ask any teacher, in a moment of candor, if he or she can get average kids, the majority of students, to make a sufficient effort in school, make good use of class time or do fairly conscientious work on homework and assignments. An alarming number of teachers don't think so. Many complain of a malaise among students, adding that only about half of their students will even do homework. Despite this, there has never been more pressure for teachers to be enormously upbeat in dealing with students and student efforts. Promotion is nearly automatic, and grades are higher than ever.

7 What this tells students, at least tacitly, is that what they are doing is good enough and that our insistence on quality is a bluff.

8 It's ironic that the reason often cited for generous grading and reluctance to fail students centers on self-esteem. In the name of self-esteem, then, we are asked to give young people something they didn't earn in the mistaken hope that they can go on to master what is presumably harder than what they have already failed to learn.

9 What they do learn is to play the game, the essence of which is that standards are not based on what students should do, or are able to do, but on what they will do, no matter how low the common denominator. And that is, as we know, pretty low; among industrialized nations, we rank embarrassingly in every academic category.

10 But you'll seldom see these deficiencies reflected in American report cards. The plain, unpleasant truth is hidden behind the good grades, lost in the peculiarly positive climate that too often prevails in our schools. If you're not sure that's true, consider this: A recent international survey showed that South Korean students rank first in mathematics, American students near the bottom. When asked where they thought they ranked, the American students ranked themselves at the top and the Koreans at the bottom.

11 It is common knowledge that so much groundless praise can breed complacency. It can. And it has.

12 For our part, the best we can do is teach young people, in an atmosphere of compassion, that self-esteem is earned, often with considerable difficulty, and equip them to earn it.

Finish timing. Record time here: ____________ and use the Timed Readings Conversion Chart in the Appendix to figure your rate: ____________ wpm.

Comprehension Check

Directions: Now answer the following questions.

1. The author's main idea or thesis is:
   - **a.** self-esteem has been sentimentalized
   - **b.** self-esteem can be taught in the classroom
   - **c.** an official California Task Force to Promote Self-Esteem and Social Responsibility recently published a book linking low self-esteem to societal problems
   - **d.** we need to teach young people that self-respect is earned, often with difficulty
2. What does the author mean when he says that "the word *self-esteem* has become an education incantation"? ______________________________

   ____
3. The author states, "The new self-esteem has less to do with forging a connection between it and achievement and more to do with simply creating good feelings." Based on this, how do you think the author defines "self-esteem"? ______________

   ____

   ____

   ____
4. T/F According to the author, self-esteem is a function of what we are capable of doing, what we've done with our ability, and what we've made of ourselves.
5. Explain why the author does or does not believe in automatic promotion? ______

   ____

   ____

   ____
6. What does the author mean when he says that students "learn to play the game"?

   ____

   ____

   ____
7. According to the author, where do American students rank academically among industrialized nations? To what does he attribute this? ______________

   ____

   ____
8. According to a recent survey, where do American students academically rank themselves in mathematics in comparison to South Korean students? Where do they really rank? ______________________________

   ____

   ____

9. According to the author, too much groundless praise can breed or cause ________

____

10. Explain what the title means. ________

____

____

Vocabulary Check

Part A

Directions: Define the underlined words in the following phrases and sentences from the article you just read.

1. The word *self-esteem* has become an education incantation. ________

____

2. We must look to pop psychology, which gave us this word ["self-esteem"]. ________

____

3. So many young people are burdened with negative, defeatist feelings. ________

____

4. They stand up and give testimonials on how swell they are. ________

____

5. It is common knowledge that so much groundless praise can breed complacency.

____

Part B

Directions: Select from the list below the proper word for each blank in the following paragraph.

candor shoddy conscientious routinely malaise

Shortcuts, such as **(6)**________heaping praise on **(7)**________work, or lowering academic standards, do not work. Ask any teacher, in a moment of **(8)**________ if he or she can get average kids, the majority of students, to make a sufficient effort in school, make good use of class time or do fairly **(9)**________work on homework and assignments. An alarming number don't think so. Many complain of a **(10)**________among students. Despite this, there has never been more pressure for teachers to be enormously upbeat in dealing with students efforts.

PRACTICE D-3: Timed Reading

Directions: Take about one minute to preview the following 465-word selection and questions. After your preview, time yourself on the reading.

Begin timing: ____________________

PUSH FOR DE-EMPHASIS OF COLLEGE SPORTS

David Holahan

1 How many exalted muck-a-mucks with advanced degrees to burn does it take to restate the obvious and then miss the whole point? Twenty-two in the case of the Knight Foundation Commission on Intercollegiate Athletics.

2 It took these wizards more than a year to determine that big-time college athletics are out of control, something high school equivalency degree holders have known for decades.

3 The Knight posse also recommended many wondrous things, including this startling caveat: Colleges should not admit athletes who are unlikely to graduate. Small wonder that news of this long-awaited report was buried on page 4 of my local sports section. Page 1 was devoted to pictures of "scholar-athletes" jumping about in short pants.

4 The principal advice of this pedantic treatise is that college presidents should take an active role in administering and overseeing their schools' athletic programs. Or, in plain language, let the big boss ride the tiger that big-time sports has become.

5 What a preposterous proposal. It presumes athletics are so important that the heads of universities should divert time and energy from overseeing education to monitoring the sideshow. The house is rotten to the core and the Knight panel recommends a fresh coat of paint.

6 What is wrong with big-time college sports is not who administers them or which department rakes in the booty or how many jocks can master majors like "family studies." What's wrong is the sports themselves, how perversely important they have become to the players, the coaches, the colleges, the alumni and the fans.

7 It would be tempting to say that money is the disease, the billions that TV networks pay schools to entertain us. But money is just the symptom. The root cause is that we simply value sports too highly. They have become the new opiate of the masses.

8 This is where the commission dropped the ball. Its 20 men and two women (men monitoring sports is a bit like foxes regulating chicken coops) should have insisted on de-emphasis. We are now in the midst of "March madness," CBS's term for the NCAA basketball tournament. Madness, indeed, with sanity nowhere in sight.

9 Even those athletes who do manage to pass their courses are doing so, by and large, so that they can continue their sporting careers. Education, if that is the right word for what these young men and women experience, is the means. Basketball, to cite the semi-pro sport du jour, is the end.

10 How sad that these teenagers head off to college thinking that being a star athlete is the most important, perhaps the only, goal to strive toward. Rarely does anything they encounter on sports-factory campuses disabuse them of this notion. They are there to run and jump and dribble. With a world of possibilities surrounding them, they limit themselves to the one thing they have already mastered. We all should be ashamed of ourselves.

Finish timing. Record time here: ____________ and use the Timed Readings Conversion Chart in the Appendix to figure your rate: ____________ wpm.

Comprehension Check

Directions: Now answer the following questions.

1. The main idea or thesis of the article is that our society has placed too much value on college sports.

a. True because ______________________________

____

b. False because ______________________________

____

2. The intent of this article is to

a. criticize the findings of the Knight Foundation Commission on Intercollegiate Athletics.

b. advocate the findings of the Knight Foundation Commission.

c. place the blame on the overemphasis of the value of college sports on the presidents of the universities involved.

d. show that many college athletes are more interested in sports than in getting an education.

3. The author's attitude toward his subject is

a. playful.

b. serious.

c. angry with a touch of sarcasm.

d. disinterest.

4. The author's question "How many exalted muck-a-mucks with advanced degrees to burn does it take to restate the obvious and then miss the whole point?" is an example of the way writers create tone.

a. True because ______________________________

____

b. False because ______________________________

____

5. We can infer from what the author says that he does not care for college sports.

a. True because ______________________________

____

b. False because ______________________________

____

6. Explain the statement that sports have "become the new opiate of the masses."

____

7. We can infer that the Knight Foundation Commission on Intercollegiate Athletics met for over a year to investigate college athletics.

   a. True because ______________________________

   ____

   b. False because ______________________________

   ____

8. What inference can we draw from paragraph 3 regarding the author's opinion of the Knight Foundation Commission? ______________________________

   ____

9. What does the author mean when he says, "With a world of possibilities surrounding them, they [college athletes] limit themselves to the one thing they have already mastered"? ______________________________

   ____

10. What inferences can we draw regarding *why* the author feels as he does about college athletics? ______________________________

    ____

Vocabulary Check

Directions: Define the underlined words in the following phrases.

1. many <u>exalted</u> muck-a-mucks with advanced degrees (paragraph 1)

   ____

2. recommended many wondrous things, including this startling <u>caveat</u> (paragraph 3) ______________________________

   ____

3. this pedantic <u>treatise</u> (paragraph 4) ______________________________

   ____

4. this <u>pedantic</u> treatise (paragraph 4) ______________________________

   ____

5. a <u>preposterous</u> proposal (paragraph 5) ______________________________

   ____

6. how <u>perversely</u> important (paragraph 6) ______________________________

   ____

7. to <u>cite</u> the semi-pro sport du jour (paragraph 9) ______________________________

   ____

8. to cite the semi-pro <u>sport du jour</u> (paragraph 9) ______________________________

   ____

9. <u>disabuse</u> them of this notion (paragraph 10) ______________________________

   ____

10. intercollegiate athletics (paragraph 1) ____________________

____

Record your rate, comprehension, and vocabulary scores on the Student Record Chart in the Appendix. Each correct answer is worth 10 percent. Discuss your results with your instructor.

PRACTICE D-4: Timed Reading

Directions: The following 1,100-word article comes from an 1991 interview that *Newsweek* reporter Ginny Carroll had with Carol Barkalow, a 1980 graduate of West Point. Captain Barkalow has commanded an air-defense platoon in Germany and a truck company at Fort Lee, Virginia, and she is the author of *In the Men's House,* a book about her life in the military. Survey the following selection before timing yourself. Read the title and answer the questions below. Then time yourself, reading as rapidly as you can with good comprehension.

1. What do you think the title means? ____________________

____

2. Why do you think women should or should not be allowed to fight in combat zones? ____________________

____

3. What reasons might the author give for allowing females to fight in combat?

____

Begin timing: ____________________

WOMEN HAVE WHAT IT TAKES

Carol Barkalow as Told to Ginny Carroll

1 I realized I wanted a military career when I was 16, the summer between my junior and senior years of high school. I had been very active in athletics. I enjoyed the discipline, the comradeship, the physicalness of sports, helping other teammates. I also wanted to serve my country. For me, the answer was the Army. My guidance counselor told me that West Point was starting to accept women. I was in the first class.

2 As plebes, we were required to greet the upperclassmen "Good morning, sir." Too often we'd hear back, "Mornin', bitch." I was naive, I guess. I thought my classmates wanted the same thing I wanted. I thought they would just accept me for that. By the time we graduated, the men's attitudes had begun to mellow somewhat. The women's attitudes had changed, too. If we weren't feminists when we went in, we were when we came out. I went back for my 10-year reunion in October 1990. There was a big difference. My male classmates had changed tremendously. They recognized us as peers. I realized they had been going through their own growth a decade ago, the hell of being a cadet. The reunion was the best time I ever had at West Point.

3 But some of those old attitudes still linger when the question of women in combat arises. It's a generational issue for the most part. Most of the senior leadership had

little opportunity to work with women as peers. Many see us as a mother, a wife, a daughter—especially a daughter. They always say they wouldn't want to see their daughters in combat. What I ask them in return is, would you really want to see your *son* in combat? And isn't it the daughter's choice? One lesson our society learned in the Persian Gulf is that it is no more tragic to lose a mother, a sister, a daughter than it is to lose a father, a brother or a son—and no less so.

4 I volunteered to go to the gulf. I was attached to the 24th Infantry Division, the unit that spearheaded the end-around attack. Our support outfit was in just as much danger as the combat element. The Iraqi weapons had just as much capability of hitting us as the men in front. The difference was that we didn't have the capability to defend ourselves like the combat troops.

5 One question that is always raised is whether women have what it takes to kill an enemy face to face—whether we can handle that particular brand of stress. After my book came out last year, a Vietnam vet named Bill Hanake came to see me. He had a leg and a foot blown off in Vietnam. I think Bill's experience is an eloquent answer to the naysayers who think women don't have what it takes for combat. Both times his unit was overrun in 'Nam, he said, it was the Viet Cong *women* who were the more disciplined, the tougher, who were the most willing to make sure their enemy wasn't going to come back at 'em.

6 Then there's the argument that men will be overprotective of women. When men are overprotective of *men,* we give them awards for valor. In May, our country awarded an Air Force pilot its second highest medal for leading a nine-hour rescue mission for a fallen flier. That wasn't looked upon as overprotective. Would it have been so if the downed flier had been a woman?

7 Some believe females would interfere with male bonding. In Saudi, I saw a new type of relationship forming between men and women, one that has traditionally been described among men. It was a nurturing relationship based upon respect, based on sharing the same hardships. The big worry before Vietnam was that blacks couldn't bond with whites. When the bullets started flying, that went away pretty fast. The same type of relationships developed in the gulf between men and women soldiers.

8 Do I believe women should be allowed to serve in the infantry? Yes, if qualified. The training and physical-strength standards should be uniform. We have standards that we must keep. Our military readiness should never suffer. But I saw a number of physically strong men very scared in Saudi Arabia. It's not just a matter of physical strength. It's mental and emotional strength as well. I think God knew what he was doing when he allowed women to bear the children and gave us the ability to handle that mental and emotional stress.

9 Pregnancy? The military doesn't have a good handle on the question. When the military looks at pregnancy, it sees it as nonavailability. We had more injuries and nonavailability among men than women in Saudi. Too often, the women are the only ones held responsible for pregnancy, not the men who helped get them that way.

10 No normal person wants to go into combat. Soldiers are the last people who want to. But we've volunteered. We understand our commitment. Everybody raises a hand, male and female, and swears to support and defend the same Constitution. Women are competent, capable and committed. We are in a integral part of the best-trained military force in the world. The services should have the flexibility to assign the best-qualified person to the job, regardless of gender. That's the bottom line.

Finish timing. Record time here: ____________ and use the Timed Readings Conversion Chart in the Appendix to figure your rate: ____________ wpm.

Comprehension Check

Directions: Now answer the following questions.

1. What is the main idea or thesis of the reading selection?____________________

____

____

2. T/F Captain Barkalow is biased toward her position on fighting in combat.

3. The intent of the selection is

a. to convince doubters that women are capable of combat fighting.

b. to convince women not to join the military.

c. to promote sales of her book.

d. to show how difficult it is for women to prove themselves in the service.

4. The author's attitude toward the military is

a. negative.

b. positive.

c. wary.

d. not able to tell.

5. T/F We can infer that Barkalow enjoyed attending West Point.

6. T/F Barkalow served voluntarily in a combat zone during what is known as the Persian Gulf War against Iraq.

7. What is Barkalow's answer to those who say that they don't want to see their daughters in combat? ____

____

8. How does Barkalow counter those who question whether women have what it takes to kill an enemy face to face? __________________________________

____

9. What does Barkalow mean when she says, "I think God knew what he was doing when he allowed women to bear the children and gave us the ability to handle that mental and emotional stress"? __________________________________

____

10. According to Barkalow, what's "the bottom line" when it comes to putting women into combat?____

____

Vocabulary Check

Directions: Define the following underlined words.

1. <u>plebes</u> were required to greet the upperclassmen (paragraph 2) ________________

____

2. recognized us as peers (paragraph 2) ______________________________

____

3. a decade ago (paragraph 2) ______________________________

____

4. the unit that spearheaded the attack (paragraph 4) ______________________________

____

5. an eloquent answer (paragraph 5) ______________________________

____

6. answer the naysayers (paragraph 5) ______________________________

____

7. interfere with male bonding (paragraph 7) ______________________________

____

8. sees it as nonavailability (paragraph 9) ______________________________

____

9. an integral part (paragraph 10) ______________________________

____

10. regardless of gender (paragraph 10) ______________________________

____

Record your rate, comprehension, and vocabulary scores on the Student Record Chart in the Appendix. Each correct answer is worth 10 percent. Discuss your results with your instructor.

Questions for Group Discussion

1. Discuss what can be inferred about the authors' biases in the articles by Van Slambrouck, Fleming, Holahan, and Barkalow.
2. Find examples of logical fallacies in other materials. Decide the effect of these fallacies on your understanding of the material.
3. Discuss the conclusion the author intends in any one of the four articles in "Putting It All Together." Now take another side and support that conclusion.
4. Did anyone's opinions change because of any of the four articles? As a group, explain why or why not.

A Final Check

At the beginning of this unit, you looked at a diagram that illustrated the three facets of comprehension. Now you have completed the unit that is represented by the left leg of the triangle.

For the diagram on page 255, fill in the blank lines in this section. Working with a partner or small group is acceptable if your instructor sets up groups.

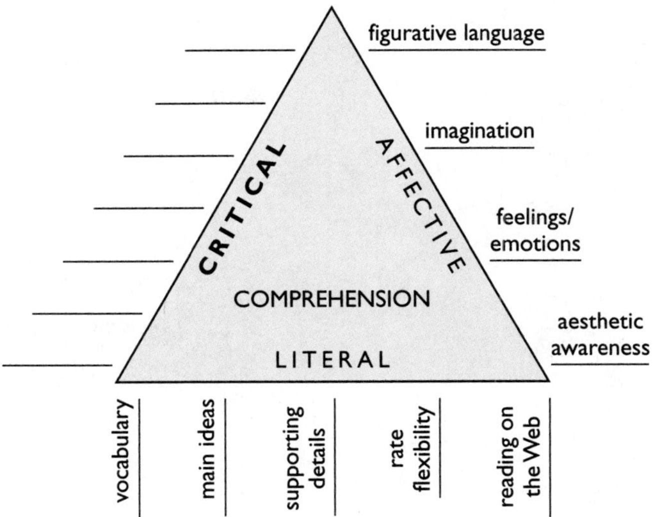

Hints: The first line has to do with information and judgments. The next four lines have to do with the author's worldview and how it influences our reading. The sixth line has to do with reading between the lines. The seventh line deals with what the reader does based on the information given.

When you have finished, check your answers with the triangle at the beginning of Unit Two.

UNIT THREE

AFFECTIVE COMPREHENSION

What Is Affective Comprehension?

Knut Hamsun wrote that "One must know and recognize not merely the direct but the secret power of the word." This unit is about the "secret power of the word," or affective comprehension.

Affective comprehension, most simply put, is your reaction to what you read at the literal and critical levels of understanding. It is your intellectual and emotional response to what you read. Why, for instance, do some people prefer to read factual materials rather than fiction? Why do some people react favorably and others negatively to a novel such as *Moby Dick?* Why do some people read fiction merely for recreation, whereas others find it personally enlightening? These differences are based on people's affective reaction to the type of material that they read.

The purpose of this book is not just to present you with various reading skills. While the development of skills is important, it is more important that you understand the distinction between the different kinds and levels of reading. As Frank Jennings says in his book *This Is Reading:*

> We read to learn. We read to live another way. We read to quench some blind and shocking fire. We read to weigh the worth of what we have done or dare to do. We read to share our awful secrets with someone we know will not refuse us. We read our way into the presence of great wisdom, vast and safe suffering, or into the untidy corners of another kind of life we fear to lead. With the book we can sin at a safe distance. With Maugham's artists in *The Moon and Sixpence,* we can discommit ourselves of family responsibility and burn our substance and our talent in bright colors on a tropical isle.

Unless we react at an affective level, a personal, meaningful level, reading becomes dull and uninteresting. It becomes nothing more than a series of isolated drills where you read and answer questions to plot on a chart.

Once you have mastered the basic reading skills, it is important to move into the world of facts and opinions, ideas, and feelings. As a good reader, you will become your own teacher, using the learned skills to rebuild and reorganize your thoughts and beliefs. That can only happen when affective reactions to what is read take place.

Affective comprehension also has to do with our tastes and appreciation of the skills involved in writing. For instance, many people prefer to read *Reader's Digest* because it takes a collection of readings from a variety of sources and condenses them for easier and faster reading. What they end up reading is seldom the original work; in fact, the language is frequently changed or written at a lower level. This may be a convenient way to read from many sources, but some readers prefer reading the original works. It's a matter of preference and taste.

Our tastes in reading often change as we ourselves change. For example, as a college student you may be required to read a book that is considered a classic. At the time in your life that you are reading it, you may be bored by the work and wonder what all the praise is about. Years later, a rereading of that book may provide you with the answers to your own questions that you weren't ready for during college. Does your present lack of appreciation for, say, Herman Melville's *Moby Dick* mean you lack taste? Do you have poor affective comprehension? Will you "appreciate" it when you're eighty years old? Why do critics think it's such a great work? Answers to these questions are all part of developing affective comprehension.

Some people try to rely solely on their intellect as a way to see and respond to the world. While reason is important, it is just as important to stay in touch with our feelings; it's what makes us human. When we lose touch with our feelings, we lose a part of our humanity, the part of us that lets us know we're alive. Reacting affectively is to react openly, to share our feelings with others, and to know that others can, have, and will feel as we do.

What Does This Unit Cover?

Much of our affective reaction has to do with our feelings. Someone once said that our feelings are our sixth sense, the sense that interprets, analyzes, orders, and summarizes the other five senses. Whether or not we feel and appreciate the fear, joy, shock, or passion an author wants us to feel through words depends on our ability to feel them in real life. The inability to react to what we read with appropriate feelings is to miss a large part of what total comprehension is all about.

This unit contains two chapters. The first practices in Chapter Seven, through the use of pictures, advertisements, and expository writings, will help you understand your affective reaction to a variety of materials. The second set of practices develops your ability to see how figurative language is used to create images and analogies as used in poetry. You have already done some drills in figurative language in Unit Two; this chapter will explore your affective reactions to words at the literal, critical, and affective levels of comprehension.

Chapter Eight provides practices in reading short fiction. Reading fiction requires a different approach from expository writing. Just as painters deal with different colors and designs to give us an image of how they see things, so do writers paint pictures with words. They stimulate our senses—taste, touch, smell, sight, and sound—with word images. How well a writer can create impressions and emotional reactions for us often depends on his or her use of figurative language.

In this unit it is important to discuss some of the questions in class. Only through interacting with others, sharing your feelings and listening to those of others, will you begin to develop your affective levels of comprehension. Good discussions are frequently frustrating because there often doesn't seem to be a "correct" answer. (It's especially frustrating to instructors who want all questions to have right or wrong answers in order to make grading your responses easier!) But sometimes there are no "right" answers; it's important to listen to others as their sixth sense (feelings) interprets their literal and critical thought processes.

What Should You Know after Completing This Unit?

As in previous units, there are some objectives you should strive to accomplish by the time you finish this unit. You should be able to:

1. Recognize how writers use figurative language to stimulate our senses.
2. Recognize images in both fictional and nonfictional writings.
3. Write a definition of affective comprehension.
4. See how closely tied together literal, critical, and affective levels of comprehension are.
5. Approach the various types of literature with an awareness of what is expected of you as a reader in each case.
6. Know all three facets of the comprehension triangle below:

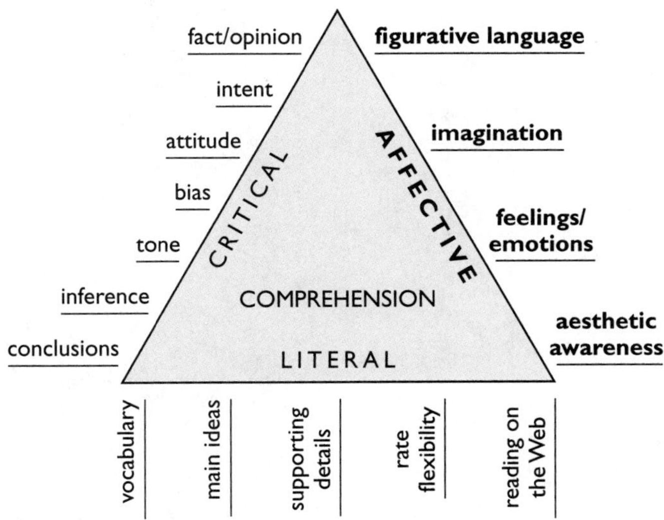

If you have personal objectives of your own, write them down and share them with your instructor.

Personal reading objectives for Unit Three:

____

____

____

____

____

CHAPTER 7

Developing Affective Awareness

A. Responding Affectively

One important element involved in developing reading comprehension is your affective or emotional involvement with what you read. Without an affective reaction of what you read, comprehension would be just matter-of-fact and rather dull. Some things, such as scientific and historical facts, can be presented and received with little or no affective reaction. But the whole range of human emotions is also communicated through the written word. The concern of this chapter is your affective reaction to what you read.

There are both negative and positive affective reactions. You may begin reading a poem, story, or essay with a positive attitude, only to discover that what you are reading isn't really interesting or moving or agreeable to you. This legitimate type of negative response comes about because of the literature itself, not because of a prereading judgment on your part. It is also possible to approach something you read with a preconceived bias, or to let your emotional reaction to what you read warp your critical judgment. Only when your affective reaction is based on critical evaluation and judgment is it a valid reaction.

Everyone reacts affectively. The idea is to develop your awareness of why your affective reaction is what it is, to investigate the reasons behind your emotional and intellectual responses. For instance, many readers lack interest in fiction and its literary effects and values. They just want the facts, the quick bottom line. They think that reading fictional literature *is* useless and unproductive, perhaps even slightly immoral. Many people think that reading literature is too pleasure oriented, too elite, or only for a select few oddballs. Some even feel that because literature is "madeup," it is not related to real life; it's untrue, humorless, and boring. These are all affective reactions, but they all are based on an unaware, undeveloped sense of aesthetics and reflect poor affective understanding. If nothing else, literature *is* a reflection of life, and because of the affective involvement necessary for reading fiction, it often can teach us more about ourselves and others than can factual writings.

The point of this chapter is to help you open up to affective communication. Practices include reacting to pictures as well as to words in order to help you understand what affective comprehension is, give you more ways to develop your affective reactions, and expose you to a variety of affective experiences. As you do the exercises in this chapter, ask yourself why you are reacting as you do. When you have finished, you should be closer to reaching objectives 3, 4, and 5 for this unit: to be able to write a definition of affective comprehension; to understand the interrelationship among literal, critical, and affective comprehension; and to approach various types of imaginative literature with the awareness of what is expected to you as a reader.

Reading and Reacting to Advertisements

You are surrounded by advertisements—on television, in magazines and newspapers, and on the radio. These ads influence us in both subtle and not-so-subtle ways. If you see twenty ads a day that encourage you to value new cars as a path to a better life, you are prone to think you need a new or different car.

We often don't think of "reading" ads, yet this is certainly of the most common reading tasks people do. Learning how to read ads is the subject of a full course, but this section will show you how two strategies help you become more effective and affective readers of advertisements.

One way advertisements and pictures work is by leading you to *evaluations*, or examinations and judgments. You evaluate when you decide one college class is better than another, when you choose one brand of pizza over another, or when you decide how to spend your free time. Evaluations are a part of your everyday life, but they can also be a problem when you make evaluations without thinking about, being aware of, or analyzing them. Advertisements may lead you to these unconscious evaluations by playing on your feelings. You may not think you're paying any attention to the advertisements or you may ignore the effect they have on you—but that doesn't lessen their impact on you. You can learn to examine ads for evaluations and then decide whether you agree with that evaluation. If the ad talks about being happy, for example, what sort of evaluation of happiness are you getting? What does the ad imply will make you happy?

A second way advertisements work is through their *use of language.* Ads tend to use few words, and each word usually has multiple *connotations,* or meanings that are associated with or underlie the dictionary definitions or *denotations.* Words such as *pleasure* or *good times* carry many connotations for most of us. You probably get a feeling of positive emotions when these words appear. If you see a female in a picture and one person refers to her as a "girl" while the other person refers to her as a "lady," what are the different connotations you would get from these words? One has the connotation of youth or inexperience, and the other connotes an older woman of a certain refinement.

Do the first two practices to make you more aware of how ads function and how you "read" them. The other two practices (A-3 and A-4) help you develop affective reactions to an essay and a modern fable.

PRACTICE A-1: An Ad

Directions: Answer the following questions about the advertisement for the American Society of Travel Agents on page 264 that shows a man in a rowboat.

1. In ads, the pictures carry much of the message. Jot down a few words that express your first evaluation of the picture of the man and the boat in the ad. ________
____
____

2. What do you assume is the intended audience for this ad (gender, age, other)? Why do you make this assumption? ____
____

3. The text "This isn't what I thought they meant by 'singles cruise'" has double meanings and connotations. What are two of the meanings?
____
____

4. What is the intention of mentioning what "the brochure" said in the first line of the text? What did the consumer find out or not find out from the brochure? ____
____

5. What does the text say a travel agent will save you? Why are these three details listed in this particular order and manner? ____
____
____

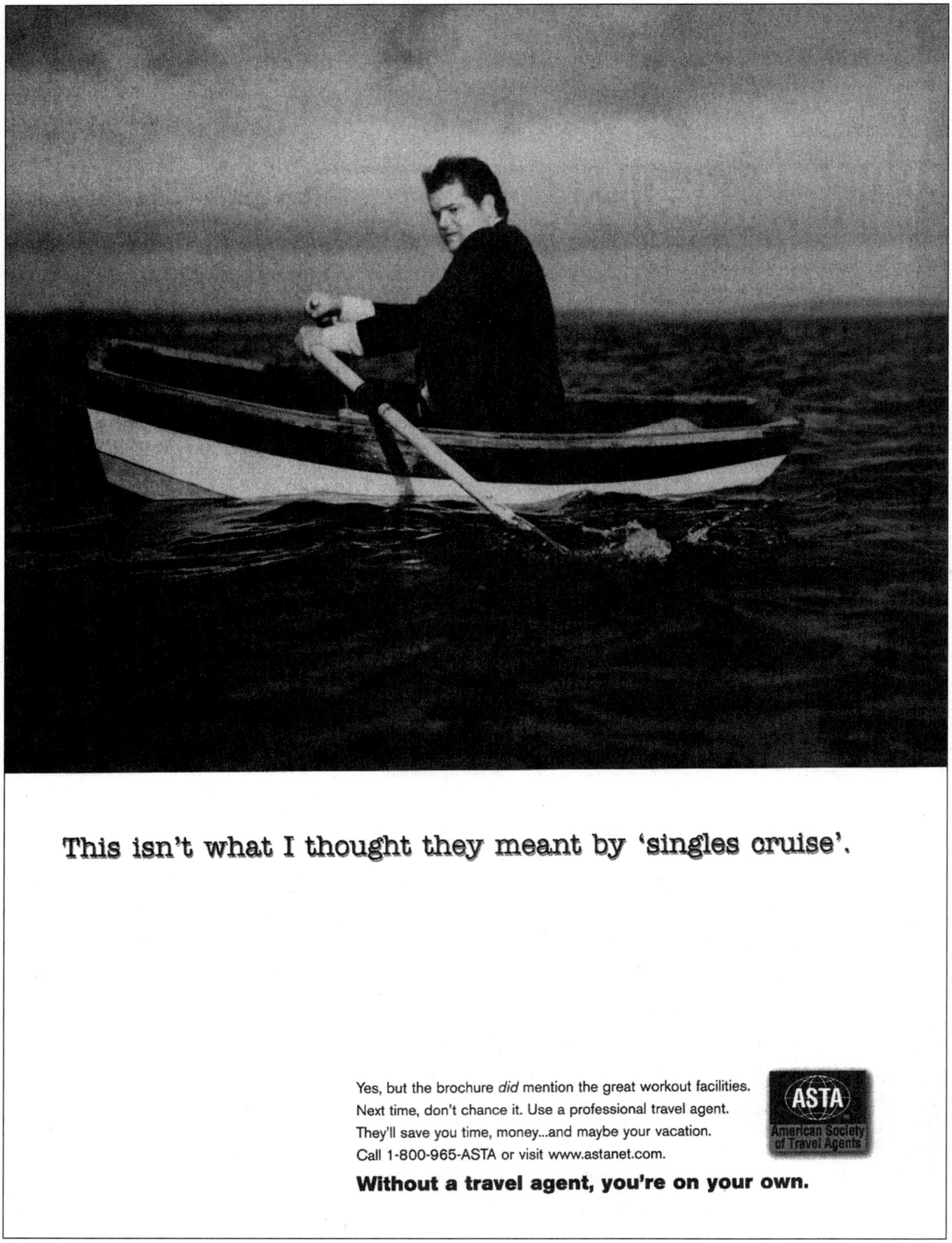

This isn't what I thought they meant by 'singles cruise'.

Yes, but the brochure *did* mention the great workout facilities.
Next time, don't chance it. Use a professional travel agent.
They'll save you time, money...and maybe your vacation.
Call 1-800-965-ASTA or visit www.astanet.com.

Without a travel agent, you're on your own.

Reprinted by permission of American Society of Travel Agents.

6. Explain the relationship of the caption under the picture and the highlighted line at the end of the text: "Without a travel agent, you're on your own." ____________

7. What, besides travel agents, is the ad "selling"? ____________

8. After examining the entire ad more carefully, now what is your affective reaction to the ad? ____________

PRACTICE A-2: Another Ad

Directions: Look at the ad for BoxLot reproduced on page 266. Then answer the following questions.

1. Jot down a few words that express your first reaction to the ad. ____________

2. How do you evaluate the woman in the ad from the bicycle she has bought and the clothes she is wearing? ____________

3. Who is the ad directed to? Explain your evaluation of audience here. ____________

4. The text "Now, my life is complete" equates a "complete life" with what? Explain.

5. What are the connotations you associate with the first line of text: "What would it take to make you happy?" How would you answer the question of what would make you happy? ____________

6. What is the intent of this ad? ____________

7. How does the text "Finders. Keepers." play on familiar refrains? What is the effect of the period between the two words? ____________

Reprinted by permission of boxLot.com.

8. After examining the ad carefully, what is your reaction to the ad now? ____________

____

____

PRACTICE A-3: An Essay

Directions: Read the following selection and then answer the questions that follow.

WHEN TELEVISION ATE MY BEST FRIEND

Linda Ellerbee

1 I was eight years old when I lost my best friend. My *very first very* best friend. Lucy hardly ever whined, even when we kids played cowboys and she had to be Dale Evans. Nor did she cry, even when we played dodge ball and some big kid threw the ball so hard you could read *Spalding* backward on her legs. Lucy was worldclass.

2 Much of our time together was spent in my back yard on the perfect swing set: high, wide, built solid and grounded for life. But one June day long ago, something went wrong. I was swinging as high as I could, and still higher. The next time the swing started to come back down, I didn't. I just kept going up. And up.

3 Then I began to fall.

4 "Know what? Know what?" Lucy was yelling at me.

5 No, I didn't know *what*. All I knew was that my left arm hurt.

6 "Know what? For a minute there, you flew. You seemed to catch the wind and . . . soar! Right up until you must have done something wrong, because you fell."

7 Wearing a cast on my broken arm gave me time to work out the scientifics with Lucy. Our Theory was that if you swing just high enough and straight enough, and you jump out of the swing at just the right moment and in just the right position—*you just might fly*.

8 July was spent waiting for my arm to heal. We ran our hands across the wooden seat, feeling for the odd splinter that could ruin your perfect takeoff. We pulled on the chains, testing for weak links.

9 Finally came the day in August when my cast was off, and Lucy and I were ready. Today we would fly.

10 Early that morning, we began taking turns—one pushing, one pumping. All day we pushed and pumped, higher and higher, ever so close. It was almost dark when Lucy's mother hollered for her to come home right this minute and see what her daddy had brought them.

11 This was strictly against the rules. Nobody had to go home in August until it was altogether dark. Besides, Lucy's daddy wasn't a man to be struck with irresistible impulses like stopping at the horse store and thinking, *Golly, my little girl loves ponies! I better get her one!*

12 So we kept on swinging, and Lucy pretended not to hear her mother—until she dropped *Lucee* to *Lucille Louise.* Halfway through the fourth *Lucille Louise,* Lucy slowly raised her head as though straining to hear some woman calling from the next county.

13 "Were you calling me, Mother? Okay, okay, I'm coming. Yes, ma'am. *Right now.*"

14 Lucy and I walked together to the end of my driveway. Once in her front yard, she slowed to something between a meander and a lollygag, choosing a path that took her straight through the sprinklers. Twice.

15 When at last Lucy sashayed to her front door, she turned back to me and, with a grin, gave me the thumbs-up sign used by pilots everywhere. *Awright.* So we'd fly tomorrow instead. We'd waited all summer. We could wait one more day. On her way in the house, she slammed the screen door.

16 *Bang!*

17 In my memory, I've listened to that screen door shut behind my best friend a thousand times. It was the last time I played with her.

18 I knocked on the door every day, but her mother always answered saying Lucy was busy and couldn't come out to play. I tried calling, but her mother always answered saying Lucy was busy and couldn't come to the phone. Lucy was busy? Too busy to play? Too busy to fly? She had to be dead. Nothing else made sense. What, short of death, could separate such best friends? We were going to fly. Her thumb had said so. I cried and cried.

19 I might never have known the truth of the matter, if some weeks later I hadn't overheard my mother say to my father how maybe I would calm down about Lucy if we got a television too.

20 A what? What on earth was a *television?* The word was new to me, but I was clever enough to figure out that Lucy's daddy had brought home a television that night. At last I knew what had happened to Lucy. The television ate her.

21 It must have been a terrible thing to see. Now my parents were thinking of getting one. I was scared. They didn't understand what television could do.

22 "Television eats people," I announced to my parents.

23 "Oh, Linda Jane," they said, laughing. "Television doesn't eat people. You'll love television just like Lucy. She's inside her house watching it right this minute."

24 Indeed, Lucy was totally bewitched by the flickering black and white shapes. Every afternoon following school, she'd sit in her living room and watch whatever there was to watch. Saturday mornings, she'd look at cartoons.

25 Autumn came. Around Thanksgiving, I played an ear of corn in the school pageant. Long division ruined most of December. After a while, I forgot about flying. But I did not forget about Lucy.

26 Christmas arrived, and Santa Claus brought us a television. "See?" my parents said. "Television doesn't eat people." Maybe not. But television changes people. It changed my family forever.

27 We stopped eating dinner at the dining-room table after my mother found out about TV trays. Dinner was served in time for one program and finished in time for another. During the meal we used to talk to one another. Now television talked to us. If you absolutely had to say something, you waited until the commercial, which is, I suspect, where I learned to speak in 30-second bursts.

28 Before television, I would lie in bed at night, listening to my parents in their room saying things I couldn't comprehend. Their voices alone rocked me to sleep. Now Daddy went to bed right after the weather, and Mama stayed up to see Jack Paar. I went to sleep listening to voices in my memory.

29 Daddy stopped buying Perry Mason books. Perry was on television now, and that was so much easier for him. But it had been Daddy and Perry who'd taught me how fine it can be to read something you like.

30 Mama and Daddy stopped going to movies. Most movies would one day show up on TV, he said.

31 After a while, Daddy and I didn't play baseball anymore. We didn't go to ball games either, but we watched more baseball than ever. That's how Daddy perfected

The Art of Dozing to Baseball. He would sit in his big chair, turn on the game and fall asleep within minutes. At least he appeared to be asleep. His eyes were shut, and he snored. But if you shook him, he'd open his eyes and tell you what the score was, who was up and what the pitcher ought to throw next.

32 It seemed everybody liked to watch television more than I did. I had no interest in sitting still when I could be climbing trees or riding a bike or practicing my takeoffs just in case one day Lucy woke up and remembered we had a Theory. Maybe the TV hadn't actually eaten her, but once her parents pointed her in the direction of that box, she never looked back.

33 Lucy had no other interests when she could go home and turn on "My Friend Flicka." Maybe it was because that was as close as she would get to having her own pony. Maybe if her parents had allowed her a real world to stretch out in, she wouldn't have been satisfied with a 19-inch world.

34 All I know is I never had another first best friend. I never learned to fly either. What's more, I was right all along: television really does eat people.

Now answer these questions, rereading any paragraphs required in the questions.

1. The essay is basically an affective reaction, in words, to the author's

a. loss of her best friend to television.

b. loss of her normal family routine after they got a television.

c. both a and b.

d. none of the above.

2. Explain how well paragraphs 11–12 do or do not capture the feelings of young children being called home from play. ______________________________

____

3. Be eight years old again and put yourself in paragraph 18. Describe how you might feel at that moment. ______________________________

____

____

4. What is the function of paragraph 25? ______________________________

____

5. What emotion(s) does paragraph 28 attempt to convey? ______________________________

____

6. How does the author feel about what she describes in paragraph 29–31? ____________

____

7. The concluding line, which states "television really does eat people," is a metaphor. Explain what she means. ______________________________

____

____

8. Does television "eat people" at your house? Explain. ______________________________

____

____

PRACTICE A-4: A Modern Fable

Directions: Read the following fable and then answer the questions that follow.

THE PRINCESS AND THE TIN BOX

James Thurber

1 Once upon a time, in a far country, there lived a king whose daughter was the prettiest princess in the world. Her eyes were like the cornflower, her hair was sweeter than the hyacinth, and her throat made the swan look dusty.

2 From the time she was a year old, the princess had been showered with presents. Her nursery looked like Cartier's window. Her toys were all made of gold or platinum or diamonds or emeralds. She was not permitted to have wooden blocks or china dolls or rubber dogs or linen books, because such materials were considered cheap for the daughter of a king.

3 When she was seven, she was allowed to attend the wedding of her brother and throw real pearls at the bride instead of rice. Only the nightingale, with his lyre of gold, was permitted to sing for the princess. The common blackbird, with his boxwood flute, was kept out of the palace grounds. She walked in silver-and-samite slippers to a sapphire-and-topaz bathroom and slept in an ivory bed inlaid with rubies.

4 On the day the princess was eighteen, the king sent a royal ambassador to the courts of five neighboring kingdoms to announce that he would give his daughter's hand in marriage to the prince who brought her the gift she liked the most.

5 The first prince to arrive at the palace rode a swift white stallion and laid at the feet of the princess an enormous apple made of solid gold which he had taken from a dragon who had guarded it for a thousand years. It was placed on a long ebony table set up to hold the gifts of the princess's suitors. The second prince, who came on a gray charger, brought her a nightingale made of a thousand diamonds, and it was placed beside the golden apple. The third prince, riding on a black horse, carried a great jewel box made of platinum and sapphires, and it was placed next to the diamond nightingale. The fourth prince, astride a fiery yellow horse, gave the princess a gigantic heart made of rubies and pierced by an emerald arrow. It was placed next to the platinum-and-sapphire jewel box.

6 Now the fifth prince was the strongest and handsomest of all the five suitors, but he was the son of a poor king whose realm had been overrun by mice and locusts and wizards and mining engineers so that there was nothing much of value left in it. He came plodding up to the palace of the princess on a plow horse and he brought her a small tin box filled with mica and feldspar and hornblende which he had picked up on the way.

7 The other princes roared with disdainful laughter when they saw the tawdry gift the fifth prince had brought to the princess. But she examined it with great interest and squealed with delight, for all her life she had been glutted with precious stones and priceless metals, but she had never seen tin before or mica or feldspar or hornblende. The tin box was placed next to the ruby heart pierced with an emerald arrow.

8 "Now," the king said to his daughter, "you must select the gift you like best and marry the prince that brought it."

9 The princess smiled and walked up to the table and picked up the present she liked the most. It was the platinum-and-sapphire jewel box, the gift of the third prince.

10 "The way I figure it," she said, "is this. It is a very large and expensive box, and when I am married, I will meet many admirers who will give me precious gems with which to fill it to the top. Therefore, it is the most valuable of all the gifts my suitors have brought me and I like it the best."

11 The princess married the third prince that very day in the midst of great merriment and high revelry. More than a hundred thousand pearls were thrown at her and she loved it.

12 *Moral: All those who thought the princess was going to select the tin box filled with worthless stones instead of one of the other gifts will kindly stay after class and write one hundred times on the blackboard "I would rather have a hunk of aluminum silicate than a diamond necklace."*

Now answer the following questions:

1. Which prince did you think the princess would choose? ________ Why?

2. Why is it important to the story that the poorest prince be described last? ________

3. Much of the humor in this piece comes from the author's use of incongruity, things that don't fit or are illogical, such as the language the princess uses compared with the fairy-tale setting. What are some other incongruous aspects of the story, language or otherwise? ________

4. Satire is used to poke fun at things. Here the author pokes fun at our human frailties. Is he satirizing the princess, the reader, or both? Explain. ________

5. If you were the princess, which prince would you have selected and why? ________

6. What does the moral at the end of the tale imply?______________________________

> ***Application 1: Responding Affectively to an Advertisement***
>
> Find an advertisement that you feel uses language or photographs to reach either your emotions or your desires. Bring it to class and share your advertisements with classmates.

B. Recognizing Images and Analogies in Affective Language

Images and Analogies

In literature, **imagery** is a term used to refer to the use of words to compare ideas, things, or feelings with something else. A writer might say, "She looks very unhappy," or, "Her face looks like she learned she only has twenty-four hours to live." The first statement is a literal one; the second is an *analogy.* The second statement allows us to *imagine* (from which the term imagery comes) how the person feels rather than just telling us. Because we can imagine what it might feel like to learn we don't have long to live, our feelings are tapped by the author through the analogy.

Imagery is important in fiction and nonfiction. Almost all good writing uses imaginative or figurative language, but it is especially important in writing poetry, short stories, or novels. It often requires that a writer carefully select words that provide strong connotative feelings in us. In the example above, "only twenty-four hours to live" connotes death within a day's time. In turn, that connotes a negative image, one we are supposed to feel.

To see more closely how this works, read the following short poem.

THE DEATH OF THE BALL TURRET GUNNER

Randall Jarrell

From my mother's sleep I fell into the State
And I hunched in its belly till my wet fur froze.
Six miles from earth, loosed from its dream of life,
I woke to black flak and the nightmare fighters.
When I died they washed me out of the turret with a hose.

Now answer the following questions as best you can.

1. Write the denotative and connotative meanings of the words from the poem in the spaces provided.

	Denotation	Connotation
a. mother	__________	__________
b. sleep	__________	__________
c. State	__________	__________
d. fur	__________	__________

2. What is the analogy being drawn between "my mother's sleep" and waking to the "black flak and the nightmare fighters"? __________

3. What images are created in the following lines from the poem?
   a. "From my mother's sleep I fell into the State" (Why is "State" capitalized?) ___
   b. "I hunched in its belly" __________
   c. "my wet fur froze" __________
   d. "Six miles from earth" __________
   e. "washed me out . . . with a hose" __________

4. What is the tone of the poem? __________

5. What is the author's attitude toward his subject? __________

6. Write a one-sentence literal statement that says what the poem implies. __________

Let's look at question 6 first. While wording will be different for everyone, the basic idea behind this poem is that "War is hell," "In war, death is common and indiscriminate," or "Some lives are treated as expendable in war." But rather than say such things at a literal level, the author chooses to make us *feel* the hell of war or the death of innocent people forced into a situation that is not their choosing. How do we know this?

The author knows that the word *mother,* literally the female parent, generally connotes feelings of love, security, warmth, and home life. *Sleep* connotes quiet and peacefulness, especially when the author says "my mother's sleep." It's a pleasant image; but it's quickly lost when he falls "into the State." The capital on the word causes us to think about government, an institution that has sent him to war. But the word also can refer to his state of mind, the change from a pleasant, safe home environment to now being at war in the belly of an airplane. It's a rude awakening from "my mother's sleep." It's also a strong analogy the author draws between the safety of home and the "black flak and the nightmare fighters." He's gone from pleasant dreams to nightmares.

Likewise, fur is soft. We use it for warmth and decoration on our clothes. But the use of the word *fur* could also remind us of the animal from which we get fur. Is the author implying through this image that man becomes animal-like by going to war? There's irony in this image. The image of "my wet fur froze" implies or suggests he may be sweating from fear. At the literal level, his perspiration freezes at six miles up in a bomber plane.

From the image, "From my mother's sleep I fell into the State," we then feel for this young man who recently was safe at home suddenly finding himself at war in a bomber (State could also refer to the actual plane itself). The image "hunched in its belly" offers a cramped feeling, like an animal hiding; in this case, he is both a hunter, looking for the enemy, and the hunted, being chased by an enemy. The word "belly" literally refers to the ball turret under the bomber where men manned machine guns to shoot down fighter planes. But "belly" (perhaps his mother's womb) is made analogous to the airplane's "womb." One is safe and one isn't; thus more contrast is made between the safety of home and the dangers of war six miles high.

The image of the last line is ugly. We are left with him dead and the almost callousness of washing out his remains from the turret in order to make room for the next person. When we put all these things together, we can say that the tone of the poem is ghastly, grim, deadly. The attitude of the author toward war is obviously negative, but more than that he wants us to see and feel for the innocent victims of the folly of war. By using figurative language, the author creates images that are hard to forget and affect us at a level a plain, literal statement never could.

The following practices will help you see how authors use affective language in a variety of ways.

PRACTICE B-1: Lines from Poetry

Directions: Following are some short passages from poetry and some quotations. Read each one and in the blanks provided write what you think is the *literal* meaning of the passage.

1. "The pen is mightier than the sword." (Edward Bulwer-Lytton) ________________

____

____

____

2. "The Lord is my shepherd; I shall not want." (Psalm 23:1) ________________

____

____

____

3. "Was this the face that launched a thousand ships,
And burnt the topless towers of Ilium?" (Christopher Marlowe)

____

____

____

4. "There is no frigate like a book
To take us lands away." (Emily Dickinson)

____

____

____

5. "God's in his heaven—
All's right with the world!" (Robert Browning)

____

____

____

6. "A little learning is a dangerous thing." (Alexander Pope) ________________

____

____

____

7. "But love is blind." (William Shakespeare)________________________

____

____

____

PRACTICE B-2: Images in a Poem

Directions: Mention the word "poem" to some readers and they immediately think of a poem like the one in this practice. It is made up of four stanzas (groups of lines), and the last word in every other line rhymes. Many poems are not structured this way, however, as you will see later. Read the following poem and answer the questions after. You may refer back to the poem as often as necessary.

Oh, My Love Is Like A Red, Red Rose (About 1788)

Robert Burns (1759–1796)

Oh, my love is like a red, red rose
  That's newly sprung in June;
My love is like the melody
  That's sweetly played in tune.

So fair art thou, my bonny lass,
  So deep in love as I;
And I will love thee still, my dear,
  Till a' the seas gang° dry. *°go*

Till a' the seas gang dry, my dear,
  And the rocks melt wi' the sun;
And I will love thee still, my dear,
  While the sands o' life shall run.

And fare thee weel, my only love!
  And fare thee weel awhile!
And I will come again, my love
  Though it were ten thousand mile.

1. What is your first reaction to this poem? What did it make you think about?______

____

____

2. Which lines in each stanza end with words that rhyme? ______________________

____

3. What is the intent of the poem?______________________________________

____

4. The title of the poem uses simile. What other simile is in the poem? ___________

____

____

5. What is the author expressing through the following images?

a. "Till a' the seas gang [go] dry"

____

b. "And the rocks melt wi' the sun"

____

c. "While the sands o' life shall run"

____

6. How do you think the person to whom this poem was intended would respond to such a declaration of love? Why? ______________________________

____

____

PRACTICE B-3: Intent and Attitude in a Poem

Directions: Robert Burns's poem in the previous practice uses many similes. The poem by Sylvia Plath in this practice uses metaphors, and unlike Burns's poem it has no divided stanzas or rhyme scheme. Read the poem aloud. As you read, pay attention to the punctuation at the end of each line. It will help you see how the author wants the poem to be read. Look for author's attitude and intent in the poem.

Metaphors 1960

Sylvia Plath (1932-1963)

I'm a riddle in nine syllables,
An elephant, a ponderous house,
A melon strolling on two tendrils.
O red fruit, ivory, fine timbers!
This loaf's big with its yeasty rising.
Money's new-minted in this fat purse.
I'm a means, a stage, a cow in calf.
I've eaten a bag of green apples,
Boarded the train there's no getting off.

(From *Crossing the Water* by Sylvia Plath, Harper & Row, 1971.)

1. What is the poem about? ______________________________

____

2. Each line in the poem is a ______________________________

____

3. To whom or what do each of the lines refer? ______________________________

____

4. What is the author's attitude toward the subject of the poem?

____

5. What is the author's intent in writing this poem? ______________________________

____

6. What does the speaker in the poem have in common with a riddle? (line 1) ______

____

7. Why do you think "nine" syllables are used? Why not another number? ________

____

8. What is the significance, if any, in the number of lines in the poem? ___________

9. What is your reaction to this poem? ___________

____

____

PRACTICE B-4: Two Versions of the Lord's Prayer

Directions: Following are two published versions of Matthew 6:9–13, more commonly known as The Lord's Prayer. Read both of them and then answer the questions that follow.

Version A

Our Father who art in heaven,
Hallowed be thy name.
Thy Kingdom come.
Thy will be done,
  On earth as it is in heaven.
Give us this day our daily bread;
And forgive us our debts,
  As we also have forgiven our debtors;
And lead us not into temptation,
  But deliver us from evil.

Version B

Our Father in heaven:
May your name be kept holy,
May your Kingdom come,
May your will be done on earth
  As it is in heaven.
Give us today the food we need;
Forgive us the wrongs that we have done,
And we forgive the wrongs that others have
  done us;
Do not bring us to hard testing, but
  Keep us safe from the Evil One.

1. Which version do you think is a more recent translation of the Bible? ___________

____

2. Why?___________

____

____

3. Which version do you prefer?___________

____

4. Why?___________

____

5. Which version uses more figurative language than the other?___________

____

PRACTICE B-5: Quick Quiz

Directions: Answer the following questions as thoroughly as you can. There are two parts to the quiz.

Part A

Below are some quotations and short passages from poetry. In the blanks provided, write what you think is the literal meaning of the passage.

1. "Ignorance is bliss." (Thomas Gray)____________________

____

____

2. "Where liberty dwells, there is my country." (John Milton)____________________

____

____

____

____

3. "Husbands are awkward things to deal with; even keeping them in hot water will not make them tender." (Mary Buckley) ____________________

____

____

____

____

____

____

4. "Early to bed, early to rise, makes a man healthy, wealthy, and wise." (Benjamin Franklin) ____________________

____

____

____

____

____

____

5. "All the world's a stage." (William Shakespeare) ____________________

____

____

____

____

____

____

Part B

Define the following terms.

1. imagery ______________________________

____

2. metaphor ______________________________

____

3. simile ______________________________

____

4. figurative language ______________________________

____

5. "the secret power of the word" ______________________________

____

6. affective comprehension ______________________________

____

Turn in the quiz to your instructor.

Name ______________________________ Section __________ Date __________

C. Putting It All Together

The following practices will help you put to use the information from this chapter and all the previous ones. As you do them, apply all the reading skills you have learned so far.

PRACTICE C-1: An Essay

Directions: Quickly read the title and first paragraph of the following essay, then answer the questions here.

1. What do you think the essay will discuss? ______________________________

____

____

2. Do you think you will enjoy reading the essay? __________________________

Why?____

____

____

Now read the essay, applying all the skills you have learned.

FRESH START

Evelyn Herald

1 I first began to wonder what I was doing on a college campus anyway when my parents drove off, leaving me standing pitifully in a parking lot, wanting nothing more than to find my way safely to my dorm room. The fact was that no matter how mature I liked to consider myself, I was feeling just a bit first-gradish. Adding to my distress was the distinct impression that everyone on campus was watching me. My plan was to keep my ears open and my mouth shut and hope no one would notice I was a freshman.

2 With that thought in mind, I raised my head, squared my shoulders, and set off in the direction of my dorm, glancing twice (and then ever so discreetly) at the campus map clutched in my hand. It took everything I had not to stare when I caught my first glimpse of a real live college football player. What confidence, what reserve, what muscles! I only hoped his attention was drawn to my air of assurance rather than to my shaking knees. I spent the afternoon seeking out each of my classrooms so that I could make a perfectly timed entrance before each lecture without having to ask dumb questions about its whereabouts.

3 The next morning I found my first class and marched in. Once I was in the room, however, another problem awaited me. Where to sit? Freshman manuals advised sitting near the front, showing the professor an intelligent and energetic demeanor. After much deliberation I chose a seat in the first row and to the side. I was in the foreground (as advised), but out of the professor's direct line of vision.

4 I cracked my anthology of American literature and scribbled the date at the top of a crisp ruled page. "Welcome to Biology 101," the professor began. A cold sweat broke out on the back of my neck. I groped for my schedule and checked the room number. I was in the right room. Just the wrong building.

5 So now what? Get up and leave in the middle of the lecture? Wouldn't the professor be angry? I knew everyone would stare. Forget it. I settled into my chair and tried to assume the scientific pose of a biology major, bending slightly forward, tensing my arms in preparation for furious notetaking, and cursing under my breath. The bottled snakes along the wall should have tipped me off.

6 After class I decided my stomach (as well as my ego) needed a little nourishment, and I hurried to the cafeteria. I piled my tray with sandwich goodies and was heading for the salad bar when I accidentally stepped in a large puddle of ketchup. Keeping myself upright and getting out of the mess was not going to be easy, and this flailing of feet was doing no good. Just as I decided to try another maneuver, my food tray tipped and I lost my balance. As my rear end met the floor, I saw my entire life pass before my eyes; it ended with my first day of college classes.

7 In the seconds after my fall I thought how nice it would be if no one had noticed. But as all the students in the cafeteria came to their feet, table by table, cheering and clapping, I knew they had not only noticed, they were determined that I would never forget it. Slowly I kicked off my ketchup-soaked sandals and jumped clear of the toppled tray and spilled food. A cleanup brigade came charging out of the kitchen, mops in hand. I sneaked out of the cafeteria as the cheers died down behind me.

8 For three days I dined alone on nothing more than humiliation, shame, and an assortment of junk food from a machine strategically placed outside my room. On the fourth day I couldn't take another crunchy-chewy-salty-sweet bite. I needed some real food. Perhaps three days was long enough for the campus population to have forgotten me. So off to the cafeteria I went.

9 I made my way through the food line and tiptoed to a table, where I collapsed in relief. Suddenly I heard a crash that sounded vaguely familiar. I looked up to see that another poor soul had met the fate I'd thought was reserved for only me. I was even more surprised when I saw who the poor soul was: the very composed, very upperclass football player I'd seen just days before (though he didn't look quite so composed wearing spaghetti on the front of his shirt). My heart went out to him as people began to cheer and clap as they had for me. He got up, hands held high above his head in a victory clasp, grinning from ear to ear. I expected him to slink out of the cafeteria as I had, but instead he turned around and began preparing another tray. And that's when I realized I had been taking myself far too seriously.

10 What I had interpreted as a malicious attempt to embarrass a naive freshman had been merely a moment of college fun. Probably everyone in the cafeteria had done something equally dumb when he or she was a freshman—and had lived to tell about it.

11 Who cared whether I dropped a tray, where I sat in class, or even whether I showed up in the wrong lecture? Nobody. This wasn't like high school. Popularity was not so important; running with the crowd was no longer a law of survival. In college, it didn't matter. This was my big chance to do my own thing, be my own woman—if I could get past my preoccupation with doing everything perfectly.

12 Once I recognized that I had no one's expectations to live up to but my own, I relaxed. The shackles of self-consciousness fell away, and I began to view college as a wonderful experiment. I tried on new experiences like articles of clothing, checking their fit and judging their worth. I broke a few rules to test my conscience. I dressed a little differently until I found the Real Me. I discovered a taste for jazz, and I decided I liked going barefoot.

13 I gave up trying to act my way through college (this wasn't drama school) and began not acting at all. College, I decided; was probably the only time I would be completely forgiven for massive mistakes (including stepping in puddles of ketchup and dropping food trays). So I used the opportunity to make all the ones I thought I'd never make.

14 Three years after graduation, I'm still making mistakes. And I'm even being forgiven for a few.

Comprehension Check

Directions: Now answer the following questions.

1. Which of the following best states the thesis of this essay?

a. College is not the place to make mistakes.

b. College is not like high school.

c. College students can be cruel sometimes.

d. College is a good place to discover who you are.

2. The tone of the essay is mostly

a. humorous.

b. serious.

c. sarcastic.

d. nasty.

3. The author's intent is to ______________________________

____

4. T/F We can infer from the essay that the author had prepared for her first days of college by reading materials on how to be a successful student.

5. What does the author mean when she says, "I realized I had been taking myself far too seriously"? ______________________________

____

____

6. T/F We can infer that the author was away from home for the first time.

7. T/F By sharing her embarrassing moments, the author gains our sympathy and reminds us of ourselves in similar situations.

8. The author mentions the "upper-class football player" twice. How does she use him to make a point? ______________________________

____

9. T/F It is difficult to relate to the author's feelings because most of us have not felt the way she does.

10. Based on what the author tells us in this essay, what advice do you think she would give to a college freshman? ______________________________

____

____

____

Vocabulary Check

Directions: Define the following underlined words or phrases.

1. I had the distinct impression that everyone was watching me. ____________

2. glancing twice, ever so discreetly ____________

3. showing the professor an intelligent and energetic demeanor ____________

4. I cracked my anthology of American literature ____________

5. a cleanup brigade came charging out ____________

6. the very composed very upper-class football player ____________

7. a malicious attempt to embarrass ____________

8. a naive freshman ____________

9. The shackles of self-consciousness fell away. ____________

10. If I could get past my preoccupation with being perfect ____________

Record your scores on the Student Record Chart in the Appendix. Count 10 percent for each correct answer. Make certain you understand any errors before going on to the next drill.

Practice C-2: A Poem

Directions: The following poem was written by Billy Collins, poet laureate for the United States in 2002–2003. Read the poem aloud two or three times. Look for the author's intent and attitude concerning the subject of the poem and your own reactions to what he has to say. Then answer the questions that follow.

Introduction to Poetry

Billy Collins

I ask them to take a poem
and hold it up to the light
like a color slide

or press an ear against its hive.

I say drop a mouse into a poem
and watch him probe his way out,

or walk inside the poem's room
and feel the walls for a light switch.

I want them to waterski
across the surface of a poem
waving at the author's name on the shore.

But all they want to do
is tie the poem to a chair with rope
and torture a confession out of it.

They begin beating it with a hose
to find out what it really means.

1. What is the speaker's attitude toward reading a poem?

____

____

2. What is the author's primary intent in this poem?

____

____

3. What senses does the author believe are necessary for understanding a poem? (Look again at the first four stanzas.)

4. Who is the "they" in the last two stanzas? ______________________________

____

5. What do you think the author means when he says he wants "them to waterski across the surface of a poem"? ______________________________

____

____

6. What effect is created by the use of the phrases "tie the poem to a chair," "torture a confession," and "beating it with a hose?"

____

____

7. What image from the poem stands out the most for you? ______________________________

____

8. What is your reaction to the poem? ______________________________

____

Discuss these answers in class. There are no right or wrong answers to these, although some may be more thoughtful than others. It's important to see how others responded to these questions. (To tell the truth, we feel that questions such as the preceding one are more important than trying to answer questions such as "What does the poem mean?")

Now, meet the author of the next selection by reading the following introduction to Langston Hughes. Another way to find current information, quotations, or pictures of this author is to use the World Wide Web. Using a search engine such as Google or AltaVista, type the author's name under "Search."

Introducing Langston Hughes

Some critics have called Langston Hughes the most representative of black American writers. Over a forty-five-year period, Hughes wrote in every major literary genre. He was a poet, a dramatist, a short-story writer, a journalist, an editor, and a translator. His earliest works were poems published in his high school magazine. His published works include fourteen books of poetry, two novels, a number of short-story collections, and several plays, including texts for stage musicals.

In 1922, Hughes dropped out of Columbia University after a year and took odd jobs. Four years later, he enrolled and graduated from Lincoln University in Pennsylvania. By then, he had published two books of poems and had became one of the leading writers of the "Harlem Renaissance," a productive period of African-American creativity in the arts during the 1920s.

In 1931, Hughes received an award for his novel, *Not without Laughter.* The award helped Hughes decide to become a writer:

> I'd finally and definitely made up my mind to continue being a writer—and to become a professional writer, making my living from writing. So far that had not happened. Until I went to Lincoln I had always worked at other things: teaching English in Mexico, truck gardening on Staten Island, a seaman, a doorman, a cook, a waiter in Paris night clubs or in hotels or restaurants . . . .
>
> Then I had a scholarship, a few literary awards, a patron. But those things were ended now. I would have to make my own living again—so I determined to make it writing. I did. Shortly, poetry became bread; prose, shelter and raiment. Words turned into songs, plays, scenarios, articles, and stories.
>
> Literature is a big sea full of many fish. I let down the nets and pulled. (From Langston Hughes, *The Big Sea,* Knopf, 1940, p. 335.)

When the Great Depression occurred, Hughes's political views were strongly to the left. But with the advent of World War II, Hughes's radicalism began to decline. He wrote radio scripts and songs supporting the war effort. In 1942, he became a columnist with the African-American weekly *Chicago Defender.* With the 1947 Broadway success of his musical play *Street Scene,* Hughes's main professional interest was the theater. But he continued to turn out several books of poems as well as fiction and nonfiction until his death in 1967.

The following practice is taken from Hughes's *The Big Sea,* the first volume of his autobiography. Your instructor or Learning Center may have a DVD of a film version of *Salvation* you may want to view and compare with what you are about to read.

PRACTICE C-3: Narration

Directions: Quickly survey the following selection, reading the title, the first paragraph and last paragraph, and the questions. Then time yourself as you read the selection.

Begin timing: ____________

SALVATION

Langston Hughes

1 I was saved from sin when I was going on thirteen. But not really saved. It happened like this. There was a big revival at my Auntie Reed's church. Every night for weeks there had been much preaching, singing, praying, and shouting, and some very hardened sinners had been brought to Christ, and the membership of the church had grown by leaps and bounds. Then just before the revival ended, they held a special meeting for children, "to bring the young lambs to the fold." My aunt spoke of it for days ahead. That night I was escorted to the front row and placed on the mourners' bench with all the other young sinners, who had not yet been brought to Jesus.

2 My aunt told me that when you were saved you saw a light, and something happened to you inside! And Jesus came into your life! And God was with you from then on! She said you could see and hear and feel Jesus in your soul. I believed her. I had heard a great many old people say the same thing and it seemed to me they ought to know. So I sat there calmly in the hot, crowded church, waiting for Jesus to come to me.

3 The preacher preached a wonderful rhythmical sermon, all moans and shouts and lonely cries and dire pictures of hell, and then he sang a song about the ninety and nine safe and in the fold, but one little lamb was left out in the cold. Then he said: "Won't you come? Won't you come to Jesus? Young lambs, won't you come?" And he held out his arms to all us young sinners there on the mourner's bench. And the little girls cried. And some of them jumped up and went to Jesus right away. But most of us just sat there.

4 A great many old people came and knelt around us and prayed, old women with jet-black faces and braided hair, old men with work-gnarled hands. And the church sang a song about the lower lights are burning, some poor sinners to be saved. And the whole building rocked with prayer and song.

5 Still I kept waiting to see Jesus.

6 Finally all the young people had gone to the altar and were saved, but one boy and me. He was a rounder's son named Westley. Westley and I were surrounded by sisters and deacons praying. It was very hot in the church, and getting late now. Finally

Westley said to me in a whisper: "God damn! I'm tired o' sitting here. Let's get up and be saved." So he got up and was saved.

7 Then I was left all alone on the mourners' bench. My aunt came and knelt at my knees and cried, while prayers and songs swirled all round me in the little church. The whole congregation prayed for me alone, in a mighty wail of moans and voices. And I kept waiting serenely for Jesus, waiting, waiting—but he didn't come. I wanted to see him, but nothing happened to me. Nothing! I wanted something to happen to me, but nothing happened.

8 I heard the songs and the minister saying: "Why don't you come? My dear child, why don't you come to Jesus? Jesus is waiting for you. He wants you. Why don't you come? Sister Reed, what is this child's name?"

9 "Langston," my aunt sobbed.

10 "Langston, why don't you come? Why don't you come and be saved? Oh, Lamb of God! Why don't you come?"

11 Now it was really getting late. I began to be ashamed of myself, holding everything up so long. I began to wonder what God thought about Westley, who certainly hadn't seen Jesus either, but who was now sitting proudly on the platform, swinging his knickerbockered legs and grinning down at me, surrounded by deacons and old women on their knees praying. God had not struck Westley dead for taking his name in vain or for lying in the temple. So I decided that maybe to save further trouble, I'd better lie, too, and say that Jesus had come, and get up and be saved.

12 So I got up.

13 Suddenly the whole room broke into a sea of shouting, as they saw me rise. Waves of rejoicing swept the place. Women leaped in the air. My aunt threw her arms around me. The minister took me by the hand and led me to the platform.

14 When things quieted down, in a hushed silence, punctuated by a few ecstatic "Amens," all the new young lambs were blessed in the name of God. Then joyous singing filled the room.

15 That night for the last time in my life but one—for I was a big boy twelve years old—I cried. I cried, in bed alone, and couldn't stop. I buried my head under the quilts, but my aunt heard me. She woke up and told my uncle I was crying because the Holy Ghost had come into my life, and because I had seen Jesus. But I was really crying because I couldn't bear to tell her that I had lied, that I had deceived everybody in the church, and I hadn't seen Jesus, and that now I didn't believe there was a Jesus any more, since he didn't come to help me.

Finish timing. Record time here: ____________ and use the Timed Readings Conversion Chart in the Appendix to figure your rate: ____________ wpm.

Comprehension Check

Directions: Now answer these questions, applying a mixture of literal, critical, and affective comprehension.

1. What is the name of the main character in the story? ______________________

____

2. He is _______ years old.

a. ten

b. eleven

c. twelve

d. thirteen

3. Where does most of the story take place?______________________________

____

4. Place a check mark in front of each statement that you believe is an example of figurative language:

___ **a.** "bring the young lambs to the fold"

___ **b.** "sat there calmly in the hot, crowded church"

___ **c.** "old men with work-gnarled hands"

___ **d.** "the whole building rocked with prayer and song"

5. T/F "The whole room broke into a sea of shouting" is an example of a simile.

6. T/F "The membership of the church had grown by leaps and bounds" is an example of a metaphor.

7. The attitude of the author toward himself as a young boy is one of

a. embarrassment. **c.** sarcasm.

b. slight amusement. **d.** hatred.

8. Why does the boy wait so long to "get saved"?__________________________

____

9. Why does the boy cry that night?___________________________________

____

10. What is the point of the story?____________________________________

____

____

____

Vocabulary Check

Directions: Define the following underlined words from the story.

1. a big <u>revival</u> at my aunt's church ______________________________

____

2. bring the young lambs to the <u>fold</u> ______________________________

____

3. <u>dire</u> pictures of hell ____

____

4. he was a <u>rounder's</u> son ______________________________________

____

5. waiting <u>serenely</u> for Jesus ____________________________________

____

6. swinging his <u>knickerbockered</u> legs_______________________________

____

7. surrounded by <u>deacons</u> ____________________

____

8. <u>punctuated</u> by a few ecstatic "Amens" ____________________

____

9. <u>ecstatic</u> "Amens" ____________________

____

10. on the <u>mourners' bench</u> ____________________

____

Record your scores on the Student Record Chart in the Appendix. Count 10 percent for each correct answer. If you are in doubt as to why any of your answers are wrong, check with your instructor.

Application 2: Recognizing Images in Affective Language

Go online to http://www.poems.com. Select another Billy Collins poem and read it, looking for unusual images created through figurative language. If you can, print out the poem and bring it to class to share with your classmates.

Questions for Group Discussion

1. In the selections in this chapter, a variety of images is presented. Which images are most memorable—and why?
2. Some of these images seem related to male narrators and some to female narrators. Find and discuss one image that could be used for both genders and one image that seems limited to one gender.
3. List one selection from this chapter that had a humorous tone and discuss what elements added to the humor.
4. Which of the selections brought out the strongest emotional reactions? As a group, discuss reasons for these affective reactions.
5. If you have viewed the Heinle Film Series DVD of Langston Hughes's *Salvation,* do you feel the author's tone and intent in the reading selection come through in the film as well? Why or why not?

CHAPTER EIGHT

Reading Affectively Effectively

A. Reading Short Stories Affectively

When you go to a football game or some other sports event, you go knowing that there will be traffic problems and parking problems, that you will be surrounded by thousands of people, that you will have to put up with all types of people and noises, and that you will probably sit far from the action. Yet you accept all that in order to become a part of the event itself. When you watch television, you know that you are going to have programs interrupted by commercials, yet in spite of these breaks, you are willing and able to get back into the program after several minutes. When you go to a movie, you are willing to sit in the dark surrounded by three walls and a big screen as light filters through moving film. In each case, you are willing to go along with what is expected of you so that for a time you can get involved in what you are seeing and feeling.

To read imaginative literature (novels, short stories, and poems), you need to be willing to go along with what is expected of you, too. In this case, you are expected to enter the world of the author who may want you to go back in the past, or forward to the future, or to share the present as the writer sees it. You must be willing to enter the imagination of the writer and attempt to see how he or she sees and feels life. In order to do this, you must understand how to read the form the writer chooses to use. Just as you have learned to identify a thesis in an essay, to identify paragraph forms and structure, to separate fact from opinion, and to recognize how language creates tone and reveals attitude and intent, so, too, you need to understand how to approach the reading of imaginative literature.

The last chapter introduced you to affective language used in short stories and poetry. You saw how important it is to read beyond the words and to relate to the "secret power" of language. Here's part of a novel by Jay McInerney, *Story of My Life*. Read it, then answer the questions that follow. Feel free to reread the passage if needed in order to answer the questions.

1 The party goes on for three days. Some of the people go to sleep eventually, but not me. On the fourth day they call my father and a doctor comes over to the apartment, and now I'm in a place in Minnesota under sedation dreaming the white dreams about snow falling endlessly in the North Country, making the landscape disappear, dreaming about long white rails of cocaine that disappear over the horizon like railroad tracks to the stars. Like when I used to ride and was anorectic and I would starve myself and all I would ever dream about was food. There are horses at the far end of the pasture outside my window. I watch them through the bars.

2 Toward the end of the endless party that landed me here I am telling somebody the story of Dick Diver. I had eight horses at one point, but Dick Diver was the best. I traveled all over the country jumping and showing, and when I first saw Dick, I knew he was like no other horse. He was like a human being—so spirited and nasty he'd jump twenty feet in the air to avoid the bamboo of the trainer, then stop dead or hang a leg up on a jump he could easily make, just for spite. He had perfect conformation, like a statue of a horse dreamed by Michelangelo. My father bought him for me; he cost a fortune. Back then my father bought anything for me. I was his sweet thing.

3 I loved that horse. No one else could get near him, he'd try to kill them, but I used to sleep in his stall, spend hours with him every day. When he was poisoned, I went into shock. They kept me on tranquilizers for a week. There was an investigation, but nothing came of it. The insurance company paid off in full, but I quit riding. A few months later, Dad came into my bedroom one night. I was like, uh oh, not this again. He buried his face in my shoulder. His cheek was wet, and he smelled of booze. I'm sorry about Dick Diver, he said. Tell me you forgive me. He goes, the business was in trouble. Then he passed out on top of me, and I had to go and get Mom.

4 After a week in the hatch they let me use the phone. I call my Dad. How are you? he says.

5 I don't know why, it's probably bullshit, but I've been trapped in this place with a bunch of shrink types for a week. So just for the hell of it I go, Dad, sometimes I think it would have been cheaper if you'd let me keep that horse.

6 He goes, I don't know what you're talking about.

7 I go, Dick Diver, you remember that night you told me.

8 He goes, I didn't tell you anything.

9 So, okay, maybe I dreamed it. I was in bed after all, and he woke me up. Not for the first time. But just now, with these tranqs they've got me on, I feel like I'm sleep-walking anyway, and I can almost believe it never actually happened. Maybe I dreamed a lot of stuff. Stuff that I thought happened in my life. Stuff I thought I did. Stuff that was done to me. Wouldn't that be great. I'd love to think that 90 percent of it was just dreaming.

---

1. Besides "a place in Minnesota," there are clues that let us know where the narrator is. Where do you think the person is? ______________________________

   ____

2. Is the narrator a male or female? What makes you think so? ______________________________

   ____

   ____

3. Describe the narrator. ______________________________

   ____

   ____

4. Who killed Dick Diver and why? ______________________________

   ____

   ____

5. What kind of life do you think the narrator has led? ______________________________

   ____

   ____

   ____

Considering that the narrator is "under sedation" and is looking out at horses through a window with bars on it, we can infer that the narrator is in a hospital, perhaps the psychiatric ward or a rest home for drug addicts. Again, we assume the storyteller has taken a drug overdose because of the reference to a three-day party, the "long white rails of cocaine," and because of the need for a doctor on the fourth day.

It's not immediately apparent that the narrator is a female, but it becomes more probable as we read. The references to starving herself, being anorectic, and riding horses certainly don't mean she is a female, but by the time we've read more, especially her reference to being her father's "sweet thing," it's a good assumption. We hear of more young women being anorectic than young men.

The narrator is probably in her late teens or early twenties, based on her language: "He goes . . . ," "I go . . . ," "He goes . . . " is the vernacular of a younger person. Her father is apparently still responsible for her, since he is the one she calls, and he is the one who called the doctor and had her institutionalized. We can assume that she comes from a wealthy family, since she had eight horses at one time and "traveled all over the country jumping and showing." Happy when she had her horses, she certainly is unhappy now, wishing she had "maybe dreamed a lot of stuff" that happened in her life, "stuff that was done to me." Her father drinks too much, and we gather that, because his business was failing at one point, he killed her favorite horse for the insurance money. We see her as a child who had plenty of material things, but not the kind of love and attention she wanted or needed. She hints she was spoiled: "Back then my father bought anything for me." The death of her horse was probably a turning point in her life, especially after learning her father's role in it. She has turned to drugs and is now in some type of hospital on tranquilizers—not a happy person.

Rather than tell us all these things literally, the author has asked us to enter the world of the girl/woman telling the story. If we are alert to the clues the author provides, we read beyond the words and begin to understand things that perhaps even the character telling the story doesn't understand or say directly. We enter the life of a fictional character, but we see reality as we know it must be for some—and sometimes for ourselves.

Now let's say that you have been assigned a short story to read in an English class. You start reading it, but you don't know exactly what you are expected to look for. You feel a bit uncomfortable because you are not used to reading imaginative literature. Here is a set of guide questions you can use with any story or novel to help you get a little more from your reading.

Literal Questions

1. Who is the main character? What is she or he like?
2. Who are other important persons in the story? What is their relationship to the main character?
3. What is happening?
4. Where and when is everything happening?

Critical Questions

5. What seems to be the point of the story (called *theme*)? If the author were writing an essay instead of a story, what would the thesis be?
6. How does the title relate to the theme?
7. What events, scenes, and/or characters are used to develop the theme?

Affective Questions

8. Explain your feelings for the characters in the story.
9. What passages seem particularly well written or effective?
10. Why do you like or dislike the story?
11. What aspects of yourself or others do you see in the story?

These questions are certainly not the only ones, nor necessarily the best ones. But they give you a starting place, a direction toward understanding what it takes to enter into imaginative literature and get something from it.

The following practices will give you a chance to become more familiar with reading and understanding imaginative literature.

PRACTICE A-1: Images in Fiction

Directions: Figurative language, as you remember from Chapter Five, is used in an imaginative rather than a literal sense. Forms of figurative language include metaphor, simile, cliché, and hyperbole. Go back to Chapter Five, Section B, if you need to refresh your memory about any of these concepts before you do the next two exercises.

Read each of the following fictional selections. On the first line that follows each selection, write in the word *figurative* if you think the selection is mostly figurative or *literal* if you think it is mostly literal. Then on the second line, write the numbers of all the sentences in the selection that you feel contain figurative language.

1. (1) Dr. Rankin was a large and rawboned man on whom the newest suit at once appeared outdated, like a suit in a photograph of twenty years ago. (2) This was due to the squareness and flatness of his torso, which might have been put together by a manufacturer of packing cases. (3) His face also had a wooden and a roughly constructed look; his hair was wiglike and resentful of the comb. (4) He had those huge and clumsy hands which can be an asset to a doctor in a small upstate town where people still retain a rural relish for paradox, thinking that the more apelike the paw, the more precise it can be in the delicate business of a tonsillectomy. (From John Collier, "De Mortuis.")

____

____

2. (1) The morning of June 27th was clear and sunny, with the fresh warmth of a full-summer day; the flowers were blossoming profusely and the grass was richly green. (2) The people of the village began to gather in the square, between the post office and the bank, around ten o'clock; in some towns there were so many people that the lottery took two days and had to be started on June 26th, but in this village, where there were only about three hundred people, the whole lottery took less than two hours, so it could begin at ten o'clock in the morning and still be through in time to allow the villagers to get home for noon dinner. (From Shirley Jackson, "The Lottery.")

____

____

3. (1) She was going the inland route because she has been twice on the coast route. (2) She asked three times at the automobile club how far it was through the Tehachapi Mountains, and she had the route marked on the map in red pencil. (3) The car was running like a T, the garage man told her. (4) All her dresses were back from the cleaners, and there remained only the lace collar to sew on her black crepe so that they would be all ready when she got to San Francisco. (5) She had read up on the history of the mountains and listed all the Indian tribes and marked the route of the Friars from the Sacramento Valley. (6) She was glad now that Clara Robbins, the "Math" teacher, was not going with her. (7) She liked to be alone, to have everything just the way she wanted it, exactly. (From Meridel Le Sueur, "The Girl.")

____

____

4. (1) Braggioni catches her glance solidly as if he had been waiting for it, leans forward, balancing his paunch between his spread knees, and sings with tremendous emphasis, weighing his words. (2) He has, the song relates, no father and no mother, nor even a friend to console him; lonely as a wave of the sea he comes and goes, lonely as a wave. (3) His mouth opens round and yearns sideways, his balloon cheeks grow oily with the labor of song. (4) He bulges marvelously in his expensive garments. (5) Over his lavender collar, crushed upon a purple necktie, held by a diamond hoop: over his ammunition belt of tooled leather worked in silver, buckled cruelly around his gasping middle: over the tops of his glossy yellow shoes Braggioni swells with ominous ripeness, his mauve silk hose stretched taut, his ankles bound with the stout leather thongs of his shoes. (From Katherine Anne Porter, "Flowering Judas.")

____

____

5. (1) The midafternoon winter sun burned through the high California haze. (2) Charles Dudley, working with a mattock in a thicket of overgrowth, felt as steamy and as moldy as the black adobe earth in which his feet kept slipping. (3) Rain had fallen for five days with no glimmer of sunshine, and now it seemed as if the earth, with fetid animation, like heavy breath, were giving all that moisture back to the air. (4) The soil, or the broom which he was struggling to uproot, had a disgusting, acrid odor, as if he were tussling with some obscene animal instead of with a lot of neglected vegetation, and suddenly an overload of irritations—the smell, the stinging sweat in his eyes, his itching skin, his blistering palms—made him throw the mattock down and come diving out of the thicket into the clearing he had already achieved. (From Mark Schorer, "What We Don't Know Hurts Us.")

____

____

PRACTICE A-2: Reacting to Fictional Passages

Directions: Following are some short fictional passages containing figurative language. Read each one and answer the questions that follow.

1. ". . . inside we ate in the steady coolness of air by Westinghouse." (From Philip Roth, *Goodbye Columbus.*)

a. The above quote is an example of figurative language. Restate the quote in literal terms.____________________________

____

b. What can you infer from the quote about the weather outside?____________

____

2. ". . . women, with their Cuban heels and boned-up breasts, their knuckle-sized rings, their straw hats, which resembled immense wicker pizza plates." (From Philip Roth, *Goodbye Columbus.*)

a. Would you call this a flattering description?____________________

____

b. What figurative phrases support your answer to *a*? ______________________

____

3. "When my parents have somebody over they get lemonade and if it's a real racy affair, Schlitz in tall glasses with 'They'll Do It Every Time' cartoons stencilled on." (From John Updike, "A & P.")

a. Literally state what the narrator is telling about his parents. ______________

____

____

b. What is the narrator's tone? Sarcastic? Friendly? Embarrassed?______________

____

4. "The flames, as though they were a kind of wild life, crept as a jaguar creeps on its belly toward a line of birch-like saplings that fledged an outcrop of the pink rock. They flapped at the first of the trees, and the branches grew a brief foliage of fire. The heart of flame leapt nimbly across the gap between the trees and then went swinging and flaring along the whole row of them." (From William Golding, *Lord of the Flies.*)

a. Why is the fire like a wild animal? ______________________________

____

____

b. List four descriptive words or phrases the author uses to give the fire life. ____

____

5. "She slides through the door with a gust of cold and locks the door behind her and I see her fingers trail across the polished steel—tip of each finger the same color as her lips. Funny orange. Like the tip of a soldering iron. Color so hot or so cold if she touches you with it you can't tell which." (From Ken Kesey, *One Flew over the Cuckoo's Nest.*)

a. From this description, can you infer whether the narrator likes or dislikes the woman? ____

b. What feelings do you get from the description of the woman? ____________

____

c. List at least three phrases that cause you to feel the way you do. ___________

____

____

6. "Lying in this third-story cupola bedroom, he felt the tall power it gave him, riding high in the June wind, the grandest tower in town. At night, when the trees washed together, he flashed his gaze like a beacon from this lighthouse in all directions over swarming seas of elm and oak and maple." (From Ray Bradbury, *Dandelion Wine.*)

a. Is the overall mood of this passage pleasing or frightening?______________

____

b. Why?____

____

c. What is meant by "the trees washed together"? ______________________________

____

d. The bedroom is being compared to what? ______________________________

e. How can you tell? ____

____

7. "The fresh-plowed earth heaved, the wild plum buds puffed and broke. Springs and streams leapt up singing. He could hear the distant roar of the river swelling in the gorge. The clear blue skies stretched out above him like the skin of a puffed fiesta balloon. The whole earth strained and stretched with new life." (From Frank Waters, *The Man Who Killed the Deer.*)

a. Is the overall mood of this passage pleasing or frightening? ________________

____

b. Why? ____

c. What time of year would you infer is being described? ____________________

____

d. Why? ____

____

____

8. "It unrolled slowly, forced to show its colors, curling and snapping back whenever one of us turned loose. The whole land was very tense until we put our four steins on its corners and laid the river out to run for us through the mountains 150 miles north. Lewis' hand took a pencil and marked out a small strong X in a place where some of the green bled away and the paper changed with high ground, and began to work downstream, northeast to southwest through the printed woods." (From James Dickey, *Deliverance.*)

a. What is the "it" that "unrolled slowly"? ______________________________

b. How do you know? ____

____

____

c. What clue does the author give as to how many people the "us" and "we" refer?

____

____

d. What can you infer from the passage is going on? ________________________

____

____

____

____

PRACTICE A-3

Directions: As a way to direct your thinking as you read the following short story, answer the questions that appear at various points. Some questions require predicting or guessing what you think will happen. Write your answers on a separate sheet to be turned in to your instructor.

1. Read the title of the next story. What do you think this story will be about? What will happen? Why?

THE STORY OF AN HOUR

Kate Chopin

1 Knowing that Mrs. Mallard was afflicted with a heart trouble, great care was taken to break to her as gently as possible the news of her husband's death.

2 It was her sister Josephine who told her, in broken sentences; veiled hints that revealed in half concealing. Her husband's friend Richards was there, too, near her. It was he who had been in the newspaper office when intelligence of the railroad disaster was received, with Brently Mallard's name leading the list of "killed." He had only taken the time to assure himself of its truth by a second telegram, and had hastened to forestall any less careful, less tender friend in bearing the sad message.

3 She did not hear the story as many women have heard the same, with a paralyzed inability to accept its significance. She wept at once, with sudden, wild abandonment, in her sister's arms. When the storm of grief had spent itself she went away to her room alone. She would have no one follow her.

2. Which of your ideas in answer to question 1 can still be correct?

3. Now what do you think will take place? Why?

4 There stood, facing the open window, a comfortable, roomy armchair. Into this she sank, pressed down by a physical exhaustion that haunted her body and seemed to reach into her soul.

5 She could see in the open square before her house the tops of trees that were all aquiver with the new spring life. The delicious breath of rain was in the air. In the street below a peddler was crying his wares. The notes of a distant song which someone was singing reached her faintly, and countless sparrows were twittering in the eaves.

6 There were patches of blue sky showing here and there through the clouds that had met and piled one above the other in the west facing her window.

7 She sat with her head thrown back upon the cushion of the chair, quite motionless, except when a sob came up into her throat and shook her, as a child who has cried itself to sleep continues to sob in its dreams.

8 She was young, with a fair, calm face, whose lines bespoke repression and even a certain strength. But now there was a dull stare in her eyes, whose gaze was fixed away off yonder on one of those patches of blue sky. It was not a glance of reflection, but rather indicated a suspension of intelligent thought.

9 There was something coming to her and she was waiting for it, fearfully. What was it? She did not know; it was too subtle and elusive to name. But she felt it, creeping out of the sky, reaching toward her through the sounds, the scents, the color that filled the air.

10 Now her bosom rose and fell tumultuously. She was beginning to recognize this thing that was approaching to possess her, and she was striving to beat it back with her will—as powerless as her two white slender hands would have been.

4. Which of your ideas about what will happen are still possible?

5. What new ideas do you have about what will happen now?

11 When she abandoned herself a little whispered word escaped her slightly parted lips. She said it over and over under her breath: "free, free, free?" The vacant stare and the look of terror that had followed it went from her eyes. They stayed keen and bright. Her pulses beat fast, and the coursing blood warmed and relaxed every inch of her body.

12 She did not stop to ask if it were or were not a monstrous joy that held her. A clear and exalted perception enabled her to dismiss the suggestion as trivial.

13 She knew that she would weep again when she saw the kind, tender hands folded in death; the face that had never looked save with love upon her, fixed and gray and dead. But she saw beyond that bitter moment a long procession of years to come that would belong to her absolutely. And she opened and spread her arms out to them in welcome.

14 There would be no one to live for her during those coming years; she would live for herself. There would be no powerful will bending hers in that blind persistence with which men and women believe they have a right to impose a private will upon a fellow-creature. A kind intention or a cruel intention made the act seem no less a crime as she looked upon it in that brief moment of illumination.

15 And yet she had loved him—sometimes. Often she had not. What did it matter! What could love, the unsolved mystery, count for in face of this possession of self-assertion which she suddenly recognized as the strongest impulse of her being!

16 "Free! Body and soul free!" she kept whispering.

6. Were you right? How did you know?

7. Now what will happen?

17 Josephine was kneeling before the closed door with her lips to the keyhole, imploring for admission. "Louise, open the door! I beg; open the door—you will make yourself ill. What are you doing, Louise? For heaven's sake open the door."

18 "Go away. I am not making myself ill." No; she was drinking in a very elixir of life through that open window.

19 Her fancy was running riot along those days ahead of her. Spring days, and summer days, and all sorts of days that would be her own. She breathed a quick prayer that life might be long. It was only yesterday she had thought with a shudder that life might be long.

20 She rose at length and opened the door to her sister's importunities. There was a feverish triumph in her eyes, and she carried herself unwittingly like a goddess of Victory. She clasped her sister's waist, and together they descended the stairs. Richards stood waiting for them at the bottom.

8. How close were your ideas to what happened?

9. What will happen now and why do you think so?

21 Some one was opening the front door with a latchkey. It was Brently Mallard who entered, a little travel-stained, composedly carrying his gripsack and umbrella. He had been far from the scene of the accident, and did not even know there had been one. He stood amazed at Josephine's piercing cry; at Richards' quick motion to screen him from the view of his wife.

22 But Richards was too late.

23 When the doctors came they said she had died of heart disease—of joy that kills.

10. Irony is defined as an inconsistency between what might be expected and what actually occurs. Discuss any irony you see in this story.

Turn your answers in to your instructor.

PRACTICE A-4

Directions: Read the title of the following story. Based on the title, make a prediction as to what you think the story will be about. As a way to guide you through reading stories, you will be asked to make more predictions as you read. As you know, reading fiction is different from reading expository writing. Learning to form your own questions and predictions as you read will help both your concentration and comprehension.

STOLEN PARTY

Liliana Heker

Translated by Alberto Manguel

1 As soon as she arrived she went straight to the kitchen to see if the monkey was there. It was: what a relief! She wouldn't have liked to admit that her mother had been right. *Monkeys at a birthday?* her mother had sneered. *Get away with you, believing any nonsense you're told!* She was cross, but not because of the monkey, the girl thought; it's just because of the party.

2 "I don't like you going," she told her. "It's a rich people's party."

3 "Rich people go to Heaven too," said the girl, who studied religion at school.

4 "Get away with Heaven," said the mother. "The problem with you, young lady, is that you like to fart higher than your ass."

5 The girl didn't approve of the way her mother spoke. She was barely nine, and one of the best in her class.

6 "I'm going because I've been invited," she said. "And I've been invited because Luciana is my friend. So there."

7 "Ah yes, your friend," her mother grumbled. She paused. "Listen, Rosaura," she said at last: "That one's not your friend. You know what you are to them? The maid's daughter, that's what."

8 Rosaura blinked hard: she wasn't going to cry. Then she yelled: "Shut up! You know nothing about being friends!"

9 Every afternoon she used to go to Luciana's house and they would both finish their homework while Rosaura's mother did the cleaning. They had their tea in the kitchen and they told each other secrets. Rosaura loved everything in the big house, and she also loved the people who lived there.

10 "I'm going because it will be the most lovely party in the whole world, Luciana told me it would. There will be a magician, and he will bring a monkey and everything."

11 The mother swung around to take a good look at her child, and pompously put her hands on her hips.

12 "Monkeys at a birthday?" she said. "Get away with you, believing any nonsense you're told!"

13 Rosaura was deeply offended. She thought it unfair of her mother to accuse other people of being liars simply because they were rich. Rosaura too wanted to be rich, of course. If one day she managed to live in a beautiful palace, would her mother stop loving her? She felt very sad. She wanted to go to that party more than anything else in the world.

14 "I'll die if I don't go," she whispered, almost without moving her lips.

1. Stop reading for a moment. Do you want to keep your prediction based on the title or change it? If so, why? What do you think will happen next? Why do you think so?

2. Read the next portion of the story.

15 And she wasn't sure whether she had been heard, but on the morning of the party she discovered that her mother had starched her Christmas dress. And in the afternoon, after washing her hair, her mother rinsed it in apple vinegar so that it would be all nice and shiny. Before going out, Rosaura admired herself in the mirror, with her white dress and glossy hair, and thought she looked terribly pretty.

16 Señora Ines also seemed to notice. As soon as she saw her, she said:

17 "How lovely you look today, Rosaura."

18 Rosaura gave her starched skirt a slight toss with her hands and walked into the party with a firm step. She said hello to Luciana and asked about the monkey. Luciana put on a secretive look and whispered into Rosaura's ear: "He's in the kitchen. But don't tell anyone, because it's a surprise."

19 Rosaura wanted to make sure. Carefully she entered the kitchen and there she saw it: deep in thought, inside its cage. It looked so funny that the girls stood there for a while, watching it, and later, every so often, she would slip out of the party unseen and go and admire it. Rosaura was the only one allowed into the kitchen. Señora Ines had said: "You yes, but not the others, they're much too boisterous, they might break something." Rosaura had never broken anything. She even managed the jug of orange juice, carrying it from the kitchen into the dining room. She held it carefully and didn't spill a single drop. And Señora Ines had said: "Are you sure you can manage a jug as big as that?" Of course she could manage. She wasn't a butterfingers, like the others. Like that blonde girl with the bow in her hair. As soon as she saw Rosaura, the girl with the bow had said:

20 "And you? Who are you?"

21 "I'm a friend of Luciana," said Rosaura.

22 "No," said the girl with the bow, "you are not a friend of Luciana because I'm her cousin and I know all her friends. And I don't know you."

23 "So what," said Rosaura. "I come here every afternoon with my mother and we do our homework together."

24 "You and your mother do your homework together?" asked the girl, laughing.

25 "I and Luciana do our homework together," said Rosaura, very seriously.

26 The girl with the bow shrugged her shoulders.

27 "That's not being friends," she said. "Do you go to school together?"

28 "No."

29 "So where do you know her from?" said the girl, getting impatient.

30 Rosaura remembered her mother's words perfectly. She took a deep breath.

31 "I'm the daughter of the employee," she said.

32 Her mother had said very clearly: "If someone asks, you say you're the daughter of the employee; that's all." She also told her to add: "And proud of it." But Rosaura thought that never in her life would she dare say something of the sort.

33 "What employee?" said the girl with the bow. "Employee in a shop?"

34 "No," said Rosaura angrily. "My mother doesn't sell anything in any shop, so there."

35 "So how come she's an employee?" said the girl with the bow.

36 Just then Señora Ines arrived saying *shh shh*, and asked Rosaura if she wouldn't mind helping serve out the hot-dogs, as she knew the house so much better than the others.

37 "See?" said Rosaura to the girl with the bow, and when no one was looking she kicked her in the shin.

3. Now, stop again. Have you found proof for your prediction? Or have you changed your mind? What did you read that helped you decide?

4. Continue reading.

38 Apart from the girl with the bow, all the others were delightful. The one she liked best was Luciana, with her golden birthday crown; and then the boys. Rosaura won the sack race, and nobody managed to catch her when they played tag. When they split into two teams to play charades, all the boys wanted her for their side. Rosaura felt she had never been so happy in all her life.

39 But the best was still to come. The best came after Luciana blew out the candles. First the cake. Señora Ines had asked her to help pass the cake around, and Rosaura had enjoyed the task immensely, because everyone called out to her, shouting "Me, me!" Rosaura remembered a story in which there was a queen who had the power of life or death. To Luciana and the boys she gave the largest pieces, and to the girl with the bow she gave a slice so thin one could see through it.

40 After the cake came the magician, tall and bony, with a fine red cape. A true magician: he could untie handkerchiefs by blowing on them and make a chain with links that had no openings. He could guess what cards were pulled out from a pack, and the monkey was his assistant. He called the monkey "partner." "Let's see here, partner," he would say, "Turn over a card." And, "Don't run away, partner: time to work now."

41 The final trick was wonderful. One of the children had to hold the monkey in his arms and the magician said he would make him disappear.

42 "What, the boy?" they all shouted.

43 "No, the monkey!" shouted back the magician.

44 Rosaura thought that this was truly the most amusing party in the whole world.

45 The magician asked a small fat boy to come and help, but the small fat boy got frightened almost at once and dropped the monkey on the floor. The magician picked him up carefully, whispered something in his ear, and the monkey nodded almost as if he understood.

46 "You mustn't be so unmanly, my friend," the magician said to the fat boy.

47 "What's unmanly?" said the fat boy.

48 The magician turned around as if to look for spies.

49 "A sissy," said the magician. "Go sit down."

50 Then he stared at all the faces, one by one. Rosaura felt her heart tremble.

51 "You, with the Spanish eyes," said the magician. And everyone saw that he was pointing at her.

52 She wasn't afraid. Neither holding the monkey, nor when the magician made him vanish; not even when, at the end, the magician flung his red cape over Rosaura's head and uttered a few magic words . . . and the monkey reappeared, chattering happily, in her arms. The children clapped furiously. And before Rosaura returned to her seat, the magician said:

53 "Thank you very much, my little countess."

54 She was so pleased with the compliment that a while later, when her mother came to fetch her, that was the first thing she told her.

55 "I helped the magician and he said to me, 'Thank you very much, my little countess.'"

56 It was strange because up to then Rosaura had thought that she was angry with her mother. All along Rosaura had imagined that she would say to her: "See that the monkey wasn't a lie?" But instead she was so thrilled that she told her mother all about the wonderful magician.

57 Her mother tapped her on the head and said: "So now we're a countess!"

58 But one could see that she was beaming.

59 And now they both stood in the entrance, because a moment ago Señora Ines, smiling, had said: "Please wait her a second."

60 Her mother suddenly seemed worried.

61 "What is it?" she asked Rosaura.

62 "What is what?" said Rosaura. "It's nothing; she just wants to get the presents for those who are leaving, see?"

5. Stop here. Which of your predictions still seem right? Which do you want to change? Why? What do you think the outcome of the story will be?

6. Finish reading.

63 She pointed at the fat boy and at a girl with pigtails who were also waiting there, next to their mothers. And she explained about the presents. She knew, because she had been watching those who left before her. When one of the girls was about to leave, Señora Ines would give her a bracelet. When a boy left, Señora Ines gave him a yo-yo. Rosaura preferred the yo-yo because it sparkled, but she didn't mention that to her mother. Her mother might have said: "So why don't you ask for one, you blockhead?" That's what her mother was like. Rosaura didn't feel like explaining that she'd be horribly ashamed to be the odd one out. Instead she said:

64 "I was the best-behaved at the party."

65 And she said no more because Señora Ines came out into the hall with two bags, one pink and one blue.

66 First she went up to the fat boy, gave him a yo-yo out of the blue bag, and the fat boy left with his mother. Then she went up to the girl and gave her a bracelet out of the pink bag, and the girl with the pigtails left as well.

67 Finally she came up to Rosaura and her mother. She had a big smile on her face and Rosaura liked that. Señora Ines looked down at her, then looked up at her mother, and then said something that made Rosaura proud:

68 "What a marvelous daughter you have, Herminia."

69 For an instant, Rosaura thought that she'd give her two presents: the bracelet and the yo-yo. Señora Ines bent down as if about to look for something. Rosaura also leaned forward, stretching out her arm. But she never completed the movement.

70 Señora Ines didn't look in the pink bag. Nor did she look in the blue bag. Instead she rummaged in her purse. In her hand appeared two bills.

71 "You really and truly earned this," she said handing them over. "Thank you for all your help, my pet."

72 Rosaura felt her arms stiffen, stick close to her body, and then she noticed her mother's hand on her shoulder. Instinctively she pressed herself against her mother's body. That was all. Except her eyes. Rosaura's eyes had a cold, clear look that fixed itself on Señora Ines's face.

73 Señora Ines, motionless, stood there with her hand outstretched. As if she didn't dare draw it back. As if the slightest change might shatter an infinitely delicate balance.

---

7. Have you found proof for your predictions? If not, what surprised you?

Comprehension Check

Directions: Answer the following questions. You may look back if you need to do so.

Literal Questions

1. Who is the main character in the story? ______________________

____

2. Summarize the story in one sentence. ______________________

____

____

3. Where and when is everything happening? ______________________

____

Critical Questions

4. What is the theme of the story? In other words, if the author were writing an essay instead of a story, what would the thesis be?

____

5. How does the title relate to the theme? ______________________

____

____

6. What events, scenes, or characters are used to develop the theme?

____

____

Affective Questions

7. What passages seem particularly effective or well written? ______________________

____

____

8. Explain your feelings for the main character in the story. ______________________

____

____

9. What aspects of yourself or others do you see in the story?

____

____

10. Why do you like or dislike the story? ______________________

____

____

Record your comprehension score in the Student Record Chart in the Appendix.

Questions for Group Discussion

1. Discuss how you each became aware that there are rich people and poor people.
2. Discuss the type of friendships you have had with people of a different economic level.
3. Have you ever felt excluded from a group you wished to be in? How did you react to the situation?
4. Have you ever excluded someone from a group that you belonged to? What was your reason?
5. How can fiction help you relate to and understand real-life situations?

The next selection is by Gary Soto. Start by reading about the author. Another way to find current information, quotations, or pictures of this author is to use the World Wide Web. Using a search engine such as Google or AltaVista, type the author's name under "Search."

Introducing Gary Soto

A respected poet, an innovator of the short essay form, and a professor of English and Chicano Studies at the University of California, Berkeley, Gary Soto has written numerous volumes of poetry and several collections of short stories and essays. Among Soto's many awards are the 1985 American Book Award and the 1985 Before Columbus Foundation American Book Award. In 1990, his *Who Will Know Us?* was nominated as an American Library Association Notable Book. He is also the recipient of a Guggenheim Fellowship and an Award for Merit from the Fresno (California) Area Council of English Teachers for inspiring the young people of San Joaquin Valley through his writing.

Soto's work not only reveals vivid moments and experiences growing up Chicano but also taps into childhood and adult experiences that we all share. He often writes of small events and experiences that affect us and remain important all our lives.

In his introduction to *New and Selected Poems* (1995), Soto tells us how he started writing.

> Having come from a family with no books, . . . I didn't know the continuity of ancient literature, the mechanics of writing, or the mesmerizing effect poetry can have on its readers. . . . By early 1973, I was devouring contemporary American poetry and Latin American poetry, a literary border crossing that I couldn't fathom. Reading Pablo Neruda, I was fascinated by his energy

and the lush, occasionally surrealistic landscapes. I was bewildered by what must have been the godly permission this poet received to write so strangely. I wanted such permission, too. . . .

A timid writer, I gazed over my meager poems in fear of grammatical glitches. . . . But by summer 1973, after my fear of writing poorly had disappeared, I knew my pulse was timed to the heart of this [San Joaquin] valley.

I began writing my first poems in 1973, and soon fell in with the poets of Fresno—Leonard Adame, Omar Salinas, Ernesto Trejo, and Jon Veinberg. We were all wrestling with words and arguing over silly and large matters. . . . Except for Jon, we were all Chicanos and, determined to realize our talents, we settled in for the long haul. We trusted our instincts and wrote poems that first appeared in college magazines. Then, as young poets will do, we got gutsy. We licked stamps and sent out poems because we wanted to be published, just as our teachers were published, in literary magazines. We were on our way on this gray and rusty tanker called Poetry. (From Gary Soto, *New and Selected Poems,* Chronicle Books, 1995, pp. 1–3.)

Practice A-5 is a short story by Gary Soto taken from his narrative collection *Living up the Street.* Notice how he takes a unique childhood experience and turns it into a universal story for us all.

PRACTICE A-5

Directions: Read the following selection, putting together all the literal, critical, and affective skills you have learned.

1, 2, 3

1 When I was seven years old I spent most of the summer at Romain playground, a brown stick among other brown kids. The playground was less than a block from where we lived, on a street of retired couples, Okie families, and two or three Mexican families. Just before leaving for work our mother told us—my brother Rick, sister Debra, and me—not to leave the house until after one in the afternoon, at which time I skipped off to the playground, barefoot and smiling, my teeth that were uneven and without direction. By that hour the day was yellow with one-hundred-degree heat, the sun blaring high over the houses. I walked the asphalt street with little or no pain toward a mirage of water that disappeared as I approached it.

2 At the playground I asked for checkers at the game room, unfolded the board under the elm that was cut with initials and, if he was there, I played with Ronnie, an Okie kid who was so poor that he had nothing to wear but a bathing suit. All summer he showed up in his trunks, brown as the rest of us Mexicans, and seemed to enjoy himself playing checkers, Candyland, and Sorry. Once, when I brought him an unwrapped jelly sandwich in my hand, the shapes of my fingers pressed into the bread, he took it and didn't look into my eyes. He ate very slowly, deliberating over each move. When he beat me and had polished off his sandwich, he turned away without a word and ran off to play with someone else.

3 If Ronnie was not there and no one else challenged me, I just sat under the tree stacking checkers until they toppled over and I started again to raise that crooked spine of checkers a foot high.

4 If there were only little kids—four or five-year-olds who could count to ten—I played Candyland, a simple game of gum drops and sugar canes down a road to an ice cream sandwich. I remember playing with Rosie, a five-year-old whose brother Raymond got his leg broken when he was hit by a car. I was not around that day, but I recall racing a friend to where it had happened to look at the dried blood on the curb. My friend and I touched the stain. I scratched at it so that a few flakes got under my nails, and no matter how I picked and sucked at them, they wouldn't come out. We both ran home very frightened.

5 Rosie sat across the picnic-like table from me, her stringy hair spiked with a few flowers, and called me "Blackie" when it was my turn to spin the wheel and move down the candyland road. I didn't hit her because she had six brothers, five of them bigger than me. To smack her would have meant terror that would last for years. But the truth was that she liked me, for she offered me sunflower seeds from her sweaty palms and let me spit the shells at her.

6 "Spin the wheel Blackie," she said with a mouthful of her seeds and sniffling from a perennial cold, a bubble of snot coming and going.

7 "OK, tether-ball-head," I countered. Both of us laughed at each other's cleverness while we traded off spitting shells at one another, a few pasting themselves to our foreheads.

8 One Saturday morning a well-dressed man let his daughter try the slide. Rosie ran over to join the little girl, who was wearing a dress, her hair tied into a neat pony tail. Her shoes were glossy black and she wore socks with red trim. Rosie squealed at the little girl and the girl squealed back, and they both ran off to play while the father sat with his newspaper on the bench.

9 I went and sat on the same bench, shyly picking at the brittle, green paint but not looking up at the man at first. When my eyes did lift, slowly like balloons let go, I took it all in: His polished shoes, creased pants, the shirt, and his watch that glinted as he turned the page of his newspaper. I had seen fathers like him before on the *Donna Reed Show* or *Father Knows Best,* and I was pleased that he was here at *our* playground because I felt that we were being trusted, that nearby, just beyond our block, the rich people lived and were welcoming.

10 He looked up from the newspaper at me and forced a quick smile that relaxed back into a line as he returned to his paper. Happily I jumped from the bench and rushed to play with Rosie and the little girl, hoping to catch the man's eye as I swung twice as high as the girls and parachuted with great abandon to land like a frog. He looked up to smile, but dropped his eyes back to the newspaper as he recrossed his legs.

11 But then it happened. The little girl fell from the swing while Rosie was pushing her. Startled by her sudden crying, the man's eyes locked on the scene of Rosie hovering over his daughter crying on the ground. He jumped up yelling, "You filthy Mexican." He picked up his daughter who had stopped crying, and then, turning to Rosie who was saying that she hadn't done anything, he shoved her hard against the chain link fence so that her sunflower seeds flew in every direction. She got up bent over, her breath knocked out, mouth open wide as a cup and a string of saliva lengthening to the ground.

12 Three of her brothers were playing Chinese checkers under the tree, and when they saw what had happened they ran to fight the man with handfuls of redwood chips that they had scooped up from the play area. Like the rest of us, the brothers, who ranged from eight to fourteen, wore T-shirts and cut-offs but with no shoes—sons of the very poor. But unlike the rest of us, they were fierce brawlers who would go at it even with older kids as they flew up like chickens against those who got them mad.

13 Yelling, "You nigger people," his raised arm blocking the puffs of redwood chips, the man was backed into the merry-go-round while his daughter, some distance away, clung to the chain link fence. He charged one brother and pushed him to the ground only to feel a handful of redwood chips against his face. Coughing, he grabbed another brother and threw him to the ground while still another threw a softball at his back. In pain, the man turned around and chased the brother, but was stopped by the coach who had come running from the baseball game on the other side of the playground.

14 "Don't touch him," the coach warned the man, who was shouting whatever wild insults came to his mind. The coach tried to coax him to calm down, but the man, whose eyes were glassy, raved rabidly as his arms flailed about.

15 I had been watching from upside-down on the bars, but got down to help Rosie gather her seeds. She was on her knees, face streaked and nose running. I pinched up three seeds from the ground before I turned to stand by the brothers who were still taunting the man with Coke bottles they had pulled from the garbage. Suddenly the man broke down and as loudly as he had screamed names, he screamed that he was sorry, that he didn't know what he was doing. He gathered his daughter in his arms, repeating again and again that he was sorry. The coach ushered him to the gate while the brothers, two of them crying, yelled that they were going to get him.

16 "You are no one, mister. You think you can do this to us because we're little," one said with his Coke bottle still cocked and ready.

17 I wanted to run for them as they left for their car, to explain that it was a mistake; that we also fell from the swings and the bars and slide and got hurt. I wanted to show the man my chin that broke open on the merry-go-round, the half-moon of pink scar. But they hurried away, sweaty from the morning sun, the man's pants and shirt stained with dirt and the little girl's limp dress smudged from her fall, and in some ways looking like us.

18 I returned to Rosie who was still collecting her seeds, and feeling bad but not knowing what to do, I got to my knees and asked if she wanted to play. I touched her hair, then her small shoulders, and called her name. She looked up at me, her face still wet from crying, and said, "Go away, Blackie."

Comprehension Check

Directions: Now answer the following questions.

Literal Questions

1. Who is the main character? What is he like? ______________________________

____

2. Who are two other important characters in the story? Briefly describe what each contributes to our understanding of what is going on. ______________________

____

____

____

3. What incident provides the central conflict in this story? ____________________

4. Where and when is everything happening?

Critical Questions

5. What is one of the major themes in the story? Don't just use one word; explain what the author is saying about that topic.

6. How is this story affected by the point of view from which we see the events? How would the story be different if we saw it from the point of view of the man with the newspaper?

7. What does the narrator mean when the well-dressed girl hurries away "in some ways looking like us"?

Affective Questions

8. Which character in this story evoked the strongest feelings from you? Why?

9. Find at least three metaphors or similes in this story and briefly explain the effect of each.

10. What aspect of yourself or others do you see in the story?

Be sure to record your comprehension score in the Student Record Chart in the Appendix.

Questions for Group Discussion

1. In many ways, Gary Soto's book is a novel about growing up. How does the narrator see himself at the beginning of the story, and how does he change after the incident with the well-dressed man and daughter?

2. The first paragraph tells us a lot about the setting and the character. Explain what the author sets up in this introduction.
3. Explain the significance of games in this story.
4. What details does the narrator use to show poverty?
5. What do the well-dressed man and his daughter represent to the narrator?
6. Rosie's brothers are "fierce brawlers." What do you think the narrator feels about their fighting?
7. If you could talk to Rosie and the narrator at the end of the story, what would you want to say or do?

B. Reading Exposition Affectively

It is just as important to read exposition with affective awareness as it is with fiction. The practices in this section are expository, using narration and description.

Practice B-1

Directions: This is a timed reading practice. Before you start, look on your Reading Record Chart and note your last timed reading rate and comprehension scores. Try to better your rate without any loss of comprehension.

Now briefly survey the article, then begin timing, applying all the reading skills you have learned.

Begin timing: ____________

TIME TO LOOK AND LISTEN

Magdoline Asfahani

1 I love my country as many who have been here for generations cannot. Perhaps that's because I'm the child of immigrants, raised with a conscious respect for America that many people take for granted. My parents chose this country because it offered them a new life, freedom, and possibilities. But I learned at a young age that the country we loved so much did not feel the same way about us.

2 Discrimination is not unique to America. It occurs in any country that allows immigration. Anyone who is unlike the majority is looked at a little suspiciously, dealt with a little differently. The fact that I wasn't part of the majority never occurred to me. I knew that I was an Arab and a Muslim. This meant nothing to me. At school I stood up to say the Pledge of Allegiance every day. These things did not seem incompatible at all. Then everything changed for me, suddenly and permanently in 1985. I was only in seventh grade, but that was the beginning of my political education.

3 That year a TWA plane originating in Athens was diverted to Beirut. Two years earlier the U.S. Marine barracks in Beirut had been bombed. That seemed to start a

chain of events that would forever link Arabs with terrorism. After the hijacking, I faced classmates who taunted me with the cruel names, attacking my heritage and my religion. I became an outcast and had to apologize for myself constantly.

4 After a while, I tried to forget my heritage. No matter what race, religion, or ethnicity, a child who is attacked often retreats. I was the only Arab I knew of in my class, so I had no one in my peer group as an ally. No matter what my parents tried to tell me about my proud cultural history, I would ignore it. My classmates told me I came from an uncivilized, brutal place, that Arabs were by nature anti-American, and I believed them. They did not know the hours my parents spent studying, working, trying to preserve part of their old lives while embracing, willingly, the new.

5 I tried to forget the Arabic I knew, because if I didn't I'd be forever liked to murderers. I stopped inviting friends over for dinner, because I thought the food we ate was "weird." I lied about where my parents had come from. Their accents (although they spoke English perfectly) humiliated me. Though Islam is a major monotheistic religion with many similarities to Judaism and Christianity, there were no holidays near Chanukah or Christmas, nothing to tie me to the "Judeo-Christian" tradition. I felt more excluded. I slowly began to turn into someone without a past.

6 Civil war was raging in Lebanon, and all that Americans saw of that country was destruction and violence. Every other movie seemed to feature Arab terrorists. The most common questions I was asked were if I had ever ridden a camel or if my family lived in tents. I felt burdened with responsibility. Why should an adolescent be asked questions like "Is it true you hate Jews and you want Israel destroyed?" I didn't hate anybody. My parents had never said anything even alluding to such sentiments. I was confused and hurt.

7 As I grew older and began to form my own opinions, my embarrassment lessened and my anger grew. The turning point came in high school. My grandmother had become very ill, and it was necessary for me to leave school a few days before Christmas vacation. My chemistry teacher was very sympathetic until I said was going to the Middle East. "Don't come back in a body bag," he said cheerfully. The class laughed. Suddenly, those years of watching movies that mocked me and listening to others who knew nothing about Arabs and Muslims except what they saw on television seemed like a bad dream. I knew then that I would never be silent again.

8 I've tried to reclaim those lost years. I realize now that I come from a culture that has a rich history. The Arab world is a medley of people of different religions; not every Arab is a Muslim, and vice versa. The Arabs brought tremendous advances in the sciences and mathematics, as well as creating a literary tradition that has never been surpassed. The language itself is flexible and beautiful, with nuances and shades of meaning unparalleled in any language. Though many find it hard to believe, Islam has made progress in women's rights. There is a specific provision in the Koran that permits women to own property and ensures that their inheritance is protected—although recent events have shown that interpretation of these laws can vary.

9 My youngest brother, who is 12, is now at the crossroads I faced. When initial reports of the Oklahoma City bombing pointed to "Arab-looking individuals" as the culprits, he came home from school crying. "Mom, why do Muslims kill people? Why are the Arabs so bad?" She was angry and brokenhearted but tried to handle the situations in the best way possible: through education. She went to this class, armed with Arabic music, pictures, traditional dress, and cookies. She brought a chapter of the social studies book to life, and the children asked intelligent, thoughtful questions, even after the class was over. Some even asked if she was coming back. When my brother came home, he was excited and proud instead of ashamed.

10 I only recently told my mother about my past experience. Maybe if I had told her then, I would have been better equipped to deal with the thoughtless teasing. But,

fortunately, the world is changing. Although discrimination and stereotyping still exist, many people are trying to lessen and end it. Teachers, schools, and the media are showing greater sensitivity to cultural issues. However, there is still much that needs to be done, not for the sake of any particular ethnic or cultural group but for the sake of our country.

11 The America that I love is one that values freedom and the differences of its people. Education is the key to understanding. As Americans we need to take a little time to look at and listen carefully to what is around us and not rush to judgement without knowing all the facts. And we must never be ashamed of our pasts. It is our collective differences that unite us and make us unique as a nation. It's what determines our present and our future.

Finish timing. Record time here: ____________ and use the Timed Readings Conversion Chart in the Appendix to figure your rate: ____________ wpm.

Comprehension Check

Directions: Answer the following questions.

1. What is the subject of this essay? ______________________________

____

2. What is the thesis or main idea of this essay? ______________________________

____

3. Explain the meaning of the title. How does it relate to the point Asfahani is making? ______________________________

____

____

4. Asfahani says that she loves her country "as many who have been here for generations cannot." Explain what she means. ______________________________

____

____

5. What happened to cause the author to try to forget her heritage?

____

____

6. What happened that caused the author to reclaim her heritage?

____

____

7. Asfahani mentions several reasons she has to be proud of her Arabic heritage. Name three:

a. ______________________________

b. ______________________________

c. ______________________________

8. T/F The author is glad she never told her mother about the teasing she received in high school.
9. T/F The author is bitter and angry about the way her brother was treated in school after the Oklahoma City bombing.
10. T/F The essay was prompted by the affective reaction the author had to discrimination and attacks on her heritage.

Vocabulary Check

Directions: Define the underlined words from the essay.

1. I knew that I was an Arab and a Muslim (2)

   ____

2. things did not seem incompatible at all (2)

   ____

3. no matter what race, religion, or ethnicity (4)

   ____

4. Islam is a major monotheistic religion (5)

   ____

5. anything even alluding to such sentiments (6)

   ____

6. the Arab world is a medley of people (8)

   ____

7. with nuances and shades of meaning (8)

   ____

8. shades of meaning unparalleled in any language (8)

   ____

9. specific provision in the Koran (8)

   ____

10. armed with Arabic music, pictures, traditional dress (9)

   ____

Record your scores on the Student Record Chart in the Appendix. Discuss your scores with your instructor.

PRACTICE B-2

Directions: Answer the questions below. Then read the essay that follows. You or your instructor may want to time your reading.

1. What is a "barrio"? ____

   ____

2. Briefly describe your neighborhood. ______________________________

____

____

Now survey the 1,350-word article to see what rate you can apply to the reading of the selection while still obtaining good comprehension. Apply all the skills you have learned.

Begin timing: ____________

THE BARRIO

Robert Ramirez

1 The train, its metal wheels squealing as they spin along the silvery tracks, rolls slower now. Through the gaps between the cars blink a streetlamp, and this pulsing light on a barrio streetcorner beats slower, like a weary heartbeat, until the train shudders to a halt, the light goes out, and the barrio is deep asleep.

2 Throughout Aztlán (the Nahuatl term meaning "land to the north"), trains grumble along the edges of a sleeping people. From Lower California, through the blistering Southwest, down the Rio Grande to the muddy Gulf, the darkness and mystery of dreams engulf communities fenced off by railroads, canals, and expressways. Paradoxical communities, isolated from the rest of the town by concrete columned monuments of progress, and yet stranded in the past. They are surrounded by change. It eludes their reach, in their own backyards, and the people, unable and unwilling to see the future, or even touch the present, perpetuate the past.

3 Leaving from the expressway or jolting across the tracks, one enters a different physical world permeated by a different attitude. The physical dimensions are impressive. It is a large section of town which extends for fifteen blocks north and south along the tracks, and then advances eastward, thinning into nothingness beyond the city limits. Within the invisible (yet sensible) walls of the barrio, are many, many people living in too few houses. The homes, however, are much more numerous than on the outside.

4 Members of the barrio describe the entire area as their home. It is a home, but it is more than this. The barrio is a refuge from the harshness and the coldness of the Anglo world. It is a forced refuge. The leprous people are isolated from the rest of the community and contained in their section of town. The stoical pariahs of the barrio accept their fate, and from the angry seeds of rejection grow the flowers of closeness between outcasts, not the thorns of bitterness and the mad desire to flee. There is no want to escape, for the feeling of the barrio is known only to its inhabitants, and the material needs of life can also be found here.

5 The *tortillería* fires up its machinery three times a day, producing steaming, round, flat slices of barrio bread. In the winter, the warmth of the tortilla factory is a wool *sarape* in the chilly morning hours, but in the summer, it unbearably toasts every noontime customer.

6 The *panadería* sends its sweet messenger aroma down the dimly lit street, announcing the arrival of fresh, hot sugary *pan dulce*.

7 The small corner grocery serves the meal-to-meal needs of customers, and the owner, a part of the neighborhood, willingly gives credit to people unable to pay cash for foodstuffs.

8 The barbershop is a living room with hydraulic chairs, radio, and television, where old friends meet and speak of life as their salted hair falls aimlessly about them.

9 The pool hall is a junior level country club where *chucos,* strangers in their own land, get together to shoot pool and rap, while veterans, unaware of the cracking, popping balls on the green felt, complacently play dominoes beneath rudely hung *Playboy* foldouts.

10 The *cantina* is the night spot of the barrio. It is the country club and the den where the rites of puberty are enacted. Here the young become men. It is in the taverns that a young dude shows his *machismo* through the quantity of beer he can hold, the scores of *rucas* he has had, and his willingness and ability to defend his image against hardened and scarred old lions.

11 No, there is no frantic wish to flee. It would be absurd to leave the familiar and nervously step into the strange and cold Anglo community when the needs of the Chicano can be met in the barrio.

12 The barrio is closeness. From the family living unit, familial relationships stretch out to immediate neighbors, down the block, around the corner, and to all parts of the barrio. The feeling of family, a rare and treasurable sentiment, pervades and accounts for the inability of the people to leave. The barrio is this attitude manifested on the countenances of the people, on the faces of their homes, and in the gaiety of their gardens.

13 The color-splashed homes arrest your eyes, arouse your curiosity, and make you wonder what life scenes are being played out in them. The flimsy, brightly colored, wood-frame houses ignore no neon-brilliant color. Houses trimmed in orange, chartreuse, lime-green, yellow, and mixtures of these and other hues beckon the beholder to reflect on the peculiarity of each home. Passing through this land is refreshing like Brubeck, not narcotizing like revolting rows of similar houses, which neither offend nor please.

14 In the evenings, the porches and front yards are occupied with men calmly talking over the noise of children playing baseball in the unpaved extension of the living room, while the women cook supper or gossip with female neighbors as they water the *jardines.* The gardens mutely echo the expressive verses of the colorful houses. The denseness of multicolored plants and trees give the house the appearance of an oasis or a tropical island hideaway, sheltered from the rest of the world.

15 Fences are common in the barrio, but they are fences and not the walls of the Anglo community. On the western side of town, the high wooden fences between houses are thick, impenetrable walls, built to keep the neighbors at bay. In the barrio, the fences may be rusty, wire contraptions or thick green shrubs. In either case you can see through them and feel no sense of intrusion when you cross them.

16 Many lower-income families of the barrio manage to maintain a comfortable standard of living through the communal action of family members who contribute their wages to the head of the family. Economic need creates interdependence and closeness. Small barefooted boys sell papers on cool, dark Sunday mornings, deny themselves pleasantries, and give their earnings to *mamá.* The older the child, the greater the responsibility to help the head of the household provide for the rest of the family.

17 There are those, too, who for a number of reasons have not achieved a relative sense of financial security. Perhaps it results from too many children too soon, but it is the homes of these people and their situation that numbs rather than charms. Their houses, aged and bent, oozing children, are fissures in the horn of plenty. Their wooden homes may have brick-pattern asbestos tile on the outer walls, but the tile is not convincing.

18 Unable to pay city taxes or incapable of influencing the city to live up to its duty to serve all the citizens, the poorer barrio families remain trapped in the nineteenth century and survive as best they can. The backyards have well-worn paths to the outhouses, which sit near the alley. Running water is considered a luxury in some parts of the barrio. Decent drainage is usually unknown, and when it rains, the water stands for days, an incubator of health hazards and an avoidable nuisance. Streets, costly to pave, remain rough, rocky trails. Tires do not last long, and the constant rattling and shaking grind away a car's life and spread dust through screen windows.

19 The houses and their *jardines,* the jollity of the people in an adverse world, the brightly feathered alarm clock pecking away at supper and cautiously eyeing the children playing nearby produce a mystifying sensation at finding the noble savage alive in the twentieth century. It is easy to look at the positive qualities of life in the barrio, and look at them with a distantly envious feeling. One wishes to experience the feelings of the barrio and not the hardships. Remembering the illness, the hunger, and feeling of time running out on you, the walls, both real and imagined, reflecting on living in the past, one finds his envy becoming more elusive, until it has vanished altogether.

20 Back now beyond the tracks, the train creaks and groans, the cars jostle each other down the track, and as the light begins its pulsing, the barrio, with all its meanings, greets a new dawn with yawns and restless stretchings.

Finish timing. Record time here: __________ and use the Timed Readings Conversion Chart in the Appendix to figure your rate: __________ wpm.

Comprehension Check

Directions: Now answer the following questions.

1. What is the thesis or main idea of this article? __________

2. What is a barrio? __________

3. What is the author's attitude toward the barrio he describes? __________

4. The phrase "from the angry seeds of rejection grow the flowers of closeness between outcasts, not the thorns of bitterness" is an example of a simile.

a. True because __________

b. False because __________

5. "... this pulsing light on a barrio streetcorner beats slower, like a weary heartbeat" is an example of a metaphor.

   a. True because ____________________

   b. False because ____________________

6. Explain Ramirez's use of walls and fences to help develop his theme of cultural isolation. ____________________

7. How does the author's use of words such as *closeness, home, family, refuge,* and *neighborhood* help us understand how those who live in the barrio feel about it?

   ____

8. What is Ramirez describing when he says, "the brightly feathered alarm clock pecking away at supper and cautiously eyeing the children"? ____________________

9. Ramirez states, "One wishes to experience the feelings of the barrio and not the hardships." What are some of those feelings and what are some of the hardships?

Feelings	**Hardships**
________	________
________	________
________	________

10. Does Ramirez give any evidence to indicate that the people in the barrio want to leave? ________ Explain. ____________________

Vocabulary Check

Directions: Define the underlined words from the article.

1. <u>paradoxical</u> communities, isolated from the town ____________________

2. it <u>eludes</u> their reach ____________________

3. to touch the present, to <u>perpetuate</u> the past ____________________

4. a world <u>permeated</u> by a different attitude ____________________

5. the <u>leprous</u> people are isolated from the rest ______________________________

____

6. The <u>stoical</u> pariahs . . . accept their fate ______________________________

____

7. The stoical <u>pariahs</u> of the barrio ______________________________

____

8. <u>complacently</u> play dominoes ______________________________

____

9. thick, <u>impenetrable</u> walls ______________________________

____

10. an <u>incubator</u> of health hazards______________________________

____

Record your scores on the Student Record Chart in the Appendix. Discuss your scores with your instructor.

Application 1: Practicing Aesthetic Awareness

Aesthetics (pronounced es-the-tiks) has to do with appreciation of beauty or what is pleasing to the senses. As a good reader, you want to become aware of the aesthetics involved in good writing. It is one thing to understand what you read, but even better to appreciate the way something was written. Your affective comprehension is enhanced when you respond emotionally not only to a written piece, but also to its artistic creation.

Find a poem, short story, or essay that you appreciate for its aesthetic as well as its entertaining value and share it with your classmates or instructor.

C. Putting It All Together

By now, you ought to have a deeper understanding of the meaning of, and the need for, developing reading versatility. Approaches to reading are as varied as the types of reading materials that exist and the reasons for reading them. This last chapter has shown you some approaches to reading imaginative literature. It brings together the general content of all three units in the book. As the Introduction told you, total comprehension is a combination of the literal, critical, and affective levels of understanding. Good comprehension brings everything you've learned separately into play. The diagram on page 320 shows the many facets of comprehension.

You should be aware, from doing previous practices, that a short poem may take longer to read and understand than a chapter in a textbook. You can read some materials quickly even skim and scan them, whereas others require rereading. Good imaginative literature seldom communicates on a literal level only. It is

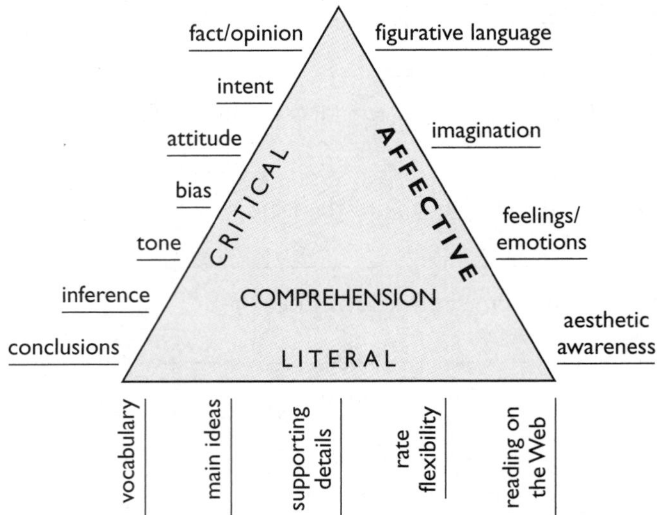

necessary to use your imagination, to interpret symbols, and to breathe life into characters, settings, and situations.

Developing reading versatility requires more than reading this book. It requires a lifetime of reading and reacting, at all levels of comprehension.

Introducing Barbara Kingsolver

Barbara Kingsolver grew up in eastern Kentucky, but never intended to stay there. Options were limited, she says: "Grow up to be a farmer or a farmer's wife." After graduating in 1977 from DePauw University in Indiana with a major in biology, Kingsolver continued her graduate studies at the University of Arizona in Tucson, receiving a master of science degree. To support herself, she worked as an archaeologist, copy editor, X-ray technician, housecleaner, biological researcher, and translator of medical documents.

Before becoming a well-known, best-selling author, she worked as a science writer for the University of Arizona and published numerous articles in such places as *The Nation,* the *New York Times,* and *Smithsonian.* In 1986, she won an Arizona Press Club award for outstanding feature writing. When some of her earlier articles appeared later in her collection of essays, *High Tide in Tuscon: Essays from Now or Never,* she was awarded an honorary doctorate of letters from DePauw University.

During the time between 1985 and 1987, Kingsolver worked as a freelance journalist. But at night, she wrote fiction. Married in 1985 and becoming pregnant a year later, she suffered from insomnia. Her doctor recommended that she scrub the bathroom tiles with a toothbrush. Instead, she sat in a closet and began to write her first novel, *The Bean Trees.* Published in 1988, *The Bean Trees* was not only well received by critics but also by the general reading public. In an interview with *Publishers Weekly,* Kingsolver says, "A novel can educate to some extent. But first a novel has to entertain—that's the contract with a reader . . . I want an English professor to understand the symbolism while at the same time I want people I grew up with—who may not often read anything but the Sears catalogue—to read my books."

Following *The Bean Trees,* Kingsolver wrote *Homeland and Other Stores* (1989), the novels *Animal Dreams* (1990) and *Pigs in Heaven* (1993), *The Poisonwood Bible* (1998), *Prodigal Summer* (2000), and another collection of essays, *Small Wonder* (2002). Kingsolver claims she never writes about herself, even though people who know her assume that some of her work is autobiographical. "I don't even write about real people. That would be stealing, first of all. And second of all, art is supposed to be better than that. If you want a slice of life, look out the window. An artist has to look out that window, isolate one or two suggestive things, and embroider them together with poetry and fabrication, to create a revelation. If we can't, as artists, improve on real life, we should put down our pencils and go bake bread."

For more information on Barbara Kingsolver, go to Google, Alta Vista, or some other browser and type in the author's name. (From http://www.harpercollins.com/catalog/author_xml.asp?authorID=5311.)

Practice C-1

Directions: Barbara Kingsolver's novel *Pigs in Heaven* has been delighting readers for several years. This selection is from the first chapter of that book and introduces us to the main character. Quickly preview this story and the questions. Who is the main character?

____

Is she married? ________________________________

Begin timing: ____________

QUEEN OF NOTHING

Barbara Kingsolver

1 Women on their own run in Alice's family. This dawns on her with the unkindness of a heart attack and she sits up in bed to get a closer look at her thoughts, which have collected above her in the dark.

2 It's early morning, April, windless, unreasonably hot even at this sun-forsaken hour. Alice is sixty-one. Her husband, Harland, is sleeping like a brick and snoring. To all appearances they're a satisfied couple sliding home free into their golden years, but Alice knows that's not how it's going to go. She married him two years ago for love, or so she thought, and he's a good enough man but a devotee of household silence. His idea of marriage is to spray WD-40 on anything that squeaks. Even on the nights when he turns over and holds her, Harland has no words for Alice—nothing to contradict all the years she lay alone, feeling the cold seep through her like cave air, turning her breasts to limestone from the inside out. This marriage has failed to warm her. The quiet only subsides when Harland sleeps and his tonsils make up for lost time. She can't stand the sight of him there on his back, driving his hogs to market. She's about to let herself out the door.

3 She leaves the bed quietly and switches on the lamp in the living room, where his Naugahyde recliner confronts her, snug as a catcher's mitt, with a long, deep impression of Harland running down its center. On weekends he watches cable TV with perfect vigilance, as if he's afraid he'll miss the end of the world—though he doesn't bother with CNN, which, if the world did end, is where the taped footage would run. Harland prefers the Home Shopping Channel because he can follow it with the sound turned off.

4 She has an edgy sense of being watched because of his collection of antique headlights, which stare from the china cabinet. Harland runs El-Jay's Paint and Body and his junk is taking over her house. She hardly has the energy to claim it back. Old people might marry gracefully once in a while, but their houses rarely do. She snaps on the light in the kitchen and shades her eyes against the bright light and all those ready appliances.

5 Her impulse is to call Taylor, her daughter. Taylor is taller than Alice now and pretty and living far away, in Tucson. Alice wants to warn her that a defect runs in the family, like flat feet or diabetes: they're all in danger of ending up alone by their own stubborn choice. The ugly kitchen clock says four-fifteen. No time-zone differences could make that into a reasonable hour in Tucson; Taylor would answer with her heart pounding, wanting to know who'd dropped dead. Alice rubs the back of her head, where her cropped gray hair lies flat in several wrong directions, prickly with sweat and sleeplessness. The cluttered kitchen irritates her. The Formica countertop is patterned with pink and black loops like rubber bands lying against each other, getting on her nerves, all cocked and ready to spring like hail across the kitchen. Alice wonders if other women in the middle of the night have begun to resent their Formica. She stares hard at the telephone on the counter, wishing it would ring. She needs some proof that she isn't the last woman left on earth, the surviving queen of nothing. The clock gulps softly, eating seconds whole while she waits; she receives no proof.

6 She stands on a chair and rummages in the cupboard over the refrigerator for a bottle of Jim Beam that's been in the house since before she married Harland. There are Mason jars up there she ought to get rid of. In her time Alice has canned tomatoes enough for a hundred bomb shelters, but now she couldn't care less, nobody does. If they drop the bomb now, the world will end without the benefit of tomato aspic. She climbs down and pours half an inch of Jim Beam into a Bengals mug that came free with a tank of gas. Alice would just as soon get her teeth cleaned as watch the Bengals. That's the price of staying around when your heart's not in it, she thinks. You get to be cheerleader for a sport you never chose. She unlatches the screen door and steps barefoot onto the porch.

7 The sky is a perfect black. A leftover smile of moon hides in the bottom branches of the sugar maple, teasing her to smile back. The air isn't any cooler outside the house, but being outdoors in her sheer nightgown arouses Alice with the possibility of freedom. She could walk away from this house carrying nothing. How those glass eyeballs in the china cabinet would blink, to see her go. She leans back in the porch swing, missing the squeak of its chains that once sang her baby to sleep, but which have been oppressed into silence now by Harland's WD-40. Putting her nose deep into the mug of bourbon, she draws in sweet, caustic fumes, just as she used to inhale tobacco smoke until Taylor made her quit.

Finish timing. Record time here: ____________ and use the Timed Readings Conversion Chart in the Appendix to figure your rate: ____________ wpm.

Comprehension Check

Directions: Now answer the following questions.

1. Describe the main character, both from details given in the story and what you infer about her.
2. Another character is the husband, who we see only through Alice's eyes. Give three details about him that help explain his character.
3. When is the story taking place, and how does that time affect the story?
4. Kingsolver is a master of figurative language. Find at least three examples of figurative language in the selection.
5. In the second paragraph, the main character summarizes her marriage by saying, "His idea of marriage is to spray WD-40 on anything that squeaks." Explain this statement.
6. Near the end of paragraph 4 is the explanation of the title of this section, "Queen of Nothing." Explain what the term means.
7. What do you infer about Alice's relationship with her daughter Taylor?
8. What is your reaction to the main character (Alice) in this selection?
9. What seems to be the point of the story (or theme) from this section?

10. What passages or sentences seem especially well written or effective to you? ______

______

______

______

Vocabulary Check

Directions: Explain in your own words each of the underlined figurative expressions listed below.

1. This dawns on her with *the unkindness of a heart attack* (paragraph 1). ______

______

2. to get a closer look at her thoughts, which have *collected above her in the dark* (paragraph 1) ______

______

______

3. Harland is *sleeping like a brick* (paragraph 2) ______

______

4. feeling the cold seep through her *like cave air* (paragraph 2) ______

______

5. the Naugahyde recliner, . . . *snug as a catcher's mitt* (paragraph 3) ______

______

6. formica countertop is patterned with *pink and black loops like rubber bands lying against each other* (paragraph 4) ______

______

7. Like rubber bands . . . *all cocked and ready to spring like hail* across the kitchen (paragraph 4) ______

______

______

8. the clock *gulps softly, eating seconds* . . . while she waits (paragraph 4) ______

______

9. Alice would *just as soon get her teeth cleaned as watch the Bengals* (paragraph 5)

______

______

10. *A leftover smile of moon hides in the bottom branches of the sugar maple* (paragraph 6)

______

______

Record the results of your rate, comprehension check, and vocabulary check, in the Student Record Chart in the Appendix.

PRACTICE C-2

Directions: Read the following short story written by the talented Southern writer Rick Bragg, from his novel *All Over but the Shoutin'*. Start with a quick preview, looking over the story and the questions that follow before you start reading. Now answer the following two questions.

1. What occupation does the main character have? ______________________________

2. Does the story all take place in one location? ______________________________

Now apply everything you know about reading with versatility. Then answer the questions that follow.

PARADISE

Rick Bragg

1 Those few months I was home in Calhoun County in the winter of 1988 and 1989, back at the *Star,* back with my family, run hot and cold in my memory. It was clear now that I had made a mistake, in believing I could somehow fix everything in my momma's life by my mere presence, in thinking I could just click into place again in that world that had changed without me. In the meantime, I had placed my ambition on hold, but it would be wrong to say that it was wasted time. A wealth of good things happened in those few months. I wrote stories again for people who knew my name and face, which is always more rewarding than writing for strangers. I even got a letter from my ex-mother-in-law, saying she liked a column I did about King, my dog. He had gotten old, weak, and walked around stiff-legged, like an old man with rheumatism, and when he finally passed away I was relieved because I knew he wasn't hurting anymore. I buried him in the goat pen, because the goats kept the weeds cut down.

2 I covered a high school football game again because the sports desk was shorthanded, and I got the names right, mostly, although the numbers still evaded me. I did get the score right, which is important. For the first time in years, I was home for Thanksgiving and Christmas and New Year's Day, and ate my momma's black-eyed peas, for luck. I even went bird hunting, but all I shot at was the sky. I saw three puppies born, and one of them, to be named Gizzard, would become both the ugliest dog on this planet and my momma's cherished companion. He was a sickly as well as a remarkably ugly puppy, but Momma kept him alive, feeding him drops of milk until he was well.

3 I ate breakfast again on Saturday at my momma's, got to know my kinfolks again. When my car broke down, Sam came to get me, again. "Ricky, if I didn't buy no better cars than you, I sure wouldn't move away from home again," he told me, once, from under the hood of my car. "I ain't comin' to get you in Florida."

4 But after a few months, it was time to go. I was twenty-nine, and while that seems young to me now, I felt like I was standing on the dock, watching the boat leave without me. I might have been content to stay there the rest of my life, if I had waited fifteen, twenty years. I just came home too soon.

5 I had a girlfriend, a good woman, who pointed out that I was pacing in the living room late at night like some circus elephant in a pen that was way too small. "Go," she

said. She was about tired of me then, anyway. It had something to do with my attention span.

6 I called the *St. Petersburg Times* on the phone and asked if they would still have me. The St. Pete *Times* was not a big newspaper in circulation—though it was twice as big as any paper I had ever worked for—but it was big in reputation. It was, consistently, year after year, one of the top ten newspapers in America. I would normally have been a little scared of it, of proving myself there. But the editor who hired me, Paul Tash, told me that it takes all manner and texture of people to make a good newspaper, and he would be glad to say he was hiring a reporter from Possum Trot, Alabama. Randy Henderson, my editor at the *Birmingham News,* had told me that, too. As long as there was at least one such person in every newspaper I went to, I knew I would be fine.

7 But it was the interview down there that sold me. The managing editor, Mike Foley, had a bust of Elvis in his office. I thought I might fit in, in a place like that. From some floors in the building, you could even see the bay.

8 On a chilly, rainy afternoon in March, I said good-bye to my momma with two hundred dollars in an envelope. I made sure she knew how to find me in case of an emergency, and told her to call me collect. I told her that Florida is just a quick plane ride away, that I could be home in a few hours if she ever needed me. That might sound silly to people who vacation in Europe and ride planes every week. To my momma, who had never been more than three hundred miles away from home in her life, who had never been anywhere close to an airplane except for the crop duster that swooped down over our house to get to the cotton fields, Tampa Bay was a million miles away. She cooked me some stew beef with potatoes and onions, which is my favorite, and tried not to cry. Before I left she gave me an envelope with a card in it, and told me not to open it until that night. It had a ten-dollar bill in it.

9 I said good-bye to my girlfriend with some roses and a promise to keep in touch that we both knew was more civility than anything else, and headed south. I got into St. Petersburg about four-thirty, too late to get a hotel room. I went straight to the beach at Clearwater and watched the sun come up, which was stupid because I had forgotten which side the water was on. It only sets over the water, genius, I said to myself, as it rose over my shoulder.

10 It was an odd place, in many ways. Pinellas County was paved from Tampa Bay to the beaches, pretty much, with all manner of people living elbow to elbow in little pastel tract houses, rambling brick ranchers and bayside mansions. To find the reasons why people ever came here in the first place, you had to live on the edge of it, by that beautiful water, or drive inland, through the sugar cane, to the heart of it. I rented a small apartment near the bay that was perhaps the most peaceful place I had ever lived. At night, when the water in the little inlet I lived on was smooth as glass, you could sit on the ground and watch the mullet jump, and egrets and other wading birds would take pieces of peeled orange out of your hands. I heard the other reporters complain about how slow it was and dull it was, how life was just one big Early Bird Dinner Special, but I loved it. The editors hurt my feelings sometimes, by sending me to do stories that I thought were frivolous, but it was hard to be miserable living by the beach.

11 The highlight of my time there, at least in the first few months, was the story of Mopsy the chicken. The little bayside town of Dunedin, north of Clearwater, had been the target of a serial killer. It seemed that a bobcat was, night after night, slaughtering the chickens of the retirees. The editor walked up to me, straight-faced, and told me that there had been a bobcat attack the night before but the chicken had miraculously survived, clawed but still clucking. The chicken's name, he told me, was Mopsy. I said something to the effect that he had to be kidding. Two minutes later, I

was motoring to the quiet and peaceful city of Dunedin. I was twenty-nine years old. I had won a whole wallful of journalism awards and risked my life in bad neighborhoods and prisons and hurricanes. I was going to interview a goddamn chicken.

12 The chicken had indeed had all the feathers raked off its ass, but when I approached it, it went squawking off across the yard. I supposed they would have to get it some counseling. I interviewed its owners instead, drove to a little parking lot by the water, sat in the car for a half-hour and rubbed my eyes. At home, Mopsy would be covered in gravy about now.

13 I went back to the newspaper office determined to get even. I would write the most overwritten crap of my life, I decided, something so purple and lurid that the editors would feel bad about sending me on the story. I began it this way:

14 "Mopsy has looked into the face of death, and it is whiskered."

15 It ran in the paper that way. All the editors told me what a good job I did, and not too long after that I got a promotion that would, I believed, take me away from stories about butt-gnawed chickens for the rest of my natural life.

16 The moral, I suppose, was this: Do not, on purpose, write a bunch of overwritten crap if it looks so much like the overwritten crap you usually write that the editors think you have merely reached new heights in your craft.

Comprehension Check

Directions: Now answer the following questions.

1. At the start of the story, the narrator has gone home to his mother's hometown. Why? ____________________

____

____

2. The narrator applies to be a writer at the *St. Petersburg Times,* a large and important newspaper. What encourages him to apply there? ____________________

____

____

3. The humorous tone of this story is an important part of it. What is one sentence or passage of the story you consider funny? ____________________

____

____

4. List at least two details that make it clear this story takes place in the South.

____

____

5. What are the narrator's feelings about being sent to write the story of Mopsy the chicken? ____________________

____

____

6. How does he get back at his editors for sending him on the Mopsy story? ________

7. Describe the narrator, using specifics from the story. ________

8. Give two examples of figurative language in this story. ________

9. Bragg is a great storyteller. Which of the stories in this excerpt is your favorite and why? ________

10. Why do you like or dislike this excerpt? ________

Vocabulary Check

Directions: Define or explain the following underlined words from the story.

1. like an old man with <u>rheumatism</u> (paragraph 1) ________

2. I got the names right mostly, although the numbers still <u>evaded</u> me (paragraph 2) ________

3. The St. Pete *Times* was not a big newspaper in <u>circulation</u> (paragraph 6) ________

4. a promise to keep in touch that we both knew was more <u>civility</u> than anything else (paragraph 9) ________

5. you could sit on the ground and watch the <u>mullet</u> jump (paragraph 10) ________

6. and <u>egrets</u> and other wading birds would take pieces of peeled orange (paragraph 10) ________

7. The editors hurt my feelings sometimes, by sending me to do stories that I thought were <u>frivolous</u> (paragraph 10) ________

8. Dunedin . . . had been the target of a serial killer (paragraph 11) ______________

____

9. I would write the most overwritten crap of my life . . . something so purple (paragraph 13) ____

____

____

10. something so purple and lurid that the editors would feel bad (paragraph 13) ___

____

Record the results of the comprehension check and vocabulary checks in the Student Record Sheet in the Appendix. If you are in doubt about why any of your answers are wrong, check with your instructor.

Questions for Group Discussion

1. As a group, come up with a summary of this chapter.
2. This chapter deals with fiction and poetry as one kind of valuable reading. Should the study of fiction be a requirement in college? Why or why not?
3. Compare and contrast "Queen of Nothing" and "Paradise." Be specific about similarities and differences.
4. You have read many selections in this chapter. As a group, analyze your favorites based on terminology from the chapter (such as *figurative language, images, emotional* or *intellectual responses,* and so on).

A Final Check

Now you should have a good understanding of how all three facets of comprehension work together in the diagram. The final area is now ready for your review. Fill in the blanks in this section on the diagram on page 330. Working with a partner or small group is acceptable if your instructor sets up groups. *Hints:* The first line corresponds to the kind of language that fosters affective awareness. The second line deals with a key element of your mind that is needed for understanding fiction and poetry. The third line has to do with what part of you is needed for full comprehension of literature. The final line is a term that refers to your sensitivity to literature.

When you have finished, check your answers with the triangle at the beginning of Unit Three.

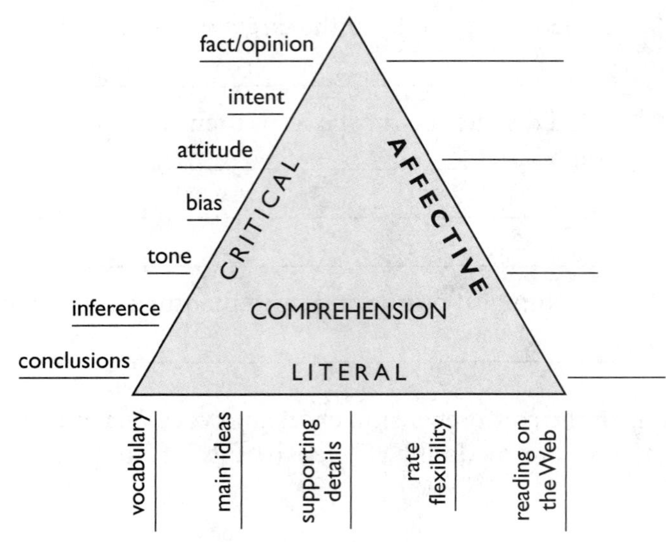
fact/opinion
intent
attitude
bias
tone
inference
conclusions
CRITICAL
AFFECTIVE
COMPREHENSION
LITERAL
vocabulary
main ideas
supporting details
rate flexibility
reading on the Web

APPENDIX I

Study-Reading Strategies

The SQ3R Study Technique

An old and proven method for study reading is the SQ3R formula. Introduced by Dr. Francis P. Robinson more than forty years ago, many versions of this method now exist, but we will present his original study method here.

The name of this study technique, SQ3R, contains reminders of each of five important steps in learning to study read:

S = Survey

Step 1: Before reading, take some time to survey what it is you are going to read. If you are beginning a new textbook, survey the book by looking at the table of contents to see what the book will cover. Check to see how the chapters are structured and what study aids are provided. See if a glossary is available to help you learn unfamiliar words. Skim over the index and see if you recognize any of the items listed. Know what is in the book that may help you better comprehend the subject.

If you have surveyed your textbook and are reading one of the chapters, survey it before you begin reading. If it is a long chapter, you might want to divide it up into different reading segments. Note the headings and captions under any pictures or graphs. If there is a summary, read it. Look at any questions at the end of the chapter. Keep them in mind as you read. All this gives you a purpose for reading and aids your concentration and comprehension.

Q = Question

Step 2: If you survey what you are going to read, it should raise some questions you want answered as you read. Having questions to answer keeps your mind from wandering. Learn to turn headings into questions. For instance, if a history textbook has a heading "Main Causes of the Civil War," turn this into "What were the main causes of the Civil War?" Read to answer the question. Also, read any questions at the end of the chapter. Just because they appear at the end of the chapter doesn't mean you can't read them first.

R1 = Read

Step 3: The first of the three Rs refers to Read. Read to answer any questions raised in step 2. But read only from one heading or section to the next. Then stop and take notes or mark the important passages. (More on this in the next step.) Your mind can only assimilate so much information at once. Our minds like to wander. So take control by reading short segments, then stopping to make sure you understand what you just read before going on.

R2 = Recite

Step 4: The second R, Recite, reminds you to "recite" back what you read. This ties in with step 3, Read. Recite by taking notes or marking the passage at the important points being made. It helps reinforce what you read and aids memory if you write notes in a notebook for that particular class. As you continue reading through other assignments in the book, you will remember better what you read before if you have notes to which you can refer in the future. Once you have made sure you understand what you've read, move on, repeating step 3, reading from one heading to the next, then stopping to "recite" through notes and markings for that passage. Repeat steps 3 and 4 until you have completed the assigned reading.

R3 = Review

After reading the entire chapter, review all of your notes. Make sure you have answered all the questions raised by your surveying and any at the end of the chapter. If you still can't answer a question, go back and find it. If you can't, make a note to ask your instructor about it. If there are no questions supplied at the end of the chapter, pretend you are the instructor and make up some questions for a test and see if you can answer them. An even better way to review is to form a study group or ask another student in the class to get together to study.

Research has shown that using the SQ3R formula or a similar method improves reading comprehension and retention. It may seem at first that it takes too much time, but once you become familiar with applying the steps to your study reading, your time will be better spent because your approach will focus your mind on what you are doing—study reading.

Surveying Textbooks

Not all textbooks are designed with study aids. Based on the S in the SQ3R formula, here is a more detailed list of what to look for when you survey your textbooks:

1. *Title page:* It will give you the full title of the book, the edition, the authors and their school affiliation, and the publishing company. The complete title often helps you understand what the book will cover in regard to the subject. For instance, an introductory textbook is going to be more general than one that specifies a particular area. A history text that states "Volume 2" on the title page indicates an entire volume of history should have been studied before that one.

2. *Copyright page:* This tells you when the book was published and the date of any previous editions, so you will have some idea how dated the information in the book is.
3. *Preface:* This explains the author's purpose for writing the book, explains for what readers the book is intended, and usually includes an acknowledgment of those people who helped with the book.
4. *Table of contents:* This shows how the book is organized, an outline of sorts. Some tables of contents are very comprehensive, some not; but at least they show you if the book is divided into units, chapters, and sections; whether or not there is a glossary, index, appendix, and so on.
5. *Index:* This is an alphabetical listing of the various topics covered in the book. Names, places, events, definitions of terms, and the like are usually listed. Looking over an index can give you an idea of the book's subject matter, plus call to mind anything you may already have studied in the past in another course.
6. *Glossary:* The glossary is a small dictionary of sorts that usually defines the specialized terms covered in the book. It can save you from using the dictionary, but better yet, it defines the words and terms as they are used in the context of the book.
7. *Appendixes:* Textbooks frequently contain an appendix (sometimes more than one) that provides supplemental information related to the topic of the book. It is provided for the reader's use but is often overlooked.

How helpful these components of a textbook are varies from book to book. All too often, they are not examined very thoroughly by students. This is unfortunate because, as you progress through a particular course, these aids can sometimes be very beneficial. It is doubtful you would buy a car without driving it, looking it over carefully to see what features it has, and even comparing it with other cars. But when it comes to textbooks, most students buy them because they are required and never bother to get to know what they offer.

Another mistake some students make is to begin reading a textbook assignment without preparing to read it. They simply turn to the assigned pages and start reading. Soon they discover their minds have wandered and they don't even remember what they have read up to that point. One of the most important parts of a good study strategy is to prepare to read an assignment. Just as you need to look over your textbooks to get to know their content, so should you look over any assignment before reading it to see how long it will take, what subject will be covered, and what aids are provided in the chapter to help you comprehend better.

Surveying Chapter Assignments in Textbooks

Research has shown that the typical reader remembers only about half of what he or she reads when given a test right after reading an assignment. Several factors contribute to this, but one of the major ones is lack of preparation before beginning to study-read. In order to get the maximum efficiency from a study-reading session, it has been found that "looking before you leap," that is, surveying or looking over what has been assigned before trying to read it, is best.

Following is a step-by-step process for surveying a chapter based on the S in the SQ3R study formula:

1. *Check the length of the assignment.* Flip through the assigned pages. Can you read it in one sitting or should you divide it up and cover a certain number of pages at a time? Don't try to take in too much at once, especially if it is a subject you don't know well or are having trouble understanding.
2. *Read the title of the chapter and the subheadings carefully.* These serve as clues to what the assignment will cover. If you know anything about the subject, your memory will be triggered by the title and headings. If you know nothing about the contents of the assignment, carefully noting the chapter title and headings will help you focus on the subject of the chapter so that your mind will not wander. If something in the title or headings is unclear, make up a question about it that you can use as a guide when you are ready to read. In fact, the more questions you have about what you are going to study-read the better, since reading for the answers will keep your mind from wandering.
3. *Look for any study aids the chapter may have.* See if there are any questions at the beginning or end of the chapter. Look them over closely before reading. Reading for answers will focus your attention on the subject matter. If there is a summary, read it to see what will be covered. Look for pictures and other visual aids. Read the captions under them. These types of aids help prepare you for better reading comprehension.
4. *Find the major idea related to each heading or subheading of the chapter.* Most chapters have three to six main ideas, and you need to identify these in your survey. If there are no subheadings, you need to look through the chapter for changes in the subject. If there are too many subheadings, you need to group them together and see if you can find the main ideas.

Marking and Underlining Textbooks

In Part A, you learned that reciting is one of the three Rs in the SQ3R study method. While oral recitation was described, it was recommended that you take some form of notes during the Read-Recite cycle. It is strongly suggested that you use one of the methods described here and in the section for note taking.

Basically, there are two ways to take notes as you read: (1) You can mark in your book, using the margins for your own remarks and underlining and circling important words and phrases; or (2) you can take notes from the text in a notebook. Section D will cover taking notes in a notebook. This section deals with marking and underlining correctly.

Take a look at the following passage and how it is marked:

> It is now believed that the earth's outer layer of rock, called the lithosphere, is divided into large, rigid plates that fit together like pieces of a huge jigsaw puzzle. There are twelve major plates (and numerous subplates), each about sixty miles thick and some almost as wide as the Pacific Ocean. They float on a layer of dense, viscous rock called the asthenosphere, which, in turn, surrounds the earth's hot core.

How helpful are all those markings going to be when you review for a test? What do they mean? The act of underlining is not in itself a helpful comprehension or recall device.

Notice the same passage marked in a more sensible way:

lithosphere, outer layer: asthenosphere, inner layer

It is now believed that the earth's outer layer of rock, called the lithosphere, is divided into large, rigid plates that fit together like pieces of a huge jigsaw puzzle. There are twelve major plates (and numerous subplates), each about sixty miles thick and some almost as wide as the Pacific Ocean. They float on a layer of dense, viscous rock called the asthenosphere, which, in turn, surrounds the earth's hot core.

Here, only the key points are highlighted. The student used what was learned about finding main ideas and supporting details. Thought went into what was to be marked for later review as well as what would be helpful for understanding the passage during the Read-Recite portion of SQ3R.

While there is no particular way to mark or underline, good note takers seem to follow two basic principles: (1) Mark only the main points and (2) be consistent in the way they mark. Here are some suggestions for marking and underlining:

1. Use pen, not pencil. Pencil marks will fade and smear in time.
2. Underline main ideas and circle important words or phrases. Studies show that, when students were allowed to underline only one sentence in a paragraph, they took more time and underlined only important sentences, which produced better comprehension and recall.
3. Underline minor, yet important, points with broken lines. Later, during a review, such markings will make it easy for you to distinguish between main ideas and minor but relevant ones.
4. Use numbers in the margins to indicate a series of points or items being discussed.
5. Use the margins to write what you feel is important, questions you have for the instructor, or notes to yourself.
6. Draw rectangles around names or places that might be used in a test or quiz.
7. Use small Post-It notes to jot key words, sticking them on the page and paragraph you want to remember.
8. From these Post-It notes, write notes on your computer. Propping your textbook on a book stand or music stand helps the process.

Remember that these are just suggestions. You may want to use your own type of marking. That's fine, as long as it is consistent and meaningful to you as you are marking and helps you later during reviews.

Marking and underlining are not as efficient as note taking *unless* you take the time to study what to underline and later review what you underlined. Underlining and marking are faster than note taking, but it doesn't do you any good to underline if you don't actually study-read as you do it.

Taking Reading Notes

Some students don't want to mark or underline their textbooks because they want to sell them when the course is over. This is understandable considering the cost of textbooks these days. Still, marking and underlining, if done correctly, are preferable to taking notes for the reasons described in the previous section. But there are times when you use books that are not yours, so a method for taking notes is needed.

The main thing to remember about taking reading notes is not to copy word for word from the book. Rephrase what the author says in your own words as much as possible. Many students make the mistake of copying right from the book, thinking that they are doing a good job of studying. Such action usually produces no results. The purpose of taking notes is to make certain that you understand what you are reading at the time and to record it for later review.

As with marking and underlining, there is no one way to take notes. But here are some guidelines for you to follow:

1. At the top of the notebook page, always write down the title of the book, the chapter title, and the pages your notes cover. There may be a time in the future when your notes aren't as helpful as you thought and you need to refer back to the book. This information will help you find the material in the book quickly.
2. Write the main ideas of the passage as your own heading, then list the supporting details under this heading. In effect, you are summarizing main ideas and supporting details just as you did in Chapter Two with paragraphs and essays.
3. Don't write anything down until you have studied a short passage and understand it. Let the writing patterns discussed in the last chapter help you sort out the key points. If an author is defining a term or concept, make certain your notes contain the definition. If the author is comparing or contrasting two items, make certain your notes reflect the comparison, contrast, and so on.
4. Remember, don't use the same words as the author unless they are necessary. If you do use the author's own words, make certain you know their meanings.
5. Keep track of words you need to look up. If the vocabulary is difficult, you may need to look up words in the glossary or in a dictionary before you can take notes.
6. Write down questions that you can't answer or that give you trouble so that you can ask your instructor about them at the next class meeting.

Feel free to modify these suggestions. Just make certain that you are not going through the motions of taking notes without really understanding what you are writing down.

Mapping: Another Type of Note Taking

Mapping is a technique used to place notes for an entire chapter on one or two notebook pages. Mapping forces you to see a chapter as a whole rather than in pieces, and it helps you store what you read in your long-term memory. As with any study device, it is only as good as you make it.

Mapping works well with the SQ3R study method. Rather than taking reading notes as discussed before, some students prefer the mapping technique. Look carefully at the map on page 337 of a chapter titled "Changing the Self-Concept." Notice how the chapter title appears in a rectangle in the center of the map. The four heading titles appear on lines drawn from each of the four quarters of the rectangle. The key points to remember about each of the headings appear on lines drawn under the appropriate heading. If there had been five headings rather than four, a different design might be drawn around the chapter title, allowing five lines for each heading. In other words, the design made around the chapter title can be drawn to fit the number of headings.

Also notice that each heading is written above or below a line depending on where you want the branches to fit. Frequently, students can map an entire chapter on one page, making it visually easy to review. In addition, mapping forces you to summarize key points.

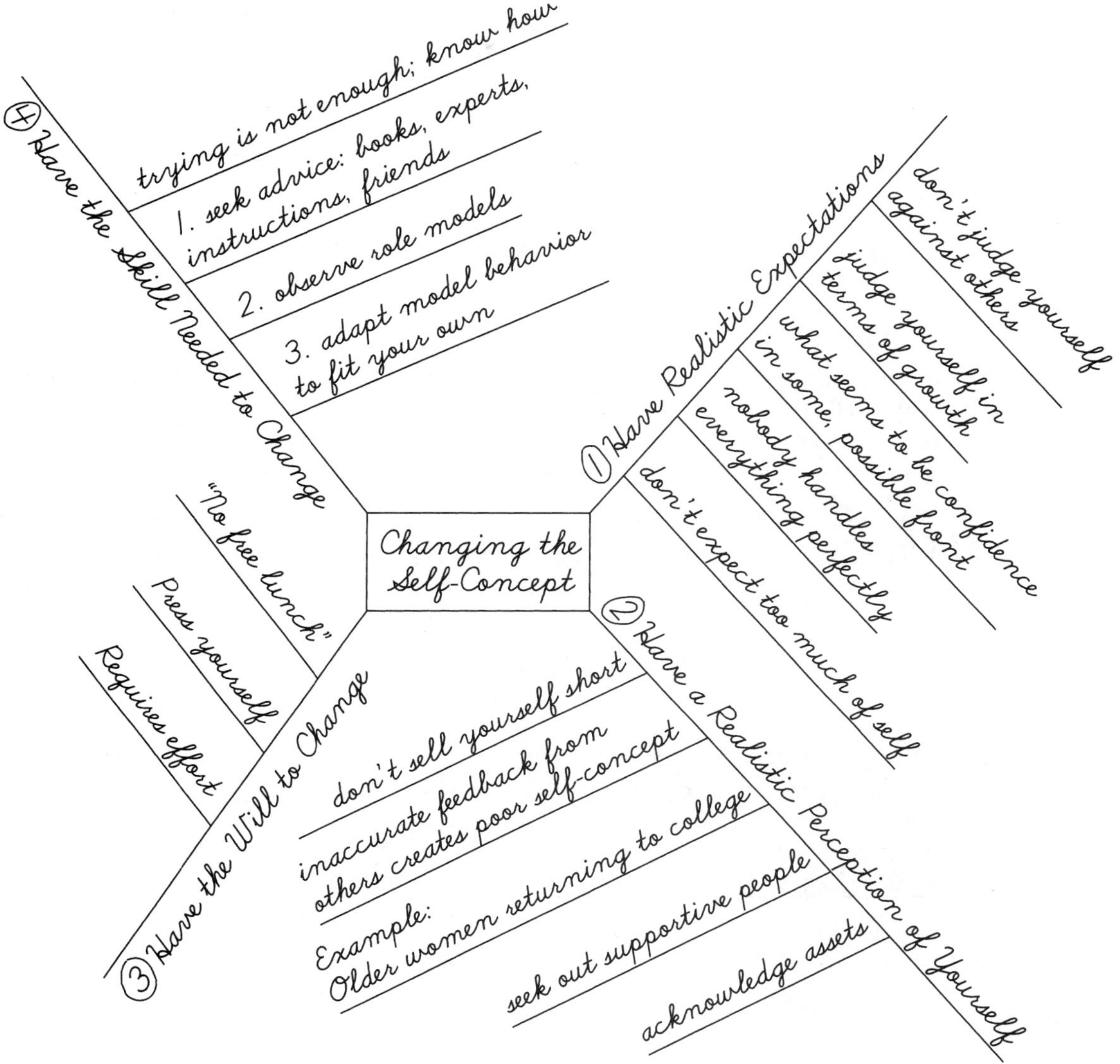

Review Quiz on SQ3R

Directions: Answer the following questions without looking back.

1. Each of the letters in the SQ3R study formula represent:
   S ______
   Q ______
   R ______
   R ______
   R ______
2. At what point in your reading should you take notes?
   ______
   ______
3. Why should you stop reading and recite at the end of each heading (or several pages, if there is no heading)? ______
   ______
   ______
4. When should you review a chapter after you have finished reading it? ______
   ______
5. What kinds of study aids should you look for in your textbooks? ______
   ______
   ______
6. Explain what method of note taking works best for you. ______
   ______
   ______

Name: ______ Section: ______

Scanning Graphic Aids

Scanning is what you do when you look for a friend's telephone number in a phone book. It is the technique used when locating a word in a dictionary, when seeking a page number in an index, or when checking to see what television programs are offered at eight o'clock. In all these examples, you know what you are looking for before you begin to read. You have to use guides and aids to find what you want rather than reading everything on the page. Good scanning ability, then, depends on knowing what you want to find and knowing the organization of the material to be read.

Scanning is something you already know how to do, but you may or may not be very proficient at it. In either case, the practices in this chapter will help you increase your scanning speed and become more aware of the organizational patterns in materials where scanning is best utilized.

Scanning graphic aids in textbooks is an important study skill. You need to learn how to scan charts, maps, graphs, indexes, and tables quickly in order to get the most information in the least amount of time. The following practice exercises are designed to help you become proficient at this skill. Try to keep to the time limits suggested.

As you do these practices, try finding a scanning technique that works well for you. Remember that you are not reading in the normal sense of the word; you are learning to develop a skill. Feel free to experiment and don't worry about mistakes. This is the place to make mistakes and to learn from them.

SCANNING PRACTICE: Charts

Directions: First take a minute to look at the chart below. Then scan the chart for the answers to the questions under the chart. Write your answers in the blanks provided. You should finish in less than three minutes.

CALORIES USED PER HOUR

		Body Size	
	120 Pounds	**150 Pounds**	**175 Pounds**
Calisthenics	235–285	270–300	285–335
Running	550–660	625–700	660–775
Walking	235–285	270–330	285–335
Bowling	150–180	170–190	180–210
Swimming	425–510	480–540	510–600
Bicycling	325–395	370–415	395–460
Tennis	335–405	380–425	405–470
Golf	260–315	295–335	315–370

HOURS/MINUTES PER WEEK TO BURN 1,500 CALORIES

	Body Size		
	120 Pounds	150 Pounds	175 Pounds
Calisthenics	5:16–6:23	5:00–5:33	4:29–5:16
Running	2:16–2:44	2:09–2:25	1:56–2:16
Walking	5:16–6:23	5:00–5:33	4:29–5:16
Bowling	8:20–10:00	7:54–8:49	7:09–8:20
Swimming	2:56–3:32	2:47–3:08	2:30–2:56
Bicycling	3:48–4:37	3:37–4:03	3:16–3:48
Tennis	3:42–4:29	3:32–3:57	3:11–3:42
Golf	4:46–5:46	4:29–5:05	4:03–4:46

Begin timing: ____________

1. If you weigh about 120 pounds, what form of exercise burns the most calories?

   ____

2. If you weigh about 150 pounds, will you burn more calories if you swim or if you run? ____

   ____

3. If you weigh about 175 pounds, how long will it take you to burn 1,500 calories per week by walking? ____

   ____

4. What activity on the chart is the slowest way to burn calories at any weight?

   ____

5. If you want to burn as many calories as you can in order to lose weight, what activity should you do? ____

   ____

6. If you don't like the activity in the answer to question 5, what's the next best activity to do to burn calories?____

   ____

7. If you weigh about 120 pounds, how many hours/minutes per week would you have to spend bowling in order to burn 1,500 calories?____________________

   ____

8. Is bicycling a faster or slower way to burn calories than tennis? ______________

   ____

Time: ________ **Number correct:** ________

SCANNING PRACTICE: Map, Graph, Chart

Directions: Using the map, graph, and chart on page 342, scan for the answers to the following questions. Circle the letter of the correct response. Answers are provided as a learning tool. Don't read them until after you have scanned.

1. The city having the lowest number of clear days during February is located in

a. California.

b. Washington.

c. Arizona.

d. South Dakota.

The correct answer can be found by looking under "Average Temperature" on the weather report chart. The city is Seattle with five clear days. To find the state in which the city is located, look on the map provided. The correct answer is Washington.

2. The city having the same number of cloudy and clear days during February is

a. Portland.

b. Denver.

c. Santa Fe.

d. Salt Lake City.

To find the correct answer, you would compare the "Cloudy" and "Clear" columns on the weather report chart to find equal numbers of cloudy and clear days. The correct answer is Santa Fe with fourteen days of each.

3. The city having the lowest average temperature during February is

a. Seattle.

b. Pierre.

c. Los Angeles.

d. Portland.

The correct answer can be found under "Average Temperature" on the weather report chart, or more quickly on the average temperature graph below it. The correct answer is Pierre with 46°, a high for that month!

4. The average temperature during February of the city shown in Colorado is

a. 63°.

b. 58°.

c. 55°.

d. 65°.

The correct answer can be found by first finding the city in Colorado on the map, then looking down the weather report chart or the graph for the average temperature of Denver. The correct answer is 63°.

WEATHER REPORT—FEBRUARY			
City	Average Temperature	Number of days	
		Cloudy	Clear
Seattle	60	23	5
Los Angeles	70	8	20
Santa Fe	75	14	14
Salt Lake City	65	18	10
Denver	63	10	18
Portland	55	10	8
Phoenix	72	8	20
Pierre	46	20	8

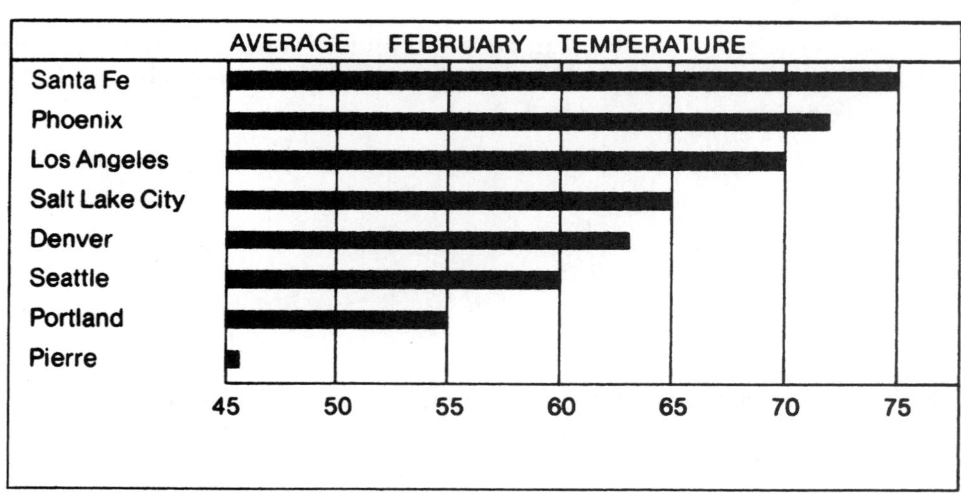

5. The city with the highest average temperature during February is nearest on the map to

a. Salt Lake City.

b. Los Angeles.

c. Denver.

d. Portland.

The correct answer can be found by looking at the weather report chart or the graph for the highest average temperature, and then locating that city on the map. Look to the adjacent cities to see which one is nearest to it. The correct answer is Denver, which is nearest to Santa Fe.

6. The number of cloudy days in Los Angeles during February is equal to the number of cloudy days in

a. Portland.

b. Santa Fe.

c. Seattle.

d. Phoenix.

The correct answer can be found by looking at the cloudy days for Los Angeles on the weather report chart and scanning the list to find which other city has the same number of cloudy days. The correct answer is Phoenix with eight cloudy days.

7. The city located nearest the Pacific Ocean had how many clear days in February?

a. 15

b. 5

c. 20

d. 8

The correct answer can be found by first looking at the map and locating the city nearest the Pacific. Then look at the clear days on the weather report chart to find the city. The city is Los Angeles, and the correct answer is twenty clear days.

8. The city having the greatest number of cloudy days during February had what average temperature?

a. 65°

b. 60°

c. 58°

d. 63°

The correct answer can be found by first looking under "Cloudy" on the weather report chart to locate the city with the greatest number of cloudy days. Then you should look under "Average Temperature" for the correct answer. The correct answer is 60° for Seattle.

9. The city appearing nearest the middle of the map is located in which state?
   a. Arizona
   b. Utah
   c. Colorado
   d. California

The correct answer can be found by simply locating the middle point of the map and looking to see what city is nearest that point. It is Salt Lake City, Utah.

10. The city farthest east on the map had how many cloudy days in February?
    a. 5
    b. 12
    c. 20
    d. 8

The correct answer can be found by locating the city farthest east on the map. The city is Pierre, South Dakota. Then look under the "Cloudy" column of the weather report chart to find the number of cloudy days. The correct answer is twenty cloudy days.

SCANNING PRACTICE: An Index

Directions: Scan the index listing on page 345 for the answers to the following questions. Circle the letter of the correct answer. You should finish in less than three minutes.

Begin timing: ____________

1. On what page would you find information about Mayan Indians?
   a. 6
   b. 44
   c. 243
2. On what pages would you find information about Meriwether Lewis?
   a. 136, 148–149
   b. 138–139
   c. 144–145
3. On what page would you find a definition of Manifest Destiny?
   a. 208
   b. 182
   c. 149
4. How many pages are listed for information on the Missouri Compromise?
   a. One
   b. Two
   c. Three

295 INDEX

5. On what page would you find information on the "Log Cabin" Bill?
   - a. 206
   - b. 207
   - c. 208
6. Are Mohawk Indians listed in the index?
   - a. No
   - b. Yes
   - c. Can't tell
7. On what pages will you find information about Lincoln's debates with Douglas?
   - a. 237–246
   - b. 233, 247
   - c. 219, 231
8. How many pages are listed for Bishop Las Casas?
   - a. One
   - b. Two
   - c. Three
9. Under what other listing besides "Massachusetts Bay Colony" could you find more information about the colony?
   - a. Founding of Maryland
   - b. Puritan colonies
   - c. Native Americans
10. How many pages are given to moonshiners?
    - a. One
    - b. Two
    - c. Three

Time: ________ **Number correct:** ________

SCANNING PRACTICE: Temperature Table

Directions: Scan the temperature listings on page 347 for the answers to the following questions. Write your answers in the blanks that follow the questions. Try to finish in two minutes or less.

Begin timing: ____________

1. What is the temperature high in Honolulu? ______________________________
2. What is the temperature low in Fairbanks? ______________________________
3. In what city is the highest temperature listed? ______________________________
4. In what city is the lowest temperature listed? ______________________________

TEMPERATURES

Temperature and precipitation table for the 24-hour period ending at 4 A.M. Pacific Time, as prepared by the National Weather Service in San Francisco:

	High	Low	Pr.		High	Low	Pr.
Albany	69	45	...	Memphis	75	61	.16
Albuquerque	81	52	...	Miami	82	78	...
Atlanta	83	61	.16	Milwaukee	60	48	.03
Bakersfield	107	75	...	Minneapolis	63	43	...
Bismark	73	47	...	New Orleans	81	69	.54
Boise	91	51	...	New York	64	58	...
Boston	71	51	...	North Platte	63	34	.05
Brownsville	79	57	2.25	Oakland	86	54	...
Buffalo	67	50	...	Oklahoma City	70	46	...
Charlotte	83	66	...	Omaha	68	53	...
Chicago	64	54	.12	Palm Springs	104	71	...
Cincinnati	86	62	...	Paso Robles	105	52	...
Cleveland	76	64	...	Philadelphia	71	61	...
Dallas	78	52	.01	Phoenix	100	70	...
Denver	74	43	...	Pittsburgh	75	56	...
Des Moines	64	53	.01	Portland, Me.	62	42	...
Detroit	70	59	...	Portland, Ore.	69	43	...
Eureka	56	48	...	Rapid City	71	47	...
Fairbanks	55	37	.02	Red Bluff	100	66	...
Fresno	103	66	...	Reno	91	59	...
Helena	83	52	.01	Richmond, Va.	76	59	...
Honolulu	85	72	.01	Sacramento	104	59	...
Indianapolis	82	62	.37	St. Louis	65	55	.30
Kansas City	67	47	...	Salt Lake City	78	53	...
Las Vegas	96	66	...	San Diego	74	62	...
Los Angeles	88	59	...	San Francisco	80	52	...
Louisville	87	63	.24	Seattle	62	47	...

5. What city received the most rain (Pr.)? ____________________

6. In how many cities was there rain? ____________________

7. Who prepared the weather listings? ____________________

Time: ________ **Number correct:** ________

Test-Taking Strategies

When taking tests, it is important that you be able to read and interpret the questions correctly. It doesn't matter how well you studied if you can't show what you learned on a test.

Tests are usually classified as either *objective* or *subjective. Objective exams* include true-false, multiple-choice, matching and completion, or fill-in type questions. Your job on an objective exam is to choose the best answer from those provided. You may be asked to select a word or phrase that correctly completes a statement. Or you may need to recall on your own some fact, date, or figure to fill in a blank. Objective tests can be scored with an answer key and frequently are machine scored. *Subjective exams,* on the other hand, usually require short to long written answers, usually called essay tests. Rather than a simple statement of fact, essay exams usually require that you demonstrate an understanding of the ideas learned rather than just a recall of facts and figures. Frequently, writing well is as important as knowing the answer in subjective tests.

In a recent research study, instructors were asked to list what they found to be the most common reasons students do poorly on tests. Here's what they listed in order of importance:

1. Most students don't know how to reason correctly.
2. Students cannot express themselves clearly in written responses.
3. Answers were not organized or stated logically.
4. Students misinterpret the questions or don't read them carefully enough.
5. Students don't know the information needed.

Many students read the assignments, listen in class, and take good notes but can't put what they learned together for an exam. Here are some pointers to help you do better on tests.

Preparing for Exams

As almost any study skills book will tell you, preparing for exams begins the first day of class. Surveying your textbooks, using the SQ3R study method, taking lecture and reading notes, mapping, attending classes, and reviewing your notes frequently are all part of preparing for an exam. Unfortunately, too many students wait until a few days before a test to get serious about it. This usually results in skipping other classes to devote time to finally studying for the test. Students then try to cram into a few hours what they think is important to memorize for the test. Cramming may get you by, but you'll soon forget whatever you memorized once the test is over—not what can be called an intelligent way to get an education. Studies show that, without frequent study-review sessions, we forget over 80 percent of what we read in less than two weeks.

Here are a few guidelines for more efficient use of time in preparing for exams:

1. *Ask your instructor about the exam:*
    - Will the exam be objective or essay? If it will be an objective exam, you will need to memorize a certain amount of material. If it's an essay exam, you can practice writing some answers to the types of questions you think the instructor might ask.
    - Can you bring a dictionary or outside materials?
    - Will the exam be "open book," that is, can you use your text when writing the exam?
    - Will the instructor provide paper, or will you need to bring your own?
    - Should the exam be done on a special form? Should you bring a "blue book" (exam booklet)?
    - Should the exam be done in pen or pencil?
    - Will the exam be primarily over lecture or textbook material?
    - Will main ideas or details be emphasized? Will you be expected to remember dates or titles, for example?

2. *Review what has been covered in some methodical manner.* For tests that emphasize the textbook, try some of the following strategies:

    - Skim over the assigned chapters in your textbook, making certain the headings make sense. Reread any sections that you may have forgotten.
    - See if you can define any words in bold type or italics. Make flashcards of new terminology you can't immediately define, and study them.
    - If there is a glossary in the book, make sure you can define those words. Frequently, objective tests are based on definitions given in the glossary.
    - Skim over the sections of the textbook you have highlighted.
    - Study the marginal notes you made while reading the assigned chapters.
    - Make up summary sheets or maps of the chapters that will be covered in the exam, and review them.
    - Answer, either in writing or out loud, any questions that appear at the end of the chapter. If you have trouble answering any of them, reread the section of the chapter that discusses the question.
    - The index of your text is another good study tool. Look through the index for any names or events that appear in the chapters over which you will be tested. If you don't remember any of the names or events listed in those chapters, turn to that page in the book and reread that section.
    - Form a study group composed of students who are willing to hold one or two study sessions. Each person in the group should be assigned a particular section of the material to be covered and either present a summary of the key points and supporting details and/or make up possible test questions to form a basis for group discussion of the test material.
    - Make up a test and answer all the questions.

    If the class and textbook emphasize solving problems (such as math, accounting, or chemistry), try some of the following study strategies:

    - Redo problems, doing enough problems from each section to show that you understand pertinent concepts.
    - Make up your own problems and work them. You could do this with a study partner and check each other's answers.
    - Find a tutor if sections of the textbook still do not make sense to you. Don't just keep coming up with wrong answers; find out why they are wrong.
    - Explain out loud the process for solving problems. Do you understand each step of the process?

    If you know the test will be partially or primarily an essay test, try the following strategies:

    - Make up essay questions and practice writing answers.
    - Use study maps for key concepts in each chapter.
    - Form a study group where each person in the group is responsible for discussing one section or one chapter, presenting both main ideas and details from that section or chapter.

For tests that emphasize class lecture notes, try the following strategies:

- Exchange photocopies of notes with other students. Use these other notes to fill in holes or misinformation in your notes so that you have a complete set of class notes.
- Make summary sheets or maps of your class notes, and study them.
- Rewrite key terminology or key concepts from your notes in a blank column or on another piece of paper. Go over these terms or concepts and see if you can define them out loud or in writing. If you cannot, go back and study that section of your notes.
- Use study groups as explained previously.

3. *Study for shorter but more frequent periods of time.* Research has shown that it's better to study for short periods of time rather than in long blocks. Long study periods may give you the feeling you are studying diligently, but the results will be an overload. Many study-skills experts even recommend that you don't study the night before a test. If you have been preparing all along, a rested mind on the day of the exam will function better than a tired one.

   - Do you have short daily study periods for at least two weeks before a major test?
   - Do you have brief weekly reviews for each class, each week of the semester?
   - Do you have all major exams listed on a calendar so you can spread out your studying over a space of weeks rather than days?

Scoring Well on Objective Tests

When the day of the big test arrives, here are some things to keep in mind:

1. *Schedule your time properly.* Look over the entire exam before you begin to answer any questions. How long is it? How many parts are there? Is there a point system indicating that one section is more important than another? Some students plunge into one section of a test and spend more time on it than they should. Time runs out before there's a chance to answer other questions that may have given them more points for a higher grade.
2. *Answer the easy questions first.* By answering first the questions you know, you help refresh and stimulate your memory. When you finish the easy ones, go back and look again at the others. Chances are that, by answering the ones you did know, you will be able to remember answers to the more difficult ones. Don't spend too much time on a question. You may want to leave some kind of mark by the tough ones and come back to them later if you have time.
3. *Look for clue words that will help you interpret the question.* In objective tests especially, clue words can make a question absolutely false or absolutely correct. The following words frequently make a statement false:

all	All objective tests are easier than essay exams.
every	Every objective test is difficult.
always	Objective tests are always difficult.
never	Objective tests are never easy.
best	Objective tests are the best kind.
worst	Objective tests are the worst kind.
none	None of the tests is easy.

When you see these words on test questions, read them very carefully to see what they are modifying. More often than not, these words produce a false answer.

Here are some clue words that tend to make a question frequently true:

some	Some objective tests are easier than essay exams.
often	Often, objective tests are easier than essay exams.
many	Many essay exams are easier than objective ones.
sometimes	Sometimes essay tests are easy.

There are clue words that can make an answer true or false depending on the point of the question. Read especially carefully questions that contain these words:

generally	Generally speaking, essay tests are more difficult than others.
few	Few tests are more difficult than essay tests.
only	Only subjective tests should be given.

Just recognizing these clue words in a question will not automatically help you answer it correctly, but knowing how they sometimes work may give you an edge.

4. *If you don't know an answer, guess—intelligently.* Unless the test directions say that you will be penalized for wrong answers, don't be afraid to guess at an answer. Here are some clues to intelligent guessing:

a. Usually, true-false tests will contain more true answers than false ones. (That's *usually,* not always!)

b. Long statements tend to be false, because in order for a question to be true everything in it must be true. The longer the question, the more chance of a false statement. However, in multiple-choice answers, long statements tend to be the correct answer.

c. Don't change an answer unless you are absolutely sure you were wrong the first time you marked it.

d. With multiple-choice questions, "all of the above" tends to be a correct answer.

e. When answers to multiple-choice questions require a number, it's best to disregard the highest and lowest numbers and go for something in between.

f. If you are in doubt about an answer, think of your instructor. What would she or he probably want as an answer based on what has been said in class?

g. If a question uses double negatives, remove the negatives to see how the question reads. For example, take out the negatives in this statement:

> It is *not un*advisable to guess when you don't know an answer on a test.

The statement then reads:

> It is advisable to guess when you don't know an answer on a test.

This makes the statement true, unless you are penalized for wrong answers.

h. When taking a matching test with two columns, read both columns before marking any answers. Make a mark near the answers you use so that you don't use them twice.

Remember, these suggestions are not always going to work in your favor. But if you have studied carefully, chances are they can help you achieve a better grade.

REVIEW QUIZ: Preparing for Objective Tests

Directions: Apply what you have just read about preparing for and taking objective tests to the following questions.

1. A recent study showed that the most common reason for students doing poorly, according to instructors, is that they don't know the information needed.

a. True

b. False because ______________________________

2. Studies show that, when we don't review on a frequent basis, we tend to forget __________ of what we study.

a. 60 percent

b. 70 percent

c. 80 percent

d. 90 percent

3. Which of the following is recommended that you do before taking an exam?

a. Ask the instructor what type of exam it will be.

b. Review what has been assigned in a methodical manner.

c. Study for shorter but more frequent periods of time.

d. All of the above.

4. Frequently, objective tests are based on ______________ given in the glossary.

5. It is never a good idea not to answer the easy questions first.

a. True

b. False because ______________________________

6. List at least four clue words that frequently make a true-false question false. _____

____

7. List three clue words that frequently are used to make a true-false statement true.

____

8. In true-false tests, long statements tend to be true, whereas the opposite is true of multiple-choice answers.

a. True

b. False because ______________________________

9. Which of the following is not recommended as a method of reviewing for a test?

a. Using the textbook's index

b. Using the textbook's glossary

c. Forming study groups with responsibilities for each member

d. Cramming

10. Subjective exams are best described as those that require ______________

____

REVIEW QUIZ: Analyzing Objective Test Questions

Directions: In the spaces provided, explain what clues appear in each of the questions in the Review Quiz that would help you guess more intelligently at the answer if you didn't know it. The first one has been done for you.

1. *Read the questions carefully. If the information is known, chances are they won't do poorly.*
2. ______
3. ______
4. ______
5. ______
6. ______
7. ______
8. ______
9. ______
10. ______

Scoring Well on Essay Tests

Preparing for an essay test is not much different from preparing for an objective test. The big difference has less to do with how much you know and more with how well you can organize and write an answer. If writing itself is not one of your strong points, the best approach you can take is to write some answers to questions you think might be on the exam.

There are at least three good sources to use in preparing for essay exam questions. As mentioned earlier, some instructors will share previous test questions. Don't be afraid to ask if any are available. Seeing what type of questions will be asked can help you anticipate probable questions the instructor might ask. Another source for possible essay questions is the text itself. Frequently, instructors base their questions on those at the beginning or end of chapters in the course textbook. Chances are that if you practice writing answers to those, you'll learn the information needed for the instructor's questions. A third source is the course syllabus. Students are often provided with handouts at the beginning of a course that list objectives and assignments and that often contain study-guide questions. These are frequently shoved into a notebook and never referred to again. Exam time is a good time to look again at such handouts.

Here are some guidelines for writing answers to essay questions:

1. *Read the questions carefully.* This seems obvious, but frequently students get involved in writing an answer to a question without regard for the total test. If directions aren't clear, ask the instructor to explain. Look for the following clue words that appear in essay exams, and make certain your answer states what is called for:

analyze	State the main ideas and show how they are related and why they are important.
comment on	Discuss, criticize, or explain (ask instructor for more specifics on this one).
compare	Show both similarities and differences, but your instructor may only want similarities.
contrast	Show differences.
criticize	Give your judgment or reasoned opinion, showing good and bad points.
define	Give a formal meaning or elaborate definition with supporting details.
describe	Give a detailed account or verbal picture in an organized or logical sequence.
discuss	Give details, and discuss pros and cons.
enumerate	List main ideas one by one and number them.
evaluate	Give your opinion, showing advantages and disadvantages.
illustrate	Explain by giving concrete details, examples, or analogies.
interpret	Use examples to explain or give meaning through personal comments or judgments.
justify	Give proof or reasons.
list	List, usually by number, without details.
outline	Give a general summary using main ideas and skipping minor details.
prove	Use argument or logic to explain.
relate	Show the connection between one thing and another.
review	Give a summary or survey.
state	Provide the main points in precise terms.
summarize	Give a brief account of the main ideas.
trace	Show in chronology the progress of history.

Students often ignore these clue words and end up writing answers that are only partially correct or even totally miss the answer the instructor wants.

2. *Answer the easy questions first.* Usually you don't have to answer essay questions in their order on the test as long as you identify which questions you are answering. By writing an answer to the easier questions first, you gain confidence and begin to call from memory other points you have studied.

3. *Write out a brief outline before you begin your essay answer.* Think through what you want to say before you begin writing your answer by making some type of outline. If you are writing answers in a "blue book," use the inside and back of the cover for your outlines. That way, if you run out of time, you can refer your instructor to your outline, which may contain parts of the answer you didn't complete and show that had you the time you would have covered those areas in your answer.

Making an outline may seem to take more time, but actually it is worth it to make certain your ideas are organized before you begin writing. It also helps you recall what you learned before trying to write it down in essay form.

4. *Get right to the question.* Don't waste time getting to the question. Let's say one of your essay questions is "Discuss the role Thomas Jefferson played in the development of American higher education." Don't waste time rewriting the question. Rather, turn the question into your first sentence:

> Thomas Jefferson played an important role in the development of American higher education in three important ways. One, . . .

Then take each of the three important ways and discuss how he helped.

5. *As you write your answers, leave room for changes you may make.* It's best to use only one side of a sheet of paper. Leave margins and skip every other line in case you need to add or make changes. If you misspell a word, don't write over it; scratch through it and write it correctly in the space above the word.

Remember that your instructor is going to be reading class sets of essay answers. A neat, clearly written essay will stand out. The easier you make it for the instructor, the better impression and the better the chances for a higher grade.

6. *Combat exam panic.* Sweaty palms, fast heartbeat, a sick feeling in the stomach, flushed face—all of these are common feelings at exam time. What can you do? Relax. Take a moment to sit up straight, close your eyes, and take some deep breaths. Let the tension out of your body. Slowly relax various parts of your body, working down from the head to the neck, shoulders, arms, upper torso, and so on down to your feet. Concentrate on your breathing; draw in a deep breath and then exhale slowly as you tell yourself you are forcing tension out of your body. Do this whenever you begin to feel tension building.

Some students have success with *imaging.* They close their eyes and see themselves taking the test and writing excellent answers to the questions. They see themselves confident and prepared. Once they see this image of themselves at work, they open their eyes and apply the confidence they saw.

Success in exams depends on accepting those anxious feelings and learning to control them. It may take several practice sessions before you master your feelings.

REVIEW QUIZ: Clue Words in Essay Tests

Directions: Define the following clue words frequently used in essay exam questions.

1. discuss ____________________
____
2. contrast ____________________
____
3. define ____________________
____
4. describe ____________________
____
5. list ____________________
____
6. evaluate ____________________
____
7. enumerate ____________________
____
8. compare ____________________
____

REVIEW QUIZ: Practicing Essay Question Answers

Directions: Answer each of the following questions.

1. An essay question reads: "List the four major causes of the Civil War." Read the following beginning answer to this question and in the space provided evaluate how well it starts.

   During the period prior to 1860, there were many problems confronting the North and the South. It began to look as though there were unresolved problems that could bring the country to a civil war. . . .

   ____
   ____
   ____
   ____
   ____
   ____
   ____
   ____

2. Discuss the difference between objective and subjective tests.

____

____

____

____

____

____

____

3. Summarize the main points discussed in this section on scoring well on essay exams.

____

____

____

____

____

What to Do with Tests after You Get Them Back

Unless you learn to evaluate what you got right and wrong on a test, you will continue to make the same mistakes again and again. When you get a test back, take some time to figure out your strengths and weaknesses on that exam. The following questions will help you learn from your mistakes.

- Were the questions you missed from the textbook or the lecture notes?
- Did you misread any of the directions?
- Did you generally miss main ideas or details?
- Were the questions you missed from one particular part of the chapter or notes (for example, are the missed questions often from the end of the class lecture)?
- Did you miss questions because you didn't know that information? If you didn't know it, why not?
- Were the test questions what you expected? If these weren't the test questions you predicted, why not?
- Did you miss questions because you didn't leave enough time to do one section of the test or you didn't finish the test?
- Is this the grade you predicted for yourself on this test? Why or why not?

Timed Reading Conversion Charts

Directions: Your reading rate (wpm) can be found by locating the name of the article you read in the list below. Then look down that column. Stop at the number of minutes and seconds it took you to read the article. For example, if you read "In Praise of the F Word" in 3 minutes and 45 seconds, your rate would be 261 wpm.

	"In Praise of the F Word"	"Putting Reading in its Proper Place"	"How Students Get Lost in Cyberspace"	"Cloning Could Halt Human Evolution"	"Self-Esteem is Earned, Not Learned"
Time	WPM	WPM	WPM	WPM	WPM
1:00	980	460	1,100	875	745
1:15	784	368	890	700	596
1:30	653	307	741	583	497
1:45	560	262	635	500	426
2:00	490	230	556	437	373
2:15	436	204	494	389	331
2:30	392	184	445	350	298
2:45	356	167	405	318	271
3:00	327	153	371	292	248
3:15	302	141	342	269	229
3:30	280	131	318	250	213
3:45	261	123	297	233	199
4:00	245	115	278	219	186
4:15	231	108	262	206	175
4:30	218	102	247	194	166
4:45	206	97	234	184	157
5:00	196	92	222	175	149
5:15	187		212	167	142
5:30	178		202	159	135
5:45	170		193	152	130
6:00	163		185	146	124
6:15	157		178	140	119
6:30	151		171	135	115
6:45	145		165	130	110
7:00	140		159	125	106
7:15	135		153	121	103
7:30	131		148	117	99
7:45	126		143	113	96
8:00	123		139	109	
8:15	119		135	106	
8:30	115		131	103	
8:45	112		127	100	
9:00	109		124	97	
9:15	106		120		
9:30	103		117		
9:45	101		114		
10:00					
10:15					

Timed Reading Conversion Charts—Continued

Time	"Push for De-emphasis of College Sports" WPM	"Women Have What It Takes" WPM	"Salvation" WPM	"Time to Look and Listen" WPM	"The Barrio" WPM	"Queen of Nothing" WPM
1:00	465	1,100	913	1,112	1,350	670
1:15	372	890	730	890	1,086	536
1:30	310	741	609	741	905	447
1:45	266	635	522	635	779	383
2:00	233	556	457	556	675	335
2:15	207	494	406	494	600	298
2:30	186	445	362	445	535	268
2:45	169	405	332	404	485	244
3:00	155	371	304	371	449	223
3:15	143	342	281	342	415	206
3:30	133	318	261	318	379	191
3:45	124	297	244	297	359	179
4:00	116	278	228	278	339	168
4:15	109	262	215	262	319	158
4:30	103	247	203	247	299	149
4:45	98	234	192	234	280	141
5:00	93	222	183	222	270	134
5:15	89	212	174	212	255	128
5:30	85	202	166	202	240	122
5:45		193	159	193	230	117
6:00		185	152	185	220	112
6:15		178	146	178	210	107
6:30		171	144	171	200	103
6:45		165	141	165	197	99
7:00		159	140	159	190	96
7:15		153	138	153	181	
7:30		148	135	148	178	
7:45		143	130	143	170	
8:00		139		139	168	
8:15		135		135	160	
8:30		131		131	153	
8:45		127		127	150	
9:00		124			144	
9:15		120			138	
9:30		117				
9:45		114				
10:00						
10:15						

Student Record Chart

Directions: Record your reading rate, comprehension, and/or vocabulary check scores for the reading practices on this chart. Each correct response counts 10 percent, with a total of 100 percent possible for each check. To find your reading rate for the timed readings, go to the Timed Readings Conversion Chart in this Appendix.

Unit One Literal Comprehension

Selection Title	Reading Rate	Comprehension Scores	Vocabulary Scores
Chapter One			
What You Should Look for in a Dictionary			
Superman and Me			
In Praise of the F Word			
Chapter Two			
Thinking: A Neglected Art			
Putting Reading in Its Proper Place			
Chapter Three			
Case Study: The State of the Onion			
How Students Get Lost in Cyberspace			

Unit Two Critical Comprehension

Selection Title	Reading Rate	Comprehension Scores	Vocabulary Scores
Chapter Four			
How Good Are Your Opinions?			
America: The Multinational Society			
Cloning Could Halt Human Evolution			
Chapter Five			
Gods Are Created in Our Own Image			
Press Freedom under Assault at Home and Abroad			
Chapter Six			
Debate over the Legalization of Marijuana: An Overview			
Self-Esteem Is Earned, Not Learned			
Push for De-Emphasis of College Sports			
Women Have What It Takes			

Unit Three Affective Comprehension

Selection Title	Reading Rate	Comprehension Scores	Vocabulary Scores
Chapter Seven			
Fresh Start			
Salvation			
Chapter Eight			
Stolen Party			
1, 2, 3			
Time to Look and Listen			
The Barrio			
Queen of Nothing			
Paradise			

Photo Credits

P 1 © Heinle/Thomson Learning
P 7 © Bettmann/CORBIS
P 50 Photo by © Rex Tystedt
P 131 © Heinle/Thomson Learning
P 165 © Getty Images
P 255 © Heinle/Thomson Learning
P 284 © CRDPHOTO/CORBIS
P 304 Photo by © Carolyn Soto
P 318 © AP/Wide World Photos

Index